# THE INDEPENDENT PIANO TEACHER'S STUDIO HANDBOOK

# THE
# INDEPENDENT PIANO TEACHER'S
# STUDIO HANDBOOK

Everything You Need to Know for a Successful Teaching Studio

By Beth Gigante Klingenstein

HAL•LEONARD®
CORPORATION

7777 W. BLUEMOUND RD. P.O. BOX 13819 MILWAUKEE, WI 53213

ISBN: 978-0-634-08083-8

Cover image by Susan Osborne

Published by:
Hal Leonard Corporation
7777 W. Bluemound Road
P.O. Box 13819
Milwaukee, WI 53213

In Australia Contact:
**Hal Leonard Australia Pty. Ltd.**
4 Lentara Court
Cheltenham, Victoria, 3192 Australia
Email:  ausadmin@halleonard.com.au

Printed in the U.S.A.

First Edition

Visit Hal Leonard Online at
**www.halleonard.com**

# CONTENTS

## PART VI
## Maintaining High Studio Standards

## PART VII
## From Preparation to Performance

## PART VIII
## Teaching Skills – Not Pieces

## PART IX
## Unique Curriculum

# P R E F A C E

My aim in writing *The Independent Piano Teacher's Studio Handbook* is to offer a holistic approach to piano teaching, one that addresses the needs of the teacher as well as the student. My hope is that this book will guide those in pedagogy courses who have yet to teach, give encouragement and insight to those who are just starting their careers as piano teachers, and present experienced teachers with new options and approaches to teaching. After 40 years of teaching, I feel I have much to share as well as much to learn. It is this spirit of lifelong learning that inspired me most to write this book.

There are four main themes that run throughout the text:

1) Acknowledging the business and professional issues that affect the independent music teacher

2) Focusing on the important skills students need in order to play musically and with proficiency

3) Developing a comprehensive curriculum in the independent studio

4) Committing oneself to professional development and arts advocacy

One important decision I made in this book was to include resources on the various topics presented within. The decision to include resources was not made lightly as books go out of print, websites change addresses and format, and new material comes on the market every month. Nonetheless, I feel that the addition of the resources will provide a huge service to pedagogy students and piano teachers alike. When reading about chamber music, world music, pedaling, theory, music history, or any other topic in the book, these resources will provide the foundation for continued learning and a model for future research. No list could be complete, but I have taken great pleasure in researching the products and professional organizations available to piano teachers and including a sampling in this book. I owe Hal Leonard Corporation a special thanks for their willingness to list the products of other publishers in this book, a decision that truly demonstrates their commitment to education.

Another significant contributing factor to this book is a series of articles I wrote for *American Music Teacher*, many for the "It's All of Your Business" column. My gratitude goes to *American Music Teacher* and its publisher, Dr. Gary Ingle, for allowing me to use those articles as the basis for the opening chapters of this book.

Because of my strong commitment to professional development and my longtime membership in Music Teachers National Association, a number of references are made to items that appear on the MTNA website. MTNA has been kind enough to dedicate a link for this publication, with easy access to each area mentioned within the text. References made to various areas of the MTNA website will appear at *www.mtna.org/HLtext* and will be listed by the chapter in which they appear.

Readers will notice that I refer to teachers as "she." Although there are numerous male piano teachers, in order to be concise and avoid clumsy wording, this book always refers to the piano teacher as female. Throughout the book, such statements are meant to imply both male and female.

It is my hope that this book will provide new and experienced teachers alike with practical and inspiring guidelines for a unique, professional, and rewarding career as an independent piano teacher.

# ACKNOWLEDGMENTS

Numerous people reviewed portions of *The Independent Piano Teacher's Studio Handbook* and offered their professional insights. I would like to offer my thanks to the following people in particular: Dr. Sarah Kahl, Dr. Diana Skroch, Dr. Sara Hagen, Dr. Jay Hershberger, Marienne Uszler, Mavis Green, Dr. Joanne Haroutounian, Dr. Dianna Anderson, Beth Leinen, and Julie Gigante.

The description of every organization and resource was checked with a publisher, editor, author, or organization. Many of these groups sent their preferred descriptions, some taken from the Internet, some modified from the Internet, and some modified from my original descriptions. I would like to thank all those who helped with product descriptions. In particular, I offer my thanks to the major editors who assisted with product descriptions: Teresa Ledford and Dr. Peggy Otwell from Hal Leonard Corporation; E.L. Lancaster from Alfred Publishing Co., Inc.; Alison Sloan from the Frederick Harris Music Co., Ltd., Peggy Gallagher from FJH Music Company Inc; and Jennifer Opdahl from Neil A. Kjos Music Company.

I would like to thank the many talented individuals at Hal Leonard Corporation for the time and effort that went into editing this book. Thank you to Dr. Peggy Otwell for inviting me to write the book and for her work with the initial edits. Thank you to Carol Klose, Dan Maske, and J. Mark Baker for their excellent editing. Their expertise has made this a far more readable and enjoyable book.

Thank you to *American Music Teacher* and its publisher, Dr. Gary Ingle, for allowing the use of my past *American Music Teacher* articles in this book, and to Julianne Miranda and Mendy McKinnis for their help in creating a link on the MTNA website dedicated to this publication.

And finally, I would like to thank my husband, Kal, and our children, Max and Emma, for their support during the writing of this book. I am blessed to have such a loving and supportive family.

# Part I

## DEVELOPING AND MAINTAINING PROFESSIONALISM IN THE INDEPENDENT PIANO STUDIO

Whether we are establishing our first studio or are seeking to enhance an existing one, a high standard of professionalism is an important and necessary goal for success.

The chapters in Part I focus on embracing standards of professionalism, creating and using professional studio documents, devising a long-range plan for studio space, acquiring the necessary equipment, and developing the basic office skills needed to operate a successful business.

# Chapter 1

# EMBRACING PROFESSIONALISM

---

**M**any of us have been confronted with that old stereotype of the neighborhood piano teacher who has minimal training and teaches a few lessons for "egg money."

Old stereotypes die hard, and, unfortunately, the reality of our training and expertise is often far greater than the expectations of many parents.

A great deal will be said in this book about the view others have of our profession as well as our own perceptions of the work we do. Running an independent studio in today's world is far different than it was 30 years ago. We are generally more educated, have far more resources available to us, and view our teaching in a more professional light. As independent piano teachers of today, we have many choices to make, and the consequences of those choices can lead us either down the path to mediocrity, or along the road to success.

I believe that successful piano teachers share the following qualities:

1) **Successful piano teachers adopt a highly professional demeanor in all aspects of studio operation.**

   Teachers who presents themselves in a professional manner employ strong organizational skills, set up a well-planned studio space, prepare lessons carefully, dress appropriately, use confident body language, and develop and maintain professional studio documents.

2) **Successful piano teachers have high expectations for themselves and their students.**

   Along with a kind and nurturing attitude, teachers need to maintain high teaching standards. Accepting mediocrity in students by not wishing to be hard on them will ultimately result in mediocrity in the studio. Successful teachers know how to balance kindness and high standards.

3) **Successful piano teachers recognize the need for business skills critical to the operation of their studio.**

   Today's independent piano teachers recognize that running an efficient and professional studio depends, not only on teaching skills, but also upon knowledge of effective business practices.

4) **Successful piano teachers are committed to continual development in all areas of pedagogy.**

   Professional teachers do not teach the same way year after year, but, rather, continually seek to invigorate lessons through new teaching tools, repertoire, programs, and pedagogical approaches.

**5) Successful piano teachers are committed to personal and professional development.**

Teachers who set aside time for continued education are committed to professional growth. Students are the beneficiaries when their teachers attend workshops or professional conferences, read professional journals and publications, and practice piano, including taking lessons themselves.

**6) Successful piano teachers feel that they are in charge of their own professional destiny.**

Teachers who are in control of their studios set and enforce workable policies and establish rates that reflect their worth, thus commanding respect in every aspect of their studio's operation. To avoid feeling victimized and frustrated, professional teachers establish policies that ensure prompt payment and prevent missed lessons.

Every chapter in this book deals with the above areas in one way or another. Perhaps the most important thing to keep in mind is that we can be in control by planning a course that will continually improve our teaching and musical expertise, our students' skills, and our studios. As a result, each of us can take delight in a constantly evolving career as a successful independent piano teacher.

# Chapter 2

# PROFESSIONAL STUDIO DOCUMENTS

O ur studio is part educational facility, part arts organization, and part small business. An excellent way to present our studio in a businesslike fashion is to develop written materials for the studio. Such materials save us time and energy, contribute to organization, enhance studio and teacher recognition, and present our studio in a more professional light.

This chapter presents some of the many options for studio documents. Samples of these documents can be found in Appendix A.

## Studio Name and Logo

Regardless of the size of the studio, it is wise to decide on a name and logo as a first step when developing written materials. Both should be chosen carefully, as they will be used on all studio documents. Today's computer technology makes it fairly easy to create one's own studio graphics. A graphic arts specialist can assist with designing and producing a studio logo, ensuring that all studio materials have a consistent font, color, format, and style.

## Business Documents

### Business Card

Besides being an efficient means of exchanging contact information and marketing a studio, a business card demonstrates that the teacher perceives herself as a professional.

A business card should be visually appealing, without an excess of information. It should include important contact information, such as studio name and logo, teacher name, address, phone number (home and/or business and cell), and e-mail address. A short phrase may be added listing the instruments or classes taught, but it is best to keep it simple. For teachers who are also active performers, a separate card could be used when marketing oneself as a performer.

### Stationery

Personalized stationery gives the studio a more professional appearance, and is suitable for all correspondence with students, parents, and colleagues. Stationery, like all studio documents, can be designed easily and stored on a computer as a template, eliminating the need to purchase expensive personalized stationery. Although basic text-weight paper is adequate, for special correspondence, linen or watermark stock is available at a reasonable price at office supply stores.

### Résumé

Unlike most business professionals, who keep an updated résumé at all times, many independent piano teachers do not view teaching as a business, and see no need for a résumé. Others might say, "But I don't have anything to put in a résumé." It is more likely that they simply have not taken the time to define and list their skills, job descriptions, and achievements.

Why would we, as self-employed piano teachers, ever need a résumé? The top ten reasons are as follows.

10. It gives us practice using annoying auto-formatting devices on the computer.

9. Like updating our will, it forces us to do some personal assessment.

8. It organizes our achievements into easily understood categories.

7. It reminds us of the name of the presentation we gave five years ago.

6. It reminds us that one of our students won three competitions instead of two.

5. It provides written proof for our children and grandchildren that, yes, indeed, we have been a functioning member of society.

4. If we decide to change careers, it saves us the anguish of wondering what we have done for the last 20 years.

3. It provides us with up-to-date information on our experience, achievements, and skills, should we wish to apply for a grant sometime in the future.

2. When we are asked to submit a personal biography, it allows us to select pertinent information with ease.

And the Number One reason why we as self-employed piano teachers would ever need a résumé is:

1. It impresses us with the full scope of our achievements, confirming the pride reflected in our studio.

The following are some of the possible sections in a résumé. All data listed should be preceded by pertinent dates, as shown in the sample résumé found in Appendix A.

**NAME AND CURRENT CONTACT INFORMATION**

**EDUCATION**

- Degrees and Institutions
- Years of Study
- Teachers and/or Professors
- Professional Certification

**PROFESSIONAL EXPERIENCE**

- Founder and Director of the _____ Piano Studio
- Positions held in a conservatory, college, or university
- Job descriptions

**PROFESSIONAL ACTIVITY**

- Publications
- Performances
- Presentations (including masterclasses and/or workshops)
- Student achievements

**CONTINUING EDUCATION**

- Conferences, workshops and/or masterclasses attended
- Courses

**PROFESSIONAL MEMBERSHIPS**

- National, state, and local music organizations
- Offices or positions held

**SERVICE TO COMMUNITY**

- Religious organizations
- Local schools
- Volunteer work

**TECHNOLOGY SKILLS**

- Facility in office software
- Facility in music software
- Studio lab (if applicable)

**REFERENCES**

- Administrator of institutions where previously employed
- Music Director or head of church or performing organization
- President of national, state, and/or local music organizations

## JOB DESCRIPTIONS IN A RÉSUMÉ

Independent piano teachers often do not list the duties performed in an independent studio on a résumé. In fact, the many skills needed to run a studio are impressive and well-worth noting under "Professional Experience." Below is a list of many of the types of activities one might include.

**ADMINISTRATIVE DUTIES:**

- Establish studio policies
- Prepare and update studio documents
- Comply with state/local business and zoning regulations
- Create budget, manage bookkeeping, and maintain financial records
- Determine and implement marketing strategies
- Conduct student/parent interviews and process registrations
- Coordinate scheduling of lessons, recitals and workshops, and prepare calendar of events
- Create press releases for studio activities
- Review and maintain music inventory
- Prepare and submit grants

**TEACHING DUTIES:**

- Develop curriculum, including repertoire, music theory, music history, sight-playing, and composition
- Teach theory and performance classes
- Organize studio recitals
- Enter students in festivals and competitions, prepare applications
- Present programs to community service organizations
- Develop curriculum for computer lab/workstation

I have a friend who, after many years as an independent piano teacher, decided to go into the business world outside of music. She rewrote her music résumé emphasizing the skills she had used in her studio, such as overall organization, budgeting and bookkeeping, curriculum development, interviewing, and communication. A cancer research group hired her immediately, where she is employed to this day. When we think of the many skills we use, and the many activities we do, our résumé can—and should—reflect that experience and expertise.

Should a teacher feel uncomfortable creating that first résumé, there are professional résumé writers who can assist with the process. Many reference books on résumés are also available for purchase or at libraries. Two excellent examples are included in the following "Resources" feature, plus a recommended website.

# Resources

The Public Library Association and the Editors of VGM Books. *The Guide to Basic Résumé Writing*, 2nd Edition. New York: McGraw-Hill, 2003.

> A carefully written résumé is a strong asset for anyone in the professional world. This book offers straightforward advice for a clearly written, eye-catching résumé. Chapters include information on the format, wording, and look of the successful résumé. A section is included on writing cover letters and advice is given for those reentering the job market.

Rosenberg, Arthur D. *The Résumé Handbook: How to Write Outstanding Résumés & Cover Letters for Every Situation*, 5th Edition. Avon: Adams Media, an F+W Publications Inc. Company, 2007.

> Résumé writing is far more than listing one's job history, and this book offers a number of do's and don'ts for the successful résumé. After guidelines are given for résumé format and content, two chapters in Rosenberg's book address "The Best Résumés We've Ever Seen" and "The Worst Résumés We've Ever Seen." The added commentary concerning what was good or bad in each example offers guidance to those wishing to write a clearly stated, eye-catching résumé. The book goes even further to include valuable tips for those learning to network, searching for jobs, and writing letters of introduction. The 5th Edition emphasizes the use of the Internet and e-résumés, and contains new information on special circumstances, such as students, over-50 workers, and employees changing fields.

**WEBSITE**

*The Damn Good Résumé*

www.damngood.com

## Studio Operation Documents

### Studio Policy Statement

The most important document in any well-run independent studio is the **studio policy statement**. It should list and explain every item that is important to one's effectiveness as a teacher. A document with a formal, professional look is far more effective than a chatty letter.

The studio policy statement should contain all the information needed for parents and students regarding teaching and administrative concerns within the studio. By stating each point clearly in the policy, a teacher exhibits the professionalism that contributes to an efficient and well-run business. Parents and students also appreciate the clarity of a formal document. The end result of a professional policy statement is more time for making music and less time spent in tackling problems.

At the beginning of each school year, the policy statement should be updated and agreed to by the parent's signature on the annual registration form, as discussed later in this chapter.

There is nothing too big or too small to include in a studio policy. The following are some possible topics to consider.

- Tuition

- Services offered

- Payment amount and schedule (monthly, by semester, or by term)

- Book and activity deposit (amount and purpose: books, festival fees, recital fees, late payment fees, etc.)

- Calendar listing important studio dates (also see Studio Calendar below)

- Make-up policy, specifying absences that are or are not covered, and an advance notice rule, if applicable

- Swap list information

- Recital and performance opportunities offered through the studio

- Information about group lessons, theory classes, and/or computer lab or workstation

- Information and rules for use of the studio music library

- References for theory, music history, or pedagogy websites, or recommended music-writing and theory software

- Practice expectations

- Importance and use of the studio assignment notebook

- Parental involvement

- Advice for purchasing a metronome and keeping the student's home instrument maintained and in tune

- Times when calls may be made to the studio

- Parking information

- Promptness in drop-off and pick-up

- Proper grooming for lessons (fingernails trimmed, hands clean, etc.)

- Rules regarding respect for the studio: shoe and boot removal in bad weather, location and use of rest room, waiting room procedures including policy regarding young siblings

There is a popular phrase, "No one can take advantage of you without your consent." The studio policy statement enables a teacher to operate the studio according to her own terms, and at the same time helps parents understand the teacher's expectations.

Some examples of clearly stated expectations:

> If the sound of gum chewing in the lesson is annoying, a stipulation like, "No gum chewing is allowed during lessons," can be included.

> If collecting payments has become a problem, a statement can be added such as, "A late payment fee of $15 will be deducted from the Book and Fee Deposit for all tuition not received by the tenth of the month."

> If students are abusing goodwill by expecting make-up lessons for any and all reasons, the policy statement can include a firmly worded and clear rule, such as, "Make-up lessons will not be given for lessons missed by the student."

It is important to have a place at the end of the studio policy statement where a parent (or guardian or adult student) can sign, agreeing to all of the terms in the policy, even before the first lesson is given. Two copies of the agreement should be signed, providing both the parents and the teacher with a copy for their records.

If the parent or guardian does not agree with the terms of the studio policy, it is best for the student to study elsewhere. Once parents sign the agreement on the registration form, they can be held to that agreement should they dispute any points in the policies at a later date. Ultimately, a teacher is responsible for setting her own policies, and as with any business, clients must abide by them. Just as a bank does not allow its customers to stop repaying a loan should they decide they do not like the terms that were agreed upon, so should teachers stand firm on the policies they set for the professional operation of their studio.

In an anonymous teacher survey, the following question was asked: "What would your ideal studio policy statement include?" Here is one teacher's unfortunate response:

> *"I think it is a waste of time to devise an ideal policy, etc.*
> *Better to concentrate on musical ideals and music making."*

This teacher sees good business policies and good music making as mutually exclusive. On the contrary, this teacher should recognize that a well-worded studio policy could free her from business worries, permitting her more time to concentrate on the important issues of making music.

## Studio Calendar

Each year a studio calendar should be compiled, listing the first and last dates of the teaching year, as well as dates when lessons will not be given (e.g., holidays, vacations, or professional commitments). Additional dates, such as performance and theory classes, festivals, competitions, and recitals can also be included. Presenting students with a studio calendar enables families to plan ahead for attendance at these special events, and saves additional communication regarding each upcoming activity. The calendar can also be incorporated into the Studio Policy Statement.

## Registration Form

Once a new student is accepted, it is important to have an adult complete a registration form for the student. This form provides the information necessary to maintain accurate student records.

Registration forms should be updated annually, and should be submitted by all students—new and returning—to reflect changes in student contact information, available lesson days and times, etc.

A typical registration form can include the following items:

- Student's name
- Date of birth (excluding adult students)
- Home address
- Billing address, if different
- Names of parents or guardians
- Daytime, evening, and cell phone numbers
- E-mail addresses
- Any personal or confidential circumstances of which the teacher should be aware such as special needs or health concerns
- Length and type of lesson preferred, with tuition cost listed for each choice
- Amount needed for book and activity deposit
- Preferred lesson days and times, with space to indicate first, second and third choices
- A brief statement about the make-up policy
- A place for parental signature indicating that the student does or does not wish to be on a lesson swap list
- A place for parental signature giving consent for student's photo to be used for publicity purposes
- A statement to be signed indicating that the parent, guardian, or adult student has read and agreed to all the terms in the Registration Form and the Studio Policy Statement

Two copies of the policy statement should be provided to the parent/guardian: one to sign and give to the teacher, and one to keep at home for future reference.

## Interview Form

Before accepting a new student, it is important to conduct an interview with the prospective student and parents. When interviewing a new student, pertinent information can be recorded on an interview form, which becomes the first document in the student's file.

Questions asked in the interview might include the following:

- Age
- Grade in school

- Years/months of piano study
- Prior number of teachers
- Reasons for taking piano lessons
- Favorite class at school
- After-school or extra-curricular activities

The form can also be used to record observations made during the interview regarding the student's playing level and musical knowledge. It is wise to develop two forms: one for beginners and one for transfer students.

### Swap List

A swap list is an excellent way to avoid unnecessary make-up lessons, allowing students to exchange lesson times with each other when they have schedule conflicts. Swap lists will be discussed in more detail in Chapter 11, along with make-up policies.

### Payment Record and Notice of Overdue Payment

A Payment Record form organizes all payment data. Information is kept for each student, including the parents' names (or names of adult paying for lessons), and contact information. Columns are organized according to the payment plan (by month, semester, or term), and payments are recorded as they are made. Teachers can notify parents of any overdue fees or late changes by sending a Notice of Overdue Payment form. Computer software that keeps track of bookkeeping will be discussed further in Chapter 4.

### Additional Studio Documents

Within a studio, additional forms may be needed to cover specific needs, such as:

- Lesson inquiry/phone inquiry form
- Waiting list
- Music/studio inventory form
- Lending library record for items such as CDs and sight-playing materials
- Student practice agreement
- Form for student/parent assessment of the teacher
- Form for teacher assessment of the student's progress
- Student Certificate of Achievement
- Scholarship Application form

## Studio Records

Documents can be developed to organize student files and maintain studio records. Some teachers choose to keep records on paper, while others elect to store information as computer files. Regardless of the means, a well-run studio depends on accurate and updated records, especially in the following areas.

## Lesson Attendance Records

Teachers must track student attendance for a number of reasons. Parents may question the number of lessons a student has received; the teacher may be concerned about the number of lessons a student has missed; or she may wish to verify that she has given the correct number of lessons within a semester or year.

Attendance can be recorded in a paper ledger or on a computer, whichever seems more efficient. In my studio, I keep a ledger in which I track each student's attendance by marking the date each lesson is actually received. (See the sample below). If a lesson falls on a holiday and will not be taught that day, I mark a "—" in the box. For unexcused absences that I will not make up, I write "UA" in place of the date. If I will make up the lesson later, I leave the box blank and enter the date into that day's slot when the make-up is actually given, as in the date "10/22" listed in the last row below.

| MONDAY | STUDENT NAME | 9/1 (LABOR DAY) | 9/8 | 9/15 | 9/22 |
|---|---|---|---|---|---|
| 3:00-4:00 | Debbie Smith | — | 9/8 | 9/15 | 9/22 |
| 4:00-5:00 | Dennis Brown | — | 9/8 | UA | 9/22 |
| 5:00-6:00 | Steven Jones | — | 10/22 | 9/15 | 9/22 |

## Contact Information

Contact information for all students must be recorded in a place that can be easily accessed. I store contact information in a database on my computer, and also print out a copy to have on hand near the phone. Important contact information includes students' names, parents' or guardians' names, home addresses and phone numbers, work or cell phone numbers, and e-mail addresses.

## Annual Student Scores

It is wise to keep an achievement record of all student scores for every annual event entered, such as National Federation of Music Clubs Junior Festival or a state theory exam. This makes it easy to determine each student's level for the following year, which is often based on the level and rating for past years. It is also wise to keep the student's date of birth and grade in school updated on this form, since there are many events for which the level is determined by age or grade.

## Individual Student Files

Student records can be filed in two different ways:

1) All registration forms for a given year can be kept in one file, all festival scores for a given year can be kept in another file, and so on. This method works well for immediate access to the complete records for a particular event, such as a state theory exam.

2) A separate file can be maintained for each student, starting with the student interview form, and including each year's registration form, signed policy sheet, theory test scores, etc. This system easily allows teachers to see at a glance the big picture for any given student.

## Studio Assignment Notebook

There are many fine assignment notebooks on the market, but a teacher can create her own to address the needs of her particular studio. This allows her to decide exactly what she wants on an assignment page and tailor the book to cover as many topics desired, such as music history or technical exercises.

The following are items that might be included in a personalized studio assignment notebook:

- An appealing personalized cover with the studio name and logo, the year, and a place to write the student's name
- Studio contact information
- A copy of any important documents the teacher wishes to include, such as:
  - the current studio policy statement
  - a summary of practice expectations, practice tips, and guidelines for an effective practice regimen
  - the current year's studio calendar
- Customized weekly practice pages with space for assignments as well as notes to parents, accumulated incentive points, manuscript paper, or a practice log
- Pages tracking music history assignments (composer of the month, history-related listening assignments, information on musical eras, etc.)
- Pages tracking completed repertoire, with subheads such as Method Books, Popular Music, and various historical periods
- List of memorized repertoire
- Performance record
- Pages for additional technique or theory information, such as scale and arpeggio fingerings and practice regimens, circle of fifths, cadence patterns, and chord spellings
- Selected definitions of commonly used musical terms

Copies of a customized studio practice book can be made and bound at a professional print shop and the cost passed on to students in the Book and Fee Deposit.

### A WORD OF CAUTION

When personalizing one's own studio documents, samples such as those found in Appendix A can serve as an excellent starting point. However, I would like to offer one word of caution. In their quest for a proven document, many teachers may choose to copy an existing form from a book or another teacher's studio, a document that may not suit the teacher's own specific needs. It is far better to study that document, compare it to similar documents, and then modify it as needed.

No one can write the perfect studio policy statement or registration form for another teacher. A case in point is a situation with one of my pedagogy students, who, when asked to formulate studio documents, patterned hers exactly on someone else's documents. When I reviewed her forms, it became apparent that they did not meet her particular needs at all. Even if someone has never taught before, I would suggest looking at other forms for ideas, but ultimately creating one's own.

## In Summary

Printed studio materials help teachers manage the independent studio efficiently. Teachers, parents and students all benefit from improved organization and clarity of expectations. Well-designed studio documents help present the studio in a way that reflects the professionalism of today's independent music instructor rather than an outdated image of the "neighborhood piano teacher."

# Chapter 3

# SETTING UP THE IDEAL STUDIO SPACE

If money were no object, how would the ideal studio look? I immediately imagine two high quality grand pianos, an extensive workstation full of computers and MIDI keyboards, a waiting room, separate studio restroom, and an area large enough to set up chairs for performance classes. Not wanting to stop there, I see a well-organized office area with a computer, printer, copier, and plenty of room for filing. The studio would have a state-of-the-art sound system, a library of books and music, and a separate entrance directly from the street into the studio (with no steps.) Add adjustable lighting and beautiful windows looking out over a forest of peaceful trees, and the studio seems complete. Although this studio reflects my fantasies more than my reality, identifying and prioritizing studio needs does help to create a long-range plan for studio space.

Perhaps one reason some teachers never move beyond their initial investment in a piano and a few chairs is that they do not think like a business professional. Instead of viewing themselves as part of the business world, some teachers prefer to be regarded solely as educator or artist. Independent piano teachers are really all three: they educate students, function as musician-artists, and operate an independent business. The business side of the independent studio is not something to deny, but rather to embrace as a tool for simplifying other areas of the profession.

Once the studio is accepted as a business, the next step is developing a plan for the use of studio income. Part of the income will be used for professional development such as attending conferences, but a portion will need to go back into enhancing the studio space itself, as well as purchasing items for studio use.

Some studio purchases, such as office equipment and supplies, serve business needs; others have a pedagogical use, such as instruments, video and recording devices, workstation and computer lab equipment, music library materials, games and other teaching tools. Whatever the requirements, one's studio needs must be prioritized, so decisions can be made about what to purchase and when.

## Home Space vs. Studio Space

Keeping studio space isolated from family life is an important goal. Some studios start out in a shared space, such as a living room or family room, but it is far better to keep the teaching and family space separate in every way possible. For many years, my students came through my kitchen and then downstairs into the studio. This was less than ideal, especially when my family was in the kitchen or when students remarked, "That's what you fixed for dinner last week." My family and I were far happier when a move to a new home allowed students to walk directly into the studio.

## Studio Area

If a teacher plans to have a home studio, she must be careful when choosing a location in which to live. As will be discussed in Chapter 15, a teacher must be in compliance with all zoning laws and homeowner rules and regulations.

An important item when considering a home studio is access.

- Can students walk directly into the studio from the street or driveway?

- Is the entrance well-lit?

- Can students enter while still in view of the parent's car, or do they enter in back of the house? Entering away from the parents' view provides a potentially dangerous scenario.

- Are outside steps free of ice and snow in winter?

Another key element is keeping the studio space attractive. In any studio, a simple coat of paint can brighten the overall look, even on the tightest of budgets. Replacing old carpet and adding wall hangings are cosmetic changes that can make a less than ideal room appear more suitable. If the studio is used as a waiting area, a modest sofa or chair and a table for reading materials are wise purchases. Something as simple as a new slipcover for an old sofa can also enhance the appearance of the room.

Even the most attractive room needs to be kept tidy. Like it or not, a stereotype exists that a music studio is always a mess. The reason this may be true is not that teachers are messy, but rather that the studio space is too small or poorly organized to allow things to stay tidy. On the other hand, when the room is in order, even the smallest area can provide an appealing studio space. Few teachers are fortunate enough to start out with their dream room, so learning to keep a studio attractive and neat, regardless of size, is crucial.

Some modern homes designed in a minimalist style include sparsely furnished rooms that are quite beautiful and calming because of their simplicity. This sense of peace is a worthy goal, and a good reason to avoid clutter. Rooms have an aura, or atmosphere, that speaks to those who enter. Students sense the atmosphere of a studio, whether it is peaceful and calming, or confused and chaotic.

Just as teachers invest years in their profession, they also must invest dollars in the studio space. As finances improve, other options may present themselves: a modest studio room can be updated, the size of the room can be expanded with an addition, or a move to a home with a more ideal studio space may be possible.

## Instruments

All piano teachers need an acceptable instrument on which to teach. The quality of the instrument will affect the quality of the lessons. Teachers should consider a piano their main and most significant investment when establishing a studio. If the starter instrument is of poor quality, such as a hand-me-down with a tinny tone, every effort must be made to replace the instrument as soon as possible. Besides an acoustic piano, many teachers today also invest in a digital instrument.

An adjustable artist's bench is important for a studio in which piano students of all ages and heights will be at the piano. A practical alternative to an adjustable artist's bench is an adjustable duet bench, which may serve more studio needs.

The area around the piano must be well-lit, and should be large enough for a comfortable (but not too comfortable!) chair for the teacher to use while observing the student. The teacher must be able to sit or walk far enough away from the student to avoid the appearance of hovering. Just as with other areas of the studio, it is best to avoid clutter in the piano area. The urge to stack things on the piano must be resisted, as stacks of music or files create a feeling of disorder.

When a teacher is able to upgrade to a new instrument, the new piano should be the highest quality acoustic piano possible, preferably a grand piano. An even better situation would be two acoustic pianos, with at least one being a grand piano. It may take 20 years to go from an upright to a grand piano, but such a purchase should be an important part of any long-range planning.

The studio piano needs to be tuned and checked on a regular basis; it is up to the teacher to set a good example for students by keeping studio pianos well maintained. By demonstrating proper care of the piano in the studio, students and parents can be guided to take the same care with their home instrument. The condition of the student's home piano is of extreme importance to successful progress. Parents often decide to buy an inexpensive instrument first, planning to upgrade if their child does well with lessons. These parents do not understand that an instrument with a poor tone quality or difficult touch inhibits their child's progress, especially if the piano is not properly maintained. Some home pianos are in an appalling state of disrepair, badly out of tune, with missing notes or sticking keys. It is the teacher's job to educate parents on the care needed to maintain their instrument so that students will be able to practice efficiently, musically, and with pleasure.

There are a number of valuable books available to assist teachers, parents, and students with purchasing and caring for their instrument.

## Resources

Fine, Larry. *The Piano Book: Buying & Owning a New or Used Piano*, 4th Edition. Jamaica Plain: Brookside Press, 2001.

This book serves as a consumer's guide to buying a piano, with specific information on grand pianos, rebuilt pianos, used pianos, and a brand-by-brand review of new and recently manufactured pianos. The book explains how to avoid sales gimmicks and offers tips for finding, appraising, and buying pianos as well as piano moving, storing, and servicing. An *Annual Supplement* to *The Piano Book* is published each year, which contains a cumulative digest of changes to manufacturers and models. More information can be found at www.pianobook.com.

Pinksterboer, Hugo. *Tipbook Piano*. Neemstede, the Netherlands: The Tipbook Company, 2001. Distributed by Hal Leonard Corporation.

This compact manual offers a wealth of information on the piano, including an introduction to the instrument and to lessons and practicing. The book serves players at all levels, providing detailed information without getting too technical. There is information about buying, selecting, and play-testing instruments, about sizes, finishes, mechanisms, and strings, about maintenance and regulation, and why regular tuning matters, and about the history and the family of the piano. A special feature of this book are the Tipcodes listed throughout, which allow the reader to view additional pictures and even short movies and soundtracks located at www.tipbook.com.

Smith, Virgil E. *Your Piano & Your Piano Technician*. San Diego: Neil A. Kjos, Jr., Publisher, 1981.

This 56 page manual covers piano care from tuning to rebuilding, and is suitable for parents and teachers alike. Chapters include: The Importance of a Properly Maintained Piano; Selecting Your Instrument; Selecting Your Technician; Working With Your Technician; Tuning; The Piano Action; Hammer Care; and Major Repairs, Reconditioning, and Rebuilding.

## Resources (cont.)

**WEBSITES**

*The Association of Blind Piano Tuners*

www.uk-piano.org

This site includes a history of the piano.

*The Piano Education Page*

http://pianoeducation.org

– Select "Links"

*Piano Home Page*

www.marthabeth.com/consumer.html

Links are included for piano action, resources, acoustics, prices, etc.

*PianoTeachers.com*

www.pianoteachers.com

– Select "How to choose a piano for your home."

*The Piano Technicians Guild*

www.ptg.org

## Educational Materials and Equipment

The most basic tool in any piano studio is the metronome. It is never a luxury, but rather, an essential tool of the trade. Another feature of a well-stocked studio is a resource library, consisting of reading material, repertoire books, CDs, videos, and DVDs, as well as educational tools such as music games, world music instruments, rhythm instruments, and flash cards. A long-range plan can be helpful in gradually building the studio library.

With the acquisition of materials, it is essential to have an organized storage system in the studio. Such organization is necessary so that the studio does not look cluttered. Home organizers emphasize inexpensive ways to organize and store materials. The following are a few items that may help teachers organize their studios:

- Closet space

- Baskets

- Colorful containers

- Enclosed shelves

- Filing cabinets

- Bookshelves (When purchasing from a discount furniture store, one can request that extra shelves be built into the cases, to store stacks of music classified by composer.)

An orderly system of storage not only helps the studio look more professional, it adds to the efficiency of the teacher. By being able to find things quickly, teachers do not spend ten minutes of the lesson saying, "Now where did I put those flash cards? I wanted you to use them this week! Just hold on, I am sure they are here somewhere… oh, darn…"

### Workstation/Computer Lab

A teacher can set up a workstation area simply by creating an area in the studio with a flat surface for writing, enough light for reading, and a place to store workbooks and assignments, such as cubbies or folders labeled with each student's name. With the addition of a CD player, iPod, or MP3 player and some headphones, the workstation becomes a listening station as well.

If the ultimate goal is to turn the workstation into a computer lab, a teacher can create a long-range plan to budget for necessary items, decide on curricular needs, organize the space, and develop a timeline for purchases. A great deal of thought must be given to how the area will be used before purchases are made.

A plan for multiple computer stations with MIDI keyboards may necessitate saving for a larger studio or perhaps a second room. Workstation uses will be discussed in Chapter 40, and workstation equipment and software will be discussed in Chapters 42 and 43.

### Waiting Area and Restroom

Having a waiting room apart from the studio itself allows parents and students to wait inside without infringing on privacy during lessons. If possible, it is advantageous to set aside a restroom for exclusive studio use. If a waiting room and separate restroom are an extravagance in a starter home or an apartment, they should be in the long-range plans of a successful studio.

## Office Area

For some teachers, the office area is outside the studio, but for many it is within the studio space itself. The office area makes a strong impression on students and parents. An orderly area says the teacher is organized and efficient, while an over-run, disheveled area says she can barely keep up.

When the office area is arranged with enough room for all office related equipment such as files and furniture, the space not only looks better, but allows for a more organized approach to paper work. Even on a limited budget, items can be purchased at a second-hand store or discount furniture store to keep the office area tidy, functional, and efficient.

Most teachers cannot afford to buy everything needed all at once, so it is important to prioritize the desired items by examining how each piece of office equipment will be used.

### Desk

As obvious as it may seem, teachers need a desk, which should be placed in a well-lit area designated for office work. The desk should have a large, uncluttered surface, with drawers that provide room to store office supplies, business records, and student files.

## Phone

**Answering machine:** This is an essential piece of equipment, used to store phone messages from students and parents when the teacher is unavailable. Many teachers leave a phone machine on while teaching so that lessons will not be interrupted.

**Studio phone line:** Some teachers have a separate phone line for the studio. Many use a recorded message: "If your message is for the Unique Piano Studio, please press 'one.'" This system allows business-related calls to be identified and accessed easily.

## Fax Machine

A fax machine allows teachers to send and receive materials that are not stored on a computer. These can include items such as competition application forms or fliers for arts events.

## Personal Computer

In this day and age, a personal computer is essential to the efficient operation of an independent piano studio. Care should be taken to purchase a computer that will fit all the studio business needs. The computer should be kept separate from student use, to protect personal or business files. Depending on the computer's operating system, individual accounts may be created allowing limited use of a specified account, thus protecting private files.

## Business Software

When purchasing a computer, teachers also must invest in software programs that will best suit the studio needs. A variety of software packages allows teachers to broaden their technology skills and become more self-reliant within the studio. Although only basic programs may be affordable at first, setting aside funds for the purchase of more sophisticated applications in the future helps spread the cost over time. Computer programs that help with business-related tasks in a studio are discussed further in Chapter 4.

## Printer

A printer allows teachers to print documents from their computer as needed. For example, with a printer, teachers can print letters and address envelopes immediately. When purchasing a printer it is not wise to buy the cheapest model, since low-end models often print at a painfully slow speed and may use ink more quickly.

## Copy Machine

A copy machine in the studio allows the teacher to make multiple copies of policy sheets, recital programs, studio newsletters, and other documents. This eliminates the time needed to travel to an office supply store or copy center. Since copiers are available in a variety of sizes, with a wide range of capabilities, it is important to predetermine one's needs before purchasing a copy machine.

## File Cabinets

Depending on the amount of material that can be stored in the desk, teachers most likely will require additional filing space. No matter how much is stored on a computer, some paper files also need to be saved, such as correspondence, invoices, receipts, and tax records. It is impossible to be organized without adequate space to store such documents. As always, the goal is to keep the studio uncluttered, so that office work can be accomplished without being overrun by paper or disarray.

## Establishing a Budget for Studio Purchases

Right from the start, teachers can organize the best possible studio based on their current budget and pedagogical needs. Just as other business owners plan for growth and change, so should the independent piano teacher try to improve studio equipment, materials, and space in some way each year.

As the years progress, many teachers will have capital for renovating studio space, building an addition, or moving to a home with a more suitable studio. The goal is to develop a workable long-range plan for purchasing instruments, equipment, workstations, pedagogical tools, and adequate studio space.

One way to plan for studio purchases is to categorize them into three groups.

- **Small purchases:** These include affordable items that could be purchased monthly and would improve some aspect of the studio, such as a file cabinet, music theory game, a software program, or new repertoire books.

- **Mid-range purchases:** Once a year a larger and more expensive item could be purchased, such as a set of world music instruments, a MIDI keyboard, or a computer.

- **Longterm purchases:** Multiple workstations, a grand piano, a second piano, or a home addition for an improved studio space are sizeable expenses that may require financing through a bank loan or savings over a number of years.

The following are some creative ways to absorb cost if the budget is tight.

- Expand the studio library by planning a system of small purchases of pedagogical resources over time.

- Take advantage of free music offered at publisher showcases for expansion of the library and access to the latest publications.

- Purchase pedagogical tools such as videos or games as part of a summer camp budget. Once purchased, these materials can be reused for many years.

- Secure a bank loan to finance a significant purchase such as a new piano or computer system.

Over time, even the most spartan piano studio can become an ideal teaching space through long-range planning, careful budgeting, and vision.

---

**MEMORABLE QUOTES**

Below are some amusing answers to the question, "What would your ideal studio include?" taken from past teacher surveys conducted in a number of different states.

"My perfect studio would have room for a secretary."

"My ideal studio would be to have four rooms – a private teaching room with a grand and an upright, a group lesson room, an electronic music lab, and a computer room. I live above the studio and the music store is across the street."

"My studio would consist of one student; I'd charge $1500 a lesson, offer no make-ups, and have summers off."

While the business of setting up the ideal studio must be based in reality, fantasizing can provide some humorous relief along the way.

# Chapter 4

# OFFICE TECHNOLOGY FOR THE STUDIO

Had anyone told me years ago that I would someday be joined at the hip to my computer, I would have laughed. Not even knowing how to type, I paid others to type my college papers and later, my recital programs and studio documents. Having resisted technology for decades, I was eventually forced kicking and screaming into the 21st century.

Anyone feeling a similar reluctance to embrace technology is missing out on its many benefits, both pedagogical and organizational. The advantages of using technology as a teaching tool will be discussed in Chapter 43, while this chapter will present ideas on using technology in studio operation.

By learning basic office and computer skills, teachers save money, free themselves from dependence on others, gain control of their studio documents and record keeping, and present their studios more professionally. The following are some ways that computer technology can assist the teacher:

- Developing attractive studio documents, such as policy sheets, registration forms, and letterhead stationery

- Producing brochures, fliers, and newsletters to market the studio

- Keeping studio records of payments, student contact information, and student levels for festivals and competitions

- Tracking tax information and completing tax forms

- Developing a studio web page

- Facilitating group correspondence with students and parents

- Accessing Internet resources such as e-mail, group forums, and informational websites

## Essential Office Software for Studio Use

### Word Processing Programs

As discussed in Chapter 2, an effective studio requires a number of essential studio documents. Being able to use a word processing program to type and update these documents saves both time and money. Word processing allows on-the-spot, easy changes to business documents (such as updating a studio policy statement) as well as quick reformatting of existing materials (for example, a student practice book). All forms and documents may be saved on the computer and reused or updated with ease, year after year. The studio logo can be inserted into any letter, document, or form that is created.

Imagine how cumbersome it would be to consult an outside typist every time a new letter or changes to an existing form were needed. If a teacher does decide to outsource the typing of studio documents, it is wise to ask the following questions before doing so:

- Do I have enough time to drop off and pick up the project during work hours?
- How much will it cost to outsource the project?
- How long will someone else take to finish the project?
- Will I get it back on time?
- Will somebody else understand what I want?

Whether relying on the kindness of friends, relatives, or strangers, teachers place themselves in a position of dependence rather than independence when they count on someone else to produce their documents.

Instructions for word processing programs are available as online tutorials on the Internet. Hardcopy texts are available at libraries as well as at office and bookstores. In addition, classes in particular software programs are frequently offered through computer retailers.

## Financial and Accounting Programs

All teachers must keep accurate financial records for both studio and tax purposes. Doing this by hand results in an outdated and time-consuming system of tracking monthly tuition payments and yearly expenses. It is much more efficient to use a financial software program to create a spreadsheet that will automatically calculate and track financial records, such as tuition payments and book expenses.

Accounting software can also generate reports on student payment activity, write and print checks, keep track of income and expenses, print invoices and mailing labels, and much more. Some accounting programs can also access information from database management programs.

## Database Management Programs

This record-keeping software helps organize contact data and other student information. Most database programs have mail merge capabilities that can print a single letter addressed to a number of recipients. They can also generate address labels and update information easily.

## Resources

*Music Teacher's Helper:* This web-based computer program is designed to assist music teachers with easy and efficient studio management. Handling everything from billing and lesson schedules to lending library items and tax reports, the program provides valuable time savers for any professional music teacher. With *Music Teacher's Helper*, each teacher gets a free studio website that the teacher, students, and parents can access, or the site can be integrated with an existing website. The program takes advantage of the benefits of having studio records online as opposed to buying software to install on a studio computer. The following lists some of these benefits.

- *Free studio website:* Teachers can put their teaching policies, photos, studio news, and more on the website. There is no need to learn how to develop a website; the websites are already beautifully designed. Putting personal information on it is as easy as using a word processor.

# Resources (cont.)

- *Student access:* Students can log in from home to see their lesson schedules, invoices, and assignments, and parents can even pay online with their credit card. Students can also get automatic e-mail reminders about upcoming lessons, classes, recitals, and loaned items that are due. *Music Teacher's Helper* also allows students to register for open lesson schedules and group events on the studio calendar.

- *Business records:* Handles business records such as invoices, tracking of payments, reports for taxes, and the tracking of lending library items (e-mail reminders sent to students when due), and student repertoire.

- *Cheaper upfront cost:* Some studio management packages can cost hundreds of dollars. *Music Teacher's Helper* is a subscription-based service, and prices depend on the number of students in a studio, starting with the *Free Forever* plan for teachers with three students or fewer, and moving to the plans for up to ten students, up to 20 students, up to 30 students, and finally to the unlimited plan.

- *Compatible with any computer:* *Music Teacher's Helper* works on any computer with an Internet connection and a modern browser, including Windows, Mac, Linux, and some mobile phones.

- *Safe information:* There is no worry about losing data if your computer crashes or transferring data to a new computer, because all studio information is online and backed up on multiple servers. Teachers can also export the data to their personal computer as a backup or print a hard copy, if so desired.

- *Instant updates:* When new features get added or bugs get fixed, everyone gets the updates immediately. There is no need to install updates of any kind, but rather they will be found just by going to the website.

- *Strong support:* E-mailed questions are generally answered within an hour, and usually faster.

To sign up, go to www.musicteachershelper.com.

Iverson, Mary Lou. *Time$ig 2005 – Studio Management Software.* Bloomington: Casa de la Musica, 1991, 2005.

A program particularly well suited to the independent studio, *Time$ig 2005 – Studio Management Software*, has been designed by accountants, music teachers, and engineers, and continues to upgrade its capabilities on an ongoing basis. The program assists music teachers by handling student profiles, scheduling, accounting and billing, rosters, notes on student progress, group or class assignments, and data for use at tax season. This software is specifically designed for music teachers, quickly generating needed reports.

- Student/teacher/studio/contest schedules
- Financial billing, including e-bills. Bills can be sent to each payer by electronic mail. Statements can also be sent by snail mail, depending on the teacher's choice.
- Calculates sales tax
- Uses either fee-per-lesson or tuition charges. The program can be customized to any studio setting.
- Student profile and progress notes; these reports include student historical data: instruments studied, ensemble groups, recitals, workshops, festivals, etc.
- Student roster: can be used for students to swap lesson times
- Detailed account status with current balances
- Tuition/lesson summary; attendance/absences
- Event schedules for contests or festivals, complete with information such as the appropriate division, selection, composer, and time allotment. This function can also be used by festival or contest chairs to assign students to a room, schedule times, assign judges to rooms, etc.
- Time$ig report includes monthly and year-to-date totals on financial information.
- Flexibility for small, large or conservatory uses

The program will accommodate a studio setting from one private teacher to unlimited teachers in a large conservatory setting. Ongoing technical support is available, as are annual software revisions and upgrades. The program is available in three versions: Solo, Intermediate, and Unlimited. Free demos are available at: www.casamusica.com/timesig.htm.

### Creative Design Programs

Designing customized studio materials allows teachers to have more creative control over their professional documents. Although a word processing program is capable of producing a variety of studio documents, specialized graphics software provides another option for creating certain types of professional and marketing materials, such as:

- Letterhead template

- Business cards

- Résumés

- Brochures

- Newsletters

- Fliers

- Studio calendars

- Recital invitations and programs

- Award certificates

- Greeting cards

Publishing or design programs include templates for many of the above documents, which can be customized to create eye-catching, personalized, and professional-looking materials.

### Digital Photo Software

Photographs taken with a digital camera are easily downloaded onto a computer. Photographs of students (with the written permission of a parent or guardian) can then be incorporated into any number of studio marketing tools such as a web page, studio brochure, or promotional flier. Software programs also allow the user to manipulate and edit pictures that have been stored on a computer.

## Using Internet Resources

### E-mail

Not having e-mail in this day and age is somewhat like doing without a telephone. E-mail is a quick and inexpensive method of communicating with parents and students as a group and individually, as well as with professional colleagues.

If a teacher is an officer or chairperson within a music teachers' organization, e-mail provides fast and easy communication to and from the membership, so that business can be conducted efficiently. Phone-tag is not a fun game to play, and snail mail (the United States Postal Service) often takes too long and can be expensive. With the click of a mouse, a group e-mail list gives immediate access to an entire board or committee. When planning a state activity, for example, group e-mails provide a fast and efficient means of reaching other planners. If a teacher does not have e-mail access, she will be unable to contribute to the organization's decision-making process, which often takes place through group e-mails.

Sometimes, sending a letter through the U.S. Postal Service has more of an impact than e-mail. In those cases, group mailings are more professionally handled and take less time with the use of database technology, as mentioned previously.

### Personalized Web Pages

More and more teachers are designing their own web pages as an additional marketing tool. Numerous web design software programs and online web design sites make it easy to create a personalized web page. Besides listing important contact information, a personal web page can include the many items that make a studio unique, such as a teacher biography, studio calendar, highlights of student activities and accomplishments, information updates for parents, a link to monthly newsletters, and a link to the teacher's e-mail address.

### Internet Research

Those who use the Internet with any regularity know what an invaluable tool it can be. Information is readily available on publishers and their materials, composers, repertoire, music topics, pedagogical developments, and professional organizations. Students can be given Internet research assignments on subjects such as composers or periods of music history, and can make use of interactive sites for theory and ear-training. Using an Internet search engine provides instant access to information that would take hours or even weeks to find in a library. However, despite their value, not all Internet sites are created equal; teachers should be selective in choosing sources that are accurate and reliable. When used wisely, the Internet brings a trillion-story library, open 24/7, right to the studio.

## Resources

Below is a short list of some of the many software programs capable of assisting the independent teacher.

Adobe®: http://www.adobe.com

> Adobe® *Photoshop*®: *Adobe*® *Photoshop*® has products to help edit and organize photographs, as well as film and video. An excellent program for teachers.

> Adobe® *Reader*®: *Adobe*® *Reader*® allows teachers to view and print PDF documents that can then be digitally transmitted to other individuals. PDF files (Portable Document Format) cannot be altered once they have been created, and are ideal for documents whose format should not be changed.

Microsoft Office®: http://office.microsoft.com

> Microsoft *Access*™: An office database management program that can be used for functions such as organizing student contact data, mail merging, and printing mailing labels.

> Microsoft *Excel*®: Allows teachers to create spreadsheets that will automatically calculate the sum of separate categories, such as tuition payments, studio income and expenses.

> Microsoft *Expression*® *Web*: A program for web page design and maintenance.

> Microsoft *Publisher*®: Can be used for creative design and marketing. Although Word can be used for a number of studio documents, Publisher allows teachers to develop even more attractive designs for materials such as studio brochures.

> Microsoft *Word*®: Allows teachers to create and update essential studio documents and correspondences.

**Microsoft *Office*® Online:** Office.microsoft.com (Select "templates").

Microsoft *Office*® Online has a helpful website with numerous templates to assist with designing any number of studio documents: student award certificates, stationery, planners, labels, legal documents, business forms, and much more.

**QuickBooks®:** Quickbooks.intuit.com

QuickBooks accounting software addresses a number of duties of the independent piano teacher. The program can create invoices, document deposits, print checks, track inventory, manage studio records, pay bills, track expenses, address envelopes, and create professional forms. The program comes with helpful tutorials.

## In Summary

Some teachers use technology, but only in a limited fashion; many others feel overwhelmed and unable to enter the world of technology at all. If teachers feel reluctant to use computers or are anxious about improving their skills, I would offer a word of encouragement: "Take a deep breath and jump right in." Plenty of people are willing to help, including friends, family, community education programs, and even our students.

There cannot be a person alive who resisted technology more vehemently than I. From the start, I felt fearful and overwhelmed. I agonized over touching the wrong button and blowing up all the computers in a ten-state region. I worried that Bill Gates would send me a letter demanding that I quit trying. I am the type of person who is fearful of turning on anything new; I had cruise control in my car for eight years before I dared touch the button. During my "it's-hard-for-me-to-change" mid-40s, however, I began teaching at Valley City State University, a university with high expectations for their faculty's use of technology. I had to touch one of those darn computers after all—and it was one of the best moves I ever made.

As difficult as it was for me, it was liberating to admit the truth, "I know nothing about technology." Fortunately, my initial fear and embarrassment did not hold me back. People were there to help, and today I would be considered fairly computer-savvy. Now I feel I have an IV connection to the Internet… I will continue to learn more, not because it is easy for me, but because of the many professional benefits I experience from improving my technology skills.

# Part II
## FINANCES

Part II discusses the numerous financial issues affecting the independent teacher. Since many independent piano teachers are underpaid, it is important to be aware of the factors causing low income in order to follow a more educated approach when setting rates.

Ultimately, teachers are in charge of their own financial health. Recognizing this responsibility will encourage them to adopt policies that will improve their financial and professional success, such as setting professional rates, devising an effective system of payment, and developing a creative approach to summer income.

Part II addresses numerous areas affecting finances—from late payments to scholarships to taxes—issues that require careful consideration and planning if the independent studio is to thrive.

# Chapter 5

# SETTING RATES

In order to understand the impact of income on our profession, it is worthwhile to observe the results of surveys completed by a cross section of independent piano teachers. However, when researching rates of the independent music teacher (IMT), it is not possible to obtain data that is 100% accurate. The reason is that many teachers cannot be reached because they have no affiliation with professional groups outside of their homes, receive no professional publications, and attend no professional events. It is impossible to identify such teachers through any kind of list, and therefore they are not included in any survey. When polling teachers who can be identified, such as members of professional organizations or subscribers to professional magazines, the results of a survey potentially become skewed. Because of their association with those institutions, teachers responding to such surveys may already be more professional and charge more appropriate rates. Nonetheless, it is still worth gathering facts about income from any available group of independent music teachers.

## Results of National Surveys

The data in this chapter has been drawn mainly from the two surveys listed below:

- **2002 IMT Business Practices Survey** by Beth Klingenstein

- **2003 *Clavier* Survey** by Judy Nelson

Additional data will come from the 2005 MTNA Member Survey.

As with all financial figures, the dollar amounts from these surveys became obsolete within a year of their publication. Nevertheless, the information collected provides a valuable comparison of the status of the independent music teacher's profession, both then and now. Since changes come about slowly in the music teaching profession, current generalizations about the profession can still be drawn from these surveys.

### 2002 IMT Business Practices Survey  BY BETH KLINGENSTEIN

This survey polled members of Music Teachers National Association (MTNA), with results published in the August/September 2002 and December/January 2002/2003 issues of *American Music Teacher* magazine (AMT). This survey was intended to help determine the factors that impact the income of the independent music teacher. The survey was sent to hundreds of teachers across the country, with questions concerning rates and workloads. All the independent teachers contacted were members of Music Teachers National Association and it is highly likely that their membership in MTNA reflects higher levels of both income and education.

From this survey, the national average revealed a teacher with a bachelor's degree, who taught for 23 years and had 30 students on her schedule. She taught 19 hours of lessons a week and worked 12 extra hours a week in the studio outside of actual lesson time. The average fee for a one-hour lesson at the time of the survey was $29. The average gross annual income from teaching was $17, 893 and the average workweek was 31 hours. Considering the years of experience and the time spent on the job, this was definitely not a good income.

## 2003 *Clavier* Survey  BY JUDY NELSON

This 2003 survey polled subscribers of *Clavier* magazine, with results published in its February 2004 issue. In her article "Studio Piano Teachers Charge Meagerly for Lessons," Judy Nelson reported the following:

> "The results of the latest *Clavier* survey of subscribers show that piano teachers charge an average of $13 per 30-minute lesson, teach 25 private students per week, and make an annual income of only $13,000 in 40 weeks of teaching. Among those who responded to the October 2003 survey, the highest fee reported for 30 minutes of instruction was $35 and the lowest was $7. The teachers in this survey had an average of 25 years of experience and have one or more degrees in music education, piano performance, and piano pedagogy. Overall, 87% of the teachers have a college degree, 35% also have a master's degree, and 4% a doctorate.
>
> In the 1980 survey of readers, the average fee for a 30-minute lesson was $5.57; when this amount is adjusted for inflation, it comes to $13. This means that in spite of reported increases in rates from surveys in the 1990s, piano teachers today on average earn exactly the same amount they did 23 years ago."
>
> © 2004 The Instrumentalist Publishing Co. Reprinted with permission.

What is remarkable about Nelson's survey is that the average piano teacher's annual income in 2003 was only $13,000, far below the incomes of other professions in that year. The other significant finding from that survey is that when rates were adjusted for inflation, teachers basically received the same income in 2003 as they did in 1980! Although today's dollar amounts are higher, when adjusted for inflation, they will most likely be on a similar par, and far below where they should be.

Although the income from both surveys reflects that of past years rather than the current year, some important comparisons put this information in an interesting light that is still valuable today.

### IMT INCOME COMPARISON

| | 2002 IMT BUSINESS PRACTICES SURVEY BY BETH KLINGENSTEIN | 2003 CLAVIER SURVEY BY JUDY NELSON |
|---|---|---|
| Average Per-hour Fee | $29 | $26 |
| Average Gross Annual Income | $17,893 | $13,000 |
| Average Years of Experience | 23 years | 25 years |
| Average Private Students Per Week | 30 students | 25 students |

In both surveys, the per-hour fee and years of experience are very similar. The gross annual income is higher in the 2002 survey because of the higher per-hour fee and larger number of students.

## Addressing Factors That Impact Income

These surveys show that income earned by the independent music teacher (IMT) is far below that of comparable professionals. How can teachers improve their income? The solution to this economic challenge lies less in society's opinion of the arts and more in each teacher's understanding of the forces determining income. Rather than feel frustrated by low income, teachers must feel empowered to take control of what they earn. Additionally, there is much that teachers can learn from each other.

To counteract the disparity in income levels, several factors that potentially impact teacher income need to be addressed by every teacher when setting rates.

### Half-hour Lessons

Teaching is made unduly challenging if only half-hour lessons are taught. Although half-hour lessons result in a shorter workweek, they mistakenly lead the teacher to feel that she works part-time. The teacher's income level decreases proportionately, but the workload remains basically the same, as each half-hour lesson must be taught with the same goals as hour lessons. No one sets lower standards for themselves or their students when they teach half-hour lessons. Personally, I wish that half-hour lessons would go the way of the typewriter. They are obsolete, especially as teachers include more music theory, sight-playing, ear-training, music history, composition, ensemble skills, and improvisation within the studio curriculum.

### Per-hour vs. Gross Annual Income

Teachers are not aware of their low income because they perceive their hourly fee as high without considering that the gross annual income (money earned in one year before deductions and taxes) is actually quite low.

The first step toward being in charge of one's income is to be able to readily answer the following questions:

- How much do you charge per lesson?
- What was your gross annual income last year?

If only the first question can be answered with ease (or with pride), the teacher may be experiencing one of the main problems the independent music teacher faces when setting rates. The IMT often focuses more on the per-hour figure and not on yearly income. When a $40 per-hour fee is considered, for example, a teacher may feel she is earning quite a lot. But if she computes her gross annual income, she may realize she is not earning as much as she deserves.

Although per-hour fees are needed in a survey as a standard unit of measure, it is far more advantageous for teachers to consider that the lesson fee covers more than the lesson itself. It is more beneficial to view the per-hour fee as a per-week fee, to take into account time spent on all the weekly activities done on behalf of the student in addition to actual lesson time. If a teacher computes her gross annual income based solely on a per-hour lesson fee rather than per-week basis, it becomes apparent that the teacher is earning far below what she deserves.

If a teacher is uncertain of her gross annual income, it can be calculated using the following simple formula, in which "per-hour" is replaced by "per-week."

## CALCULATING GROSS ANNUAL INCOME

| NUMBER OF STUDENTS | PER-WEEK FEE PER STUDENT | NUMBER OF TEACHING WEEKS | TOTAL GROSS ANNUAL INCOME |
| --- | --- | --- | --- |
| 20 | $20 | 40 | $16,000 |
| 20 | $50 | 40 | $40,000 |
| 20 | $80 | 40 | $64,000 |

**Formula:** Number of students a week x per-week fee per student x number of teaching weeks in the year = Gross Annual Income.

As discussed later in this chapter, when deductions are taken from the gross annual income, the net income will be even lower.

### Per-hour vs. Tuition

Many teachers represent their rates as "per-hour" rather than as "tuition." Words have a great deal of power. One of the most important words the IMT can use is tuition. When I am asked, "How much do you charge per lesson?", I do not answer with a per-hour rate. Instead, I discuss all the things that I offer in my studio and what the tuition will be to study with me. Tuition helps families realize they are not paying a high per-lesson fee, but rather a payment that covers a broad range of activities. Also, if students miss a lesson, they are more likely to understand this does not impact their tuition payment. It is similar to a college student missing a biology lab; the tuition will not be adjusted because of the absence.

### Full-time vs. Part-time

The argument might be made that the average teacher in my survey is a part-time teacher and therefore an average income of $17,893 is not that bad. In reality, $17,893 is not an adequate income for someone with 23 years of experience who is teaching 30 students. It can also be argued that this teacher is not part-time. No one who teaches 30 students and performs all the extra duties this requires is part-time.

Too often teachers consider only the time spent actually teaching lessons as their work time when deciding if they teach full-time or part-time. Keep in mind that the typical full-time load for a college instructor of applied lessons is 18 hours a week during a nine-month year. Colleges and universities know that there are many other duties that go along with the job, and the IMT should recognize this as well.

If a teacher has not given adequate thought to all of the services she provides for her students, she should examine (and even add to) the following list:

- Attend professional meetings, such as those of local music organizations
- Hold offices in music organizations
- Arrange recitals
- Schedule lessons
- Purchase music and supplies
- Accompany students (duets, concertos, etc.)
- Attend state and national conferences
- Prepare computer lab or workstation assignments
- Hold theory classes
- Conduct performance classes
- Keep financial records
- Learn new repertoire and practice regularly
- Prepare and grade assignments done at a workstation
- Learn and teach computer software
- Collect payments
- Devise an appropriate curriculum for each student, plan individual lessons
- Provide college recommendations
- Plan studio policies
- Maintain time for continuing education
- Publish studio documents
- Counsel students
- Obtain permits and comply with local zoning and business license ordinances
- Prepare and file studio tax information

There are other negative and often unpredictable side effects of labeling oneself part-time. Recently a teacher contacted me because her husband of 30 years was divorcing her. He had copied her studio calendar and all the hours she had filled in with student activities to prove to the court that she could increase her income by teaching more lessons instead of doing those "extra" activities. What he did not understand was that these duties went along with the 20 hours of lessons this woman gave. They were not something that could be replaced by 40 hours of nothing but lessons.

In my survey on rates and workloads, there were surprising answers to what constitutes part-time. Many teachers marked themselves as part-time teachers, and yet had heavy teaching loads.

- 35% of part-time teachers had 20–29 students
- 10% of part-time teachers had 30–39 students
- 17% of part-time teachers had 40 or more students

## 2002 IMT BUSINESS PRACTICES SURVEY
### BY BETH KLINGENSTEIN
## RATES AND WORKLOADS

|  | PART-TIME | FULL-TIME |
|---|---|---|
| Percentage identifying with each group | 55% | 44% |
| Highest number of students | 48 | 80 |
| Average number of students | 22 | 40 |
| Average hours spent teaching private lessons | 14 | 25 |
| Average total hours spent on all music activities | 23 | 39 |
| Average fee per hour lesson | $26 | $32 |
| Average gross income from teaching lessons | $10,928 | $27,132 |
| Average gross income from all music activities | $12,460 | $32,670 |

As seen in the table above, somewhere in this great land is a teacher with 48 students who considers herself part-time!

In a separate survey, the 2005 MTNA Member Survey conducted by MTNA in conjunction with Beyond Data, Inc., about half of the respondents viewed themselves as teaching full-time. The full survey is available on the MTNA website: http://www.mtna.org/HLtext.

## 2005 MTNA MEMBER SURVEY
### WORKLOAD

|  | PART-TIME | FULL-TIME |
|---|---|---|
| Percentage identifying with each group | 44% | 51% |
| Average number of private students | 17 | 30 |
| Average hours spent teaching private lessons | 14 | 23 |

For all those considering themselves part-time, it would be wise to re-examine their studio workload. Teachers need not teach 40 hours a week or 12 months of the year to actually teach full-time. Even if a teacher does work part-time, how would her salary compare to those working part-time in other professions, such as nursing?

## Salaries of Other Professions

Many teachers are unaware of the average income paid in other professions and unwittingly accept an income that is comparable to that paid in fields requiring lesser skills. How does the salary of the independent music teacher compare to that of other professionals? Helpful comparisons giving national averages for the salaries of various professions are listed on Internet sites such as the following:

### U.S. DEPARTMENT OF LABOR: WWW.BLS.GOV/OES

The statistics listed in the following table are from the Department of Labor (DOL) site. (Go to www.bls.gov/oes and scroll down to "Archived," then select "Employment and Wage Estimates" for the desired year.) They do not reflect current figures, which change annually, but rather show figures that relate to the survey years mentioned in this chapter. The most intriguing comparisons are between the following two factors:

- The growth rate within some professions

- The 2002 salaries when compared to the gross annual income of the IMT in the surveys published in 2002 in American Music Teacher and in 2003 in *Clavier*.

The salaries listed below are not the highest in a profession, but rather the mean, or average. Notice the figures in 2002 and compare them to the average income of the independent music teacher quoted in the surveys. Also notice the increases that each of the professions below experienced in 2002 and again in 2005.

### AVERAGE GROSS ANNUAL INCOME OF THE IMT

| | |
|---|---|
| 2002 Business Practices Survey by Beth Klingenstein | $17,893 |
| 2003 *Clavier* Survey by Judy Nelson | $13,000 |

### U.S. DEPARTMENT OF LABOR STATISTICS

| | 2002 | 2005 |
|---|---|---|
| Dentist | 133,350 | 133,680 |
| General practitioner | 136,350 | 140,370 |
| Lawyer | 105,890 | 110,520 |
| Pharmacist | 75,140 | 88,650 |
| Physical therapist | 60,180 | 65,350 |
| Dental hygienist | 57,790 | 60,620 |
| Librarians | 44,430 | 49,110 |
| Elementary school teacher | 44,080 | 46,990 |
| Plumber | 42,630 | 44,850 |
| Athletic trainer | 36,070 | 36,520 |
| Carpet installer | 34,920 | 37,100 |
| Massage therapist | 33,720 | 40,210 |
| Pharmacy technician | 23,200 | 25,350 |
| Receptionist | 21,970 | 23,120 |
| File Clerk | 21,190 | 22,840 |
| Janitor | 20,150 | 21,120 |
| Manicurist | 18,810 | 20,400 |
| Maid and housecleaner | 17,330 | 18,180 |

Comparing these figures with those in the 2002 IMT Business Practices Survey shows that in 2002 the IMT income was lower than a pharmacy technician, janitor, receptionist, file clerk, and even a manicurist! What does this say about how the independent teacher's work is valued? Even the fairly new professions of massage therapist and athletic trainer are far above the average IMT salary. In 2002, the only profession on the DOL list that teachers topped (and just barely) was a maid! It should be remembered that these surveys do not take into account the many teachers who could not be identified through memberships or magazine subscriptions. Because the income of these teachers may very well be lower than those surveyed, the IMT income estimates are probably even lower than shown.

It is even more appropriate to view the average IMT income in relationship to the more substantial salaries of pharmacists or lawyers. Like pharmacy and law, for example, music teaching is a field that reflects a high level of skill and training and provides a specialized service. Imagine if music teachers billed like lawyers do:

- $80 half-hour phone call consultation
- $100 college recommendation
- $200 one-hour interview

### BUSINESS WEEK STATISTICS

On its website (http://swz-businessweek.salary.com), *Business Week* includes a *Salary Wizard*, reflecting median salaries (in other words, 50% earn higher and 50% earn lower) of various professions. This can be used as a tool to check the salaries of specific professions in a teacher's geographical area, simply by selecting a profession and a location.

## Level of Education

Teachers do not take into account their educational level when setting lesson fees. In the 2002 IMT Business Practices Survey, shown in the following table, the per-hour rates and therefore the gross annual income increased slowly but consistently as the level of education increased. Unfortunately, the average gross annual income for the most educated group of music teachers in 2002 was still less than $30,000, far below other professional salaries that year.

## 2002 IMT BUSINESS PRACTICE SURVEY
### IMPACT OF EDUCATIONAL LEVEL

| HIGHEST LEVEL OF EDUCATION | PERCENTAGE OF THOSE POLLED | AVERAGE FEE PER HOUR LESSON | AVERAGE GROSS ANNUAL INCOME FROM TEACHING | AVERAGE HOURS PRIVATE LESSONS | AVERAGE GROSS ANNUAL INCOME FROM ALL MUSIC ACTIVITIES |
|---|---|---|---|---|---|
| PRE-COLLEGE | 2% | $22 | $12,000 | 18 | $12,000 |
| SOME COLLEGE | 24% | $25 | $13,159 | 17 | $14,248 |
| BACHELORS DEGREE | 43% | $28 | $16,067 | 18 | $17,898 |
| MASTERS DEGREE | 24% | $33.50 | $23,899 | 22 | $32,373 |
| DMA/PHD | 3% | $37.75 | $24,750 | 18 | $29,712 |

A similar disparity exists today. When setting rates, teachers need to give themselves credit for their degrees, as well as for all the continuing education they have received through workshops, conferences, and professional seminars.

## Years of Experience

Another startling statistic from the 2002 IMT Business Practices Survey is the impact of years of experience on income. The average annual income for teachers with 30–35 years of experience was only $16,682, even lower than the overall survey average. Although income rises steadily as the educational level increases, there is no consistent rise in income as the years of experience increase; rather, income levels fluctuate unpredictably, with some of the most experienced teachers receiving the lowest wages.

This fluctuation may be due in part to the fact that older teachers set their rates much lower when they first started teaching, and raised rates in increments that were too small, leaving them behind. In terms of experience, the highest paid group consisted of teachers with 21–25 years of experience. Perhaps their income reflects an updated view about rates as well as a respect for their years of experience.

## 2002 IMT BUSINESS PRACTICES SURVEY
### YEARS OF EXPERIENCE AND INCOME

| YEARS OF EXPERIENCE | AVERAGE FEE PER ONE-HOUR LESSON | AVERAGE HOURS PRIVATE LESSONS PER WEEK | AVERAGE GROSS ANNUAL TEACHING INCOME | AVERAGE GROSS ANNUAL INCOME FROM ALL MUSIC ACTIVITIES |
|---|---|---|---|---|
| 5 YEARS & UNDER | $23 | 13 | $12,899 | $13,885 |
| 6–10 YEARS | $28 | 19 | $17,129 | $18,734 |
| 11–15 YEARS | $26 | 16 | $15,155 | $16,246 |
| 16–20 YEARS | $32 | 17 | $15,434 | $18,720 |
| 21–25 YEARS | $30 | 21 | $22,738 | $25,205 |
| 26–30 YEARS | $28.50 | 21 | $18,454 | $21,409 |
| 31–35 YEARS | $28 | 20 | $16,682 | $34,754 |
| 36–40 YEARS | $28 | 18 | $16,033 | $17,550 |
| 41 YEARS & OVER | $31.50 | 20 | $20,768 | $21,550 |

Teachers must make parents aware of their years of experience, reflect that experience when setting rates, and earn a gross annual income that reflects the value of all they have achieved.

## Population

Many teachers are not aware of the impact that area population has on income. The 2002 IMT Business Practices Survey shows that the factor affecting income the most is not education or experience, but rather the population of the community in which the individual teaches. Teachers in cities with a population of over 700,000 earned more than double the income of teachers from communities of 10,000 or less.

In 1994, I moved from the metropolitan Washington, D.C. area to a small town in rural North Dakota, and moved from a community with an average weekly fee of $34 per student to one with an average weekly fee of $6 per student. All the experience and degrees in the world would not have allowed me to charge the same fee in North Dakota as I had in the D.C. area.

Some might say, "Ah, but it is much less expensive to live in North Dakota than in Washington, D.C." Yes, that is true. But Ford Motor Company does not say, "You live in North Dakota, so your van will be 1/3 off." Toys-R-Us does not offer Christmas toys at half-price to North Dakotans. In rural areas, many important items are not less expensive; in fact, some might cost even more. Interestingly enough, piano technicians in North Dakota charged almost the same fees as technicians in Washington D.C. It was only the piano teachers who were far behind, much more so than the difference in cost of living would warrant.

When teachers justify low wages in a small community due to cost of living, they may be selling themselves short. The 2003 *Clavier* survey makes note of this as well: "Although fees and attitudes about fees vary from teacher to teacher, in general, location governs the amount a teacher can charge for lessons: parents in rural areas of the country are often unable or unwilling to pay high fees, while those in affluent areas near large cities accept them."

## 2002 IMT BUSINESS PRACTICES SURVEY
### IMPACT OF POPULATION ON IMT SALARY

| POPULATION | PERCENTAGE OF TEACHERS | AVERAGE FEE PER HOUR LESSON | AVERAGE GROSS INCOME TEACHING | AVERAGE GROSS ALL MUSIC INCOME |
|---|---|---|---|---|
| 10,000 & LESS | 22% | $23.50 | $13,168 | $15,139 |
| 10,001–100,000 | 33% | $29 | $17,402 | $19,899 |
| 100,001–700,000 | 25% | $27.50 | $15,971 | $17,626 |
| 700,000 & OVER | 14% | $37.25 | $29,441 | $31,226 |

A word of caution also needs to be offered to teachers in urban areas who often earn much higher rates. A teacher in New York City or Los Angeles earning $80,000 a year in 2003 may have felt that she was receiving a good salary. However, it would not have been commensurate with other professions in the area. Even though such a salary may sound high compared to the national IMT average, it should be viewed within the context of the cost of living in New York City or Los Angeles.

## Self-Employment

Since independent music teachers are self-employed, they lack adequate income models; few guidelines exist for establishing income for the self-employed. When setting rates, being self-employed actually works against piano teachers; they are not hired for a job with a pre-set corporate pay scale that also includes set, incremental yearly raises. The IMT works alone, and often does not even know what other teachers in the same area charge. To be informed, as recommended later in Chapter 13, conducting regular surveys on rates and workloads within local music associations enables teachers to share extremely valuable data about area rates, policies, and business practices. These surveys should always be conducted anonymously to protect the privacy of the participants.

Another issue that affects the income of the IMT is that each teacher must pay self-employment tax, a Social Security and Medicare tax paid by individuals who work for themselves. People who work for an employer pay only half of the amount due; the employer pays the remainder. Self-employed workers must pay the full amount themselves. Taxes will be covered in further detail in Chapter 8.

## Missed Lessons

If income is constantly adjusted due to missed lessons, a reliable income is impossible to achieve. A lenient or vague make-up policy, or one that lacks firmness by offering numerous exceptions, ultimately leads to a lowered income. When teachers set a firm and clearly written make-up policy and stick to it, parents and students understand and respect their expectations. Teachers are then able to receive a steady, predictable income. More will be said about this in Chapter 11.

## Method of Payment

Teachers often use an inefficient method of billing, further impacting income. If teachers charge by the lesson, or if they charge a monthly fee adjusted for variables like missed lessons, vacations, and holidays, income becomes unpredictable.

Teachers have it within their power to create a reliable income. They can determine the annual income per student, then implement a standard payment plan that does not vary. This not only saves on bookkeeping but also establishes a consistent annual income. Various methods of payment will be discussed further in Chapter 6.

## Out-of-date Rates

Many teachers initially set rates too low, reflecting those of the 1980s or '90s, rather than the 21st century. Piano teachers need to bring their rates in line with those of the current decade (and century!). While it is a natural impulse for a young teacher to set a lesson rate equal to what her parents paid for her lessons in the past, that should not be the automatic choice. One of the hardest income errors to recover from is setting rates too low at the start. Teachers should use present-day economics and today's market when determining lesson fees.

## Infrequent or Inadequate Rate Adjustments

Assuming that rates have been set appropriately to begin with, they need to be adjusted to match the increase in each year's cost of living. This necessary increase is not a real raise. Actual raises should be higher than any adjustment for cost of living, and are taken to reflect factors such as additional years of experience, additional skills, a change in educational level, and continuing education. If rates are originally set too low, then large increases will be necessary in order to catch up. When raises are too small, income will fall behind.

With a simple statement in the policy sheet, teachers can alert parents to expect an annual increase in rates: "Tuition will be adjusted annually." If teachers do not increase their rates annually, what they will experience is a pay cut because, as the cost of living increases, actual earnings decrease.

The U.S. Department of Labor, Bureau of Labor Statistics website (www.bls.gov/bls/inflation.htm) provides a helpful means of determining cost-of-living increases, listing valuable current information on the value of the dollar and the cost of living.

- The *Consumer Price Index* measures inflation as it is experienced in our daily lives.

- The *CPI Inflation Calculator* is used to "calculate the value of current dollars in an earlier period, or to calculate the current value of dollar amounts from years ago."

- The *Chained Consumer Price Index* provides an approximation of the cost-of-living index.

## Lack of Benefits

Using the year 2002 as a consistent point of comparison, the average salary for an elementary school teacher in this country was $41,980. When benefits were added to that salary, its value increased even more. The IMT does not receive the health, dental, and retirement benefits that make many other jobs financially appealing. Rather, the lack of these benefits presents the IMT with an additional burden that must be considered when setting rates; teachers must compensate for the lack of benefits when considering the tuition rates they set.

I have a niece who taught sixth grade in the Minneapolis area during the 2002 school year. Teachers in her school district with a Masters degree and seven years' experience earned salaries of $56,000 or more, plus extensive health, dental, and retirement benefits. These benefits alone were worth thousands of dollars. A fair assumption is that in 2002 there were few piano teachers in Minneapolis with a Masters degree and seven years of experience who had reached that income level.

## Expenses

IMT net salaries are lower than many professions because of the numerous business expenses and taxes incurred when running an independent music studio. Although business expenses are deductible, as will be discussed further in Chapter 8, paying for travel, professional development, studio space and maintenance, and purchases for the studio, all affect net annual income (the amount earned after all business-related expenses have been deducted). Many teachers overlook this fact, and do not consider these expenses when setting rates.

## Mental Attitude

The image that piano teachers have of their work and themselves is probably the most significant area needing examination when setting rates. The following are a few of the harmful mindsets that hinder independent teachers in their quest to set appropriate rates.

- **Independent teachers often suffer from poor self-esteem.** They feel guilty about charging what they deserve because they have not developed a strong sense of pride in their profession and the contribution they make to their communities. Knowledge is power. Knowing that the IMT's average salary is far below that of a carpet installer will empower teachers to charge a fee that is more commensurate with their expertise.

- **Teachers feel they cannot charge more because their services are not "necessary."** Unlike the services of a plumber or a lawyer, they reason that no one needs piano lessons. It must be argued that society does indeed need music, and the teachers of children provide the only means for music to survive in any culture.

- **Teachers often reason, "I don't need the income because I am being supported by my spouse."** This is one of the most disturbing mindsets of all, because not all teachers are so fortunate; some do need to support their family on the income from their studio. There are no guarantees in life: one day, any teacher may actually need that income, and then she will personally suffer if she has set her rates too low. By charging artificially low rates when the money isn't "needed," everyone in the profession suffers. Teachers who support a family have difficulty competing with the lower rates of those who charge less when they are supported by a spouse.

  In other professions, it is illegal for an employer to base salaries on whether or not they are primary or secondary income. It is important in music teaching that the worth of one's work not be based on whether it is a primary or secondary means of support.

- **Teachers may think "I am teaching 'for the love of it' and not for the money."** This implies that it is wrong to be paid for something one loves to do. Doctors do not receive lower wages if they love what they do, and neither should the IMT.

- **Some teachers operate out of fear that they will lose students by charging too much.** They believe, "Parents don't want to pay more for lessons!" This is true. No one wants to pay more for gas, doctor visits, or food either, but that does not keep prices from rising. No other business keeps rates set artificially low because parents don't want them to increase.

- **Teachers may fear that a deserving student will not be able to afford lessons if their rates are too high.** This fear can cause teachers to keep fees artificially low, and the net result is that they offer all their students a reduced rate. Instead, piano teachers should be paid what they are worth by charging professional rates, and then awarding scholarships to deserving students in need of financial assistance.

  This well-meaning desire to set low rates in order to keep lessons from being "exclusive" actually harms the profession. The result is that the profession itself becomes exclusive, available only to the rich, creating a situation in which the only people who can afford to teach are those who are independently wealthy or who have wealthy spouses. That is exclusive! If it is not possible to support one's family on one's income, is music teaching a profession or merely an avocation? Rather than set one-price-fits-all bargain rates, teachers benefit from setting professional rates and offering scholarships when needed, as stated above.

## Gender

The fact that teaching piano privately has traditionally been a female profession impacts wages; traditionally female professions tend to be lower paid than traditionally male professions. This is not offered as a criticism of either women or men, but rather as an historical fact. Fortunately, this is changing in today's world, but not as much or as quickly as some might believe. In the piano teaching world, the majority of teachers are still female, often earning less than their male counterparts. Women could benefit from advocating for equal wages, and should not allow gender to dictate their salary.

The 2005 MTNA Member Survey, which primarily measured satisfaction with MTNA membership and services, also included data relevant to the comparison of salaries by gender.

As in the two surveys previously cited, the respondents, by their very membership in MTNA and willingness to participate in the survey, reflected a higher interest in professional issues and a potentially higher level of income than teachers at large. Additionally, the average annual income in the 2005 MTNA Member Survey was much higher than in the other two, perhaps because this survey is the only survey that included respondents receiving income from colleges and universities (almost 20%).

**PART II**

### 2005 MTNA MEMBER SURVEY – GENDER COMPARISON
#### AVERAGE ANNUAL INCOME OF ALL MEMBERS: $27,000

|                       | MALE     | FEMALE   |
|-----------------------|----------|----------|
| Total Membership      | 13%      | 87%      |
| % Respondents         | 14 %     | 86%      |
| Average Annual Income | $36,000  | $26,000  |

It is worthwhile to read the entire 2005 MTNA Member Survey at: http://www.mtna.org/HLtext.

## In Summary

Self-assessment is crucial for the IMT when setting lesson fees. Whether living in a rural or urban environment, each independent piano teacher must do some soul-searching by contemplating the following questions carefully.

- Am I paid what I deserve?

- Does my income reflect the value of all that I do?

- Do I really work part-time?

- Does my salary fall where I want it to in comparison to other professions?

- Are my years of experience and level of education reflected in how much I earn?

- Am I compensating for the lack of benefits and for extra expenses when setting my rates?

- Can I support my family on my income?

- Am I afraid I will lose students if I raise my rates?

- Am I truly proud of what I do for my students and the service I give to my community?

# Resources

Butler, Mimi. *The Complete Guide to Making More Money in the Private Music Studio.* Haddonfield: Mimi Butler Publisher, 2008. Available at www.privatemusicstudio.com.

> Focusing on increasing income in the independent studio, chapters cover teaching in the schools, teaching home-schooled students, hiring additional teachers, teaching areas other than music lessons, organizing money-making activities, and developing summer music camps.

Butler, Mimi. *The Complete Guide to Running a Private Music Studio.* Haddonfield: Mimi Butler Publisher, 2008. Available at www.privatemusicstudio.com.

> Offering chapters on getting started, location, marketing, taxes, interviews, scheduling, make-ups, recitals, and more, this book serves as an excellent foundation for the business side of running a successful independent studio.

Gigante, Beth. *A Business Guide for the Piano Teacher.* San Diego: Neil A. Kjos Music Company, 1987.

> This brief business guide for the independent teacher covers student interviews, policy sheets, setting rates, make-ups, group lessons, scheduling lessons, bookkeeping, payment plans, zoning, projecting a professional image, and more.

Newsam, David, and Barbara Sprague Newsam. *Making Money Teaching Music.* Cincinnati: Writer's Digest Books, an imprint of F+W Publications, Inc., 1995.

> This book is an in-depth look into the finances of making a living by teaching music. Chapters offer suggestions for finding teaching opportunities, teaching at home, setting up a business, marketing, teaching to various age groups, student relations, finances, and personal and professional growth.

## ARTICLES

Klingenstein, Beth. "Being a Starving Artist Isn't All It's Cracked Up to Be" *American Music Teacher*, August/September 2002, Vol. 52, No. 1, pp. 82–83.

Klingenstein, Beth. "Do We Need an Attitude Adjustment?" *American Music Teacher*, December/January 2002/2003, Vol. 52, No. 3, pp. 66–67.

"MTNA Member Survey." *American Music Teacher*, April/May 2006, Volume 55, No. 5, p. 83.

Nelson, Judy. "Studio Piano Teachers Charge Meagerly for Lessons." *Clavier*, February 2004, Vol. 43, No. 2, p. 7.

## WEBSITE

*Piano Home Page*
> www.marthabeth.com/business.html

# Chapter 6

# A DEEPER LOOK AT TUITION AND PAYMENT PLANS

The previous chapter covered general issues impacting the income of the independent piano teacher as well as the importance of setting professional rates. The next area to be examined will be the practical aspects of dealing with financial issues, such as billing procedures in the successful operation of the independent music studio.

## All-inclusive Tuition vs. Tuition with Additional Fees

How are teachers compensated for the many areas of their work? They can charge an all-inclusive tuition, resulting in a higher but comprehensive rate that covers all studio activities and student fees, or they can set a base tuition rate, which they then supplement with additional fees.

An all-inclusive tuition generates a single, reliable income. Teachers can inform parents of the many services included in the tuition (such as theory, performance or chamber music classes, or computer lab sessions). Under this plan, students cannot opt out of those services, hoping for a lower rate. Although tuition should be set high enough to cover all studio activities, parents will not feel overwhelmed by additional fees with everything included in a single charge.

If the teacher feels it necessary to break down the tuition into a group of fees, the following might be some areas to consider. However, it is important not to list too many fees above and beyond the basic tuition.

- **Studio fee**, for studio-related expenses, such as printing and mailing studio documents and correspondences, maintaining a web page, and servicing pianos.

- **Recital fee**, covering the cost of programs, hall rental, and reception expenses.

- **Late fee**, charged whenever a tuition payment has not been paid by the due date. The policy statement should list the amount of the late fee and the date after which it will be applied, giving parents an added incentive to pay tuition on time.

- **Registration fee**, to compensate for the time involved in registering students each year. Some teachers collect non-refundable registration fees at the end of the spring term, so students can reserve a lesson slot for the fall. In surveys, teachers reported registration fees ranging from $10 to $150. As an example of the additional income generated by this fee, $50 charged to 30 students would bring in $1500 a year.

- **Computer lab or workstation fee**, charged when that service is included in the studio curriculum. The advantage of a separate fee is that the lab/workstation can be made optional, with individual students deciding if they wish to participate.

- **Special programs fee**, to cover expenses and teacher time for activities such as chamber music or sonatina festivals, summer camps, monthly performance classes, and composition workshops.

- **Lending library fee**, to cover books loaned to students until new ones are purchased, sight-playing material, CDs, and the replacement of worn books. One word of caution about lending music: if composers and publishers are to stay in business, their music must be purchased. Teachers must therefore decide judiciously when and why to lend music rather than have students purchase it.

- **Book and activity deposit**, used during the course of the year to cover book expenses and any fees the student may incur. This deposit is not income and should not be reported as such. It does not belong to the teacher and is used entirely for the student's own expenses. Costs to be deducted from the initial deposit include all books and supplies, as well as festival, audition, and competition fees, thus avoiding the need to collect any small payments throughout the year. Late payment fees can also be deducted from this fund.

All book and fee expenses should be tracked on duplicate-copy invoices available at any office supply store. When the deposit is used in full, a copy of the invoice should be sent to the parents showing how the money was used. If the student is moving or discontinuing lessons, any funds left in the account should be refunded.

## Payment Plans

### Methods of Payment

While it is crucial to set rates at an acceptable level, it is also important to use a system of collecting payments in keeping with today's professional studio. A brief historical summary of methods of payment provides a basis for decisions concerning payment collection.

#### PER-LESSON PAYMENTS

In years gone by, students came to the studio with the payment for that day's lesson in hand, usually in cash. No bills were sent, and no longterm debts were incurred. Some teachers use this payment system to this day.

This method requires very little bookkeeping, assuming that students bring each week's payment with them. When the student misses a lesson, however, the teacher does not get paid. The teacher cannot count on a steady income and earnings are greatly impacted by sick or unreliable students. The teacher often finds it difficult to pay her own bills, since money dribbles in slowly throughout the month.

#### MONTHLY PAYMENTS

Eventually, teachers started charging by the month. At first, many teachers adjusted each month's income to reflect the exact number of lessons in that month (three lessons due to a holiday or five lessons due to a fifth Wednesday, for example). Teachers also adjusted the total amount due by deducting for any missed lessons from the past month or by adding on any book expenses and fees incurred during the month.

This system requires a great deal of bookkeeping and provides an unpredictable income. The amount owed each month fluctuates with holidays, missed lessons, and book expenses. Because of the variable rate, teachers also need to send parents monthly statements.

### SET MONTHLY PAYMENTS

A huge step forward was the implementation of set monthly payments. This method ensures a steady income, unaffected by missed lessons, holidays, or the numbers of Wednesdays in the month. A yearly income per student is established and that income is then divided into a set number of equal monthly payments. For convenience, $40 a week and ten months of lessons are used as the base in the following example:

- 40 weeks of teaching x $40 a week = $1600 annual income per student

- Ten monthly payments: $1600 ÷ 10 = $160 a month per student over a ten-month period

With this system, income is not adjusted per month, regardless of the number of lessons in any given month. Instead, the amount due is presented as tuition, which has been divided into equal monthly payments. In order for standard monthly payments to work they must not be altered for any reason. Teachers using this system must therefore build in all additional fees mentioned in the previous section, to avoid sending invoices for any additional monthly charges. The one exception to this is the book and activity deposit, which should be billed separately.

A firm make-up policy must also be developed, establishing when lessons will or will not be made up, with the understanding that missed lessons will not result in an adjustment in monthly tuition payments. In this way, parents know what to expect and teachers earn a steady monthly income, unaffected by missed lessons. Make-up policies will be discussed further in Chapter 11.

The disadvantage to the set monthly payment system is that the teacher may receive a lower income during the summer months.

### EQUAL PAYMENTS FOR 12 MONTHS

The easiest method for producing a steady twelve-month income is to go back to the annual income figure of $1600 in the previous example, and divide that figure by twelve months instead of ten. The monthly income will be slightly lower with twelve monthly payments as opposed to ten monthly payments, but now a steady income will be received during all twelve months. Even if a teacher decided to travel to Italy during the month of August, for example, she would still receive the same monthly income as in October or April.

Such a system needs to be clearly explained in a policy statement. An adult's signature agreeing to this system is required, to ensure that payments will continue to be made through the summer months.

### SEMESTER OR TERM PAYMENTS

Some teachers choose to bill for tuition on a semester or term basis, collecting payments at the beginning of each. Semesters usually divide the year into two, while terms can consist of any number of weeks. This system requires careful budgeting to avoid the financial stress of having income depleted long before the end of the semester or term.

## Comparing Payment Plans

Using a base of $1600 per student per year, how would the same income look when computed using the different payment plans discussed above?

## COMPARISON OF PAYMENT PLAN INCOME

| PAYMENT SCHEDULE | ANNUAL INCOME PER STUDENT (40 WEEKS X $40 PER WEEK) | INCOME PER PAY PERIOD PER STUDENT | TOTAL INCOME FOR 30 STUDENTS PER PAY PERIOD | TOTAL ANNUAL INCOME FOR 30 STUDENTS |
|---|---|---|---|---|
| 12 EQUAL MONTHLY PAYMENTS | $1600 | $133 for each of 12 months | $4000* for each of 12 months | $48,000 |
| 10 EQUAL MONTHLY PAYMENTS | $1600 | $160 for each of 10 months | $4800 for each of 10 months | $48,000 |
| FOUR TERM PAYMENTS | $1600 | $400 for each of four 10-week terms | $12,000 for each of four terms | $48,000 |
| TWO SEMESTER PAYMENTS | $1600 | $800 for each of two 10-week semesters | $24,000 for each of two semesters | $48,000 |

*Rounded up

## Summer Income

Teachers might wish to supplement September to June income with additional summer programs. More will be said about this in Chapter 39, but the following are some ideas to consider in generating summer income.

### Required Summer Term

Some teachers require students to attend a set term of summer lessons. A six-week summer term, for example, might include standard lessons or cover a specific topic such as jazz, Mozart, the music of a favorite pop artist, duets, or hymns. By focusing on an area of special interest to the student, the teacher can inspire more eager participation during the summer months. Tuition for a summer session can be required, whether the student attends or not, in order to reserve a slot on the fall roster of students.

### Summer Camps

Another way to generate income in the summer is to hold a summer music camp. The camp might cover activities for two to six hours a day and last for any pre-set number of days. One or more camps could be offered during the course of a summer. The camps provide an exciting learning experience for students and important supplemental income for teachers. Music camps will be discussed in further detail in Chapter 39.

### Combined Sources of Income

When teachers charge tuition in ten monthly payments, they can make up for the lack of income in the other two months by collecting tuition for a summer program in July, and setting the due date for additional annual fees in August. For example, a $100 lab fee ($3 per week) billed in August to each of 30 students annually would generate $3000 for that month. This would help parents spread out their financial responsibilities and would provide teachers with income during a non-teaching month.

## Innovative Methods for Collecting Payments

There are those who feel that the independent teacher should not be in the business of collecting fees any more than a doctor personally sends invoices requesting payment. Just as the doctor uses others to do the billing, there are collection resources available to the independent teacher.

### Professional Agencies

Some teachers turn to agencies specifically designed to collect tuition for the independent music teacher. These agencies receive a list of students with parents' names, addresses, and phone numbers plus the tuition owed. The agency then sees that payments are collected in full while charging a small fee to the independent teacher. The service saves the teacher time while minimizing book-keeping and the stress of collecting unpaid tuition.

### Authorized Direct Bank Payments

For convenience, parents can request that monthly tuition payments be automatically withdrawn from their bank account and sent directly to the teacher. There are several options, including direct payments and e-banking. It is important to speak with a banking representative to determine the process.

## Collecting Overdue Funds

Teachers should never "ask" for overdue payments or apologize when requesting payments. No one has the right to determine if the money is needed or not, or to debate who needs it the most at that particular time, the teacher or the parent. Lax parents should be reminded that by signing the Studio Policy Statement, they have accepted responsibility for making tuition payments on time as well as for the consequences of late payments.

When payments are late, the steps for collection may include the following:

- Deduct a late fee from the student's book and fee deposit.

- Send the parents a notice that a late fee has been applied, accompanied by an invoice for the amount due and a self-addressed envelope for easy return. Such an invoice should not be in letter form.

- If invoices are ignored, send a letter stating the consequences of not paying the bill. A first letter should be worded very solicitously; any additional letters should be worded in an increasingly firm manner.

Usually parents will pay their bill upon receiving the initial invoice. Rarely, even after repeated notices, have I had difficulty collecting payments. In the rare instances that parents have neglected to pay me, I have taken them to small claims court. This is not something that I relish, and I do this only as a last resort. In each case, the parents have paid immediately upon receipt of the papers from the court. Since I have their signatures on signed studio policy statements and registration forms agreeing to the amount due, as well as copies of any letters I have sent requesting overdue funds and notifying them of my intention to bring the case to small claims court, I know that I have more than enough documentation to win my case. Despite its unpleasantness, the alternative is worse.

A teacher stands to lose a substantial amount of income if, for example, a family with three students falls behind three months in payments, then stops coming to lessons. Too many stories are told of teachers who feel obligated to absorb unpaid tuition; small claims court gives teachers an effective tool for collecting lost wages. The amount requested through small claims court should always include any court fees.

## Family Discounts and Scholarships

One final thought about tuition payments concerns giving discounts to families with more than one child studying in the studio. On the surface, this may seem reasonable and even generous, but teachers should be reminded that many professionals do not provide discounts for their services to multiple family members. Neither can it be assumed that a family with three children is more financially strapped than a family with one. The three may be the children of a well-paid corporate lawyer, while the one may have a single parent who is struggling to make ends meet.

In addition, families can be even more work, not less; teachers certainly do not do less for multiple siblings, and sometimes face additional challenges in scheduling, repertoire, rivalries, etc. A family discount, in effect, offers the teacher less pay for more work.

If a teacher wishes to adjust the rate in certain circumstances, rather than offering general discounts, a better solution is to award scholarships on a case-by-case basis. This will enable the teacher to address special needs while still maintaining professional rates in the studio.

Teachers who wish to offer reduced rates or scholarships to students in need may wish to affiliate with The MusicLink Foundation. The unit of measure for this non-profit organization is the Free and Assisted Lunch Program at school. If a student is eligible for the Free or Assisted Lunch Program, they are automatically eligible for reduced rates from a willing teacher, usually about half the normal fee. The teacher is not compensated by MusicLink for the lower rates, but rather agrees to offer the scholarship herself. This program documents teachers who give eligible students a scholarship in a manner that avoids asking embarrassing questions about family income. Both the teacher's policy statement and registration form should reflect the offer of reduced rates for eligible students. MusicLink students are eligible for a number of extra benefits, including music camp scholarships. Interested teachers may wish to visit the MusicLink website at www.musiclinkfoundation.org.

## Power in Numbers

I first became interested in business issues and rates after a group discussion at my local music teachers association on common studio concerns. The discussion was enlightening and empowering. Others had faced what I was facing and could offer solutions to my problems. I did not need to reinvent the wheel all on my own!

I recommend that all teachers take part in discussions of this kind. Sharing information gives teachers a better picture of acceptable rates and workable studio policies. The independent teacher benefits from group discussions when addressing business concerns. Local and state music organizations would do well to survey their members every two years on business practices, workloads, and rates. Only by better understanding the economics of the profession in one's own area can teachers begin to gauge their own economic success. Surveys will be discussed in Chapter 13 and a sample survey appears in Appendix B.

## MEMORABLE QUOTES

The following quotes are taken from anonymous surveys in a number of different states.

### How do you feel about your rates?

"I'd starve to death if I had to depend on it."

"This is only a hobby."

"I teach because I love it; my husband pays the bills."

Two responses in the same year and same city:

"I am happy with $14 an hour."

"I receive $36 an hour and feel underpaid."

"I am trying to raise my fees, but feel that it's difficult since other teachers in the area often charge less. Many people don't inquire about educational background, only who charges the least."

"The money I make is excellent considering it's a second income. It has always bothered me that it would be extremely difficult for me to support myself and child if something happened to my husband."

"I don't earn what I am worth."

"Inadequate salary—am looking for other work."

"I planned to raise my rates but several teachers in my area charge lower rates than mine so I postponed it."

"Since I do not have a degree in music nor depend on it for my livelihood, I am satisfied with lower rates."

"Too low! There is so much thought, training, and paperwork that it doesn't balance. Also, hobbyists and people who do it for fun undercut fees."

"I make about half now of what I made working 16–20 hours as an RN."

"I have another professional job, so I don't need the income and I don't charge anything for lessons."

"It's hard to charge professional rates when one nearby teacher asks for donations rather than a set fee for lessons."

### What are some suggestions for increasing income?

"Teach group or partner lessons."

"Teach new markets: at-home adults, home-schooled students, early-childhood music, daycare groups, and private schools."

"….bake sales, take in laundry, ironing…."

# Chapter 7

# MARKETING

We can set up the most beautiful studio in our town, have all our documents in order, and create a place for everything, but if we do not let people know that we are in business, all that hard work will not reap the benefits we anticipate.

In the not-so-distant past, it was considered in poor taste to advertise our studios in any way other than by word of mouth and referrals. Today marketing is seen as an important part of building and operating our business, and we should expect to budget a certain amount of time and money toward it. Whether we are an established teacher, a new teacher, or are starting a new and unique program, we can all benefit from the wide variety of creative marketing strategies currently available for our use.

## Brochures

### Studio Brochures

By developing an effective studio brochure, teachers can have a ready means of marketing the studio to prospective students and parents, as well as to the general public. An attractive brochure enables a teacher to present the studio in a professional light, highlighting her education and years of experience, professional affiliations, outstanding achievements, students' achievements, and studio activities.

Teachers need to address some basic questions before creating a brochure:

- What do I want my students and their parents to know about me?
- What is special about my approach to music?
- What is special about my musical background?
- How can I present my studio as a unique center of learning?

A brochure can be as simple as an 8½" x 11" piece of paper folded into thirds. One column can list the areas of instruction offered in the studio, such as:

- Private or Group Lessons (Piano, Voice, Trumpet, etc.)
- Music Theory
- Technique
- Music History
- Sight-Playing and Ear-Training
- Performance Classes
- Recitals
- Music Computer Lab

- Listening Workstation

- Ensemble Playing

- Chamber and/or Collaborative Music

- Jazz Improvisation

- Composition

Another panel of the brochure might contain a brief b
experience, professional affiliations and positions, and
her students.

A third panel could include a brief summary of the insu uctor
professional photo, as well as a picture of an actual teaching situation (with parental per...
the studio. The brochure can be updated annually as needed. A sample studio brochure can be found
in Appendix A.

### Event Brochures

Brochures can highlight a special activity within the studio, such as a chamber music program or a
summer camp. They can be distributed at libraries, schools, supermarkets, places of worship, and
other public venues. Students can hand them out to friends and relatives as well.

## Community and Local Newspapers

### Press Releases

A teacher can use a press release to announce the opening of a new studio, an upcoming recital, or
the establishment of a new program within the studio, such as a summer camp. In a press release,
the teacher can also feature student achievements and awards, or announce a special studio event,
such as a mall performance.

Two items should appear at the top of a press release:

- The preferred date for the article to appear in the newspaper ("For Immediate Release"
  or "For Release on May 11," for example)

- Contact information (Contact: Karen Turner, the Unique Piano Studio, 555-555-4321;
  uniquepianostudio@somewhere.net)

It is wise to include a title for the article, bearing in mind that the newspaper has the right to edit
the title and/or the article. A press release should be short and clearly written, and include any pertinent information such as the time and location of upcoming events. Some newspapers have a word
limit, or a certain day of the week when they print arts- or student-related articles.

I submit articles to our paper on a regular basis, and make it a point to befriend the person in charge
of the arts section. I make sure that I respect the editor's time by avoiding last-minute requests for
publication.

North Dakota, I can submit an article on any activity I would like and know
ted. However, when I lived in the Washington, D.C. area, *The Washington Post* was
ed in my studio. In a large metropolitan area, it is easier to publish studio news in
munity papers. Major newspapers are often interested in human-interest or arts-related
it is always worth a try if a teacher feels she has something worth printing. One can also
t an interview with a reporter if the program seems important enough to announce.

### Paid Advertisements

Although newspapers may not always be willing to print a press release, they will print a paid advertisement. Since the cost for a paid advertisement is based on the number of words in the ad, the copy
should be short and to the point. In addition to listing the types of services offered (for example,
piano and voice lessons or instruction in music theory), it is essential to include basic contact information limited to the studio name and phone number or studio e-mail address. If space allows, the
advertisement can also include a short phrase to grab attention and a brief statement about qualifications, such as "20 years' experience."

## Other Print Advertising

### Posters

Attractive posters created on a home computer can be used to advertise the studio and its offerings.
Posters can be placed around town on public bulletin boards, in the windows of willing businesses,
in places of worship and public libraries, etc. It is recommended that only the business name and
phone number appear, rather than personal contact information.

### Fliers

Fliers present another option for marketing the studio or publicizing a special event within the
studio, such as a summer camp or recital. Besides a brief description of the event, the flier can
include the dates, cost, and contact information. Creative fliers such as bookmarks and magnets are
another means of advertising the studio in a unique way.

Fliers are an ideal means of marketing to large groups of people. For example, if a teacher is advertising a program for fourth graders only, she can deliver a stack of fliers for each fourth-grade class
in nearby schools. Classroom teachers can then hand out a flier to each student. Fliers can also be
sent to schools in nearby communities, parent groups, pre-schools, home-school associations,
daycare centers, and religious groups. Some places of worship even allow inserts in their bulletin
announcing special seasonal concerts or recitals.

### Studio Newsletters

Another effective way teachers can market their business is through a studio newsletter. By mailing
the newsletter to current or prospective students and parents, the teacher can advertise the many
activities of the studio and announce any current student or teacher achievements.

## Marketing Through Professional Teacher Organizations

### Referral Services

Some music teacher groups have a referral service for members who request to be included on a list
of teachers with openings. Usually a member of the group is designated to field requests from

prospective students and find a teacher in the community who fits their needs. To promote their studio, teachers who are new to an area should seek out local and state music teacher organizations, attend meetings, and volunteer to work on a committee with high visibility. In this way, other teachers in the area will get to know them and feel comfortable referring students to them.

When I was a member of the Northern Virginia Music Teachers Association, during the September meeting, new teachers would be called upon to stand up and introduce themselves, summarize their educational background and other qualifications, and mention whether or not they had openings for new students. Unfortunately, many of those new teachers never attended subsequent meetings and therefore never received referrals from the teachers with waiting lists. The new teachers who did attend came to be known within the organization and received more than enough referrals.

When seeking new students, teachers should be aware that online networking is another effective means of referral. In addition to several independent referral sites online, many state and local music organizations have websites that include a link to their members listed by area, so that parents and other teachers can readily find a teacher in their particular location.

### Professional Organization Newsletters or Directories

Teachers may take advantage of the newsletters of local or state music teachers' organizations to market a program or highlight an achievement within a studio. An article about a student who wins a competition or receives a scholarship, for example, is a marketing tool that reflects well on that student's teacher. Studio ads can also be placed in the local or state directory.

### Networking and Word-of-Mouth Referrals

Although teachers must pursue modern means of marketing our studios, word of mouth is still a valuable way to market the studio. When teachers have satisfied customers, when their students love studying with them, or when students win competitions or do well in festivals, they will tell their friends. Their parents will express satisfaction and encourage other parents to send their children to the same studio.

## Internet and Other Media Marketing

### Web Pages

Web pages are an excellent tool for marketing an independent music studio. Because of their non-linear format, web pages can be attractively organized and can include easy access to a variety of information about the teacher, her students, and the studio itself. The following are some areas of information that can be included on a web page:

- Studio contact information

- Links to registration forms, policy statements, and payment schedules

- Link to the studio newsletter

- The teacher's biography, listing degrees and major achievements

- A brief history of the studio

- Photos of students and studio activities

- Video clips of student performances

- Weekly announcements

- Information regarding special programs such as chamber music festivals, composition programs, or summer camps

- Link to an article featuring the student of the month

- Links to educational sites

### Television and Radio

Most teachers think that an advertisement on television or radio is financially out of reach, but radio stations do run Public Service Announcements (PSA). Teachers should investigate this outlet to help make the public aware of their studio, especially since many smaller radio stations are more than willing to help local arts programs and are required to include a certain number of PSAs in their programming. In addition, local open-access cable television stations will broadcast videos of special events that take place in the community.

### Public Performances

Whenever teachers organize a program in a public setting, they are advertising their studio. This may not be the main goal in presenting the program, but it is an inevitable outcome. A student performance in a mall, senior center, place of worship, museum, or library draws attention to the teacher's studio. If the venue allows, the teacher can set up a large poster on an easel featuring information such as the name and contact information of the studio. She can also provide business cards or brochures for the public at the event.

---

### A WORD OF CAUTION: PERMISSION FOR USE OF STUDENT PHOTOGRAPHS AND VIDEO CLIPS

Pictures or videos of students must never be used in any marketing situation without first receiving written permission from a parent or guardian. Teachers can obtain this permission at the beginning of the term by reserving a place on the registration form or policy statement where the parent or guardian can give signed consent for the student's photo to be used for publicity purposes.

---

## Resource

Johnston, Philip. *The PracticeSpot Guide to Promoting Your Teaching Studio.* Pearce, Australia: PracticeSpot Press, 2003.

Filled with numerous suggestions on marketing the independent studio, this one-of-a-kind book covers areas such as preparing professional documents, taking advantage of local advertisements, offering discounts for referrals, targeting a niche, partnering with other professionals, using the Internet, and much more.

# Chapter 8

# TAXES, INSURANCE, AND RETIREMENT FUNDS

**B**ecause independent music teachers are self-employed, they must be informed about how to deal with taxes and insurance in the operation of their studio. Failing to abide by state and national tax laws can lead to heavy financial penalties; underinsuring health or business can mean financial ruin. The information in this chapter will introduce the means by which teachers can avoid both situations in order to maintain a professionally run studio, as well as a brief summary of possible retirement funds.

## Taxes

Although tax laws change frequently and vary from state to state, there are aspects of record-keeping and tax preparation that must be considered by all independent music teachers, regardless of their situation or location.

### Keeping Accurate Records

In order to calculate taxes correctly, teachers need to keep careful records of all income and expenses. Haphazard record keeping can mean the loss of credit for deductions as well as penalties in possible future audits. Permanent records should show gross income, deductions, and credits. The principal support for entries is the business checkbook. It is strongly recommended to keep a separate bank account for the business.

#### RECORDING INCOME

All income should be documented on a computer or in a paper ledger to include the source of a deposit and whether the deposit was received by check, credit card, or cash. Keep copies of all deposit slips, noting on each slip the source of deposit. By recording tuition payments as they are received, the teacher will have no doubt as to who has paid and when, and the month or semester covered by the payment.

Before cashing or depositing tuition checks, teachers should always record them on a long, duplicate-copy deposit slip, which can be obtained from the bank. Each check should be listed with the name of the parent or guardian, the term covered by the payment, and the check number and amount. The deposit slip can also serve as a backup record, in the event that the teacher inadvertently omitted the payment in the studio ledger.

Income from activities other than teaching must be recorded as well. Such areas might include:

- Accompanying
- Performing for religious services
- Other performances
- Presentations
- Publications

- Adjudication

- Royalties

- Editing

## RECORDING EXPENSES

All payments relating to the studio or teaching should be made by check or credit card to document business expenses. In an audit, a canceled check by itself may not be enough proof of a business expense. Match each invoice to the canceled check by writing the check number on the invoice. It is recommended to avoid checks payable to "cash" and also to avoid paying non-business expenses from the business account.

An easy system for maintaining expense records is to keep a folder for all paid receipts, with envelopes or dividers marked for each area, such as music books, office supplies, subscriptions, etc. This makes it easy to calculate the total amount for each type of expense when preparing taxes.

A more organized system is to enter expenses, along with income, directly into a ledger or accounting program as they occur, keeping receipts as documentation.

## Tax Forms for the Self-employed

### FORM 8829: EXPENSES FOR BUSINESS USE OF YOUR HOME

If the business use of a home meets a Use Test, the business use percentage of expenses is generally deductible on Form 8829. This form is used to calculate the percentage of the home space used exclusively for business on a continuing basis. Based on that percentage, deductions can be made for expenses such as utilities, home mortgage interest, house insurance, home repairs/maintenance, rent, depreciation, and real estate taxes. The amount of deduction is then included on Schedule C.

### SCHEDULE C

Anyone who is sole owner of a business is required to file a Schedule C form to report income or losses from business activities. Independent music teachers are required to report all studio income as well as any studio expenses on this form.

The following is a checklist of some of the possible expenses that might appear on Schedule C:

- Piano tuning and instrument repairs

- Computer software programs used in studio operation/computer lab

- Teaching tools, such as music games

- Depreciation on studio furnishings, instruments, computer equipment, copier, etc.; limited to the percentage of business use vs. personal use

- Office, studio, and bathroom supplies

- Expenses related to studio telephone, cell phone, pager and answering machine

- Postage

- Studio decorations, including seasonal items

- Studio or recital rental fees

- Printing expenses related to recital programs and studio documents and correspondence

- Advertising (brochures, mailings, etc.)

- Gifts or awards for students and colleagues

- Professional services (legal, accounting, graphic arts, computer)

- Business license and related taxes

- Subscriptions to professional publications or reading materials for waiting room

- Dues for professional organizations

- Bank service charges for studio account

- Mileage to any professional event, recital, music store, or seminar (Document business mileage by recording the date, event, and miles on a ledger kept in the car.)

- Conference or workshop costs such as registration fees, hotel, travel, and meals

- Other business-related meals

- Liability insurance and insurance on instruments used in the business

### SCHEDULE SE

Teachers whose net earnings are above a designated minimum are required to file a Schedule SE form and pay the Self-Employment Contributions Act (SECA) tax on the net earnings of the business. SECA, the counterpart to the Federal Insurance Contributions Act (FICA), is the means by which self-employed persons pay Social Security taxes, due on all wages. Since an employer is not withholding or matching the independent teacher's Social Security or Medicare taxes, the teacher must do so using Schedule SE. The formula for computing the self-employment tax is different than that used to compute the Medicare portion of the SE tax; a tax professional can be consulted to compute theses taxes correctly.

### FORM 1040 ES: QUARTERLY TAX FORM

The income taxes and self-employment taxes required from all independent teachers are usually paid in estimated quarterly installments using Form 1040 ES. Quarterly installments are due on the 15th of April, June, September, and January. Estimated payments must total either 90% of the current year's tax liability or 100% of the prior year's tax liability, depending on the taxpayer's adjusted gross income. The quarterly estimated payments are computed by dividing the total tax liability into four equal payments.

## Other Deductions

Another deduction that may be available to self-employed individuals is a deduction for health insurance premiums paid on behalf of the sole proprietor, spouse, and dependents. This amount may be deducted on Form 1040 as an adjustment to income. Certain restrictions apply, as each individual may have different circumstances; therefore, a tax advisor should be consulted.

## Consulting Tax Experts

Although many teachers might want to avoid the cost of hiring a tax professional, it is beneficial to do so and it is a tax-deductible business expense. In many cases, tax professionals can alert teachers to take deductions they might not have known were acceptable. In addition, they can help teachers avoid penalties incurred through improper deductions.

## A WORD OF CAUTION

Unfortunately, there are some teachers who do not report their income fully when filing taxes. They accept payments from students in cash, not recording them as income. This will only come back to haunt these teachers. First, it is illegal not to declare income. Secondly, teachers who do not declare full income will have difficulty qualifying for a loan for large purchases like a new home, car, or piano. Additionally, teachers who do not declare their income accurately are paying less into Social Security and will receive reduced Social Security benefits upon retirement.

Some teachers declare false deductions, such as hotel expenses that were not really for business trips. As I understand it from people who have been audited and found to be in error, Uncle Sam is a stern disciplinarian with a long and suspecting memory.

# Resources

*Brief Tax Guide for the Independent Music Teacher.* Cincinnati: Music Teachers National Association, 2004.

Compiled by accountants, this booklet covers the depreciation of musical equipment, business entertaining, social security taxes, and many more areas of interest.

The guide can be purchased by going to http://www.mtna.org/HLtext.

Riley, Peter Jason, CPA. *The New Tax Guide for Artists of Every Persuasion.* New York: Limelight Editions, 2002. Distributed by Hal Leonard Corporation.

Written as a tool to help artists best understand the unique aspects of taxes as they apply to the arts, this book is not intended to tell people how to prepare their taxes, but rather how to prepare for their taxes. Recommending that artists have taxes prepared by a professional, this book addresses actors, directors, musicians, visual artists, and writers. The chapters that apply to musicians in this book include Income; What Can I Deduct?; For Musicians and Singers Only; Setting up a Business Entity; The Audit Process, Bookkeeping and Your Taxpayer Rights; Choosing a Tax Advisor; and Tax Planning. A helpful Appendix section includes resources, mileage charts, a monthly expense spreadsheet, and an exemptions claimed record.

## Insurance

### Types of Insurance

#### HEALTH INSURANCE

A high percentage of independent music teachers rely on a spouse's job for health insurance. When that option is not available, however, some teachers choose to go without health insurance rather than incur the high expense on their own. Fortunately, affordable group policies are available through professional organizations such as alumnae and teacher associations, insurance agencies, and through some banks, clubs, or organizations. Such options are worth researching by any teacher without health insurance.

## HOMEOWNER'S OR RENTER'S POLICY

Since most independent teachers work out of the home, it is important to have a homeowner's or renter's policy to protect this important asset. If the house should burn down, not only would the home be lost, but the teacher's livelihood would be taken away as well. Coverage through a homeowner's or renter's policy must have an additional office or professional endorsement to cover a home studio. An even better option would be to acquire a Business Owner Policy (BOP), for coverage of a home business. Special care should be taken to insure studio space against natural disasters, such as flooding, which are not normally covered under a homeowner's policy. Everything in the studio needs to be insured, even if this means taking out an additional rider to cover the replacement value of expensive instruments and equipment.

Teachers who rent a home and/or studio space still need to protect the contents from fire, flood, and theft by securing a renter's policy.

## LIABILITY POLICY

Independent teachers are vulnerable to various kinds of lawsuits because of the nature of their profession. If someone trips on a step and breaks a leg, the teacher could be found liable for damages. If a student has an allergy to dust, animals, or peanuts, and the teacher has assured the family there will be no problem in the studio, in today's litigious world a lawsuit might be brought against the teacher if the student were unable to breathe during a lesson. Therefore, all teachers need to protect themselves with liability insurance.

Teachers are vulnerable to another type of lawsuit, or even worse, criminal charges. Often children are taught in an enclosed or isolated area. With no one else in the room, teachers are naturally required to behave in a most professional manner. Even so, teachers have had their teaching careers ruined because of false accusations of misconduct. Such an accusation can result in a lengthy and expensive legal battle and possibly in having to pay a large settlement.

A recent e-mail sent to a number of teachers read, "I know of two teachers of long-standing reputation, whose careers were recently damaged by false accusations from unstable students. One (teacher) still sits in an adjacent state's penitentiary, awaiting a decision on an appeal. His career is entirely over, after over 30 years of excellent teaching…"

One way to protect against false accusations of misconduct is to have a parent or guardian sit in on all lessons. Another way is to tape all lessons. If a digital camera is used, recorded lessons can be stored on small digital tapes or transferred to DVD for easy storage.

## UMBRELLA POLICY

An umbrella policy provides liability insurance over and above the normal policy. Liability insurance augmented by an umbrella policy should be seen as a necessary business expense. A $1.5 million dollar policy is not excessive. Some music organizations and school districts have group rates for anyone who teaches, with no restrictions on who may join. Even policies purchased independently are well worth the investment. They are not excessively expensive, provide peace of mind, and contribute to financial stability.

## MALPRACTICE INSURANCE

Malpractice insurance is another possible addition to a professional liability policy. Although malpractice insurance is not an insurance that most teachers hold, it is not outside the realm of possibility that someday piano teachers may be sued for teaching badly. In his article, "Sued for Malpractice?" (*American Music Teacher* December/January 2001/2002, Vol. 51, No. 3, pp. 24-25), Dale Wheeler opens with a tongue-in-cheek scenario about a piano student suing a teacher for "not adequately preparing him technically and emotionally for the rigors of the recent competition." In many professions, there have been lawsuits concerning work poorly done. One would hope the day will not arrive when a piano teacher will be sued because a student develops carpal tunnel syndrome or plays poorly after six years of lessons, but Wheeler's article is well worth reading.

### RECORDS FOR INSURANCE

For insurance claims, teachers should keep photos of equipment, receipts, and dates purchased in a location separate from the studio, such as a safe-deposit box. The rental fee for a safe-deposit box used for business purposes is a tax-deductible expense.

# Resources

### INSURANCE RESOURCES

*Music Teachers National Association*

www.mtna.org/HLtext

MTNA partners with the Trust for Insuring Educators (TIE) and Forest T. Jones & Company to offer various types of insurance to members, including:

- Professional Liability
- Private Practice Professional Liability
- Group Term Life
- 10-Year Level Group Term Life
- Group Disability Income Protection
- Group Accidental Death & Dismemberment
- Identity Theft Protection
- Personal Auto
- Long Term Care Insurance Evaluation Service
- Comprehensive Health Care Insurance

*The Alumni Insurance Program*

www.alumniinsuranceprogram.com

The Alumni Insurance Program lists health insurance available to alumni from universities and colleges across the country. The organization may be emailed at info@alumniinsuranceprogram.com.

### LEGAL RESOURCES

*Brief Legal Guide for the Independent Music Teacher.* Cincinnati: Music Teachers National Association, 1999. Compiled by attorneys, this booklet guides music teachers through zoning, copyright, insurance and other aspects of owning and operating a business. The booklet can be purchased at www.mtna.org/HLtext.

### VOLUNTEER LAWYERS FOR THE ARTS

www.vlany.org

Volunteer Lawyers for the Arts organizations exist in many states, and can assist a teacher who is experiencing legal problems but is unable to afford an attorney. Lawyers in this organization provide *pro bono* legal services and mediation for individual artists as well as arts and cultural nonprofit organizations.

*Music Teachers National Association Legal Consultation*

www.mtna.org/HLtext

MTNA offers legal consultation services free of charge exclusively to MTNA members. Assistance is available in the following areas:

- Zoning issues
- Bill collection
- Business formation (additional fees may be required for filing in some states)
- Non-compete agreements
- Buying and selling existing studios
- Music purchases and resale to students
- Copyright and ASCAP issues
- Ethics issues
- Liability issues
- Tax issues

## Retirement Funds

Since independent music teachers do not have a company retirement plan, it is advisable that each contribute to an independent retirement fund. Even if a teacher feels that she is struggling financially, regular contributions to a retirement fund should be viewed as a necessary yearly expense, one that will be greatly appreciated when the retirement years are reached.

The most common retirement plans available to self-employed individuals would include an individual retirement arrangement (IRA) or a simplified employee pensions plan (SEP-IRA).

An IRA is a personal savings plan that allows a taxpayer to accumulate money, tax deferred, until retirement. Contributions to the IRA may or may not be deductible, depending on the individual circumstances. However, the earnings from a traditional IRA are tax deferred until distributed to the taxpayer.

A SEP-IRA is often used by self-employed individuals, as they have the same contribution limits as profit sharing plans, but none of the complex and costly compliance and reporting rules applicable to qualified retirement plans. Contributions made to a SEP-IRA are non-forfeitable (meaning that they belong fully to the individual owning the account and may not be rescinded) and subject to the same distribution rules as traditional IRAs.

# Part III

## ESTABLISHING LESSONS

From the first phone inquiry to the first lesson, teachers must be able to communicate effectively with prospective students and parents. Before signing on new students, it is important for the teacher to meet with the prospective students and parents so all parties can decide whether the teaching situation meets their individual needs and expectations. Part III discusses this interview process, as well as further communication with parents, scheduling lessons, and devising a make-up policy.

# Chapter 9

# INTERVIEWS AND COMMUNICATIONS
# WITH PARENTS

Although some teachers accept new students sight unseen, a growing number interview all students and parents before accepting them into the studio. An interview offers valuable information about the student's expectations, readiness for lessons, and ability to work with the teacher. It also reveals parents' expectations, their perception of the child, and how they might interact with their child at home.

An interview allows students and parents to experience the studio atmosphere and the teacher's approach, whatever that may be: warm, exacting, caring, detailed, relaxed, professional, etc. The student interview is just the first of many communications teachers will have with the parents, so care must be given to set the right tone from this very first meeting.

## The Initial Phone Inquiry

During the first phone inquiry regarding lessons, a teacher should gather basic information about the student, such as name, age (if younger than 18), grade in school, beginner or transfer student, and years (or months) of prior lessons. The teacher might also ask why the student will be taking lessons. Answers such as, "We just want her to have a few years of lessons," "He has always loved the sound of the piano," or "She wants to be a concert pianist" all help the teacher evaluate the situation and decide on whether or not to pursue the next step by scheduling a live interview.

For a student transferring from a teacher in the area, the initial phone conversation is the time to ask if the student has terminated lessons with the former teacher. It is highly unprofessional to consider accepting a student who is still studying with another teacher, unless that teacher has suggested or agreed to the change. Confirmation of this should be made by discussing it directly with that teacher, not merely trusting a statement by the parents. If for any reason the parents indicate that the original teacher is unaware of the family's desire to change, the interview should be postponed until the intent to discontinue has been made known to the other teacher.

Once the transfer is cleared with the other teacher, or it has been determined that the student is a beginner or a transfer student new to the area, an interview can be arranged. It should be suggested that the transfer student be prepared to play a few pieces of contrasting styles at the interview.

## Conducting the Live Interview

Although many questions can be asked over the phone, a face-to-face interview provides the best vehicle for more personal questions, as well as observations of the student at the piano. Even if a teacher is setting up a new studio or needs as many new students as possible, automatically accepting students over the phone means the teacher will miss the opportunity to gain significant information about the student, as well as present herself and her studio in the proper light.

Whether or not to charge for audition time is a matter of personal choice, but any fees should be clearly stated and agreed upon before the interview takes place. Depending on the teacher's style, an interview can take between a half hour and an hour to complete.

## The First Part of the Interview: Teacher and Student

At the start of the interview, the teacher can explain that the first part will be spent interacting only with the prospective student, and the second part in discussion with the parents (or guardian, if that is the case). The teacher should suggest that, during the first part, the parents silently observe how the student and teacher interact, without interruption from the parents. She can stress that talking one-to-one with the student and hearing his responses to questions will help her evaluate the student more accurately.

This separation of interview time is extremely valuable. The first part is meant as a time to hear the student play (or in the case of beginners, observe how they respond to suggestions). This part of the interview also allows the teacher to hear the student's thoughts first, without having anything filtered through the adult's perspective. If the student fumbles a bit in her piece, it is not helpful to hear Mom say, "She usually can play the piece much better than that! We've been out all day, and she's a bit tired."

I never realized why parents sometimes seemed to have difficulty sitting quietly until I took my first child for a pre-kindergarten skills test and was asked just to observe. Oh, how I wanted to interject, "He usually can build the blocks much higher than that! We've been out all day and…"

### BEGINNING STUDENTS

When a student is new to piano, the initial interview should help the teacher put the student at ease while checking for basic responses and skills. The teacher might begin with general questions about school, hobbies, extra-curricular activities, and favorite types of music. An interview form (see Appendix A) is a valuable guide for asking and recording answers for future reference.

Although the teacher may have asked the question of the parent over the phone, she should ask the student himself why he wants to take lessons. Answers from students do not always match those given by their parents: for example, "I really want to play the flute, but Mom and Dad said I have to play the piano for three years first," may mean that some serious discussion is needed about the best course of action.

I remember a young boy who desperately wanted to play the piano, but I never asked why. I was only happy to hear how much he wanted the lessons. The parents had saved for a year for a piano and were now ready to pay for lessons, happy that they would finally be able to fulfill their son's dream. After about two months of lessons and noticeably declining interest, I finally asked the boy why he had wanted so strongly to take lessons and yet didn't seem interested now. Was it too hard? Was I moving too fast? Too slow? He responded with great sadness, "My best friend takes piano lessons and his teacher always gives him sticker sheets. I have a sticker collection but you don't give stickers." Asking why students want to take lessons and hearing it from their own mouths is a step I learned not to skip. Hundreds of sticker sheets later he was doing remarkably well in his lessons.

When the student is a beginner, the teacher should check the student's coordination, basic aural and rhythm skills, and the ability to listen or follow instructions.

PART III

Options include:

- Clapping a rhythm and asking the child to clap it back

- Playing pitches and asking which are high and which are low

- Having the child sing back easy melodic patterns, intervals, or a children's song

- Having the child play a simple pattern on all of the black keys, lowest to highest

- Checking the student's readiness for a good hand position

- Teaching a short pre-reading piece to see how the child responds

- If CD or General MIDI (GM) disk accompaniments are used in the studio, playing one and asking the student to clap or tap along with it

During this time, the child's enthusiasm or lack thereof, ability to follow instructions, and overall responsiveness will become apparent. This part of the interview can end with questions from the student.

### TRANSFER STUDENTS

For transfer students, the interview starts in much the same fashion, asking friendly questions about school and hobbies, and why the student wants piano lessons. Questions follow concerning the student's piano background, such as how many years of lessons she has had and how many different teachers. If a change in teacher is occurring for reasons other than a move, it is important to hear the child's version of why the switch is being made.

After the opening conversation, the interview turns to gathering information about how the student approaches the piano and responds to suggestions. This section starts with the student playing those few selections of contrasting styles that were mentioned on the phone. The teacher can observe a great deal about musicality, accuracy, technique, etc. while listening. After each selection, compliments can be given on strengths followed by a few musical suggestions, providing an opportunity to gauge how well the suggestions are taken and whether change is easy or difficult for the student.

Next, the interview can continue with questions concerning music theory and music history to measure the student's understanding of the pieces just played, explaining that these questions are being asked randomly in order to get a feel for what has been taught so far. This process should begin with easy questions so that the student feels comfortable, with questions becoming more challenging only if the student seems able to respond.

The following questions are examples of what may be asked:

- What is the key of this piece?

- What does the time signature mean?

- What chord is the dominant in this piece?

- What is the form and style of this piece?

- Can you tell me when the composer lived?

- Do you know what period of music this is from?

Next, ear-training and rhythm can be tested by asking the student to sing back a melody or clap back a rhythm. Reading abilities may be tested by asking the student to sight-play a duet with the teacher. The student's keyboard skills can also be assessed by asking for fiver-finger patterns, scales, or arpeggios in various keys.

Depending upon the age of the student, in-depth questions can then be posed, such as what the student sees as personal strengths or challenges at the piano, or longterm goals for improvement. The first part of the interview can be concluded by asking if the student has any questions or concerns.

## The Second Part of the Interview: Involving the Parents

Once the student and teacher complete the first portion of the interview, attention is turned to the adults. Now the teacher can give parents the opportunity to ask any questions concerning what they have observed. During this discussion, the teacher can outline her teaching philosophy, as well her personal goals, such as creating a friendly and supportive environment in the studio while having high expectations for students.

At this point, the teacher should specify her practice expectations. Parents and students need to have a clear understanding of what these expectations are before lessons begin. Practice plans vary from studio to studio, and practice expectations can increase as students mature. In some cases, teachers ask students to commit to a practice time of their own choosing, and sign a contract agreeing to practice for that amount daily.

Finally, the teacher should go over each point in the studio policy with the parents, rather than asking them to read it at home. I personally read the entire policy word for word with the parents. This will confirm that all points are understood, especially those concerning rates, payments, and missed lessons. If this is not done, parents will often sign the policy statement without reading it. Parents must agree to all studio policies in order to have their child study in the studio. If the parents object to any part of the studio policy as it is read, the teacher can offer to recommend another teacher.

This is also a time for the teacher to observe the parents.

- Do the adults seem flexible or rigid?

- Do they seem supportive of their child?

- How do they perceive piano study?

- What was the nature of the problem with the last teacher if the student is transferring from a local teacher?

- Do the parents' expectations fit in with the teacher's philosophy?

I remember interviewing a charming and talented young boy who studied with five local teachers in five years. When talking with him, I could not understand why he had switched teachers so often, and he didn't seem to know either, as he had liked all of them. Finally I turned my attention to his mother, and realized what the problem was. His mother was opinionated and overbearing, and had a long list of demands that she expected me to perform to her exact specifications. Within five minutes I decided there was no way I would teach this child, because there was no way I could tolerate his mother.

This may seem like I was punishing the son for the sins of the mother, but I knew that, for my own peace of mind, I could not accept him. I also knew of a teacher who lived near this family who was not only a very good teacher, but a real no-nonsense dynamo as well. I referred the family to her and she taught him successfully for many years. She was fond of the student and more than capable of handling his mother, so the story had a happy ending for all concerned.

At the end of an interview, if the teacher is not willing to accept the student, she can refer the family to another teacher. For any student she chooses to accept, it is best to ask the parents and student to go home and discuss their impressions privately before making a final decision.

## Interviewing Adult Students

Although the questions asked in the interview with adult students are similar in most ways to those for younger students, a few other areas need to be discussed. Most adult students want to play the piano as a hobby, but some beginners truly do not understand that they will not be playing the piano proficiently within the first month. I once interviewed a young woman who had always wanted to play the piano. She asked how long it would take her to learn to play Chopin, and did not believe my answer. "It didn't take me very long to learn how to type. Once you know where the keys are, what else is there to know?" The interview is the time to discover the adult student's expectations for lessons and to offer realistic encouragement concerning study as an adult.

Adults often have heavy demands on their time, and may miss more lessons than children. The interview provides an opportunity to be completely clear about the consequences of missed lessons.

## Additional Communications with Parents

Once a student has been accepted into the studio, written correspondence provides the most time-efficient and reliable form of communication with parents. Letters should be mailed to parents rather than given directly to students, as students sometimes lose notes or forget to show them to parents. There is a much stronger chance that a letter mailed directly to the parents will actually be read by them. Group letters can be easily addressed by using a Mail Merge feature on the computer.

If parents need to be notified about an important issue such as a change in rates, no other information should appear in the letter. Such important information has the potential to be overlooked when it is offered in a long letter that may be briefly scanned. A letter about an increase in rates might read:

> Dear Mr. and Mrs. Smith:
>
> As of June 1, the monthly tuition for students taking 45-minute lessons will be $_____.
>
> Sincerely,
>
> Karen Turner

In addition to mailed letters, other tools for communicating with parents may include the following:

- **A web page:** Upcoming events, yearly calendars, reminders about tuition, and a link for e-mail messages are some of the possibilities to include on a web page. A word of caution: not everyone uses the Internet, and those who do may not check the web page daily, so important announcements may need to be reinforced through an alternative medium.

- **Group e-mails:** E-mailing students and parents allows teachers to send information to the complete studio in a timely and efficient way. A group of all parent e-mail addresses can be created at the beginning of the year for convenient e-mails to all families.

- **Newsletter:** A studio newsletter provides information of interest to the parents. To be on the safe side, vital information such as a change in policy must be reinforced with a separate communication.

If either a web page or e-mails are used as a means of communicating important information, parents must be reminded often to open all e-mails or to check the web page on a regular basis.

**PART III**

## USE OF SURNAME IN THE STUDIO

In these casual times, "Mr. Smith" and "Uncle Dave" have become "Sam" and "Dave" to many children. However, professional studios benefit from a less casual approach, including addressing piano teachers by their surname. Some may consider such a suggestion to be old fashioned. I make this recommendation, not from any desire for the good old days, but rather, because addressing a teacher formally enhances a more professional and courteous relationship between student and teacher. When sixth graders call their teacher at school "Mrs. Jones" and their piano teacher "Debbie," it speaks volumes about the difference in respect each teacher is given. Just as addressing teachers by their surname is still the standard in public schools, so should it be in the piano studio as well. Being addressed by a surname is especially important for young teachers who may not be that far removed in age from their older students.

If teachers are comfortable with parents addressing them by their first names, the parents should also be addressed using first names. Early in my career I had not learned that lesson. I remember talking to a father years ago and having him say, "Well, when you are my age, you will understand." I asked how old he was, and he told me "Thirty-two." At the time I was thirty-one. So not only did I have a great deal to learn before the ripe old age of thirty-two, I also realized that by calling him Mr. Anderson while he called me Beth, I had inadvertently set up an implied deference in my relationship with him that did not reflect the more equal relationship I should have been building.

## Resource

Butler, Mimi. *The Complete Guide to Raising Parents in the Private Music Studio.* Haddonfield: Mimi Butler Publisher, 2008. Available at www.privatemusicstudio.com.

Butler addresses the challenges faced by private music teachers when dealing with the parents of their students. Chapters address communicating with parents, motivating and educating parents, collecting money, deciding to include parents in lessons, difficult parents, Butler's responses to the top ten parent excuses, and more.

# Chapter 10

# SCHEDULING LESSONS

PART III

This chapter offers ways to generate schedules for various lesson formats efficiently, along with creative solutions for maximizing available teaching time.

## Setting Up Weekly Lessons

For many independent piano teachers, developing a lesson schedule each fall is one of the most time-consuming and least pleasant tasks of operating the studio. Scheduling lessons over the phone, calling parent after parent, and constantly revising to accommodate changing preferences and availability can frustrate even the most experienced teacher. Whatever the lesson format—private or group—teachers can avoid scheduling woes by collecting written preferences from students and developing a master schedule from that information.

### Private Lessons

While private lessons are the easiest to schedule, students should not automatically assume that they will receive the same lesson time from year to year. The teacher's own schedule may change, as well as the obligations and needs of other students.

There are several formats that teachers can use to collect data on students' availability for private lessons. The yearly registration form can include an area for students to indicate their first, second, and third preferences for lesson day and time. From that list, teachers can collect the information necessary for efficient scheduling. Another option is to include a chart listing all available times and days when mailing the registration material, and request that the students mark their choices on the chart. The chart should include early morning hours if the teacher offers lessons before school as an alternative to extended evening hours.

Once all the requests are submitted in writing, the teacher can enter every student's first, second, and third choices on a master schedule, as shown in the following example. For convenience, this version includes only 60-minute lessons, whereas each teacher's master schedule would reflect the actual lesson length, times, and days being offered.

## SAMPLE: TEACHER'S COMPILATION OF PRIVATE LESSON PREFERENCES

| LESSON TIME | MONDAY | TUESDAY | WEDNESDAY | THURSDAY |
|---|---|---|---|---|
| 3:30–4:30 | #1 Debbie Smith<br>#3 Joe Hoffman<br>#3 Nancy Becker | #3 Debbie Smith<br>#2 Joe Hoffman<br>#2 Don Foster | #2 Patty Ross<br>#1 Joe Hoffman<br>#3 Kay Stein | #1 Patty Ross<br>#3 Joe Hoffman<br>#1 Mary Lee |
| 4:30–5:30 | #2 Debbie Smith<br>#2 Steven Jones<br>#1 Dennis Brown | #1 Nancy Becker<br>#1 Don Foster<br>#3 Patty Ross<br>#2 Kay Stein | #2 Nancy Becker<br>#3 LindaAnderson<br>#3 Patty Boyle<br>#1 Kay Stein | #3 Patty Ross<br>#2 Patty Boyle<br>#3 Dennis Brown |
| 5:30–6:30 | #1 Steven Jones<br>#2 Sara Wagner | #1 Linda Anderson<br>#1 Sara Wagner<br>#3 Don Foster | #1 Jody Park<br>#1 Patty Boyle | #2 Dennis Brown<br>#2 Mary Lee |
| 7:30–8:30 | #3 Steven Jones<br>#3 Sara Wagner | #2 Linda Anderson<br>#2 Jody Park | #3 Jody Park | #3 Mary Lee |

The next step is to assign lesson times through a process of elimination, giving priority to first choices whenever possible, striking out each student's alternative choices once a time has been assigned, and circling the final selections.

After the scheduling is completed, the teacher can send parents a written letter to inform them of their child's lesson time for the new term, and to remind them of the date of the first lesson.

This system also avoids phone debates about busy schedules and preferences. When students submit the requests which work for them, they understand they will not necessarily receive their first choice.

## Group Lessons

Group teaching has become increasingly popular in recent years. Some teachers have turned solely to group instruction, while others offer a combination of group and private lessons. One of the advantages of offering only group lessons is that they shorten the workweek, with all students being able to complete lessons in a more condensed amount of time.

The pedagogical value of teaching group lessons and the equipment needed will be discussed in Chapters 41, 42, and 43; however, the following factors must be considered before committing to group lessons:

- Are there enough students to support multiple levels of groups?

- Will there be enough levels for students to be able to move up or down if needed?

- Is the studio adequately equipped for conducting group instruction?

Scheduling groups presents far greater challenges than scheduling private lessons. In today's busy world, students of all ages have multiple after-school commitments. The registration form mentioned earlier had room for students to list their first, second, and third choices for lessons from a list of available teaching times. However for group lessons, students may need to mark all available times, giving the teacher more options in assigning students to the appropriate group.

The chart below could be used for studios where only group lessons are offered, or for weeks when group lessons are offered instead of private lessons, as discussed later in this chapter.

### SAMPLE PREFERENCE SIGN-UP SHEET FOR GROUP LESSONS

**Please mark all available times for group lessons in order of preference.**

Name: *Sue Smith*

| LESSON TIME | MONDAY | TUESDAY | WEDNESDAY | THURSDAY |
|---|---|---|---|---|
| 3:30–4:30 | #1 | #2 | | #3 |
| 4:40–5:40 | #5 | | | #4 |
| 5:50–6:50 | #6 | | | #7 |

Notice that a ten-minute break is scheduled between groups to give the teacher time to organize each class as well as to allow for the multiple comings and goings of groups of students.

## A Combination of Group and Private Lessons

The following are a few possibilities for combining group and private lessons in the studio:

- Teach private lessons on most weeks and allocate a specific number of weeks throughout the term for group lessons.

- Alternate teaching group lessons one week with private lessons the next.

- Teach two lessons a week for each student, one private and one group.

If students take a combination of group and private lessons, they will either need to fill out charts requesting times for each type of lesson, or mark two sets of choices on a chart designed for both uses. Because of the complexity of the scheduling, each student should mark all of the available options for both private and group lessons, as shown in the following example.

## SAMPLE SIGN-UP SHEET FOR GROUP AND PRIVATE LESSONS

**Please mark all of your available times for both private lessons and group lessons. The type of lesson that is offered at any given time or day is listed in each box. The 5:00 lesson time is available for both private and group lessons.**

**Name:** _Sue Smith_

| LESSON TIME | MONDAY | TUESDAY | WEDNESDAY | THURSDAY | FRIDAY |
|---|---|---|---|---|---|
| 3:30–4:15 | Private #1 | Private | Private | Private #3 | Private |
| 4:15–5:00 | Private #2 | Private | Private | Private | Private #4 |
| 5:00–5:45/6:00 | Private Group #1 | Private Group | Private Group | Private #5 Group #3 | Private Group #2 |
| 6:45–7:45 | Group #4 | Group | Group | Group #5 | Group |
| 7:45–8:30 | Private #5 | Private | Private | Private | Private |

After the teacher receives all of the lesson request charts, she should schedule the group lessons first, as they require more matching.

Offering a group and private lesson each week has many pedagogical advantages, but can be extremely difficult to schedule, and requires a great deal of careful planning. The biggest challenge in offering both a group and a private lesson each week lies in matching students according to level of experience, so that the groups are effective. Naturally, the teacher must accept fewer students if each student receives two lessons per week, lowering the available pool of students for the group lessons, and therefore making the matching process even more challenging.

### Overlapping and Partner Lessons

Lesson times can be overlapped to provide students with enjoyable and productive time together, in addition to private time with the teacher. Overlapping lessons are most effective when the two students are of similar levels and can be conveniently scheduled back to back for just such a purpose.

#### SAMPLE SCHEDULE: OVERLAPPING PARTNER LESSONS

| STUDENT | TOTAL LESSON TIME | PRIVATE LESSON | OVERLAPPING PARTNER LESSON | PRIVATE LESSON |
|---------|-------------------|----------------|----------------------------|----------------|
| A | 60 minutes | 3:30-4:00 | 4:00-4:30 | |
| B | 60 minutes | | 4:00-4:30 | 4:30-5:00 |

The overlapping part of the lesson can be used for theory, sight-playing, duets, rhythm drills, keyboard skills, and other activities. In the above example, the teacher teaches the equivalent of two hours of lessons in one-and-a-half hours and is able to earn more income in less time, as well as teach certain topics more efficiently.

The same approach could be taken with a 45-minute lesson, allotting 15 minutes for the overlapping lesson and a 30-minute private lesson on either side.

Teachers may also choose to have lessons that are completely partnered, with two students taking their complete lesson together each week. The pedagogical benefits of offering overlapping and partner lessons are discussed further in Chapter 41.

It cannot be stressed strongly enough that compatibility is one of the key ingredients to successful overlapping or partner lessons.

- Are the students at similar levels of study?

- Do they seem to learn at similar rates of progress?

- Are they well suited to each other in temperament?

- Do they get along well with each other?

## Studio Classes

### Performance, Theory, and Other Large-Group Classes

Performance classes can be scheduled by ability level (beginner, intermediate, and advanced), but a mix of levels will offer students a valuable listening experience. Performance classes can be scheduled whenever time allows. Depending on the number of students in each class, the classes could be an hour to an hour-and-a-half long.

Theory classes must be scheduled by level; less advanced students will feel frustrated if they are in a class with more experienced students, and advanced students will be bored if they are held back.

The size of the class will depend on the teacher's expertise as a group instructor. Theory classes can be scheduled on any given day, and may be offered every week, every other week, or even once a month. The farther apart the classes, however, the less likely students will retain information. Weekends often work well for theory classes, but keep in mind that students' sports events will definitely impact weekend classes.

Large-group classes can be used to teach any subject that requires more time than private, partner, or small group lessons allow. Music history, world music, rhythm and movement, ear-training, improvisation, composition, and chamber music are several types of activities or subjects that are effectively taught in large groups. These classes can be scheduled as often as the teacher desires: twice a month, once a semester, or the first Wednesday of the month, for example. They can last from one to three hours. One particularly effective way to set up group classes is to schedule them for a total of 2.5 hours, with two hours of actual class time devoted to a specific subject or activity, separated in the middle by a half-hour break for pizza, snacks, or a musical game.

One example of creative scheduling that incorporates group classes for large numbers of students is to assign 30 students who normally receive 45-minute private lessons to three large groups of ten students each; then, divide two 17-week semesters into 13 private lessons and four large-group lessons per semester. During the group-lesson weeks, students benefit from more teacher time (2.5 hours), and the teacher teaches fewer hours (7.5 hour instead of 22.5), leaving more time for professional development and curriculum planning.

## Workstation or Computer Lab Time

Time at a workstation or computer lab is most efficiently scheduled directly before or after a private lesson. As shown in the following example, each student receives a private lesson while another is at the workstation.

### SAMPLE WORKSTATION SCHEDULE

| STUDENT | TOTAL LESSON TIME | WORKSTATION | PRIVATE LESSON |
|---------|-------------------|-------------|----------------|
| A | 90 minutes | 3:45-4:15 | 4:15-5:00 |
| B | 90 minutes | 4:15-4:45 | 3:30-4:15 |

# Expanding Teaching Hours

Music studios today are quite different from studios 20 years ago. Recent societal changes permit children to be educated in the home and adults to work in a home office with flexible daily working hours, opening up many new opportunities for the independent music teacher to schedule lessons throughout the day. Teachers can therefore offer several different types of lessons to a diverse student population.

## Home-Schooled Students

With the rise in the number of home-schooled students, teachers have the opportunity to include daytime hours that formerly were unavailable. By so doing, a greater number of students can be taught, or a schedule can be developed that better suits the teacher's preferences. On surveys, music teachers have listed teaching hours as one of the greatest drawbacks to the profession. Expanding teaching hours into the day by accepting home-schooled students offers an excellent alternative to the late evening hours of a busy studio and less intrusion into the teacher's family's schedule.

Through the local home-schooling association, teachers can publicize the availability of daytime private, group, or partner lessons in the following ways:

- Sending fliers or brochures about the studio to the association

- Contacting the person in charge of the association by phone

- Arranging for a personal interview with someone in a leadership position within the association

### Time-release, Lessons for Credit, and Teaching in the Schools

To make use of daytime hours, teachers can explore school release-time for lessons or school credit for private lessons. Some states have laws allowing or forbidding time-release and school credit, but more often this is decided by individual school boards.

MusicLink has a StudyLink independent study program that offers a system for awarding credit for private music lessons. More information about the StudyLink program can be found at www.music linkfoundation.org.

Some schools allow the IMT to teach on school grounds, excusing students from class to take piano lessons. This is more common in rural areas than urban, and in private schools than public. More often, time-release permits students to travel to the teacher's studio for study.

### Adult Lessons

Teaching adult lessons offers another option for maximizing one's studio time throughout the day, especially since many adults work out of their home and have flexible hours. School-age students normally schedule lessons after school and into the early evening hours; however, adults may be available for daytime lessons or in later evening hours. When scheduling daytime lessons, it is wise to arrange a number of lessons back-to-back rather than individual lessons at random, unrelated times. Random scheduling tends to break up the day, making non-teaching hours less productive or relaxing.

## In Summary

There are numerous scheduling options besides the traditional private lesson. In my own personal experience, I found scheduling lessons for adults to be particularly gratifying. Teaching adult students gave me time to be with adults, something that I enjoyed immensely since most of my students were children. My teaching day was extended and my income increased.

Perhaps the best suggestion is to "think outside the box." By using some imagination, teachers can devise a system that works best for their needs and the needs of their students.

# Chapter 11

# MAKE-UP POLICIES

Most of us have had the experience of someone taking advantage of our generosity. Parents don't mean to drive us to the brink; they just don't know what an inconvenience make-up lessons can be. To avoid schedule disruptions and lost income, we need to let parents know that we do not allow unlimited make-up lessons, nor are we responsible for the consequences of missed lessons. For our studios to run smoothly, we must each decide on an acceptable make-up policy and enforce that policy consistently.

## The Need for a Make-up Policy

Why do teachers even need a make-up policy? Why not just decide each case on an individual basis when a student misses a lesson? Without a make-up policy:

- Parents will take advantage of a teacher's generosity.

- Miscommunication could result in disputes harmful to the parent-teacher relationship.

- Uncompensated missed lessons will affect the teacher's income.

- The teacher may grow to resent that-little-rascal-Susie-for-missing-her-music-lesson-again-this-week-and-while-we-are-on-the-subject-why-aren't-her-parents-taking-music-as-seriously-as-soccer-anyway?

Parents actually appreciate clear policies. When a teacher is up front about policies such as make-up lessons, parents have the information needed to decide if that teacher is right for their child. Once a family agrees to lessons in a given studio, they are choosing to accept the teacher's policies, including the make-up policy.

Teachers also need to feel assured that the students they accept will commit to weekly attendance. When a teacher is not clear about such expectations, parents may even feel they do not need to pay for missed lessons. This would adversely affect the teacher's income, something that few teachers can afford and none should accept.

Misunderstandings about missed lessons foster the wrong atmosphere in the studio. No teacher wants to resent students and parents for being inconsistent and inconsiderate. Over time there is a strong possibility that such resentments would negatively affect the lessons, to the point where the teacher might even consider dropping the student, replacing her with one who is more reliable and interested.

## Valid Reasons for Make-up Lessons

Each teacher should develop as firm a policy as possible, but not one so firm that the teacher will be uncomfortable enforcing it. Constantly making exceptions will erode the effectiveness of the policy and gradually negate it.

Teachers have developed a variety of ways to accommodate make-up lessons. The least efficient is to offer them for any and all reasons, as long as notice is given in advance. This may seem efficient, but the possible reasons for missed lessons are endless. For example, it is understandable that a student would want to attend her grandmother's 80th birthday party, but it may also be impossible to accommodate choices such as this.

Another approach teachers use in offering make-up lessons is to allow them only in certain cases, such as:

- Illness with 24-hours advance notice

- Extreme weather conditions

- Family emergencies

- School conflicts

- Unavoidable conflicts

- Family vacations

- Any reason, with a limit of three per year

While all of the above may seem like valid reasons for making up a missed lesson, some of the conditions must be narrowed down because the vague wording allows for too many options. Offering three make-up lessons a year, for example, may sound manageable; however, a busy teacher with 30 students who allows three make-up lessons per student is agreeing to a possible 90 make-up lessons a year! "Unavoidable conflicts" may also seem like a reasonable allowance, but it is amazing what will be construed as an "unavoidable conflict." Teachers must remind themselves that if a student chooses some other activity over lessons, the teacher is not obligated to compensate the student for that choice. These scenarios reinforce the need for a teacher to be very clear about make-up lessons in the studio policy statement.

## The Swap List

A better option than providing make-ups for all conflicts is to ask interested parents, guardians, or adult students to sign an agreement to be on a swap list. The list should include students' names, lesson times, and phone numbers for distribution to other students on the list; however, *written* permission must always be obtained from an adult before any phone number is published. The lesson times for students who do not wish to be on the list should be noted on the schedule with the words "Not available," to avoid students requesting a make-up lesson at that time.

When a student has a conflict, such as Grandmother's birthday party, she can call others on the list to swap that week's lesson rather than miss either the party or the lesson. The student then notifies the teacher of the swap in advance so that everyone is clear about the revised schedule. If a swap cannot be arranged or the student has decided not to be on the original swap list, that lesson would be forfeited and no refund is due.

A sample swap list is included in Appendix A.

## Other Ways of Scheduling Make-up Lessons

When the number of make-up lessons owed to students becomes overwhelming, a teacher can select from a number of creative options to solve the problem.

- **Group make-up lessons:** If weather has caused missed lessons, the teacher can offer a longer group make-up class covering areas such as performance, music history, or theory. This solution would provide the students with more hours of instruction than their usual weekly lesson time, and allows the teacher to make up multiple lessons in a reasonable amount of time.

- **Smaller group or partner lessons:** Teachers can save time by combining students in pairs or small groups for make-up lessons.

- **Make-up weeks:** Make-up lessons can be scheduled in one week at the end of the year or semester, designated on the studio calendar as "Make-Up Week."

### Successful Wording of a Make-up Policy

The wording used in a make-up policy either clarifies and strengthens the policy, or confuses and weakens it. The following are some examples of wording that is firm and clearly stated.

- "Payment includes all scheduled lessons, regardless of attendance, and no lessons will be made up for any reason."

- "Each student is allowed one make-up lesson per term for sudden extreme weather conditions or for illness with 24-hours notice. For other conflicts, please use the swap list."

- "No deductions or make-ups will be given for lessons missed by the student. To accommodate conflicts, students may opt to be included on a swap list that allows them to exchange lessons times when needed."

- "When a student cancels a make-up lesson, the lesson is forfeited."

- "Lessons missed due to weather will be made up by scheduling an additional performance party during the term."

The following are examples of inefficient, vague, or poorly worded make-up policies.

- "Lessons will be rescheduled because of emergencies, weather, illness, conflicting school activities, or out-of-town trips ONLY. Except in cases of last-minute emergencies, 24-hours' notice must be given." (This teacher sounds like she is trying to be firm, but in actuality, this is a non-policy where every possible scenario is eligible for a make-up lesson.)

- "Missed lessons cannot be made up. However, if the student is ill, arrangements can be made…" (First there are no make-ups, then there are…)

- "Lessons missed due to emergencies will be made up. Lessons missed for reasons other than emergencies will be made up at the teacher's discretion." (The parents have no way of knowing which lessons will be made up. With the phrase, "at the teacher's discretion," the teacher hopes to maintain control of what could be an uncontrollable situation, but actually leaves parents unsure of what to expect. Every time there is a conflict they will need to ask, "Will we be getting a make-up lesson?" Most teachers would feel uncomfortable about continually defending each reason for granting or not granting a make-up lesson, and the parents and teacher may disagree about which reasons are acceptable.)

In order for a make-up policy to be effective, it must be presented in writing in the teacher's annual studio policy. If parents should later object to not receiving a make-up lesson, the teacher can remind them that by signing the policy statement, they agreed to the teacher's conditions for make-up lessons.

In one of my workshops on studio policies, a teacher explained that her policy clearly stated that refunds would not be given for missed lessons. However, a student missed a lesson and his parents deducted the cost of the lesson from the following month's payment. The teacher was too embarrassed to ask the parents for payment for the missed lesson. I advised her to send the following to the parents:

- A written invoice for the overdue funds

- A charge for late payment

- A photocopy copy of the policy statement showing the parents' signatures indicating their agreement to all policies

These parents did not have the right to change this teacher's policies any more than they have the right to change the payment policies at a lawyer's office or loan payments at a bank.

I would like to share an experience from my early years of teaching, when I was offering make-ups for every possible reason. During a single week one summer, 11 students in a row missed their lessons. By the eleventh phone call I was hyperventilating and decided I needed to take action. I wrote the following letter and mailed it to all of my students:

---

**A SPECIAL LETTER TO SUMMER STUDENTS:**

Last Tuesday, I had seven lessons scheduled. Three people canceled lessons when they were due to arrive, and four more canceled with only minimal notice. Everyone wanted a make-up lesson. The following day my first four Wednesday students did the same thing.

Eleven lessons in a row went untaught. A day and a half went by during which I was unable to work, nor was I free for other activities. I know it is hard to keep a schedule in the summer, but please respect my time. In August, please keep lesson times as scheduled. I will not give make-ups or rearrange lesson times for the following reasons, ever again:

> I/she/he has not practiced enough.
> I am still baby-sitting.
> The car just broke down.
> She/he is not back from the pool yet.
> I don't know where Mom is.

These excuses may seem valid, but when given so late, my time is lost. No other lesson can be arranged. Your hour cannot be used by anyone else and remains your hour.

I am too well bred to utter the words and think the thoughts that flowed forth after the eleventh caller on Wednesday. Please help me to avoid my darker side and to remain,

The Happy Piano Teacher,
*Mrs. Klingenstein*

---

Two weeks after mailing the letter I received a call from a mother requesting make-ups for her three family members because their car was broken down. I answered that I was sorry that they would miss their lessons, but as stated in my new policy, I would not be making up the lessons. She called back in five minutes and said they would make the lessons after all because she had borrowed the neighbor's car. This taught me a lot about "unavoidable conflicts." It also taught me that when parents are given a firm policy, they are more likely to respect the teacher's time.

The presence or absence of a workable plan for make-up lessons impacts teachers' professionalism as well as their peace of mind. Parents, students, and teachers all benefit from clearly written conditions concerning make-up lessons. In the long run, teachers will save themselves hours of time and frustration by planning and implementing a fair, effective, and enforceable make-up policy.

## MEMORABLE QUOTES

In an anonymous survey, teachers were asked, "How do you feel about your make-up policy?" The following are some notable answers.

"I don't like making up lessons missed for avoidable reasons. However, people refuse to pay for lessons they don't receive." (This teacher also had trouble collecting payments for lessons that were taught, and had generally weak studio policies.)

"I am strict about make-ups and therefore have very few cancellations. I offer no make-ups and they still pay." (This teacher had a very clear make-up policy that she enforced, leaving her with few problems.)

"I get taken advantage of."

"It is difficult to enforce, and sometimes I feel as though I'm too nice, but if I followed it like I should, it would work well!"

"I feel taken advantage of when people who cancel insist on 'taking it off of next month's check.' I remind them of my written policy and they act like they never heard it. A few say, 'I'm not paying for lessons I didn't get.'" (As stated earlier, if parents deduct for a missed lesson, the teacher should send them a written bill and remind them they have signed the policy statement agreeing to all the teacher's conditions. This is the teacher's business; she sets the rules.)

# Part IV

## IMAGE

As individuals and as members of a profession, independent music teachers must be aware of the image they project, both to the public and to themselves. Part IV stresses the importance of maintaining a professional image as skilled and trained pedagogues with high professional standards.

Among the topics discussed are the public perceptions others have of music teachers and our profession. Also covered is the value of assessing one's professionalism by comparing data from local and state surveys on studio policies. Finally presented is the immediate impression that the teacher makes on students and parents through body language, speech, and dress.

# Chapter 12

# PUBLIC PERCEPTIONS OF THE INDEPENDENT MUSIC TEACHER

When I started teaching piano I was still in high school. I enjoyed teaching and was proud of my students and their musical progress. When it came to the professional aspects of running my studio, however, I made every mistake possible. I charged $2.00 an hour and was paid weekly as each student came to the studio. I did not keep written records of payments or attendance, and gave make-up lessons for any and all reasons. With no formal studio policies, the parents of my students did not have any guidelines to follow about payments or attendance. My less-than-professional approach to teaching, coupled with my youth, resulted in my being perceived as the stereotype of a neighborhood piano teacher: not very professional, not that educated, not organized, and not worthy of a decent salary.

As I look back on those early years, I find it hard to believe that I approached teaching in such an unprofessional manner. At times I called parents to remind them that they hadn't paid for a lesson, only to be informed that they had indeed paid. With no records, how was I to know? Although I started teaching very young, I soon had a full studio of active students who wanted their lesson times rearranged on a regular basis. I obliged every conflict, to the point of barely having enough hours in the day to accommodate all of the requests. It never occurred to me to limit those requests.

In college and graduate school, I continued to teach as I advanced in my own piano studies, focusing on my growing musical and technical skills. At no point was there even one word from a professor about what I would do with those skills. What suggestions did they give me for running a private studio? None.

When I finished graduate school, I was completely on my own. Fortunately, by then I had years of experience teaching piano. Teaching privately suited me well and I was eager to start an independent studio as my primary source of income. Unfortunately, my approach to the business side of teaching was only marginally more professional than back in my high-school days. I still did not inspire others to view my work with respect and high regard.

## Misconceptions

As in any profession, there can be a wide range of perceptions and misperceptions about what the independent music teacher does. Some of these misconceptions can be quite damaging, demeaning the profession and lessening teachers' ability to earn a respectable salary. If teachers were to answer the following questions, it would become evident that even they would have varying views about the profession.

- Is piano teaching seen as an important and rewarding career?

- Is piano teaching considered to be a job to fall back on if nothing else works?

- Is teaching viewed as part-time work or is it viewed as a career?

- What exactly does the independent music teacher do?

- What are the average work hours per week of the IMT?

- What factors affect income level?

- What specific educational requirements are necessary to teach effectively?

- What skills does the IMT use?

- What possible stereotypes exist that detract from the image of the profession?

Teachers who convey the importance of their profession and the intensive skill and training required for their occupation are regarded by students, parents, and the community as highly qualified and deserving of respect. The opposite is also true. Teachers who perceive their occupation as one requiring little training, involving marginal skills, and deserving of only minimal pay, will be regarded by others as such.

One striking personal experience that demonstrates these two opposite perceptions dates back about 20 years. A young woman who had recently graduated from high school spent the summer with my husband and me. Knowing that she had taken ten years of piano lessons, I asked about her teacher. "Oh, she is not like you; she is not a professional. She's retired." Curious about a teacher who still gave lessons after retirement, I asked a few questions. How many students did she teach? "Fifty." Did her students ever give recitals? "Oh, yes. She has recitals twice a year where she rents the town hall, the piano, and an organ. Then she fixes a huge buffet for all the students and parents."

As the young woman continued to describe the many activities of this busy teacher, whose rates were about one-fifth of mine, I started to think, "I'm never going to retire. I don't have the energy for it!" How did this house guest come to perceive me as a professional while she thought of her hard-working teacher of so many years, not only as non-professional, but even as retired? There was clearly something in our behavior that was shaping the perceptions of those around us.

Besides shaping the image we personally project, we must also battle societal stereotypes that continue to plague our profession. Even educated people can have major misconceptions about what it takes to be a piano teacher. Some people still think that anyone who studied piano can take up the profession.

I encountered a vivid example of this in an article that appeared in 1983 in the *Washington Post* written by a counselor named Jean Lawrence. In the article, "Mother Burnout," Lawrence had some interesting advice for tired moms: "Concentrate on a talent by joining a local choir or theater group; or try painting, sculpting, taking music lessons, or *giving* music lessons."

After reading that article I thought to myself, she should have included, "Go to see a counselor, or *be* a counselor." After all, just like giving music lessons, it must not take any specialized training, right? Here was an irritating perception about our profession held by an educated woman; anyone can jump in and teach music lessons as long as she had a few lessons herself. Nothing could be farther from the truth.

Misconceptions about independent music teaching abound in our society. The following lists a few.

- It's not really a job.

- That's part-time work.

- Anyone who has had piano lessons as a kid can teach piano lessons.

- People who teach in their homes can't do anything better.

- You can't earn a living from teaching at home.

Parents, students, and music teachers themselves can inadvertently contribute to these misconceptions, but only teachers are capable of changing them.

## A Survey on Perceptions of Teachers

In 2002, I conducted a national survey comparing the perceptions independent music teachers have of their own profession with the perceptions of the public at large. The results were not necessarily what I had expected. Not only does the public view our profession in a less-than-flattering manner, but in many cases, so do we.

The survey was sent to music teachers chosen at random from each state and the District of Columbia, as well as to non-teachers randomly selected from the Internet, in locations ranging from small rural areas to large metropolitan cities. I stressed that the responses were to reflect *perceptions* of the independent piano teaching profession. Non-teachers responding to the survey did not need to know the "facts," and there were no "correct" answers. To me, such perceptions were important; they would represent the perceptions that piano teachers must confront on a daily basis.

### Training

*"What has the average piano teacher studied to teach successfully in an independent studio?"*

## STUDIES

| NON-TEACHER RESPONDENTS | PIANO TEACHER RESPONDENTS |
|---|---|
| • Education courses | • Education courses |
| • Music theory courses | • Music theory courses |
| • Basic music courses | • Psychology |
| | • Piano literature |
| | • Piano lessons |
| | • Piano pedagogy |
| | • Music history |
| | • Business skills |
| | • Technique |
| | • Harmony |
| | • Ear-training |
| | • Performance |
| | • Child development |
| | • Accompanying and ensemble playing |
| | • Injury prevention |
| | • Music technology |
| | • Stage presence |
| | • Sight-playing |

These responses prove that, although we as teachers may understand that it takes a broad range of specialized study to teach successfully, the public at large is almost clueless about the depth of our training. It is up to us to change the way we are perceived by informing parents and students of our areas of study, expertise, degrees, and the services that that we offer in our studio.

## Responsibilities

*"What are the duties and responsibilities of the independent music teacher?"*

The public at large seemed equally uninformed about the duties teachers perform in addition to actually teaching lessons. When asked to list these duties, only a small percentage of non-teachers responded; their answers fell into two basic areas: professional responsibilities and people skills. This was a recurring trend throughout the survey. On the other hand, teachers covered a much longer list, and the percentage responding in each category was much higher.

**PART IV**

### TEACHING DUTIES

| NON-TEACHER RESPONDENTS | TEACHER RESPONDENTS |
| --- | --- |
| Professional responsibilities: | Professional responsibilities: |
| • Preparing lessons | • Preparing lessons |
| • Arranging recitals | • Arranging recitals |
| • Evaluating students | • Evaluating students |
| | • Scheduling lessons |
| | • Buying music and supplies |
| | • Accompanying |
| | • Keeping records |
| | • Collecting bills |
| | • Providing appropriate materials for each student |
| | • Writing college recommendations |
| | • Keeping up with one's own continuing education |
| | • Participating in professional organizations |
| | • Entering students in competitions |
| | • Preparing students for auditions and festivals |
| | • Taking students to concerts |
| | • Teaching ear-training and rhythm skills |
| | • Adjudicating, marketing the studio, planning studio policies |
| | • Publishing a studio newsletter |
| | • Communicating with parents |
| People skills: | People skills: |
| • Encouraging students | • Being a role model |
| • Assisting students with life lessons such as setting goals and developing a strong work ethic | • Encouraging students |
| | • Counseling |
| | • Being a friend to students |

Most teachers included their duties in the professional category, but it was disheartening that some teachers actually answered by listing only people skills or by listing few professional duties. It was surprising that practicing was hardly mentioned at all. Counseling was the duty listed by the highest percentage of teachers. While people skills are indeed very important to our profession, they do not heavily outweigh the professional responsibilities listed above.

## Additional Skills

*"What skills besides musical skills do you think a private music teacher uses
in order to teach music successfully in a home studio?"*

### NON-MUSICAL SKILLS

| NON-TEACHER RESPONDENTS | TEACHER RESPONDENTS |
|---|---|
| • People skills | • Organizational skills |
| • Patience | • Technology skills |
| • Ability to work with others | • Business skills |
| | • Knowledge of learning styles and how to accommodate them |
| | • Communications and listening skills |
| | • Knowledge of child psychology and development |
| | • Ability to challenge and motivate students |
| | • Empathy |
| | • Public relations skills |
| | • Sense of humor |
| | • Writing skills |
| | • Creativity |
| | • Flexibility |
| | • Fortitude (Ability to ignore a growling stomach when teaching past the dinner hour.) |

## Work Hours

*"Do you consider piano teaching a full-time or part-time job?"*

The response from both groups to this question was astounding: 75% of each group stated that teaching piano in an independent studio is a part-time job. Considering how overworked so many independent teachers are, how can teaching be perceived as a part-time job? Perhaps the clue to understanding this misperception may be found in the answer of one teacher: "Probably it's part-time, but for me it feels like full-time." My response to that is, "If it looks like a duck, and walks like a duck, and quacks like a duck, it probably is full-time."

### Annual Income

*"Take a guess at the annual income (for example, $35,000) for these professions.*
*Don't worry about being totally accurate. This question is to measure your perception*
*of these annual incomes."*

Although rates and the outside factors that can influence rates have already been discussed in previous chapters, it is interesting to compare the perceptions of teachers and non-teachers concerning the annual income of the IMT. The following answers reflect perceptions of the average income in 2002 and are therefore outdated. Nonetheless, the responses were revealing.

## PERCEPTIONS OF INCOME

| OCCUPATION | NON-TEACHER RESPONDENTS | TEACHER RESPONDENTS |
|---|---|---|
| Lawyer | $93,611 | $113,700 |
| Electrician | $47,500 | $52,220 |
| Plumber | $46,111 | $50,000 |
| Truck driver | $42,222 | $38,840 |
| Elem. school teacher | $28,833 | $34,000 |
| Janitor | $24,722 | $25,420 |
| Private music teacher | $20,000 | $19,940 |

Responses in the table above show that independent piano teachers are perceived as earning less than a plumber, truck driver, and janitor, as well as approximately one-fifth of a lawyer's salary. Why is our income perceived to be so low? It cannot be because we are paid per client—so are plumbers and lawyers. It cannot be because we do not need training—we have far more training than most, if not all, of the professions listed above. Perhaps it is because we do receive a low income. When actual rates from the **2002 IMT Business Practices Survey** by Beth Klingenstein (see Chapter 5) on rates and workloads are compared to the list above, they are even lower than the perceptions of income from either of the above groups! But why is this deplorable disparity of income accepted? Who will change it? Each teacher needs to take steps to assure a salary worthy of her training and expertise, or the low-income status of independent music teachers will never change.

## Memorable Perceptions

To determine whether old stereotypes influence current perceptions of the independent piano teacher, I asked the following question of both teachers and non-teachers in my survey:

*"When you think of the typical music teacher who teaches lessons in a home studio,*
*what image comes to mind?"*

**Here are some responses from the public at large.**

- "White female in her 30s to 40s, working part-time to supplement income for the family. Middle aged and married." (The stereotype of working a part-time job for extra money is strong.)

- "An older lady, usually 40+ years old." (The humor of this answer is increased by the fact that it was submitted by a woman in her 30s. Oh, how quickly she will reach those "older" 40s!)

- "A musical person with one or more children at home, no matter what the degree of music or experience in teaching. A great job for moms who want to stay at home." (This implies that there need not be any standard for training.)

- "A very warm person, with a genuine love for all kinds of music, friendly, and patient. Middle aged, middle income, female who works for extra money, but could squeeze the budget and be fine otherwise. Gentle, patient, caring, has a love for the instrument."

**Some of the positive perceptions of the typical IMT provided by the music teachers themselves include the following.**

- "A very busy person. Usually is also a wife and mother, a church worker, and involved in other music and club activities. She has to be a good organizer to do the planning and preparation."

- "Incredibly overworked, but deeply satisfied. Gentle, patient, funny, truly enjoys the students, able to communicate high expectations."

- "I think of a teacher like myself—degreed and takes their job seriously. They don't teach for 'extra money.'"

- "A happy, self-employed, educated, caring professional, practicing his/her art in a comfortable setting. Extremely satisfied in sharing music with others."

**Some less positive perceptions provided by music teachers themselves are listed below.**

- "50-year-old female, married or widowed. Some-college level study. Loves children. Supports art in the community. Dependent on husband's income for livelihood. A sweet, but not 'with it' lady."

- "The image of overworked, underpaid, and under-appreciated does seem appropriate. Often sells oneself short."

- "Music everywhere, in closets, under benches, on tables, in file cabinets. Not dressed professionally, casual home attire."

- "A teacher who has had 6–8 years of private instruction (pre-college), uses the same methods for all students, is teaching to improve financial status, teaches mostly beginning students."

- "The lady down the street, doing this job as a hobby for a little extra income."

- "Little gray-haired lady with glasses perched on her nose."

- "Likely a widow/widower or low-income person, non-professional and untrained."

**The following question was asked only of teachers:**

*"Do you have any interesting anecdotes about the perception your students, their parents, or someone outside the profession has had about the independent music teacher or of the job of teaching in a home studio?"*

The responses provided a number of humorous or astonishing answers.

- "Oh, you are a piano teacher. Do you work?"

- "In a conversation with a 'friend' at a public gathering, she asked me what I charge for lessons and then noted, 'You must be a millionaire!' At the time I was charging $7 a lesson and had about 40 students."
  (I did the math: $7 x 40 students = $280 a week x 40 weeks = $11,200 a year.)

- "What else do you do?"

- "Where do you work when you are done teaching piano?"

- "[I] ran into an old high school classmate in a supermarket parking lot. I knew he had become a lawyer and judge. Pleased to see me, he asked if I was 'still teaching piano.' I replied 'Yes, I am, are you still practicing law?'"

- "Can you please reschedule my lesson at a more convenient time since your teaching schedule is so flexible?"

- "I think some people think that teaching a 30- or 45-minute lesson weekly is all we do."

- "People are always surprised at my studio because it's in an attached garage, separate entrance, and kids never get into my house. I run it like a business because it is!"

- "When I was a chemist, people always said, 'You must be smart!' Now when I tell them I am a piano teacher, they say, 'How nice.'"

- "One of my new adult students left me a message when she couldn't reach me at 9:00 a.m. She said that I was probably sleeping in since I work at home. I was, of course, out of the house and busy already."

## In Summary

Although there are decades of stereotypes to overcome, each teacher ultimately determines how she will be perceived. If we feel that changing all of society's stereotypes is more than one person can do, we need to remind ourselves that we are the only ones who can do this. Therefore, we can and we must take the responsibility. By so doing we will help establish a positive perception of our profession. We must project an image that will impress others with our skill, education, and talent. If the old stereotypes have not yet died a natural death, it is up to each of us to lay them to rest.

## Resources

### ARTICLE

Klingenstein, Beth. "Shaping Perception: Taking Responsibility for our Profession." *American Music Teacher,* December/January 2001/2002, Vol. 51, No. 3, pp. 20–23.

# Chapter 13

# CLARIFYING IMAGE: THE VALUE OF TEACHER SURVEYS

How do we know if we are conducting our studios in a professional manner? How can we evaluate our business policies and compare them to those of other independent music teachers in our locale? In order to answer these questions, it is helpful to access data summarizing the decisions of our peers in addressing professional issues.

During my early years of teaching, I found that discussing work-related problems with my colleagues provided an excellent way to discover how other teachers addressed the same challenges of studio operation that I faced. Our local organization, the Northern Virginia Music Teachers Association (NVMTA), devoted one of its meetings to a group discussion of business issues, and we were so energized by the shared ideas during that session that we decided to go one step further and conduct a teacher survey of business practices among our members.

Surveys offer invaluable insights into teaching practices in our geographical area and provide us with a deeper look into accepted business practices, professionalism, and successful studio programs.

## Do's and Don't's of Music Teacher Surveys

The purpose of a survey is to gather information, much like the data on average wages per occupation that is collected by the Department of Labor. However, in any survey of business practices, especially one concerning rates, no recommendation can be made for a set wage or a set annual percentage of increase in income, or for any other economic policies that affect the IMT. Such actions are considered price-fixing, are illegal, and must be avoided.

Several types of data can be collected legally in a teacher survey, and provide a great resource for teachers in comparing their business policies with those of colleagues in their particular geographic location. Some of the areas to include in a survey might be:

- Educational background
- Years of experience
- Population of community
- Number of students taught
- Hours per week spent teaching
- Rates calculated per hour
- Annual income

- Method for billing (weekly, monthly, semester, etc.)

- Hours per week spent on other studio activities (bookwork, learning new repertoire, meetings, etc.)

- Extra services offered (work station, chamber music, group lessons, theory classes, performance classes, summer camps, etc.)

- Make-up policy

- Use of book and fee deposit

- Use of swap list

- Use of technology in the studio

- Sources for summer income

Surveys should be conducted anonymously, as teachers are more likely to share personal information when not giving their names. Unfortunately, some teachers have been reluctant to share information concerning rates, even on an anonymous survey. This makes it difficult to establish data from which teachers can draw comparisons with regard to the rates they charge.

## The Northern Virginia Music Teachers Association (NVMTA) Surveys

From 1979 through 1994 when I moved to North Dakota, I conducted surveys of the teachers in NVMTA. Comparing two of these surveys—1985 and 1987—offers some valuable insight into how the members of the organization used the results of the earlier survey to make more informed choices concerning their studio policies just two years later. The survey made no recommendation to adopt a new policy or rate.

When I compiled the results of the 1985 survey, I was astonished that 40% of teachers responding felt they charged too little. Most teachers (63%) raised their rates only every two to three years and the average hourly fee had increased only one dollar in the two years previous to the survey.

By contrast, the 1987 survey was surprisingly optimistic. In the two years following the 1985 survey, 81% of the teachers raised their rates and the average hourly fee increased by $3.80. Sixty-three percent of the teachers were content with their fees. The number of teachers who offered only half-hour lessons (the length most disliked) was down from 31% to 14% and most teachers were content with the lesson lengths taught. Services offered, such as theory classes, workshops, and such, increased in every category, reflecting a more comprehensive, professional approach to teaching. Use of a renewable deposit method of billing for books nearly doubled, from 16% to 30%.

In general, the 1987 survey reflected a much greater level of professional satisfaction among member respondents, and an increase in professional approaches to the varied aspects of studio policy. These choices were made independently; teachers drew their own conclusions from the results of previous surveys.

Below are the changes in the average per-hour fee of the members of NVMTA from 1979 to 2006.

## NORTHERN VIRGINIA MUSIC TEACHERS ASSOCIATION SURVEY RESULTS
### AVERAGE PER-HOUR FEE

| YEAR | 1979 | 1981 | 1983 | 1985 | 1987 | 1989 | 1992 | 1995 | 1999 | 2001 | 2003 | 2006 |
|------|------|------|------|------|------|------|------|------|------|------|------|------|
| HOURLY RATE | $15 | $17 | $20 | $21 | $25 | $27 | $31.50 | $35 | $40.50 | $46 | $49.50 | $59.33 |

It is quite likely that the healthy increase in rates is due in part to the heightened awareness of rates brought on by the organization's surveys, and would have been much less significant without the comparative data. No mention was ever made in the surveys about what individuals should charge, and yet by keeping rates an open topic for discussion rather than a deep, dark secret, the income of the teachers in the Northern Virginia area has been one of continual growth, surpassing many of the increases in other geographical areas.

Included in Appendix B is a sample survey that may be reproduced and modified to meet the needs of any music teachers' organization. The sample includes questions covering issues such as rates, lesson length, services offered, policies, and insurance.

Having learned a great deal from teacher surveys, I highly recommend that local and state associations survey their members regularly on business and professional issues.

# Chapter 14

# PROJECTING A PROFESSIONAL IMAGE

---

Let us imagine a worst-case teaching scenario, which, unfortunately, is more common than we would like to believe. Ms. Jones teaches a lot of lessons, including a few before school—no need to worry about wearing bedroom slippers that early in the morning, right? She loves her casual approach to style, so blue jeans and an oversized T-shirt provide comfort during a long day of teaching and parenting, and the students seem to like the relaxed look. Since the piano is in the family room, toys are strewn around the room, but that's okay. Her students understand she has kids: after all, they run in and out of the room often enough when she is teaching.

Stacks of music are everywhere and the room is disorganized, but eventually she usually finds what she is looking for. The phone is constantly ringing, and since there is no one watching the kids, Ms. Jones frequently yells for her daughter to get the phone. Sometimes she actually leaves the room to get her daughter; after all, she needs to check on the kids from time to time as well as get dinner in the oven.

When Ms. Jones isn't barking directions at her kids, she babbles about any old thing, chattering on and on while the student sits quietly. It's a good thing Ms. Jones knows how to fill those awkward silences! As she leans back in her reclining chair, Ms. Jones rarely looks at her students when teaching them. She keeps her eyes on the music or the piano so as not to miss a trick, except when she starts to drift off and think of other things… then who knows where she might be looking? Good thing the students can't notice while they are playing the piano.

Ms. Jones obviously needs a course in professionalism.

## Home Life vs. Work Life

The importance of separating home and work space, time, and activities cannot be overemphasized. In order to keep home life from interfering with work, independent piano teachers must find a way to maintain a professional image and project professionalism in the studio, despite the demands of raising a family or dealing with personal responsibilities.

Many problems can arise when home life is interjected into the work environment. Teachers must ensure that family or personal responsibilities do not encroach on work hours.

**Problem:** Children run into the room and say they are hungry.

**Solution:** Hire a sitter to watch young children during work hours, utilizing childcare the same as one would for any other job. Young children should not be left unattended, and no teacher should be attending to children while working.

**Problem:** The teacher takes a minute to put the dinner in the oven.

**Solution:** If dinner needs to be put in the oven, an actual break should be scheduled between lessons to attend to dinner duties.

**Problem:** A friend calls during a lesson.

**Solution:** Phone calls during teaching hours can be handled in one of three ways:
- Voice mail for all calls
- Breaks between lessons to allow time to check phone messages
- A separate line for student phone calls allowing the teacher to respond to important business-related calls

**Problem:** The studio room is also used by the family, and toys are scattered throughout.

**Solution:** Toys and clutter must be put away during lessons. Bins, baskets, or closets can be used to organize the studio space so that no toys are visible during teaching hours.

## Making Your Home Your Place of Business

Teachers need to remind themselves that while teaching, they are at work, and must treat their job with the same importance as if they worked in an office building. The following exercises can help teachers gauge the businesslike atmosphere of the home studio.

**Exercise 1:** Pretend your studio is part of an important corporation, and that the CEO of the company is coming to observe your studio in one week. What changes should you make before the CEO arrives? What will you need to clean or reorganize? Assume that you have no funds to alter the studio, but still need to be more organized. Decide what you can do within the next week and then do it!

**Exercise 2:** Imagine that after the CEO's visit, he/she has decided to give you a small but very important sum of money ($200) to help you organize your studio more efficiently. What will be the very best way for you to spend the money? Will you add a second phone line? Purchase storage shelves or a new file cabinet? Get a better desk? Then devise a plan to actually save $200, and purchase those much-needed items!

**Exercise 3:** The CEO is coming back, this time to observe your teaching for one week. Will anything in your behavior need to change? Are you inadvertently mixing family and teaching time? Will you need to be more careful about starting and ending lessons on time? Will you have to stop answering the phone or going to the kitchen? Will you need to dress differently? Make a list of all behaviors that need to be modified, and then change!

# Body Language

We all express ourselves using body language: where we look as we speak, facial expressions, and the way we hold our body. Body language often sends a stronger message than actual spoken words. For the IMT, understanding the significance of body language is crucial, as non-verbal cues set the tone for lessons, student interviews, and professional meetings. Students, parents, and colleagues might be responding to a message that teachers do not even realize they are sending. It is therefore crucial to examine one's own non-verbal cues and to develop body language that promotes positive learning and helps teachers achieve their goals.

## Gestures

Gestures often strengthen a message, but nervous gestures, such as fiddling with hair or biting nails, undermine the image a teacher wishes to project. Imagine how such gestures would come across in an interview with a new family.

Some gestures conflict with the verbal message that is being sent. Gestures such as crossing arms over one's chest during a lesson send a hostile message, even if the words are friendly. Teachers are often unaware of habitual gestures, such as finger pointing. Yet constant finger pointing may cause a student to feel scolded or uncomfortable. Videotaping lessons might reveal any habitual gestures that need to be modified.

## Facial Expressions

Facial expressions, the most spontaneous form of expression, usually express how a person truly feels. Genuine and receptive expressions invoke responsiveness in the listener, while insincere or unfriendly looks will turn a listener away.

Facial expressions can work to our benefit during lessons, putting the student at ease and reflecting our enjoyment of teaching. When we smile, we also look more confident and self-assured.

I know that, as I walk down the hall of the music department where I teach, I often concentrate hard on the many things I have on my mind. But I have learned that this concentration sometimes translates into a scowl, and that I need to be aware of the messages my facial expressions are sending.

## Eye Contact

Speaking to a student or parent without making eye contact produces any number of negative reactions. It might appear that we are distracted, shy, embarrassed, lacking in confidence, untrustworthy, or uncaring. Looking directly into someone's eyes helps us to be perceived as honest, sincere, and confident.

Videotaping a lesson yields valuable observations about our use of eye contact. How much time is spent engaged in direct eye contact with students? Are instructions given while looking at the book, the piano keys, or the student? Students will feel disengaged if conversation is normally directed to the music book or the piano keys. They might not have a sense that we care about them if we rarely seem to be speaking directly to them. Maintaining eye contact is not a difficult thing to do, but can easily be left out of a busy piano lesson if we are not careful.

**PART IV**

## Posture

A few years ago, the university where I teach interviewed candidates for the position of vice president. One candidate sat slumped backwards against the chair, with one foot crossed over his knee, his chin very high and his head cocked to one side. He used gestures such as pressing the fingers of one hand against the other or looking at his nails as he spoke. The impression he gave was one of arrogance, and it was hard to listen to him objectively. His body language as he sat was so strongly negative, that I truly did not hear his verbal message, and absolutely did not want him to be our VP!

Posture while sitting, standing, and walking reflects our attitude toward life, as well as how we feel about ourselves. Posture sends a message about whether we are active or passive, flexible or rigid, confident or self-conscious, happy or sad, and much more.

**Negative:** Sitting on the edge of a chair makes us appear anxious or uncomfortable. Leaning back against a chair with arms draped over the back of the chair gives us the appearance of being nonchalant or uncaring.

**Positive:** Sitting up straight and leaning forward a bit shows that we are engaged in the lesson, giving the student our full attention.

**Negative:** Standing in front of a room while fidgeting from one foot to the other and nervously wringing our hands makes us appear insecure.

**Positive:** Standing with feet firmly planted, and shifting eye contact to different areas of the audience when speaking, demonstrates ease with being in front of a group.

**Negative:** Shuffling awkwardly and hesitantly toward the stage with head held down makes us appear scared or insecure.

**Positive:** Walking confidently with firm, measured steps, shoulders squared, and head held high sends the message that we are confident and eager to do our appointed task.

In addition to being aware of one's own body language, a teacher must also be able to interpret body language in the student. Being aware of nonverbal clues allows the teacher to be more receptive to a student's feelings during the lesson.

**Student's body language:** Sara does not look directly at the teacher, sits slumped, and answers questions in a whisper.

**Superficial meaning:** Sara is a quiet girl.

**Possible message:** Sara may be feeling insecure and may be in need of special encouragement or clearer instruction.

**Student's body language:** David seems easily distracted, fidgets, and seems unable to focus.

**Superficial meaning:** David has trouble paying attention.

**Possible message:** David may be feeling bored and insufficiently challenged. His learning style may be different than what the teacher assumes. A varied approach may be needed to actively engage him in the lesson.

## Verbal Cues

### Vocal Tone

There is an expression, "The way you say what you say, and the way you look when you say it speak so loudly that I can't hear what it is that you're saying." Imagine a piano teacher who wants to be taken seriously, but has a timid, soft, fading, or whining voice. Imagine this teacher speaking softly and hesitantly while saying:

*"I really think you should be practicing more, and that, um, it would help you learn these pieces better."*

*"But I need to be paid and you owe me the money for the last two months already. Would you please pay me soon?"*

Not a very convincing message, is it?

If the tone of one's voice is inconsistent with the message, people will often respond more strongly to the tone of voice and believe the message less, as shown in the following examples.

*"I'll be happy to help your daughter more with her recital pieces,"* said while scowling with arms crossed.

Or the ever popular, *"I'm not angry!"* said in a loud, harsh voice while frowning with brows furrowed.

*"I'm sure I could chair the composition committee,"* delivered while slumped, with eyes cast downward and speaking in a shaky, timid voice.

The message, "I'm sure I could chair the composition committee," would be much more believable if it were said with enthusiasm and head held high, while standing erect with feet firmly planted.

If a student seems bored at the lesson, what is it that causes the boredom? Is it because the teacher rambles on and on in a monotone voice with no energy? Is the teacher saying, "This is a great piece," with no excitement? Does the teacher present fascinating information concerning a certain type of music, but in a dull, flat, voice? Any of these scenarios could cause the student to tune out the teacher.

To get an immediate sense of the importance of vocal delivery, try the following exercises.

**PART IV**

**Exercise 1:** Read the following paragraph aloud in a flat, dry monotone voice. Then read it with enthusiasm and energy.

> Having studied the music of the Baroque period, there is a great deal I would like to share about that era. In the next six weeks we will be discussing Baroque music in your lessons, including famous composers of the time, musical dance forms of the Baroque period, and the use of counterpoint in keyboard music.

Depending on how this little introduction is delivered, students could either be intrigued or bored to tears.

**Exercise 2:** Record a lesson and listen to your tone of voice and how it projects.

**Exercise 3:** To demonstrate the significance of vocal delivery, say the following word, altering the vocal inflection to produce multiple meanings:

> *"David!..."* from an angry mom

> *"David..."* from a sweetheart

> *"David..."* from an annoyed coworker

Besides using a tone that reflects the message accurately, the voice should be projected at an appropriate level. This denotes confidence and a belief in what is being said. Loud or soft voice levels, and fast or slow speech send entirely different messages.

- If we speak too softly to students, we are conveying that what we have to say is not important enough for them to hear.

- If we mumble or speak hesitantly, we undermine any attempt to assert ourselves.

- If we speak too slowly in a lesson, students may start to daydream or lose interest.

- If we speak too quickly, we may frustrate a student who is having trouble understanding a new concept.

- By speaking too loudly, we may be perceived as being aggressive, rude, or overbearing. A student may grow to resent us or stop responding in the lesson.

- If we constantly interrupt a student, after a while she will feel less inclined to answer questions or express herself in the lesson.

Teachers are far more likely to be heard, understood, and appreciated by pausing occasionally and varying vocal tone as well as the pace of their speech.

## Vocal Pitch

Like vocal tone, the pitch of one's voice adds meaning to the message. Pitch provides emphasis, creates variety and interest, and establishes emotional intensity.

Using a lower pitched voice allows all speakers, but especially women, to project maturity and authority.

Some people end sentences with a rise in voice inflection. This makes each statement sound unsure?... Upward inflection or allowing the voice to rise at the end of a sentence implies that the speaker is asking a question, is insecure, or is seeking approval.

> *"I think it is important to fix the timing in this piece?"*
>
> *"I want you to count out loud?"*
>
> *"Maybe I don't know what I am talking about?"*

On the other hand, a downward inflection at the end of a sentence leads students to believe that the teacher is certain of her suggestions and should be taken seriously.

### Inappropriate, Mispronounced, and Filler Words

All teachers are naturally expected to use appropriate language at all times, avoiding objectionable or inappropriate words that may be offensive. It is never acceptable to use swear words, slang stereotypes, or questionable humor in any professional setting.

Poor grammar makes any teacher appear less educated. A teacher who says, "She don't do what she should in her lessons," would have a hard time convincing parents that she is well-qualified in her field. While some adults have grown up in areas where certain grammatical errors, such as double negatives, are common, teachers can work to rid themselves of such habits.

Mispronounced words also send a negative impression. For example, if one is uncertain of the pronunciation of *Der Freischütz*, it is better to use the English title, *The Marksman*. Another unfortunate consequence of mispronounced words is that any errors will be replicated by students.

Without being aware of it, many teachers often use filler words such as "um," "uh," "like," "you know," and "OK." Using these words weakens any speaker's effectiveness. Taping oneself speaking can reveal overuse of filler words.

> *"OK, let's open your Performance Book. OK, did you do page 27?*
>
> *Yes? OK, that's great!*
>
> *OK, ready to start? Count one measure before you start, OK, and then keep counting through the whole piece, OK? OK."*

The first time I taught a supervised lesson as a graduate student, I said "OK" 84 times in the first half-hour and, yes, my observing professor was counting.

## Listening Skills

Effective piano teachers are good listeners. Imagine a lesson with a teacher who chatters away and never stops explaining. Now imagine a lesson with a teacher who maintains a friendly interactive communication with the student, asking questions frequently and listening intently to the student's responses. In order to hear a student's concerns and know that she understands the material presented, a teacher must stop talking and be a good listener.

A valuable listening technique is to summarize what the student has said to assure her that she has been heard and to check our own understanding.

*"As I understand it, you are concerned about this passage because you are having difficulty playing the sixteenth notes up to tempo."*

## Personal Space

Personal space, or the space around us, is an extension of ourselves. In less formal situations, less personal space or distance is needed. In more formal professional situations, close physical contact should be avoided.

An important challenge faced by the independent teacher is the fact that the private piano lesson is a professional yet intimate situation. For that reason, caution is necessary when defining personal space in a teaching situation. In a lesson, the teacher can be close to the student, but must be careful not to be inappropriately close. The teacher might feel the need to adjust a student's hand or arm position by constantly reaching over and touching her; however, she must first ask permission: "May I show you what I mean by moving your arm?" Once that permission is granted, touching to guide the arm or hand is acceptable, but must still be limited.

A teacher must also remember that she is teaching a child in a closed room without adult supervision, so unless another adult is present, it is probably advisable to avoid that big hug at the end of the lesson. Unfortunately, as mentioned in Chapter 8, teachers have not been immune to being charged with abuse because of something as innocent as a hug given when an adult is not present. All teachers must be cautious about any physical contact with their students.

Some students need more personal space than others. Teachers need to be mindful of this and treat each student individually. If closeness is forced upon a person, that person will feel uncomfortable and the instinctive reaction will be to draw away. To prove this point, try the following exercises.

**Exercise 1:** As you chat with another piano teacher at a meeting or in a music store, start to move closer and closer as you speak. That person will probably start to back away from you. Finally, explain what you were doing and why, and ask the other teacher how it made her feel. Most likely, she did not like it when you invaded her personal space. We need to remember this with our students as well.

**Exercise 2:** Videotape a lesson, observing the following aspects of personal space.
- How close do you sit to your students?
- Do you constantly touch their arms and hands, and if so, do you know how they feel about that?
- Do you hover over your students as you stand, implying a position of power?
- Do you sit so far away from them that you do not seem engaged?
- Do you respect their personal space, and do they respect yours?

## Dress

The way we dress and our personal appearance affect the way we feel about ourselves and the way others respond to us. Like it or not, people will make judgments about our competence, background, education, abilities, and confidence based on the way we look, dress, and carry ourselves. We might believe that the person we are matters more than how we look, and ultimately that is true. Our appearance, however, sends a strong message, especially as a first impression.

A good example of this truth is demonstrated in television makeover shows. It is amazing how changed people look after receiving professional advice on clothes, makeup, and hair. But even more astounding is how different their new look makes them feel about themselves.

Consistently looking our best sends a message to our students that we respect ourselves and what we do. Although we may work at home, it is not acceptable to dress in tank tops, tee shirts, or jeans, even if they look good in casual situations. On the other hand, it is also unacceptable to dress as a wannabe movie star. The adage, "When in doubt, don't," certainly applies to clothes. I have heard stories of lessons being taught in bathrobes. It is my sincere hope that these stories are highly exaggerated.

Having taught in a private studio as well as in a university, I feel it is even more important to dress well in the private studio. In a university there is an assumption that those who have been hired to teach are knowledgeable and are to be respected; in an independent studio, this respect must be earned.

## Putting It All Together

The following exercises are designed to assess body language, vocal delivery, and dress.

**Exercise 1:** Record yourself speaking and notice how you project yourself through your voice. Talk about your musical background on the tape for five minutes, and on the playback, ask yourself the following.

- Does my voice sound harsh?
- Is it too soft or shy?
- Do I sound my age?
- Do I project the emotions I mean to convey?
- Do I sound nervous?
- Do I project confidence?
- Does my voice rise at the end of sentences?
- Do I use filler words frequently?
- Do I hold my listener's interest?

If you are not happy with the answers, decide what you need to alter, work on the necessary changes, tape yourself again, and assess your progress.

**Exercise 2:** Videotape yourself dressed professionally and speaking for five minutes about your qualifications as a piano teacher. When you watch the tape, observe your body language, posture, hand gestures, movements, and facial expressions. Ask yourself the following:

- Am I sending the message I intend to convey?
- Do I look confident?
- What does my attire say about me?
- Do I appear nervous?
- Am I sending any mixed messages?

**Exercise 3:** The next time you listen to a professional speaker, observe the qualities that you find most effective or least effective in projecting the intended message. Decide what the speaker is doing that adds or subtracts from your appreciation of what is being said. When you speak, try to mirror that which you see as positive, and avoid that which you dislike.

**Exercise 4:** Go to the mall and observe the body language of those around you. Notice gestures, posture, facial expressions, method of standing and walking, and nervous habits. What messages are these people sending? What messages might you inadvertently be sending with your own body language?

**Exercise 5:** It is not only what we say, but how we say it that sends a message. Practice saying each of the following words and phrases with a variety of tonal inflections, to show honesty, anger, happiness, excitement, and frustration. Also use a variety of facial expressions, hand gestures and body postures, and notice the change in the message being sent each time, even when the words themselves are not changing.

- Good morning.
- Yes.
- No.
- Where?
- I am tired.
- Please.
- How many times?
- I'll do it.
- I'm sure I could do that.
- I am not angry.

**Exercise 6:** Go into a high-class restaurant, store, or office dressed in jeans, an old tee shirt, and sneakers, and take note of how people respond to you. Later, return dressed in a sharp-looking suit or dress and polished shoes. Was the response any different? How do you think parents will respond to you during an initial interview based on how you dress? How does your approach to dress, vocal inflections, and body language impact how you are perceived?

## MY LEAST PROFESSIONAL MOMENT

An example from my own experience as a teacher clearly demonstrates the importance of projecting a professional image in all aspects of one's work. Although this story is personally embarrassing, it stands as a humorous example of the consequences of mixing family needs with work time.

One morning I received a phone call while I was playing with my young children. A family had just moved into the area, and the father was looking for a piano teacher for his daughter. He had been referred to me and I was delighted, since the daughter sounded like a very good student. As we were talking, my son, who was two-and-a-half years old at the time, came over to me and began jumping up and down frantically.

Without changing my tone of voice, holding my hand over the mouthpiece, or even pausing mid-sentence, I said, "Do you need to poop?" To which the man on the phone replied in a hesitant voice, "Noooo…" To which I replied as I looked at my son, "If you need to poop, tell me now." To which the father replied, "No, really. I am fine…"

I finally regained access to my brain cells and apologized to the father for addressing my son during our conversation, but I never heard from that family again. The daughter did not study piano with me. That day I fit the stereotype of the frazzled mom who teaches a few lessons for extra money, and who cannot separate home from work. Although by this time in my career I was well aware of the importance of maintaining a business-like studio, by answering a phone call when my young children needed attention I placed myself in an awkward situation. It would have been far better for me to have taken the father's number, returning the call at a more convenient time.

I have told this story countless times. It serves as an amusing reminder of the many problems that can arise when home life is interjected into the work environment.

**PART IV**

# PART V

## ZONING LAWS AND ETHICAL ISSUES

As the saying goes, "No man is an island," and no teacher operates in a vacuum. Legal and ethical issues affect every teacher and, by extension, every student. Many independent music teachers are unaware of legal and ethical matters that can seriously affect the operation of the home studio. Part V discusses some of these concerns, including zoning laws and ethics arising from copyright laws.

# Chapter 15

# ZONING AND BUSINESS LICENSES

As small business owners, too many teachers are unaware of the zoning laws in their own communities. Although music teachers may feel far removed from the world of legal battles, in reality, noncompliance with zoning laws can result in losing the right to teach in a home studio. Knowledge is power, and independent piano teachers must know how to ward off legal action that might be instigated by neighbors objecting to a home business in their area.

Let us examine two scenarios.

## Scenario 1

1) Ms. Williams is buying her dream home. She finally has enough money to purchase a home with a wonderful studio area.

2) She meets her prospective neighbors before purchasing and explains that she wishes to teach in her new home. They are all delighted to have a piano teacher in the area.

3) She moves in, teaches happily for years, gaining a large studio of dedicated students.

4) New neighbors move next door who dislike the comings and goings of the studio. They complain to the authorities.

5) The authorities contact Ms. Williams and inform her that she is operating her business illegally. She does not have a business license, and she has not signed the required home occupation agreement stating that she will comply with local zoning laws.

6) Her studio is shut down permanently. She must move from her dream home and studio.

## Scenario 2

1) Ms. Williams is buying her dream home. She finally has enough money to purchase a home with a wonderful studio area.

2) She meets her prospective neighbors before purchasing and explains that she wishes to teach in her new home. They are all delighted to have a piano teacher in the area.

3) She contacts the local zoning board, signs the necessary home occupation agreement, and is issued a business license. She checks with the local homeowner's association and does a thorough check to be sure she is in compliance with any city ordinances affecting home businesses.

4) She moves in and teaches happily for years, gaining a large studio of dedicated students.

5) She makes sure to comply with all zoning laws regarding parking, noise, and number of students. Each year she pays the fees and taxes related to her business, and updates any necessary legal forms.

6) New neighbors move next door who dislike the comings and goings of the studio. They complain to the authorities.

7) The authorities tell the neighbors that Ms. Williams is in complete compliance with all zoning laws and they have no legal grounds for a complaint against their neighbor.

8) Ms. Williams continues to teach happily in her dream studio despite the fact that she has grumpy neighbors.

## Zoning Laws

Zoning laws are enacted to protect a community from unwanted development. Although these laws have earned a bad reputation, in and of themselves they are beneficial to a community. For instance, zoning laws prohibit liquor stores from being built across from high schools; garbage dumps from being placed in the middle of residential neighborhoods; and adult video stores from being built near elementary schools.

For the independent music teacher, however, zoning laws might present unexpected restrictions. Problems begin when teachers are unaware of the laws and suddenly find their ability to teach in their studio threatened.

Zoning laws vary from community to community and can be changed from year to year. If lessons are taught in the home, teachers must abide by any applicable zoning laws. The independent teacher might be required to comply with any of the following conditions.

- Limit the number of students allowed in a studio on any given day (e.g., a maximum of eight students in a day).

- Limit the number of students allowed in the studio at any one time (e.g., a maximum of four at a time, or this may be decided on a case-by-case basis).

- Allow only people living in the home to work there (no outside teacher may be hired).

- Set specific guidelines for impacting neighborhood traffic and parking.

- Display no external business signs.

- Restrict noise generated through any shared walls as in a townhouse or apartment.

- Limit available teaching hours.

Occasionally, the limitations of strict zoning laws can be dealt with by enlisting the support of other area music teachers, parents and students. In Virginia, for example, 200 people appeared at a Fairfax County meeting when the county commissioners were considering a new zoning law that would limit home businesses to four clients a day. Those attending the meeting to protest the new ordinance were mainly independent piano teachers, but also included band and choral directors, parents, and students. After hearing hours of testimony from over 20 attendees, the proposal was tabled.

Curiously enough, there were no representatives from other professions that also would have been affected by the law (hairdressers, daycare operators, accountants, lawyers, etc.). The commissioners complimented the music teachers on their dedication and commitment to their profession, and the chair of the committee closed with, "We'll certainly think twice before we propose anything that will get the attention of the music teachers again!"

PART V

Some teachers with zoning problems have argued that they are operating an educational facility or school rather than a business. However, the zoning office might require that the teacher grant degrees or credits as part of the curriculum in order for the studio to be declared a school. Should the studio be designated as a school, independent teachers might then find it difficult to meet city codes that apply to schools, such as restroom facilities, sprinkler systems, etc. In addition, some communities hold private studios to the same codes as schools, regardless of their designation.

## Business License

In many communities, a license is required to operate any type of business, including one operated from the home. A signed document stating that the applicant is aware of the zoning laws and will comply with them may be required before a business license will be granted. This agreement might be called a letter of approval, an occupancy permit, a special use permit, or a home occupation agreement. A trade name for the studio may also need to be registered with the local Clerk of Court before the business license can be issued. Each community handles occupancy issues differently, and some may say that if no more than five students at a time are taught, an occupancy permit is not required. A community's laws might state that if more that five students at a time are taught, the studio becomes an educational facility and building codes must be met (such as an enclosed stairway, a certain number of exits, smoke detectors, etc.).

A business license often requires payment of an annual fee, which may be determined by the gross annual income of a studio. If a teacher has been teaching without a license where one is necessary, she may be required to pay a penalty. This penalty may be a flat rate, or may be prorated based on the studio income over, say, the past three years.

By obtaining a business license and meeting zoning requirements, teachers protect themselves from possible complaints by neighbors about teaching in a home studio. However, if a neighbor issues a complaint and the teacher has not complied by filing the correct zoning papers and acquiring a business license, she may be forbidden to teach in her home ever again.

If the city finds a teacher in violation of zoning laws, the teacher can be served with a citation requiring her to stop conducting business from the home, effective immediately. In a worst-case scenario, the teacher might even be served a summons to appear in court for violating a zoning ordinance if she continues to teach.

## Related Taxes

Once a business license has been issued, the recipient may be required to pay a "tangible business tax" or "personal property tax" on personal property such as instruments, music, or office equipment declared as a deduction on income tax forms. After a business license has been granted, forms for personal property tax are usually automatically mailed to the business owner each year. Unpaid taxes could result in a penalty.

## Additional Ordinances and Homeowners Association Codes

Complying with city or county zoning boards may be only a first step. Depending on the type of residence, a teacher may also be required to comply with other specific ordinances or codes set by a homeowners association, a condominium association, or an apartment building owner. Any of these could forbid a home business, determine the maximum number of clients, or limit traffic, parking, noise, or signage.

## Variances and Appeals

In many communities, teachers may appeal or apply for a variance if the zoning laws are overly restrictive. For example, a teacher might appeal if the law allows only five clients a day in a home business and the teacher would like to teach seven students a day. A fee often accompanies the appeals process.

The following are two cases that prove the importance of thoroughly researching the zoning and variance laws before setting up a studio in a particular community:

- Carolyn Inabinet describes her difficulties in dealing with her local zoning board. She writes, "My attorney informed me that a use permit or variance from the City was only half the picture for residential property and use permits. Any residential property has CCRs—codes, covenants and restrictions—whether or not there is an active home-owners association." Inabinet's need for a new home and studio eventually lead her to a house with no deed restrictions, and she made an offer for that property contingent upon receiving a use permit.

Inabinet, Carolyn. **"Beyond Piano Instruction: A Decade of Evolution and Revolution."** *American Music Teacher*, December/January 1997/1998, Vol. 47, No. 3, p.18.

- A highly publicized zoning case was that concerning Nancy Stokes, a teacher from DeKalb, Georgia. As stated in the article "Teachers Are Not Criminals: The Stokes Zoning Laws," "Nancy Stokes, before purchasing a home in DeKalb County with her husband, Lane, in 1993, says she obtained written permission from the local homeowners association and verbal permission from several neighbors to start a studio." In 2000, two neighbors complained about her teaching, citing its impact on traffic and parking, although it was minimal on Stokes's street. Following the complaint, a special land use permit that was not required in 1993, but which was required as of 1999, was denied to Stokes, rendering her teaching illegal.

Ingle, Gary, and Dena Eben. **"Teachers Are Not Criminals: The Stokes Zoning Case."** *American Music Teacher*, December/January 2001/2002, Vol. 51, No. 3, pp.14–19.

Stokes's saga, like that of Inabinet, is well worth studying. Both of these women paid exorbitant lawyer fees and suffered years of anxiety as they worked to resolve the zoning nightmares they faced. I offer these stories not to create anxiety, but merely to highlight the fact that none of us wants to face a situation where we are told that our studio is illegal and we must stop teaching.

**PART V**

## CHOICES AND CONSEQUENCES

1) We can be aware of all zoning laws and homeowner codes, acquire all of the correct documents that we need, and pay all of the fees and taxes that are required. We will then be protected by the law.

2) We can avoid compliance with zoning laws by allowing ourselves to be ignorant of them, afraid to check them, or because we just do not agree with them. We may then be susceptible to a neighbor's complaints and the possibility of having our studio shut down. We may be vulnerable to discovering that we are not legally able to teach in our home, or may legally teach only a fraction of the students we had intended. We may find we live in an area where we are unable to support ourselves because of overly restrictive laws. We may also discover that we have invested a great deal of time and money into building our studio in our dream home, only to be told we must close our studio.

3) We can disagree with our area zoning laws because they are overly restrictive. However, we can comply with them as we work with fellow teachers to change them.

All of this may sound overwhelming, but business licenses and zoning laws ensure that a neighborhood stays residential and that it is protected from unwanted businesses. Anyone who has ever been to a town with no zoning laws can attest to how truly unattractive such a community can become.

Before moving into a neighborhood or purchasing a home, each of us must check the requirements for a business license and all zoning laws, homeowner association rules, and codes that apply to an independent music studio. As home businesses continue to flourish, zoning laws will of necessity change, hopefully becoming more favorable to a home business. We must all stay current with changes in our community as they occur.

## Resource

**WEBSITE**

*Free Advice*
www.freeadvice.com

This site provides information on a variety of legal topics. For information on zoning laws:

- Go to www.freeadvice.com

- Select "Real Estate Law"

- Select "Zoning"

- Select "Home-based business"

# Chapter 16

# ETHICS IN TEACHING

As in every profession, the independent music teacher must maintain high moral and ethical standards, choosing the high road and following a respected professional code of ethics in all aspects of studio operation.

## Code of Ethics

Many local music teacher associations as well as national organizations have a non-binding Code of Ethics stating important guidelines and ethical standards for teachers. A typical Code of Ethics might instruct teachers to do the following:

- Respect their colleagues, avoiding unprofessional criticism of other teachers, their teaching methods or their studios

- Always represent their own qualifications accurately and honestly

- Never actively solicit students from another studio

Ethical piano teachers share the following qualities:

- They provide their students with a safe environment. This means that they make sure that the studio space both inside and out is safe (no icy, broken steps), that the emotional space is safe (no verbal abuse), and that the child's physical space is safe (no improper touching of any kind). (See Chapter 8 under "Liability Policy," and Chapter 14 under "Body Language.")

- They respect their profession and colleagues by charging professional rates that reflect the training and skill of all in their field. They realize that their rates impact every other teacher in the community, including teachers who must earn a working income. (See Chapter 5.)

- They are aware of local zoning laws and abide by them. If the laws are unjust, they work with local legislators and administrators to change them or obtain legal variances. (See Chapter 15.)

- They obey tax laws, reporting all income from professional activities (including teaching, adjudication, workshops and performances), and paying any taxes due if the studio has a business license. (See Chapter 6.)

- They follow copyright laws assiduously. (See below.)

- They are not satisfied with what they already know. New teachers realize there is much more to learn, and experienced teachers recognize that the world of piano teaching is constantly changing and evolving. The most skilled performer and the most experienced teacher can still grow musically and professionally. Ethical teachers honor their obligation to pursue continual growth.

## Copyright Laws

If there is one area in which ethical behavior can be easily compromised in the music profession, it is in adhering to copyright laws.

### Photocopies

The ethical piano teacher does not photocopy music for students. Every instructor needs to know when photocopying is allowed and when it is illegal. The temptation to make quick copies in certain circumstances is great, for example, when assigning one piece out of a large anthology. But photocopying music for students sets a bad example and has unpleasant consequences for the teaching profession. It is easy to believe that a few pieces photocopied here and there will have minimal repercussions. On the contrary, collectively breaking the law in this way deprives composers and authors of their rightful income through royalties, and prevents publishers and music retailers from making the income necessary to stay in business. Ultimately, everyone will suffer: composers, publishers, music dealers, teachers, and students.

### Arrangements

Many teachers are unaware that it is unlawful to create arrangements of copyrighted music. One must receive permission from the publisher before undertaking such a project.

### Performances

Live performances of copyrighted music are subject to copyright laws. The Copyright Act of 1976 made several exceptions to copyright requirements. For example, live performances without commercial advantage to anyone are not subject to copyright restrictions.

### Recordings

Teachers need to be aware of the legalities concerning recordings of student performances. For example, single recordings can be made for evaluation purposes, but multiple copies may not be made and sold. Legal copies of already recorded music (such as CDs) can be made when they are for educational purposes and retained by the teacher, but copies may not be sold to students.

### Multimedia

In this increasingly digital world, copyright issues become even more complex. Teachers must check copyright laws before posting recordings or videos on a studio web page or any other Internet site.

# Resources

*Brief Legal Guide for the Independent Music Teacher.* Cincinnati: Music Teachers National Association, 1999.

Compiled by attorneys, this booklet guides music teachers through zoning, copyright, insurance, and other aspects of owning and operating a business. The booklet can be purchased by going to www.mtna.org/HLtext.

Leach, Joel. **Music Copyright Basics.** Van Nuys: Alfred Publishing Co., Inc., 2003.

In *Music Copyright Basics*, Joel Leach addresses copyright issues as they pertain to the music profession. Teachers concerned with copyright laws can learn about the basics of copyright, the copyright submission process, copyright ownership, copyright and earnings potential, and international copyright laws. The book also includes important copyright forms, a glossary of relevant terms, and information on public domain.

Moser, David. **Music Copyright for the New Millennium.** Vellejo: ProMusic, an imprint of artispro.com, 2002. Distributed by Hal Leonard Corporation.

Written by an entertainment attorney and covering copyright laws as they pertain to musicians and the music industry, the major chapters in this valuable guide to copyright laws include History of Copyright; Ownership of Copyright; The Reproduction Right; Duration of Copyright; and Infringement of Copyright. This book is particularly helpful for musicians in the industry who compose and perform.

## WEBSITES

*Copyright: The Complete Guide for Music Educators*

www.menc.org

– Select "Resources"
– Select "Copyright Center"

*Piano Home Page*

www.marthabeth.com/music_copyright.html

– Select "Copyright and Music"

**PART V**

# PART VI

## MAINTAINING HIGH STUDIO STANDARDS

All piano teachers, regardless of their experience or background, benefit from a dedication to high studio standards. Continual commitment to musical, pedagogical, and professional growth is a key ingredient to success in the studio.

Teachers are responsible for keeping their teaching fresh and innovative, for their own benefit as well as that of their students. If the studio atmosphere is lacking in energy or inspiration, any sense of boredom, stress, or exhaustion felt by the teacher will inevitably affect the students as well.

Part VI suggests ways to maintain an inspired studio, expand teaching materials, and incorporate an understanding of learning styles into effective teaching. Also presented are options for renewing oneself through professional development in areas such as continuing education, professional certification, and membership in professional organizations.

# Chapter 17

# THE STUDIO ATMOSPHERE

Although most piano teachers hope to feel inspired by the joys of teaching music, at some point, most of us have experienced some degree of boredom or frustration when teaching. My worst experience occurred when a high school transfer student came to my studio with what seemed to be no understanding of, or natural response to, the inner beauty of music. I felt her lessons challenging and tried to teach her all I could about dynamics, rhythm, rubato, pedaling, technique, stylistic elements, and so on. For weeks and months, we discussed what makes music beautiful. Every time she began working on a new piece, she would return with the same incredibly flat, boring sound.

She never, in the three years that she studied with me, transferred any of her skills without my asking, "What would you like to do with the dynamics?" I did not feel like an inspired or inspiring teacher. Every time she came back with that same painfully boring sound, as if she had never heard anything about phrasing in her life, I felt agonizingly bored and boring as well. I did not feel that I was contributing to a lifetime love of music or music making, or even to a positive moment within her week. Much to my shock, she went on to minor in music…

## BSE Syndrome

Although dedicated teachers wish their studios to be thriving centers of learning and enthusiasm, that is harder to achieve than it sounds. New teachers may feel anxious about lacking the experience needed to develop an effective curriculum, and seasoned teachers may experience burnout. At times, even the most enthusiastic educator can fall prey to the dreaded "BSE Syndrome:" Boredom, Stress, and Exhaustion.

How does BSE syndrome creep into our teaching? Take boredom, for instance: some of us may face a time when we feel we have lost our "zing." As students respond less and less to suggestions, we feel less inspired to teach, until the lessons have reached a point of painful repetition. On the most frustrating level, musical ideas are presented and forgotten, while mistakes and corrections are made week after week in a seemingly endless cycle. A day where the bulk of the teaching is spent fixing fingerings, correcting notes, and reviewing rhythms can leave a teacher feeling bored and uninspired.

Such lessons are not what make us treasure our moments with students, and hopefully, those are not the memories students will carry to adulthood. Nor will fixing mistakes in any way ensure a student's musical growth. True, notes do need to be learned, and fingerings and timings do need to be accurate, but corrections alone lead to a chicken-and-egg scenario. Why aren't we more enthusiastic? Because the student isn't trying, because we aren't enthusiastic, because the student isn't trying, because…

Stress is the next part of BSE Syndrome. A newer teacher may feel stress or frustration at being unable to fix a certain problem. She may fear that she is ineffective, and might feel frustrated that her students do not seem to be progressing adequately. She may be at a loss as to how to proceed when working alone in a private studio. A more experienced teacher may simply feel exhausted after years of trying, and may wonder why students don't seem to care.

Friends have asked me, "What could possibly be stressful about *your* work?" Others may perceive me sitting in a lesson, smiling at a little cherub as I teach a few not-so-difficult pieces once a week for a half hour. I do this a few times a day, and then go and fix dinner for my family, and poof, the day is done. How can that make anyone feel overworked and stressed?

It can be stressful to fit more things into one day than time allows. It can be stressful to be pulled in a thousand different directions. It can be stressful to feel that work is never done. What are some of those things that are so hard to fit into the day?

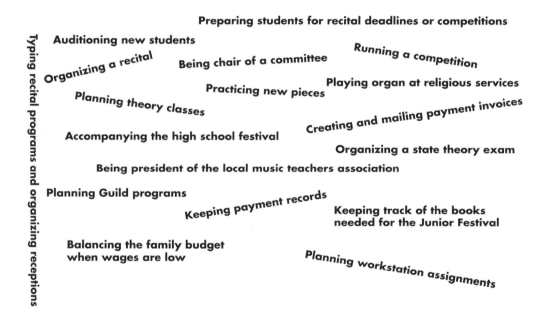

Add to that finding enough time in the day to cover all the extra needs of students and family, which are often in direct conflict for the little free time available. An involved and caring teacher can easily feel stressed and overworked, resulting in the third aspect of BSE Syndrome: Exhaustion.

That is the dark side. The cup is half empty and leaking badly. Now, for the bright side: there is an antidote to feeling bored, stressed, and exhausted.

## The Need to Change

Although it may sound simple, the solution is to change. As participants in the 21st century, piano teachers can embrace change without feeling they are forfeiting all that was once good. Innovations in piano instruction have flourished in the last few decades, including MIDI keyboards, computer programs, workstations, group lessons, summer camps, a growth in piano pedagogy materials and degree programs, and thousands of new publications by modern day composers.

When independent piano teachers embrace change, they do so not just to do something different, but to do something better. Change reflects a commitment to innovation, creativity, personal growth, and high standards within the studio. Change might include embracing new repertoire, new skills, new programs, or just a new attitude toward teaching. On the other hand, if a teacher always does things in exactly the same way, she is not being innovative, nor is she rejuvenating her professional life.

A basic truth exists in the saying, "You can't change the other person's behavior; you can only change your own behavior." If teachers are to stimulate students so that they respond with enthusiasm, they must periodically renew their passion for teaching by adopting an invigorated and healthy attitude, coupled with a dedication to constant renewal.

Attending sessions at national conferences provides a wealth of ideas on how to reinvigorate our teaching. However, after returning from a national conference, a teacher might think, "There are so many creative things that other people do. I can hardly keep up!" To avoid being overwhelmed in the effort to improve the studio and maintain higher standards, it is important to develop a plan that incorporates one or two new ideas at a time.

## Time Management and Clutter Control

How do teachers find time for innovation in the course of an already overwhelming schedule? Would adding new approaches to teaching just create more stress and exhaustion? After all, there is a straw that will break any camel's back… A good starting point is to make practical adjustments to everyday tasks, so they are carried out with maximum efficiency.

- Minimize bookwork by adopting more effective systems for billing, record keeping, marketing, and correspondence.

- Establish a firmer make-up policy to decrease time spent on unnecessary make-ups.

- Create a lesson swap list and allow students to rearrange their own lessons, to eliminate feeling obligated to accommodate student conflicts.

- Reorganize files (computer and paper) and store them conveniently to save time locating items such as phone numbers, forms, student records, etc.

- Organize studio space efficiently to reference items like music, CDs, and teaching tools quickly.

- Eliminate clutter to avoid feeling frozen into inactivity due to studio mess.

- If needed, hire a personal organizer (a tax-deductible business expense) to reorganize the studio space for maximum efficiency.

- Minimize lesson interruptions by installing an answering machine and instruct family members about work time vs. family time.

- Eliminate infringements on time with a firm policy statement regarding late arrivals and students who are not picked up on time.

Rather than face time-management struggles alone, teachers can tap into the expertise of their colleagues in gaining ideas for making the most of their time. For example, local music teacher groups can schedule a program in which members share time-saving ideas and organizational techniques with each other.

Research is another way teachers can discover helpful time-management skills. Numerous websites on the Internet offer a wealth of options for customizing an individual approach to time-management and clutter control. There, teachers will find help from experts who have developed proven systems for deciding how to prioritize and manage clutter that not only devours time, but dominates studio space as well.

## Making Choices

Effective time-management is based on learning to make choices. "I can't possibly get everything done" is more a reflection of personal choices than a statement about the amount of time in a day. Teachers accustomed to allowing too many activities to take over the day need to find a more discerning approach to scheduling.

A helpful exercise in deciding how best to reorganize one's time is to write out a schedule for each workday, listing every activity and its duration, as well as any free time. From this list, a teacher can identify activities that cause stress and reduce studio health. If there are any such activities, how important are they? Could they be reduced? Could they be eliminated?

Another helpful step in time-management is listing the top priorities for time commitment—choices that focus energy on personal and professional fulfillment. Such a list should include time for work and self-improvement, but also time for family, friends, and fun. A healthy studio schedule includes time for regular vacations, as relaxation is essential for a refreshed return to work. Independent piano teachers deserve and need time away from music and students.

I first faced questions concerning time-management during a seminar for directors of community schools of the arts, which turned out to be more like ten days of arts boot camp. One assignment was called "Get a Life." We were asked to list the total time spent each week on family, friends, work, religious activities, and fun. When my paper was returned, it had a big red "F" on it, followed by the bold words, "Get a life!"

What are some of the ways teachers can "get a life?" The answer lies in making wise choices that will provide more time and less stress. If the local high school needs an accompanist and the town's only piano teacher is the best accompanist, it does not mean that she has to do all the high school accompanying. It is okay to say, "This is what I am willing to do..."

The same is true with music organization activities. All teachers need to volunteer for local, state, or national music organization duties and offices; even busy teachers need to give some volunteer time. However, no individual should do it all. An overwhelming sense of duty must be kept in check. Conversely, if a teacher feels no sense of duty to the musical community, she unfortunately contributes to the stress of her colleagues as they pick up the slack caused by her negligence. That same teacher may also be contributing to the boredom of her own teaching by not committing to any outside activities. The key is to find a balance between professional and personal commitments.

Another drain on time is the size of the independent studio. Teaching too many students eliminates the time available to experiment with new ideas. Perhaps a teacher feels a sense of obligation: "If I don't teach them, who will?" However, this same feeling of obligation can lead to, "There is no one else to play at church," or "I am the only one willing to run the festival." It is not healthy to feel obligated to help everyone, everywhere, every time. In the long run, the teacher's students will suffer, as will her family and her mental and physical health.

One reason teachers take too many students is financial need. "I hardly make enough money as it is, and need all the income I can earn." Instead of teaching endless hours to the point of exhaustion, teachers can increase personal income by teaching fewer students and charging more professional rates, or teaching the same number of students in fewer hours through class or partner lessons. (For more ideas along these lines, see Chapter 10). Earning more from fewer students creates time to develop a more effective approach to curriculum without being overwhelmed with financial concerns. When a more creative approach to teaching is implemented, parents need to be made aware of the innovations; the teacher is providing more and she is worth more.

## The Studio Climate

Every studio has a climate that is instantly recognizable by students; some studios reflect a serious approach to teaching, some center more on fun, and others are a mixture of work and play.

Personally, I have had a problem with the issue of "fun" in music study. I find it somewhat irksome when college students complain that a class isn't fun. There are more important reasons to study than because it is fun, are there not? What about studying because it is valuable, or important, or because the material being studied is worthy of the highest regard? If students of any age only want to have fun in their lessons, are they not trading "yee-haw" moments for a deeply profound and gratifying musical experience?

And yet... why shouldn't learning be fun? Why is it that a first grader is so eager to answer questions, yet no self-respecting seventh grader will raise her hand? Why do so many piano students drop out of lessons after only a few years? Is it because the lessons are not fun? Are they boring? Too difficult? Surely there is something teachers can do to keep these students in love with music.

Work that is fun must still be done well. Introducing an element of fun does not mean compromising on quality. An imaginative teacher can create innovative and fun ways to teach theory, rhythm, or music history. By having fun, the seriousness of the goal is not diminished; rather, the process becomes so enjoyable that the student learns with enthusiasm.

One piano teacher I know sets a theme for each semester and then makes a board game centered on that theme. One semester the theme was the Romantic era. Students moved from space to space on the board using points awarded for activities such as completing Romantic pieces and researching their composers, writing papers related to the 1800s, watching movies about the time period, listening to CDs of Romantic music (extra points for opera and chamber music), and attending concerts and writing reviews of the Romantic music on the program.

Each semester, this teacher's students are enthusiastic about the board game, and although their only reward is completing the game, the students eagerly anticipate arriving on the last space. Since each student works on material appropriate to her level, the board game does not need to be adjusted for varying ages or levels. With one creative and motivational tool, this teacher has incorporated fun into her studio while enabling her students to learn far more than they would if she just told them about Romantic music.

## Recreational Music

In her article, "The Future of Music Teaching? Recreational Music Making," Brenda Dillon describes recreational music making as "music making for the joy of it in non-stressful environments." Recognizing that far too few members of our society partake in music, Dillon suggests that recreational music making (RMM) is an avenue for experiencing the fun and joy of music making. Students interested in RMM do not participate to become professional musicians or win competitions. Rather, these are adult students who are playing because they have always wanted to play the piano and have finally decided to learn. They want to enjoy lessons and to experience the type of music that most appeals to them. Dillon describes a "student-centered approach" as highly effective, allowing students to feel more fulfilled by their music making.

For independent teachers who accept these older students, Dillon sees the potential for increased revenue and expanded teaching hours. Such teachers also have the opportunity to enhance their own love of music as they work with this new group of learners.

**PART VI**

## Resources

There are RMM Teachers Training Seminars offered through the National Piano Foundation. For more information, visit the following:

*National Piano Foundation*
    www.pianonet.com
        – Select "Recreational Music Making"

*International Music Products Association (NAMM)*
    http://rmm.namm.org

## Fun as a Motivational Tool

I once conducted a national survey in which teachers were asked to share their ideas for fun summer programs and studio activities that increased student enthusiasm, as well as teacher income. Although the activities were designed to be implemented in the summer, many could be applied year-round.

- Themed music camps, one to two weeks in length. (Music Camps will be discussed in Chapter 39.)

- Music Fun Day: theory games, music-related crafts, chamber music, performing, and picnicking.

- Arts Extravaganza: each student works on a piece of his own choice and illustrates his interpretation of the music through some other branch of the arts (e.g., poetry or creative writing, painting or drawing, choreography, a skit, or a craft project). All projects are presented in an end-of-the-summer Arts Extravaganza Show.

- A required six-week summer semester in which each student focuses on the theme of his choice, such as jazz, improvisation, or composition. Alternatively, students who cannot attend the special session are required to make a payment in order to reserve a lesson time for the fall term.

- Team contests in areas such as memorization, sight-playing, or keyboard skills, with awards for the winning teams presented at an end-of-the-summer party.

- Highlights of the Semester program to share the semester's special projects and achievements.

- Sessions that focus on using percussion instruments to strengthen rhythm skills. Students can play rhythms of new pieces on drums, or groups of four students can read four rhythm parts at once as a percussion quartet. Students can also play rhythm-in-a-round and imitation games, improvise rhythms on drums, and play follow-the-leader games using various percussion instruments or drum pads.

- Group lessons or workshops taught in teams featuring teachers who specialize in areas such as period dances, tribal drumming, and composition.

- A Carnival or Fun Fair with booths as an entertaining way to test theory, keyboard skills, etc. Several teachers and their students can participate in activities such as:

    – A dart game to determine the key for a scale or pentachord to be played

    – A booth for students to fish for theory questions color-coded by level to reinforce state theory and keyboard skills

    – Tickets awarded for correct answers, used to buy inexpensive treats, music items, or food at the fair.

- An incentive gameboard modeled after a semester theme. Students move around the board by means of points earned for achievement in areas such as practice, memorization, sight-reading, composition, and music appreciation. Every ten spaces, a card is read with an assignment for a special project; for example, playing scales at a more challenging tempo. Completion of the project helps to move around the board faster.

- A "one-week piece" assigned at the lesson, to reinforce sight-playing and independent learning skills. The student chooses the piece by perusing materials two levels below her current repertoire, then learns the piece on her own in one week. This activity also helps the teacher assess strengths and weaknesses and avoids spoon-feeding.

- "Music money" or tickets, earned throughout the school year and spent on treats or small items in a "music store" at monthly group lessons or at an end-of-the-year Fun Fair.

- A grab bag of small treats and items for weekly achievements, such as memorizing a piece, playing scales accurately, etc.

- A party featuring team relays and hunts, using flash cards and a timer to identify the notes, key signatures, or rhythms. The activity can be followed by pizza or ice cream sundaes.

- Achievement clubs
    - The 200 Club: those who practice 200 or more minutes per week
    - The One Minute Key Signature Club: those who identify all key signatures on flash cards within one minute

- "Student of the Month" or "Team of the Month" awards in scales, sight-playing, memorization, exceeding practice quota, extra projects, etc. Points can also be applied to "Student of the Year" or "Team of the Year" awards in the same areas.

- Ribbons, statuettes, certificates, and other trophies, awarded at recitals for noncompetitive achievements. Students can earn awards by reaching personal goals, such as 150 pages of sight-playing; ten memorized pieces; or scales, cadences, and arpeggios in all keys.

- Music games for group lessons or studio parties, or music software games that can be played at a workstation.

Although some of the above activities may seem more appealing than others, they all center on making study fun or motivational. Some teachers use competitive or team activities to motivate; others choose activities based solely on personal achievement. Some offer material rewards; others offer recognition. This is an area that is open to a great deal of creativity and personal choice.

An Internet search of "music games" also provides a wealth of material for fun and rewarding activities for the independent piano studio.

**PART VI**

# Resources

Athey, Margaret, and Gwen Hotchkiss. *A Galaxy of Musical Games for the Music Class.* Prentice Hall Trade, 1998.

Although out of print, *A Galaxy of Musical Games for the Music Class* is still available on the Internet. This time-tested book was developed for a classroom setting, but can be easily adapted for group settings within the independent piano studio. The table of contents lists the title, appropriate grade level, number of players, equipment needed, and skills involved for each game. The games are grouped in Chapters; Chapter I: Games for Rhythmic Response; Chapter II: Games for Reading and Writing Rhythm; Chapter III: Games for Reading and Writing Melody; Chapter IV: Games for Learning Music Notation; Chapter V: Games for Ear-Training; Chapter VI: Games for Developing Singing; Chapter VII: Games About Composers and Music Literature; Chapter VIII: Games About Musical Instruments; Chapter IX: Games for Any General Review; Chapter X: Musical Word Games. An appendix includes information on how to create the suggested equipment needed for various games.

## Resources (cont.)

Lundin, Stephen, John Christensen and Harry Paul. *Fish!*® New York: Hyperion, 2000.

Lundin, Stephen, John Christensen, Harry Paul and Philip Strand. *Fish! Tales*®, New York: Hyperion, 2002.

The bestseller, *Fish!*® introduces *The Fish! Philosophy*®, while *Fish! Tales*® gives real-life stories of businesses that have applied this philosophy to enhance the workplace environment and the enthusiasm of employees. Based on the work environment created in Seattle's Pike Place Fish Market, these books champion having fun while being fully committed to a job well done. Meant to enrich the work environment in group-settings, the *Fish!*® series of entertaining and heartwarming short books applies well to the art of piano teaching.

### SOURCE CITED

Dillon, Brenda. "The Future of Music Teaching? Recreational Music Making." *American Music Teacher*, August/September 2007, Vol. 57, No. 1, pp.21–23.

### WEBSITES

*Morton Subotnick's Creating Music*

www.creatingmusic.com

*Theory Time Product Catalog*

www.theorytime.com

# Chapter 18

# TEACHING MATERIALS AND LEARNING STYLES

**K**eeping abreast of new method books and new repertoire is essential for teachers who are dedicated to high standards within the studio. This commitment to new music came into my life soon after I finished graduate school. I had just moved to Virginia, and a local teacher drove me to my first Northern Virginia Music Teachers Association meeting. Along the way, we talked about our favorite teaching pieces. As she mentioned some of hers, she referred to a few composers who were unknown to me. She was shocked that I didn't know the works of Jon George, John Robert Poe, or William Gillock, and invited me to her studio for a day of sharing.

That teacher gave me a gift that I will never forget. Besides exposing me to the work of some wonderful composers, I acquired an interest in new repertoire that I have carried with me ever since. No longer content to teach only the works of masters from the past, I now continually review new publications from living composers. Finding new gems to teach is like trying a new restaurant every week and discovering a delicious new meal at each one. Such experimenting is far better than eating the same meal at the same restaurant week after week, no matter how good it is!

## Method Books Then and Now

Method books have changed drastically over the last 50 years, and a short review of some of the disadvantages of the earliest method books offers insights into why authors have taken new directions in recent years.

### Earlier Methods

Although they provided a systematic approach to piano instruction, early method books had some major shortcomings.

- Material was presented with little, if any, reinforcement.

- Notes were immediately presented on the staff, usually with a middle-C approach.

- The same hand position was used for a long period of time, making it difficult to learn to read outside that position.

- Fingering was given for every note, resulting in a dependence on finger numbers for reading.

- Books were published with an unappealing black-and-white look.

- Difficult concepts were presented at a quick pace, with little regard to age-appropriate learning.

- There was little, if any, material on improvisation, harmonization, or theory.

- Supplementary books rarely existed.

### Contemporary Methods

Method books have progressed dramatically since those early years. Current methods take a vastly different approach.

- Methods usually introduce notes written off the staff, to enable students to become familiar with the keyboard before reading notes on the staff later.

- Methods incorporate a variety of approaches to reading, including multi-key, intervallic, and middle-C.

- Books are printed with colorful and appealing artwork.

- Books present difficult concepts at a manageable pace, with attention given to age-appropriate learning, based on advances in pedagogy.

- Today's methods present concepts systematically, with an integrated approach to rhythm, technique, and reading that is then reinforced throughout the books.

- Methods often include skills such as improvisation, harmonization, transposition, and composition.

- Supplementary materials are plentiful, including books for repertoire, technique, theory, sight-playing, workbooks, jazz, games, etc.

Perhaps the biggest change in method books in recent years is the addition of CDs and GM disks. These offer the student the opportunity to perform pieces while being accompanied by a variety of sounds, from orchestral to jazz. This innovative use of technology (discussed further in Chapter 43) assists students with musical skills such as rhythm, dynamics, and phrasing, while enhancing the sounds students create at the piano.

## Evaluating Method Books

If the same method book has been used for several years, experimenting with a totally new series can freshen the approach to lessons for teacher and student. Even if the teacher loves the method she is currently using, she may find that a different course of study has real value for certain students. Experimenting with a variety of methods makes it possible to match method books to individual learning styles, especially if the methods have dramatically different approaches.

There are several helpful questions teachers should ask when reviewing a method.

- When does the student begin reading notes on the staff?

- Does the method employ a middle-C, intervallic, or multi-key approach to note-reading?

- What method of counting is used (numeric, syllabic, metric)?

- When do the pieces move out of a five-finger position?

- Does the method allow the student to explore the complete range of the piano?

- How much fingering is indicated in the score?

- Is there adequate reinforcement of new concepts?

- What is the rate of progression? Does the student advance steadily? Quickly? Slowly?

- Are concepts presented in a logical sequence?

- What are the sources of the pieces (original compositions, folksongs, arrangements of larger works)?

- Are the pieces varied in style?

- Are the pieces harmonically interesting?

- When and how clearly are musical concepts introduced?
    - Dynamics
    - Tempo markings
    - Phrasing
    - Articulations
    - Pedaling
    - Harmony
    - Form

- How much theory is presented?

- Are transposition, harmonization, or composition introduced?

- Is the student encouraged to improvise?

- Is ear-training included?

- Are duets included in the book and, if so, what is the quality of the duet parts?

- Is the course for group or private lessons, or both?

- How many levels are there?

- What supplementary materials are included? How many books are in each level?

- Are the materials visually appealing?
    - Are they colorful?
    - Are there pictures?
    - Is the size of print satisfactory for a young student?
    - Does the book look daunting because of too much information on a page?

- Is the method better suited for certain age groups? (Younger students, older students, adult students.)

- Are CDs or GM disks available?

Music stores sometimes allow a teacher to preview books at home. A valuable summer project would be to review a number of method books, comparing answers to the questions above. Such research provides a broader understanding of the pedagogical approaches to piano instruction that are currently available.

## Resource

**WEBSITE**

*Annotated Bibliography of Sources on the History of Piano Pedagogy*

– Visit **www.francesclarkcenter.org**

– Select "National Conferences"

– Under "Resources," select "Historical"

– Download the PDF file *Annotated Bibliography of Sources on the History of Piano Pedagogy*

## Keeping Abreast of New Teaching Repertoire

About 15 years ago, a father said to me, "I don't want my daughter to learn any more 20th Century music. You just teach it because it is easier to perform and I don't like it." As tactfully as I could, I told the father that it actually was not easier to perform, and that I would continue to teach current music. Serious students, such as his daughter, have an obligation to learn repertoire from all periods of music, including the most recently composed. If he was unhappy with his daughter learning contemporary music, he would have to find another teacher. He did not find another teacher, and his daughter continued to learn current compositions, which she and I both found most rewarding.

A teacher's commitment to explore new repertoire creates a rich inventory of pieces from which to choose. Making a commitment to buy and study at least one new book of beginning, intermediate, or advanced repertoire on a regular basis keeps lessons from becoming stagnant and avoids the overuse of standard warhorses.

There are a number of excellent composers writing original music for all levels, in a variety of styles. Additionally, many publishers are furnishing new volumes of jazz and popular music that are pedagogically sound and appeal to the interest of today's young pianists.

Besides new repertoire, every year new editions of works of the masters emerge that are well worth reviewing for use with students. Many of these new editions offer careful suggestions for the performance of stylistic elements such as ornamentation and pedaling, as well as historic background. Of particular value for teachers are many new anthologies with pleasing collections of masterworks.

To help expose teachers to exciting new literature, local music teacher associations can devote a meeting to presenting new and favorite teacher repertoire. Showcases and workshops offered by publishers and music retail stores also help acquaint teachers with the latest student literature.

# Resources

Hinson, Maurice. *Guide to the Pianist's Repertoire*, 3rd Edition. Bloomington: Indiana University Press, 1987, 2000.

Hinson has compiled a comprehensive guide for those seeking information on solo piano repertoire, including information on level, publisher, and special musical features. Composers are listed in alphabetical order, with individual works cited under each composer's name. The works are graded by difficulty level: Easy, Intermediate, Moderately Difficult, and Difficult. Brief descriptions of individual works are included, and in some cases, short biographies follow the composer's name. The section on collections is divided into four groupings: General; General: Contemporary; Tombeaux, Hommages (collections written in honor of a composer); and Collections of Various Nationalities. A number of helpful indexes appear at the end of the book including an index of Black Composers and one for Women Composers.

Kirby, F.E. *Music for Piano: A Short History.* Portland: Amadeus Press, 1995, corrected reprint 1997, 2000. Distributed by Hal Leonard Corporation.

This historical survey focuses on music for piano solo but also includes important compositions for piano duet and two pianos. Scholarly yet readable, it covers the entire repertoire from the Renaissance to the late 20th century and incorporates a bibliography of 1,100 sources for further study.

Magrath, Jane. *The Pianist's Guide to the Standard Teaching and Performing Literature.* Van Nuys: Alfred Publishing Co., Inc., 1995.

An annotated bibliography, this book organizes material by historical period: Baroque, Classical, Romantic, and 20th Century. Works include brief descriptions as well as a level rating from 1–10 covering beginner to early advanced material. The descriptions usually include general information about style, and may include additional information on pedagogical and musical elements.

**WEBSITE**

*Piano Lessons in Your Home*

www.pianolessonsinyourhome.com

- "Company" has a pull-down menu
- Select "Music Resources"

**PART VI**

## Matching Learning Styles with Appropriate Methods and Repertoire

The topic of learning styles has become increasingly prominent in pedagogical discussions on successful teaching. Among the experts who have categorized learning styles and personality types in their own unique fashion are:

- Myers-Briggs (Katharine Cook Briggs and Isabel Briggs Myers)
- Dawna Markova
- David Keirsey
- Keith Golay
- Howard Garder
- Anthony Gregorc
- David Kolb

Why is it important for piano teachers to understand learning styles? The most obvious reason is that they will be able to teach more effectively by first understanding how each student learns. Conversely, teachers will better understand the impact their own learning style has on their teaching style. Finally, when a teacher marries an understanding of her students' individual learning styles with a broad knowledge of method books and repertoire, she is better able to serve the needs of each individual student.

## Common Learning Styles

There are three learning styles that are most often described in relation to piano students: visual, aural, and kinesthetic.

### VISUAL

Visual learners learn from seeing. They respond well to facial expressions and body movement, benefit from taking notes, and learn well from written material. Piano students who are visual learners may read music well and like to use workbooks. They may visualize the written page when playing from memory. Teachers who are more visual might ask, "Do you see the shape of this phrase?" or say, "This looks like fun."

### AURAL

The aural learner learns from hearing. Aural learners listen to voice inflection and respond well when explanations are given verbally. Piano students who are aural learners like to hear their pieces performed, and respond well to recordings and aural demonstrations. They may prefer to "play by ear" rather than read music. The aural teacher might ask, "Can you hear how to shape this phrase?" or say, "That sounds like fun!"

### KINESTHETIC

The kinesthetic learner learns from doing. Hands-on approaches work well and physical activities provide a good learning tool. These students remember best by doing rather than by reading or hearing. The kinesthetic teacher might ask, "Can you feel the shape of this phrase?" or say, "That seems fun to do!"

## Learning Temperaments

Besides these approaches to learning, different descriptions have been given to individual temperaments. David Keirsey describes four in his book *Please Understand Me: Character and Temperament Types:* Rationalists; Idealists; Artisans; and Guardians.

Keith Golay takes these four types a step further and assigns animal names. In his article "Introducing the Animal Kingdom – it's a jungle out there!" written for *American Music Teacher*, Golay goes on to apply these personality types to music students and teachers. The following information is based on excerpts from that article.

### RATIONALIST – OWL

Rationalist–Owl students "like to learn, and want to know how to do things and to know about things… They seek a reasonable explanation for things… As a piano student, this person will want to know specific techniques and understand why things are done the way they are."

Owl teachers are "very practical and logical in their approach… This teacher focuses on using those teaching approaches that best fit each student and will use innovation whenever possible."

### IDEALIST – DOLPHIN

The Idealist–Dolphin student "is cooperative and interested in doing what the teacher requests. This student wants a harmonious relationship with the teacher and other students. They want to be recognized as unique and someone who is special… Music becomes a way of self-expression."

The Dolphin teacher "focuses on bringing out the best in each student by developing a personal relationship with students. This teacher is naturally empathetic toward students and easily gives encouragement."

### ARTISAN – APE

"As a student, the Artisan-Ape needs a great deal of physical movement and novelty. They need stimulation and variation. They easily become bored… If caught by an activity, like playing the piano, they will practice for hours on end."

The Ape teacher "takes the position that one becomes skillful with experience… The idea is in order to learn it, you have to do it… This music teacher will focus on improving the student's performance."

### GUARDIAN – BEAR

"The Guardian–Bear student tends to be cooperative and conforming. They learn early on to do what the teacher asks and desire to meet the teacher's expectations. They like skill and drill and follow routine. This piano student likes to practice scales and will find comfort in knowing exactly what to do."

Guardian–Bear teachers "follow standards that are handed down. They utilize a body of teaching material and procedures that has stood the 'test of time.' …Their charge is to transfer from one generation to the next the understandings and skills that were taught to them."

**PART VI**

# Resources

Keirsey, David and Marilyn Bates. *Please Understand Me: Character and Temperament Types.* 5th Edition. Del Mar: Prometheus Nemesis Book Company, Distributed by Oxford Psychologists Press, 1984.

> One of the most popular books ever written on personality types, *Please Understand Me* addresses the various personality types that can be encountered in family, colleagues, and friends. Keirsey and Bates seek to have the reader understand and accept the different personality types encountered in others, rather than fruitlessly trying to change them. The book starts with a 70-question Keirsey Temperament Sorter, a test that helps the reader to determine his or her own personality type.

Keirsey, David. *Please Understand Me II: Temperament, Character, Intellilgence.* Del Mar: Prometheus Nemesis Book Company, 1998.

> This book updates and expands Keirsey's original book, and also includes a new focus area defining four kinds of intelligence. The book contains the Keirsey Temperament Sorter as a self-test for determining personality type.

### WEBSITES

*Ageless Learner*

www.agelesslearner.com

– Scroll down to "Introductions"

– Beside "How Adults Learn," select "learning styles"

# Resources (cont.)

*learning-styles-online.com*

   www.learning-styles-online.com

      – Select "Overview of Learning Styles"

*The Myers & Briggs Foundation*

   www.myersbriggs.org

*Piano Home Page*

   www.marthabeth.com/pedagogy.html

      – Scroll down and select "Learning and Teaching Styles"

*Piano Pedagogy Forum*

   www.music.sc.edu/ea/keyboard/PPF/7.2/7.2.PPFgarcia.html

## SOURCE CITED

Excerpted and reprinted with permission of Music Teachers National Association.
Golay, Keith. **"Introducing the Animal Kingdom – it's a jungle out there!"** *American Music Teacher*, Vol. 52, No. 2, October/November 2002, pp. 40–44.

> Every teacher increases the chance of effectively teaching a variety of personality types by better under-standing individual approaches to learning. I highly recommend reading Golay's complete article and doing additional study on learning styles. In addition, this volume of *American Music Teacher* has a number of arti-cles on learning styles.

# Chapter 19

# PROFESSIONAL DEVELOPMENT, PROFESSIONAL ORGANIZATIONS, AND PARTNERSHIPS

Continuing education is required in many professions, including public school instruction, real estate brokers, etc. Although such study is not required by law for independent music teachers, it is vital to their growth and the success of their studios.

Music teachers who continually improve their pedagogical and performance skills experience unlimited rewards in their teaching. On the other hand, those who do not continue developing professionally encounter a glass ceiling that limits their teaching level and can cause motivated students to become bored to the point of quitting lessons or changing teachers.

An example of this self-limiting approach to teaching comes to mind as I recall one of my former college piano students. She came from a small farming community, and although she did not major in music, she was highly motivated during her college piano study, progressing from Clementi sonatinas to challenging repertoire by Debussy and Schumann.

As I complimented her on her progress and growth at the end of her senior year, she replied, "I just wish I could have had more lessons before I came to college." We again discussed her reason for stopping lessons in elementary school. "Once I reached level four in my method books, my teacher said 'That's it. You are done now, there are no more books.' "

How sad that this teacher did not know more about the expansive world of piano literature! How unfortunate that she felt there was nothing more for this gifted student to learn! It is certainly understandable that she, like many teachers, may not have felt comfortable teaching above a given level. There is nothing wrong with knowing one's limitations, but it would have been better for this teacher to say, "I feel we have progressed well together, but now it would benefit you to go to another teacher. Although there are no other teachers in our town, there is a fine teacher an hour away, and I hope you and your parents will consider going to her for lessons." This statement would have shown that the teacher acknowledged her limitations but had the student's best interest at heart, aware that there was much more for the student to learn.

If this same teacher had been willing to improve her skills and her knowledge of literature and pedagogy, she could have raised her glass ceiling to a higher level. All teachers, novice or seasoned, can continue to learn regardless of a lack of degrees—or an abundance of them.

## Lessons and Practice for Teachers

As the years go by, it is inevitable that teachers tend to develop a teaching pattern that stresses the same things in lessons in an increasingly similar fashion. One way for teachers to avoid sliding into a routine is to continue improving their own performance skills. Many teachers discontinue lessons after the last degree is earned; some even stop lessons while still in high school. No matter how long it has been since the last lesson, there is not a piano teacher alive who would not benefit from additional piano study and practice.

Piano study revitalizes the teacher's ability to present musical concepts creatively. Taking lessons enables a teacher to see the piano through another's eyes, and experience how students feel when facing a challenge. Lessons with a skilled teacher also have the potential to improve and expand a teacher's approaches to technique. When the teacher's own approach to keyboard study is energized and invigorated through lessons, the likelihood is strong that her students will feel the same excitement.

With or without lessons, every piano teacher benefits from daily practice. For those teachers who wish to perform in public, dedicated practice is essential. In the music profession it is not enough to read books, as a history professor might. Music teachers must also maintain their craft, like a tennis coach or a language instructor. When teachers set aside time for daily practice, they not only improve their skills, but even more importantly, they revitalize their love of music making. That feeling of personal gratification at the piano often gets lost if time at the keyboard is focused solely on students.

When teachers perform in recital, their students benefit from their example. Although lack of time and interest may be excuses for not attending their teacher's performances, students should be encouraged to attend. Early in my career, I became aware of the lack of student attendance at my own recitals and developed a workable plan to alleviate the problem. I sent a letter to all parents stating that during my recital week, no lessons would be given. Attendance at my recital would be required and would take the place of that week's lesson. This policy not only ensured that students would attend my performance, it also gave students an opportunity to hear live performances of advanced repertoire, enabled parents to observe a new dimension of their child's teacher, and gave me extra time to devote to practice, concentration, and relaxation the week before the event.

## Reading Materials

### Books on Professional Topics

Books provide valuable knowledge and inspiration for the conscientious piano teacher. Works have been published on every topic of interest: memorization, practice habits, music history, performance anxiety, wellness, learning styles, motivation, approaches to teaching, and composers and their lives, to name but a few. Two tips for effective reading are:

- Develop a reading list designed for personal growth.

- Reserve time to read books as part of a sustained commitment to professional development.

Although some teachers may wish to purchase books and build a professional library, others may prefer to take advantage of a local library when seeking resources. Many libraries have access to an inter-library loan program and online resource material, often including access to a nearby university system's libraries. A number of local music organizations maintain helpful lending libraries, providing an additional resource for interested teachers.

The following Resources section lists a few of the many professional l
websites available to teachers.

# Resources

Amabile, T.M. *Growing Up Creative: Nurturing a Life of Creativity*, 2nd Edition. Hadley: Crea
Foundation, 1992.

> Amabile sets five areas for study in the preface: describing what children's creativity is and ho
> nize it; the basic components for children's creativity and stages of the creative process; the importance of
> motivation in creativity; how home and school environments can destroy children's creativity; and several
> specific techniques that parents and teachers can use to keep children's creativity alive. The book ends with
> a chapter on games, exercises, dialogues and ideas, followed by a list of suggested readings.

Hinson, Maurice. *The Pianist's Bookshelf: A Practical Guide to Books, Videos, and Other Resources.* Bloomington:
Indiana University Press, 1998.

> This helpful guide to available resources is arranged by topic: Accompanying (chamber music included),
> Aesthetics, Analysis, Biographies, Construction and Design, Group Piano, History and Criticism, Lists of
> Piano Music, Ornamentation, Pedagogy, Performance Anxiety (Stress and Tension), Performance Technique,
> Piano Duet, Transcriptions, and Two or More Pianos. Authors of materials are arranged alphabetically within
> each topic. Each entry has one to a few paragraphs of description.

Lyke, James, with Yvonne Enoch and Geoffrey Haydon. *Creative Piano Teaching.* Champaign: Stipes Publishing LLC,
1996.

> A general guide for piano teachers, this book touches on the core information that is essential when
> teaching piano. Although no one area is covered in extreme detail, this book includes chapters by a
> number of authors and offers a well-rounded approach to such areas as technique, memorization, methods,
> repertoire, ensemble and jazz repertoire, stylistic elements for each period of music, issues pertaining to
> elementary, intermediate or adult students, music technology, professional issues in the independent studio,
> and much more.

Meyers Ross, Cynthia, and Karen Meyers Stangl. *The Music Teacher's Book of Lists.* San Francisco: Jossey-Bass
Publishers, An Imprint of John Wiley and Sons, Inc., 1994.

> This book includes helpful lists in nine major categories: Rudiments, Music Theory, Composers and Their
> Works, Instruments and Instrument Ensembles, Opera and Vocal Music, Music History, Popular Music,
> Dance, Integrating Music with Content Areas. The lists provide a quick and easy resource to materials as
> diverse as cadences, modes, Italian composers, music symbols, Pre-Baroque composers, chord names,
> operas of Verdi, jazz terms, top tunes of the 1990's, Civil War songs, national anthems of various countries,
> seasonal music, and much more.

Uszler, Marienne. *Play It Again, Sam... What, Why, and When to Repeat.* Fort Lauderdale: The FJH Music
Company Inc., 2003.

> From the *Teaching Keyboard Effectively Yourself* series, this brief book provides practical advice on how to
> use repetition to its fullest advantage when teaching. Sections include: Reinforcing a Concept, Making
> Concepts Concrete, Materials That Reinforce, Materials That Prepare, and more. The last chapter includes a
> list of additional readings.

Uszler, Marienne. *Time Flies: How to Make the Best Use of Teaching Time.* Fort Lauderdale: The FJH Music
Company, Inc., 2004.

> From the *Teaching Keyboard Effectively Yourself* series, this short book provides suggestions on using
> teaching time efficiently. Tips are given on using a teaching timeline, planning group lessons, controlling
> "talk" during lessons, stretching teaching time, and much more. The last chapter includes a helpful list of
> further readings.

PART VI

## Professional Magazines and Journals

Articles from music teacher magazines and journals provide a wealth of teaching ideas and a good starting point for professional growth. Subscription fees to professional periodicals are tax-deductible as well. Rather than putting a magazine aside for that elusive free moment, a better option is for teachers to allocate an hour (or more) a week for continuing education, taking time to learn from skilled teachers who share their expertise in magazine articles.

Teachers can take this one step further by documenting one good idea from the reading and applying it in their studio. Keeping a list of briefly summarized ideas from specific magazine issues (and organizing magazines in an accessible order) allows teachers to easily revisit articles for review at a later date. The following are some of the many excellent professional periodicals to consider.

# Resources

*American Music Teacher.* Published by Music Teachers National Association. Subscription included with membership in MTNA.

> www.mtna.org/HLtext

*Clavier Magazine* for teachers and Clavier's *Piano Explorer* for students

> www.claviermagazine.com
>> – Select "Clavier" or "Piano Explorer"

*International Piano*

> www.pianomagazine.com

*Keyboard Companion.* Published by the Frances Clark Center for Keyboard Pedagogy

> www.keyboardcompanion.com

*Music Clubs Magazine* for teachers and *Junior Keynotes* for teachers, students and parents. Published by the National Federation of Music Clubs. Subscription to Music Clubs Magazine is included in senior member dues.

> www.nfmc-music.org
>> – Select "Periodicals"

*Music Educator's Journal* and *Teaching Music.* Both of these journals are published by the National Association for Music Education (MENC) and subscription are included with membership.

> www.menc.org
>> – Select "Resources"
>> – Select "Periodicals"

*Piano Guild Notes.* Subscription included with Guild participation.

> No web address available.

### Websites

The Internet offers a wide spectrum of teaching resources for almost any topic related to music or teaching. Using a search engine, teachers can locate not only articles on pedagogy, but related topics such as composer backgrounds, video and sound files, scores, historical timelines, tutorial websites, etc. The following are some of the many websites available.

# Resources

*Music Teachers National Association Discussion Boards*

www.mtna.org/HLtext

*Music Teachers National Association Wellness Bibliography*

www.mtna.org/HLtext

*Piano Education Page*

http://pianoeducation.org

– Scroll down and select "Links" for links to music-related sites.

– Scroll down the page for numerous sites, listed by category.

*Piano Home Page*

www.marthabeth.com/piano.html

*Piano Lessons in Your Home*

www.pianolessonsinyourhome.com

– "Company" has a pull-down menu.

– Select "Music Resources" for a comprehensive list of music-related links.

*PianoTeachers.com*

www.pianoteachers.com

*Steve's Piano Service*

www.stevespianoservice.com

– Select "Music Links" or "A Short History on the Piano"

– This site also has information on piano repair.

**PART VI**

## Membership in Professional Organizations

Aside from my music degrees, there is nothing that has shaped me more as a teacher, performer, and career musician than my membership in professional music organizations. I have attended meetings regularly since my graduate school days and continue to learn from monthly programs. Holding office and chairing committees in professional organizations has afforded me the opportunity to improve my skills as an organizer, speaker, and collaborator.

A lifelong membership in professional music organizations adds to a lifetime of continual learning. Membership keeps piano teachers from being too independent and isolated in their studios, and allows self-employed teachers to benefit from the networking, shared ideas, and mutual concerns of a professional organization.

Memberships in professional organizations offer an abundance of benefits, including the following:

- Monthly meetings with presentations, lectures, and masterclasses

- State and national conferences

- Opportunities to network with other teachers

- Professional magazines and publications

- Teacher certification

- Opportunities for leadership

- Group benefits such as insurance programs and legal services

- Libraries of professional materials

- Access to websites of specific organizations

- Mentors willing to help all teachers, even those new to the profession

- Assistance with zoning issues

- Grant opportunities

- Advocacy materials

- Standardized student theory testing

- Standardized student keyboard skills testing

- Student performance and composition festivals and competitions

Teachers have sometimes said to me, "I just don't get anything out of belonging to a national organization when I teach in my home, so I am not going to pay those dues!" I am always dismayed when I hear this. If a teacher never reads the magazine that comes with membership, never attends local programs, does not go to state or national conferences, has no desire to enter students in activities sponsored by the organization, and has no intention of learning about new compositions or improving her pedagogical skills, then I guess that statement is true. But if a teacher has the desire to improve her teaching so that she can offer her students her best, then memberships in professional organizations are priceless.

Although some teachers may feel the dues are expensive, when compared to the dues of professional organizations in fields outside of music, they are actually modest. Dues are another tax-deductible expense that can be budgeted into the annual cost of running a home-based business.

The following are some of the many music teacher organizations to consider. Contact information for each may be found in Appendix C.

### The College Music Society (CMS)

The College Music Society is a consortium of college, conservatory, university, and independent musicians and scholars interested in all disciplines of music. Its mission is to promote music teaching and learning, musical creativity and expression, research and dialogue, and diversity and interdisciplinary interaction.

### Music Teachers National Association (MTNA)

This organization is designed with the teacher of applied lessons in mind, both in independent music studios and in colleges and universities. MTNA sponsors conferences, competitions, non-competitive studio programs, and a teacher certification program. *American Music Teacher*, a bimonthly journal published by MTNA, offers invaluable articles dealing with all areas of teaching. The MTNA Foundation Fund sponsors special award programs as well as grant programs. Members in the national association are also members of their MTNA state affiliate and usually of a local association as well. The MTNA website is particularly helpful, with links to information such as membership, publications, resources, programs, services, products, and certification. MTNA has also partnered with insurance providers to assist its members with insurance.

### National Association for Music Education (MENC)

The world's largest arts education association, MENC offers a multitude of services for music educators. Although many of its members are public school teachers, there are a number of valuable services for the independent teacher as well. The MENC website includes links to a wide realm of helpful information including music books and periodicals, information on the MENC conference and links to Music Standards, advocacy resources, technology information, and programs sponsored by MENC.

### National Federation of Music Clubs (NFMC)

Dedicated to finding and fostering young musical talent, the NFMC conducts annual non-competitive Junior Festivals, as well as competitions offering more than $750,000 in state and national prizes.

The Federation champions American music with awards and commissions. Awards are given annually to recognize educational institutions for their promotion and presentation of American music. The Federation also supports legislation affecting the welfare of musicians, music education and development of American musical life. It sponsors music therapy programs in hospitals, nursing homes and prisons, and recognizes and promotes outstanding American music and composers annually through programs such as American Music Month (November), Parade of American Music, and Crusade for Strings.

NFMC members are informed of NFMC activities and educational music information through *Music Clubs Magazine*, the official publication of NFMC, and *Junior Keynotes*, targeted toward Junior members. Both are published three times a year.

## Professional Conferences

Several music teacher organizations hold an annual national conference specifically for their members. Some of the many benefits teachers can derive from these conferences include the following:

- Observing masterclasses given by the finest teachers in the world

- Attending sessions that lend insight into a multitude of topics, possibly some that a teacher might not have previously considered

- Hearing inspiring concerts and recitals given by both professionals and students

- Meeting composers of student repertoire and discussing their music with them

- Focusing on areas of special interest through day-long workshops dedicated to a particular topic, such as technology, pedagogy, or professionalism in the independent studio

- Networking with colleagues, discussing solutions to mutual problems, and developing professional relationships

- Keeping up-to-date on current music publications through publisher showcases and exhibits

I have often heard teachers say, "I can't go to the conference. It is too expensive," or "I'd never be able to make up the missed lessons." Although conferences can be expensive, as teachers who are dedicated to professional growth, it is important to resist the urge to avoid professional conferences because of cost. Instead, money and time for professional development need to be budgeted as a legitimate and necessary business expense that pays back ten-fold in improved knowledge, skills, and earning power.

One way to plan for the time and expense of a conference is to incorporate it into the studio calendar and amortize the cost as part of the term's tuition. Before the new teaching year begins, schedule a non-lesson week to allow for conference attendance. It is still possible to charge for that week as part of annual tuition, letting the parents know it is not a "week off," but a workweek that is spent for the benefit of their children. This will, in effect, result in a paid week in which to attend the conference, with no lessons needing to be rescheduled. Although the cost of attending a conference is tax-deductible, sharing a hotel room, bringing breakfast food, and traveling with other teachers all help to lower expenses.

One teacher I know writes the parents of her students after attending a conference and outlines all the sessions she attended at the conference. She introduces the list with the statement, "These are the sessions I attended on behalf of your children during the conference week." In this way, the teacher conveys the value of that week in terms of its benefits to her students.

Informing parents of the benefits of attending a conference also becomes a form of self-marketing. Parents will not understand the value of all a teacher does unless the teacher tells them, and defining the benefits of a professional conference reinforces that the teacher is a caring and committed educator.

## National Music Teacher Organization Conferences

The following are a few of the music teacher organizations that conduct national conferences yearly for their members.

- The College Music Society

- Music Teachers National Association (MTNA)

- National Association for Music Educators (MENC)

- National Federation of Music Clubs (NFMC)

See Appendix C for contact information.

## Additional National Conferences

In addition to the conferences for members of the organizations listed above, there are two national conferences specifically dedicated to piano pedagogy.

### THE NATIONAL CONFERENCE ON KEYBOARD PEDAGOGY (NCKP)

Designed exclusively for piano teachers, this biennial conference focuses entirely on the pedagogical issues affecting piano teaching. As stated on their website:

> The National Conference on Keyboard Pedagogy is a continuation of the original National Conference on Piano Pedagogy, founded by Richard Chronister and James Lyke, that convened between 1979 and 1994. The history of piano pedagogy in the American university is inextricably linked to the National Conference through people, initiatives, and institutions. Now an ongoing project of the Frances Clark Center, the National Conference on Keyboard Pedagogy meets in early August of odd-numbered years.

### WORLD PIANO PEDAGOGY CONFERENCE (WPPC)

This annual piano pedagogy conference offers teachers the opportunity to experience valuable lectures, masterclasses, teaching demonstrations, and concerts presented by pedagogues and specialists from all over the world. WPPC's website offers piano teachers an extensive online resource center. One area, *The WebZine*, includes features such as News & Articles, Ask the Expert, Movement & Wellness, and Forums. The vision of the World Piano Pedagogy Conference, as stated on their website, is to:

- Offer a forum for promotion and dissemination of quality piano teaching and teacher training for independent studios, pre-college institutions, colleges, conservatories, and universities.

- Design programs and presentations to enhance teacher training, specifically for the needs of the music student and the young professional.

- Offer quality presentations by piano and keyboard educators, performers, composers, piano and keyboard manufacturers, music publishers, and the rest of the music industry.

- Enable interaction and information sharing among piano teachers and pedagogues from the U.S. and abroad through demonstrations, discussions, and analysis of piano teaching and pedagogy topics.

- Document the conference on videotape for current and future generations of piano teachers.

**PART VI**

## Networking and Partnerships

A vast range of professional resources awaits those who learn to network and partner with others. Networking fosters connections and establishes friendships in the field of music as well as in related fields. Colleagues are able to turn to each other for assistance with professional or pedagogical questions. By networking, teachers can make themselves known to those who may someday be looking for a teacher with their skills or a studio with their programs.

### Activities Made Possible Through Partnering

The benefits of interdependence are overlooked far too often in the independent studio. Independent music teachers need not walk alone as they move down their career path. There are a number of fruitful activities conducted in partnerships that can increase the effectiveness of private teaching, including the following:

- Developing programs in partnership with an outside entity
- Offering collaborative student performances
- Co-sponsoring events
- Using another group's facilities
- Working with another organization for funding or grants
- Offering studio services to another group's clients
- Working for arts advocacy issues with other teachers or arts groups

### Partnering with Local Music and Educational Organizations

Independent music teachers can multiply the effectiveness and visibility of their studio by creating programs and activities with the many education and performance organizations in their area. Some of these are listed below.

- Public and private school music programs
- Other independent music studios
- Home school associations
- Special education programs
- College and university fine arts departments
- Community colleges and schools of the arts
- Local orchestras, choirs, and community bands
- Piano technician guilds

### Establishing Partnerships with Community and Civic Organizations

Within the community, partnerships can be initiated with any of a number of organizations:

- Places of worship

- Senior citizen programs

- Retirement homes

- Hospitals

- Area hospice programs

- Public libraries

- Social Services

- Parks and Recreation departments

- Summer recreation programs

- YMCA and YWCA

- Girl Scouts and Boy Scouts

- Chambers of Commerce

- Convention and Visitors' Bureaus

- City Councils

- Local businesses

- Service clubs (e.g., Rotary, Elks, and Kiwanis)

**PART VI**

### The Importance of Partnering with Local Music Retailers

A partnership with the local music store is particularly valuable, as teachers benefit from the many services a local music dealer has to offer. Teachers need to keep in mind that the effectiveness of local dealers will be diminished if teachers purchase from them only on rare occasions or make illegal copies of music for students.

Some of the ways local music stores assist teachers include the following:

- Providing music for sale at association meetings and state conferences

- Providing presentations on new publications for the benefit of local teachers

- Giving training workshops on electronic keyboards, software, or other technology areas

- Stocking an abundant supply of music for easy access

- Sponsoring competitions

- Including fliers about music activities with their monthly invoices

- Displaying business cards for teachers

- Providing a current list of available teachers to parents inquiring about lessons

- Holding local association meetings in store facilities

- Hosting recitals

How does a strong partnership with music teachers benefit the local music dealer?

- The support of independent teachers is vital to the health of a music dealer's business, as their business depends on developing a strong client base.

- When teachers shop regularly at the local music store and encourage their students to shop there, dealers are able to keep more music in stock.

- When teachers purchase from local dealers, the dealer knows those teachers and can better serve their needs.

- Music-store business cards can be displayed in studios.

- The store's promotional materials can be shared with students.

- Local teachers can include information about special music-store promotions in their studio newsletter.

- Dealers can request an advertisement in local associations newsletters.

Just like a person who takes medication wants to know his pharmacist well and be known by his pharmacist, piano teachers need to know their music dealer well and have their needs known by the dealer. As the partnership grows stronger, the possibilities for collaboration increase, and a true win-win situation is created.

# Chapter 20

# TEACHER CERTIFICATION THROUGH PROFESSIONAL ORGANIZATIONS

**M**any independent piano teachers have prepared themselves well professionally by obtaining degrees and the training needed to operate a successful studio. However, there are a number of teachers currently teaching with little or no formal training. One reason is that there are no actual standards that must be met in order to teach piano independently in the United States. It is true that anyone with any skill level can establish a studio without earning certification, passing an exam, or obtaining a degree. There is no minimum level of performance required, nor even a basic knowledge of the fundamentals of music or pedagogy.

There is a movement, not on the part of the government, but from within the music profession itself, to encourage a system for acquiring certification or diplomas for the independent music teacher. Such recognition assures potential students that a teacher has met professional standards and is committed to personal growth. Just as a patient would insist that a doctor has met medical standards before practicing, there is the hope that parents will insist that a piano teacher has met core musical, pedagogical, and professional standards.

There are a number of resources available for teachers interested in validating their professional expertise through certification or professional diplomas. The following is a description of a few of these options, with contact information listed in Appendix C.

## Music Teachers National Association (MTNA)

Teachers wishing to become recognized as highly qualified in their profession may obtain national certification through Music Teachers National Association (MTNA). The designation "Nationally Certified Teacher of Music (NCTM)" indicates that a teacher has undergone a set of rigorous requirements in all areas of teaching and is committed to continual professional growth.

### The Certification Process
Candidates must meet five standards in order to achieve and maintain the status of Nationally Certified Teacher of Music (NCTM).

- Standard I: Professional Preparation

- Standard II: Professional Teaching Practices

- Standard III: Professional Business Management

- Standard IV: Professionalism and Partnerships

- Standard V: Professional and Personal Renewal

Areas of focus within the standards include the following:

- Competency in music theory, music history/literature, pedagogy/teacher education, and performance

- The ability to plan and execute a creative course of study for all students

- The ability to use a wide variety of musical resources, equipment, technology, materials, methods, music, and teaching styles and strategies

- The ability to establish a nurturing learning environment

- The ability to use multiple tools for student assessment

- The ability to develop comprehensive and sequential lesson plans

- The application of professional and ethical business practices

- Contributions to the musical and professional growth of one's community

- The ability to build partnerships with colleagues within the musical community

- A commitment to professional growth through continuing education

Teachers are eligible to apply for certification after teaching for two years and must satisfy requirements depending on their professional preparation. Academic and performance preparation may be verified through coursework or proficiency and performance testing. Candidates with approved applications choose to demonstrate their teaching competence through a certification examination, a portfolio, or administrative verification. To satisfy the requirements for coursework, a candidate with a college or university degree that included classes in required areas may submit transcripts for verification; however, a candidate need not have a degree or college experience in order to become certified. Teachers can access further information on guidelines and requirements for certification on the MTNA website: www.mtna.org/HLtext.

All teachers who are certified through MTNA are listed in the MTNA Certified Teacher directory, which can be accessed by visiting the certification site on the MTNA website.

In order to maintain their NCTM status, teachers must undergo a required renewal process every five years, thereby demonstrating a commitment to continuing personal growth and professionalism. Requirements include verification of activities through the use of documented points, a portfolio of professional activities, or administrative verification of professional activities. After the third successful renewal teachers may apply for Permanent Certification, which recognizes a true commitment to personal growth and professional excellence.

## Self-assessment

MTNA has developed a booklet entitled *Assessment Tool*, which is available from www.mtna.org/HLtext. This affordable booklet asks valuable questions that directly concern one's teaching, studio operation, and pedagogical approach to lessons.

The booklet first appeared in the August/September 2004 issue of *American Music Teacher*, and consists of three parts:

1) Self-Assessment Tool

2) Peer Assessment Tool

3) Client Assessment Tool

## Associated Board of the Royal Schools of Music

The Associated Board of the Royal Schools of Music (ABRSM) is the world's leading music examining board. ABRSM offers a Diploma Syllabus for musicians, including assessment in the following areas:

• Music Performance

• Music Direction (for directors of instrumental or vocal ensembles)

• Instrumental/Vocal Teaching

In addition, ABRSM offers courses in professional development for teachers. All information for the current Diploma Syllabus can be found on the ABRSM website.

## The Royal Conservatory of Music (RCM)

Based in Toronto, Canada, The Royal Conservatory of Music (RCM) serves as an excellent model for teacher certification. One of several Canadian conservatory programs, RCM has extended its examination and certification offerings to American teachers through its National Music Certificate Program. (See below.)

Like the ABRSM, the Royal Conservatory of Music offers a system of testing and evaluating students and teachers, with ten grades of student examinations followed by examinations for associate diplomas in two possible areas: performance and teaching. Upon completing the necessary requirements, an individual is awarded an associate diploma and is certified as an Associate of the Royal Conservatory of Music (Toronto) (ARCM).

## Resources

*Piano Pedagogy Certificate Program.* Mississauga, Ontario: The Frederick Harris Music Co., Ltd., 2005.

This syllabus for the Piano Pedagogy Certificate Program is designed as a progressive pedagogy curriculum, with preparation for certification on three levels:

Elementary Certificate

Intermediate Certificate

Associate of the Royal Conservatory of Music (ARCT) Diploma

Examination requirements are included in this syllabus, along with a helpful bibliography of materials applicable to the examinations.

PART VI

## Resources (cont.)

*The Piano Syllabus, 2008 Edition.* Mississauga, Ontario: The Frederick Harris Music Co., Ltd., 2008.

Designed as a guide for the Royal Conservatory of Music and National Music Certification Program examinations, the repertoire in this syllabus is listed in progressive levels and includes selections of Baroque, Classical, Romantic, and 20th and 21st Century repertoire. An added bonus is a list of Technical Requirements for each level of testing, including Technical tests (scales, triads, arpeggios, etc.), Ear Tests, Sight-Reading, and Theory Co-Requisites. By dividing the repertoire and skills into distinct levels, this syllabus allows piano teachers to follow a well-planned system for progress in each area. The syllabus also includes the requirements for the Performer's and Teacher's ARCT exams.

**WEBSITES**

*Associated Board of the Royal Schools of Music*

www.abrsm.org

*Music Teachers National Association*

www.mtna.org

*Royal Conservatory of Music Examinations*

www.rcmexaminations.org

## National Music Certificate Program

Teachers and students in the United States may now participate in an internationally recognized system of assessment and evaluation called the National Music Certificate Program, in association with the Royal Conservatory of Music Examinations, a division of the Royal Conservatory of Music (RCM) in Toronto, Canada. The curriculum is based on that of the RCM, with the goal of creating a national standard of music excellence for both teachers and students in America.

As in the RCM examinations, practical piano examinations are given that encourage high standards in performance, technique, ear-training, and sight-reading. Parallel exams in theory include testing on rudiments, harmony, counterpoint, and analysis, as well as in music history. Examinations begin with two preparatory levels and then progress to levels one through ten, with carefully chosen testing in all levels of skills. More details for student examinations are available in Chapter 25.

As in the Canadian system, a teacher may seek either a performer's diploma or a teacher's diploma, allowing a teacher to become certified as an Associate Royal Conservatory of Music Teacher (ARCT). In order to receive ARCT status, the teacher must be tested and meet the necessary requirements in performance, rudiments, music history, counterpoint, harmony, and analysis.

Receiving a diploma and ARCT status is a form of certification that attests to the skill and proficiency of the teacher. Teachers who pass the appropriate practical piano examinations and theory examinations and receive a teaching or performance diploma can be confident that they have received a solid background in piano and are well-prepared for the pedagogical requirements of the profession.

## Resource

**WEBSITE**

*National Music Certificate Program*

www.nationalmusiccertificate.org

## PARENTS AND PROFESSIONAL CERTIFICATION

Many parents in the United States do not yet seek any form of certification as a requirement for their child's piano teacher. However, more and more parents are inquiring about educational and professional qualifications. Teachers must be proactive rather than complacent by seeking opportunities for continuing education and certification in order to demonstrate their commitment to growth in their profession. Regardless of one's educational background, certification provides a valuable process for assessing and verifying one's professional skills and pedagogical growth.

**PART VI**

# PART VII
## FROM PREPARATION TO PERFORMANCE

All piano students perform on some level, ranging from performing for family and friends to performing in competitions. Before students can perform effectively, they must first be taught three fundamental skills: how to practice, how to memorize, and how to perform. The time spent teaching students how to practice and how to memorize will be well spent, regardless of whether they find themselves performing in a living room or a concert hall. Part VII explores the art of teaching students to practice conscientiously, memorize effectively, and perform with confidence.

# Chapter 21

# THE ART OF PRACTICE

## The Need for Effective Practicing

Many doctors' offices display wall charts that measure degrees of pain. What if a chart existed that measured successful practicing? It might look something like this:

**Please assess the effectiveness of your practice sessions since your last lesson:**

**10** 100% accuracy; full retention
**9**
**8** 80% accuracy; high level of retention
**7**
**6**
**5** 50% right/50% wrong; remembered half of what was learned
**4**
**3** Painfully slow improvement; some retention if lucky
**2**
**1** Nothing has improved in the least; no recollection of having been at the last lesson

How many piano students have been told, "Go home and practice this," with no specific guidelines for productive practice? Students will not practice effectively if teachers take too much for granted. The teacher who gives little guidance, or vague, generalized instructions, will not equip the student with the tools she needs to produce positive results when practicing on her own. Success will be elusive at best.

Conversely, the teacher who micromanages a student's piano study—whose students play beautifully only after she has corrected every note, demonstrated every rhythm, marked every fingering, and specified exactly how to play the dynamics and phrasing—has succeeded at "showing" but not teaching. By pointing out every detail in each week's lesson, a role of perpetual dependence and neediness develops. Ultimately, such dependency means the last piece the student is taught will be the last piece played with accuracy. In order for students to be independent, teachers must ensure effective learning will occur by first teaching productive practice habits.

From the student's perspective, good practice habits enable her to create beautiful sounds with discipline, musical intelligence, and independence. From the teacher's perspective, teaching a student how to practice shifts the focus of lessons from teaching notes and timing to teaching students *how* to learn and perform repertoire without being spoon-fed.

## Practice Guidelines

The goal of intelligent practicing is to learn a piece accurately and musically from the very beginning. Students can learn new pieces with impressive accuracy if they first learn how to practice. There are many effective practice techniques and numerous acceptable methods for presenting them. The following section includes suggestions for sequential and effective practicing.

### Engage in the discovery phase

An initial discovery phase that takes place before practicing begins allows the student to benefit from a pre-practice analysis of the new piece. The student may use this phase to identify and explore important areas of musical content, including:

- Historical elements such as time period and type of composition
- The form of the piece, noting repetition of sections
- The basic tonal structure of the piece
- Patterns in the music: rhythmic, melodic, and harmonic
- Technical challenges and fingering
- Musical elements such as phrasing, pedaling, articulations, and dynamics

During the discovery phase, the student shares her understanding of the job ahead with the teacher. This phase also provides the teacher the opportunity to discuss the musical and technical challenges facing the student. Questions posed by the teacher concerning details of the piece during this phase will help the student clarify her understanding of the piece and will set her on the right path for subsequent practice sessions.

### Sight-play the piece

Teachers often want to be sure a student likes a piece before she takes it home to practice, and therefore may believe it is important for her to hear the piece while at the lesson. This is understandable, but the student should always sight-play the piece herself (or sections of the piece if it is a particularly long composition) *before* the teacher plays it, or before listening to a recording. This allows the student to make independent discoveries about details of the piece without relying too heavily on listening to someone else's performance of it.

Sight-playing a new piece before hearing it reinforces the student's reading skills and encourages her to become an independent (and hopefully lifelong) learner of music. She will come to see the initial reading of the piece as her responsibility, time to gain basic information about the task ahead, while determining her personal feelings about the piece.

### Develop a plan for an aural approach to study

Students often get so involved with the notes on the page that they stop listening to the sounds they produce. Too often, true listening seems to go by the wayside. A conscientious teacher can guard against this by including listening activities in the lesson and practice plan. Each teacher must weigh the benefits and drawbacks to each activity, asking the following questions as she develops an aural facet to practice for her students:

**PART VII**

- At what point is it appropriate for the teacher to play the piece for the student?

- How often should the teacher model musical concepts in an assigned piece?

- When should recordings be introduced?

- How many recordings of a certain repertoire selection should the student hear?

- What recordings of similar repertoire (same composer, same era, or same type of piece) should the student hear?

- How can the teacher ensure that the student understands that listening to the performance of others is an important guide for her own personal choices, and not merely a model to be imitated without thought?

- How often should the student record and listen to her own practicing?

- What types of assessment tools can the teacher develop so that the student is able to listen insightfully to commercial recordings (CDs, MP3s, etc.), teacher performances, her own practicing, and recordings of her performances?

For more information on these topics and questions, please see Chapter 31, Developing the Ear.

## Assess practice sessions

Recorded practice sessions provide students with a strong assessment tool. As students listen to the recording, questions can help assess the effectiveness of the practice session.

- How do dynamics sound?

- Do phrases have a musical shape and direction?

- Is the tempo well-suited to the piece?

- Are balance and voicing effective?

- Is the pedal used appropriately?

- Are articulations produced consistently and in a stylistic manner?

A recorded practice session also demonstrates if practice time is used wisely. Bringing a recording of home practice to the lesson allows the teacher and student to assess practice techniques taught during the lesson.

## Understand expectations for accuracy

Teachers have varying expectations for accuracy from practice. Some insist on a high level of accuracy right from the start, expecting students to observe not only rhythms and pitches, but also musical details such as dynamic markings, articulations, and pedalings from the earliest stages of practice. Others feel the early stages of learning are meant to be exploratory and allow for experimentation of musical elements such as dynamics and articulations. Changing the articulations—playing a staccato passage legato, or a legato one staccato—is offered as a technical, musical, and creative tool for the student to explore.

Regardless of which approach a teacher takes, one thing seems true: no teacher wants a student to struggle with accuracy or arrive at each lesson with numerous errors. Low expectations for accuracy and musicality result in a student who thinks, "I just want to get the notes right now and I'll get the counting later," or "I'll think about articulations after the whole piece is learned." Addressing dynamics or articulations after the piece is "learned" is far different than experimenting with creative options during the learning process. Deciding to learn the rhythm after the pitches is similar to stating, "I just want to put up the walls now and I'll lay the foundation later."

Some teachers feel it is too much to expect complete accuracy early in the learning process, fearing students will become frustrated if expectations are too high. Certainly no teacher wants to foster feelings of frustration or inadequacy in a student, and teaching students solid practice habits actually has the opposite effect. When students know how to practice productively, they will feel less frustration and more satisfaction. Accuracy becomes a reasonable and realistic goal.

There are several reasons why a student may learn new pieces with only marginal accuracy:

- **The piece is too difficult:** If the piece is too difficult, it is wise for the teacher to admit the error in assigning the piece and put that piece on hold for a more appropriate time.

- **The student does not like the piece:** If the student dislikes a piece, it benefits everyone to look for a better choice. Students do not need to be tormented with a sonata that they dislike just because it is "time for a sonata." One caveat: the time for a student to request a new piece when the current one isn't liked is within the first week or two, not after six weeks of practice.

- **The student has not learned careful practice habits:** It is up to each teacher to ensure that her students have learned to practice effectively. It can take weeks and months of patience before a student consistently demonstrates good practice habits. Effective practicing is not a skill students will intuitively understand with no training.

- **The student has not learned basic musical or technical skills:** Teachers are also responsible for covering the basic skills required to learn pieces accurately and musically. Without a thorough mastery of basic skills, every lesson will be spent fixing mistakes instead of relying on a solidly learned foundation (discussed further in Part VIII).

- **Personal issues impede progress:** Family problems or school demands can easily disrupt steady progress and interfere with practice goals. These problems may be more difficult to address and require patience and understanding as solutions are sought that allow piano practice to improve.

If external factors beyond the teacher's control are not present, if repertoire is chosen carefully, if students are taught how to practice with discipline, and if they have a solid understanding of basic skills, students will be able to learn pieces with impressive accuracy right from the start.

## Make musical choices right from the start

Although I have stressed the importance of accuracy when practicing, the ultimate goal of accuracy is a musical and personal interpretation of the piece. Students need to be shown how to make good musical decisions about articulations, style, pedaling, dynamics, balance of melody and harmony,

**PART VII**

and other musical elements from the first moment they approach a piece. This will help ensure that musical reasoning becomes the background for every decision they make during practice. Naturally, as practicing continues, these musical decisions will evolve, come more into the foreground, and be refined.

## Be goal-oriented

Each time a student practices, she should have a practice goal in mind:

> "I will learn four measures flawlessly."

> "I will learn the second half of the third page at m.m. 144."

> "I will re-finger the passage that has given me trouble whenever I play at tempo."

Setting a specific goal and then achieving that goal gives the student a sense of accomplishment. Meeting specific goals steadily chips away at the immense amount of work to be done. Rather than focusing on the enormity of a long piece and all the pages yet to come, the student should focus on one attainable goal at a time. Once that goal is achieved, the student can set the next goal.

## Decide on hands-alone or hands-together practice

Teachers disagree on the value of hands-alone versus hands-together practice. Some teachers feel it is wise for a student to learn new pieces one hand at a time and then hands together; others feel it is best to learn the pieces hands-together from the start. Some teachers insist on hands-alone practice only to clear up trouble spots. To confuse the issue even more, some students seem to benefit more from one or the other approach, depending on their natural coordinative abilities and technical development. Every teacher must ultimately decide what she prefers, weighing advantages and disadvantages of each. It may be that a teacher will prefer a combination of both strategies, reserving the flexibility to recommend what works best for each student in her studio.

### HANDS-ALONE PRACTICE

**Advantages:** Students focus more on the exact details of each hand before facing the challenge of putting the hands together. They are less likely to ignore the music of one hand because they are distracted by what is happening in the other. Special attention can be given to the technique required of each hand.

**Disadvantages:** Students must use three steps rather than one to learn the piece (right-hand alone, left-hand alone, and hands-together). Also, hands-alone practice does not aid sight-playing and reading fluency. These skills require hands-together practice.

### HANDS-TOGETHER PRACTICE

**Advantages:** Students learn the piece as it is written from the beginning, rather than in steps. They are more likely to understand the musical content as a whole, and are more comfortable with the interaction of the hands right from the start. Practicing hands-together reinforces the student's ability to sight-play.

**Disadvantages:** Students may have difficulties with challenging sections, or may feel overwhelmed with certain passages. The content of each individual hand may not be learned or understood as solidly.

My personal choice is to have students learn new pieces hands-together. When my students follow the practice guidelines listed in this chapter, they are able to learn the music in each hand accurately while reading hands-together. Hands-together practice gives them a truer picture of the music, saves time in the long run, and improves their sight-playing abilities.

I do, however, teach my students the benefit of judicious hands-alone practice. Practicing with one hand at a time provides an invaluable tool for clarifying musically complex sections, conquering technically challenging passages, and solidifying memorization.

## Practice new material slowly

When the fingers finally are put to the keys, the teacher must impress upon the student the value of practicing new material at a slow tempo. Slow practice makes sense only when the student truly understands why it is needed: accuracy is expected and cannot be achieved when learning the material at a too-fast tempo. Slow practice gives the student the opportunity to notice the details of the music and to play with precision right from the start. It is not acceptable to learn a piece with 70% accuracy this week and 75% accuracy next week. Rather, the goal is to practice at a slow enough tempo to allow for impressive accuracy right from day one. Such accuracy is indeed attainable when a student has been given the right tools.

The biggest problem regarding slow practice is the word "slow." When I ask my students if they practice slowly, most insist that they do. When asked to demonstrate slow practice, they are off and running. The teacher can answer two important questions readily by observing a student practicing *slowly* during a lesson:

- How slow is "slow" to the student?

- How long does slow practice continue before the tempo increases?

Often, a student may practice slowly only briefly and then dramatically increase the miles-per-hour long before the material is learned, and far too soon for it to be secure. Miles-per-hour provides a good analogy for piano practicing: racing down a highway at 100 MPH affords less time to notice details and an increased likelihood of an accident. The same thing is true with practicing. Fast practice affords less time to notice details and increases the likelihood of an accident, or rather, of numerous accidents.

While slow practice is essential when first learning material, it also provides the best means to repair any trouble spots that crop up later. Technically challenging material also demands slow practice; a tough passage must be addressed slowly before it can ever be performed at tempo.

Naturally there comes a time for the student to increase the practice tempo; how else would she ever learn to play a fast piece up to tempo? How will she get a true sense of her final phrasing or dynamics if the piece is always practiced under tempo? What technical problems might she need to solve at a fast tempo that did not exist at a slower one? While it is understood that practice at tempo lies ahead, most students should devote far more time to slow practice before attempting any increase in tempo.

The metronome will be discussed in Chapter 26, but the value of working with this device is worth mentioning here. The metronome helps students to establish and maintain a slow tempo in the early stages of practice and also serves as a tool for setting systematic, incremental increases in speed as the piece is gradually learned at tempo.

**PART VII**

I have had this particular reminder on my studio bulletin board for many years:

*Slow practice – fast progress*

*Fast practice – slow progress*

*No practice – no progress*

## Practice new material in small, manageable sections

Initially dividing pieces into small sections gives students a manageable amount of material for daily practice. During early stages of learning, practicing a piece from beginning to end wastes valuable time. There is too much information for the brain to take in; mistakes will be made and mistakes will be learned.

When a student begins new repertoire by practicing the complete piece over and over, a few things may improve, but many reading errors, technical problems, and poor fingering choices may be cemented into the performance of a piece as well. Even worse, the student can become quite attached to those errors, liking an incorrect rhythm so much that it just cannot be undone.

In order for students to successfully practice in small sections, there are two areas worthy of clarification:

- The meaning of the word "small": Small might mean two measures, it might mean four measures, or it could mean one beat. If the student has bitten off more than she can chew, the section must be cut down to a size where the material can be learned accurately.

- The need to overlap sections: Each section that is practiced must begin with a few beats leading into that section and end with a few beats leading out of that section. These will be practiced along with the small section itself. As each new section is practiced, so are the overlapping beats, thus keeping the transitions from section to section seamless. Without practicing overlapping beats, students can learn individual sections flawlessly but get stuck transitioning from one section to the next.

## Use intelligent repetition

Intelligent repetition is a key ingredient in careful practicing. Playing a section once a day for 15 days will provide only a small fraction of the learning success achieved by practicing the same section 15 times in a row, in one practice session. But students must be taught the art of mindful repetition. It is not enough to tell them to practice five times in a row, or even to say "play it over and over again until you know it."

The difference between thoughtless repetition and mindful, engaged repetition is enormous. Repetition while on autopilot wastes time and ultimately leads to boredom, while producing minimal results. Conversely, mindful repetition produces maximum results and is defined with words like "focused, engaged, thoughtful, musical, purpose-driven, intelligent, exacting, and goal-oriented." Such repetition produces maximum results because the mind is totally engaged with the details of the music. As the section is repeated, there is time to concentrate on all details: fingering, pedaling, notes, timing, phrasing, dynamics, articulations, balance, melodic lines, and harmony.

Not only must repetition be mindful, it must be employed for longer than most students realize. Most students stop practicing a section far too soon. After playing the section correctly a few times, students often feel they have mastered it, when in fact they have just experienced some good luck or momentary success. Sections need to be practiced correctly many times in order to learn them securely.

### Spend time with the big picture

Setting goals and practicing small sections within a piece are valuable practice strategies, but understanding the big picture is just as important. Sections need to be put together like a set of musical building blocks, with the blocks forming a flexible sculpture that can be worked and reworked. As the piece gets closer to performance readiness, the student will likely find that the remaining practicing is highly gratifying. Teachers should gently guide students in this very personal and creative process, always with the goal of helping them to be as independent as possible.

### Enjoy the process, not just the product

Perhaps the best advice for effective practicing is to enjoy the process. If students can be taught to take pleasure in practice and to understand the gratifying benefits of dedicated and deliberate practice, they will be sold on its rewards. Practicing becomes productive and fulfilling rather than boring or frustrating.

### Understand that all practice and no play makes Jane a dull girl

Not all practicing need be serious or goal-oriented. Setting aside piano time to "goof off," play duets with friends, jam, sight-play, revisit old favorites, and "play" rather than practice, is fun and gratifying. Such time serves as a reminder that the better one practices, the more fun one can have!

## Observation of Student Practice

When the above practice guidelines are presented to a student, it then becomes important to monitor that they are indeed being used. If a student comes to a lesson insisting that she has practiced a section according to all of my guidelines, but it just isn't improving, I often ask her to practice for me in the lesson for 15 to 30 minutes. She is told that I will not be saying anything while she practices and will not answer questions or make comments, but will merely observe her as she works.

The results are revealing. One student may attempt too large a section to master well. Another may practice far too quickly. Another may be careless about details, and not seem to care about accuracy. Many play a section a few times and then move to the next section long before the first is mentally cemented, leaving little chance for retention. Some seem truly confused about how to practice.

Even when I have given my students guidelines for practicing, I know I must teach this important skill repeatedly until the student demonstrates a musical, thorough, mindful, and consistent approach. If a student doesn't "get it" after I first explain the details, it isn't my invitation to give up, but rather a sign that I need to engage in some mindful repetition of my own. When I finally observe a student execute 15 to 30 minutes of careful practice, I can be assured that she has finally internalized the how-to's of good practice.

## Parental Involvement with Practice

Parental involvement with practice can be a sensitive topic. Unsupportive parents may ignore their children's involvement with music, never showing any appreciation for their efforts. On the other extreme is the overly involved parent, one who shows the child how to play every piece and demonstrates every rhythm. Neither of these extremes is desirable. It may be obvious that teachers want parents to show interest in their child's musical training, but it needs to be equally clear that too much involvement actually sabotages a child's musical success.

Although parents may be well intentioned, too much help actually works against the student; she will grow to need help in order to learn. I can recall a few transfer students who came to their first lessons delightfully well prepared. When it came time to sight-play a piece or tap a rhythm, those students were suddenly at a loss, and demonstrated abilities far below that displayed in their prepared pieces. It wasn't hard to discover that their parents played their pieces for them and showed them how to execute every passage. The students did not need to figure out anything on their own and consequently couldn't!

Just as teachers must be diligent about training students in the art of practicing, they must also be conscientious about training parents to be a supportive parent. Part of that support means stepping back and allowing the student to learn independently.

# Resources

Bernstein, Seymour. *With Your Own Two Hands.* Portland: Manduca Music Publications, 1981.

> Focusing on myriad issues concerning piano practice, this book is divided into three sections. Part One covers various elements of practicing, such as why we do and don't practice, concentration, and sub-areas including fingering, mistakes, and sight-reading. Part Two deals with tempo, listening, and many aspects of technique, such as arm weight, finger motion, and pedaling, and Part Three discusses performing and performance issues concerning anxiety and memorization.

Breth, Nancy O'Neill. *The Parent's Guide to Effective Practicing.* Milwaukee: Hal Leonard Corporation, 2007.

> This guide is a tool for parents to help their children build good practice habits. It brings together a variety of widely used practice tips, written in a way that is easy for children to understand. Parents who use this guide regularly, even if they have limited time or little knowledge of music, can greatly improve the quality of their children's practice sessions.

Breth, Nancy O'Neill. *The Piano Student's Guide to Effective Practicing.* Milwaukee: Hal Leonard Corporation, 2004.

> *The Piano Student's Guide to Effective Practicing* offers helpful suggestions for utilizing practice time and building productive practice habits. It helps solve specific problems with 58 concise practice tips, clearly-explained drills, and tactics for mastering challenging passages. The practice tips are matched to appropriate overall categories including accuracy, articulation, balance, continuity, coordination, evenness, expression, fingering, memory, pedal, rhythm, and speed.

> Practice tips abound that offer creative approaches to learning and polishing a piece. Requiring students to own this one short guide, and then working with them until they understand how and when to follow the suggestions, helps foster the independence needed when practicing.

Bruser, Madeline. ***The Art of Practicing: A Guide to Making Music from the Heart.*** New York: Bell Tower, 1997.

Bruser describes the difference between regimented, tedious practice and the kind of practice that is a joyful expression of self. Her book presents practice as a means of cultivating free and natural movement, listening techniques, and an open mind to acquire a personal understanding and enjoyment of the music being studied and performed. The book is divided into three parts: The Starting Point, A Ten-Step Approach, and Natural Command, with chapters such as Struggle and Freedom, Basic Mechanics, The Spark of Inquisitiveness, Pure Perception, and Playing by Heart.

Corragio, Peter, with Jon J. Murakami, illustrator. ***The Art of Piano Performance: Perfect Practice.*** San Diego: Neil A Kjos Music Co., 1997.

Written in a comic book format with cartoon characters, this book offers practical guidance to intermediate students on establishing practice habits that lead to timely and accurate learning.

Johnston, Philip. ***Practiceopedia.*** Pearce, Australia: PracticeSpot Press, 2006.

Billing itself as "the complete illustrated guide to mastering music's greatest challenge…" this book offers 367 pages of practice techniques, tricks, and tips. ***Practiceopedia*** is written for students and parents and offers a multitude of suggestions in an easily accessible format for student musicians. Teachers will appreciate the emphasis on enabling students to develop their own workable practice habits. Visit www.practiceopedia.com for a complete tour of the book.

Provost, Richard. ***The Art and Technique of Practice.*** San Francisco: Guitar Solo Publications, 1992.

The 45 pages in this short book emphasize that successful practice involves physical, musical, mental, and aural elements. The first chapter discusses the setting of goals and organizing productive practicing. Subsequent chapters deal with preparation techniques, memorization, visualization, note-reading, interpretive practice, problem solving when practicing, repertoire maintenance, and developing reading and listening skills. This book offers a quick-reading summary of good practice habits.

Snitkin, Harvey, Ph.D. ***Practice for Young Musicians: You are Your Own Teacher***, Revised and expanded edition. Niantic: HMS Publications, Inc., 1997.

Although older students might find the approach a bit young, this book offers students a well-paced and easy-to-read guide to practicing. The five sections in the book include Part One, You Are Your Teacher; Part Two, Planning Your Musical Travel; Part Three, Methods of Practicing: The Rewards of Good Planning; Part Four, The Arrival: Your Destination; Part Five, Your Teacher's Manual: Teaching Tips and Suggestions. The book offers students a well-thought-out plan for diligent, productive, and independent practicing.

**PART VII**

# Chapter 22

# THE ART OF MEMORIZATION

---

Memorizing can often be the most painful part of preparing a piece for a performance, and the most stressful part of performing itself. If a student is ill-trained, it can also be extremely time-consuming. When memorization is required, students often complain; even college piano majors sometimes grumble, "Why…?" Because of this, an increasing number of teachers today forego requiring memorization for student recitals in the hopes of establishing a more relaxed experience for the student or to accommodate the limited practice hours of overscheduled students. Although this approach can indeed take away some of the time and stress of being required to perform from memory, it also deprives students of the benefits of learning to memorize:

- Memorization fosters a more complete understanding of the total content of a composition.

- Students who memorize develop a higher level of discipline during practice. Understanding this, some teachers insist on memorization even though their student will be allowed to use music in the recital.

- Memorization enhances musicality. A carefully memorized piece has been studied far more thoroughly than an unmemorized piece, allowing the performer to become more intimately involved with the musical content.

- Performers of securely memorized music are able to focus more deeply on the beauty, emotion, and excitement they are creating. Many teachers feel that once students detach themselves from the written notes, they are more able to play the music in an expressive manner. Think of an actor, holding the script onstage and reading lines while trying to act. It is when the lines are memorized that the person is able to act to their fullest ability.

- No one knows which students will become serious about music. If a student wishes to perform in a competition, audition, or solo recital, performing from memory will be necessary. Students who decide to major in music, but who have never performed from memory in a recital during the formative years, will have a difficult time memorizing college-level repertoire. It is short-sighted of teachers to limit a student's potential or musical options by never requiring memorization.

## Types of Memory

The pianist relies on various interdependent types of memory when performing memorized repertoire: analytic/cognitive, tactile/kinesthetic, aural, and visual.

### Analytic/Cognitive
Analytic or cognitive memory is used to understand and remember the details of a composition. The brain is engaged to memorize the musical content and structure of a piece. Using analysis to commit a piece to memory means employing cognitive skills: applying the power of the brain to analyze,

understand, and recall the music. Students who have developed a clear analytic understanding of the content of a piece while memorizing have internalized the elements essential to a strong performance.

### Tactile/Kinesthetic

Performances go by far too quickly for the mind to think about each individual note. Tactile memory is an essential tool for pianists, as the body eventually must know instinctively what to do next. Even the strongest approach to analytic memory does not negate the need for a secure tactile or muscular sense of the piece. Initially approaching a piece using analytic memory does not deny the need for tactile memory; it just delays developing that intuitive, kinesthetic sense until after the content of the piece is learned thoroughly, giving the student a grounded and secure grasp of the musical content. As a piece is more securely learned, tactile/kinesthetic motions become more automatic, allowing for increased spontaneity and creativity at the keyboard.

### Aural

Having a strong aural memory of the forward motion of a piece shapes the expectations for the sounds that are to be produced. When a melodic interval or harmonic progression is anticipated before it is played, aural memory is used to reinforce cognitive memory. Students who hear a third in the melody or a minor chord in the harmony before it is played have a far greater chance of success and a much smaller risk of "blanking out."

### Visual

Many visual learners have a visual memory of the piece, actually "seeing" the music as they play, including a mental image of each page of the music or each movement on the keyboard. Security at the keyboard is greatly strengthened for those with this visual recall.

## Teaching Memorization

How is the initial memorization done? Students are often told, "Now go home and memorize this," when they actually need to be given specific guidance about how to tackle such a confusing task. In my early teaching I would ask my students "to go home and memorize" a piece. They often returned with real delight, "Well, I just tried playing it without the music and found out it was already memorized!" This is not memorizing. It is remembering, and the problem with remembering is that you can forget. Such recall is not an active process, but rather a passive one, like remembering someone's name now but forgetting it later.

Memorization can be approached in a variety of ways, but the one way that does not work well is mindless repetition. When a piece is played over and over again with fingers flying and the mind only marginally focused, the student sets herself up for inevitable memory slips. In recital, suddenly she *does* think and her mind *is* engaged. She starts to question every upcoming passage, or wonder about the next chord, and voila! Blank out.

Solid memorization is a combination of analytic/cognitive, tactile/kinesthetic, aural, and visual memories all working together. Every student and teacher will have a stronger or dominant form of memory, but learning to use all forms produces a more solidly memorized piece.

## Memorization Using Analytic/Cognitive Skills

One presenter I heard at a state music teachers' conference a number of years ago suggested memorizing the piece as it is first learned, thereby combining learning and memorizing into one procedure. The thinking behind this system is that when memorization takes place while the piece is first being learned, the memory is more cognitive and less tactile. Conversely, if a piece is repeated over and over before memorization begins, the fingers learn where to go but the content of the piece may not be understood as thoroughly as it should be.

I decided to try this new approach to memorization and I followed the presenter's advice on concurrent learning and memorization by incorporating many of my own guidelines for effective practice. I began by thoroughly studying the first two measures of a new piece. I looked for melodic patterns, reviewed the harmonies, and planned my fingerings. I studied dynamics, articulations, and pedalings. The first few beats of measure three were included as I studied measures one and two, so that I had an overlapping section between the two measures I was currently working on and the two I would study next.

As I played these two and a half measures slowly a number of times, I kept my mind totally engaged on all aspects of the musical content, reviewing notes, rhythms, patterns, harmonies, fingerings, dynamics, pedalings, and articulations as well as listening to the sounds I was producing. In other words, my brain was actively learning all the details of those measures while my hands were first beginning to develop a tactile memory of the piece. The memorization process started immediately, including an aural and visual memory of the measures. I did not stop working on those few measures until I could consistently play them from memory with complete accuracy. I then continued to learn and memorize the rest of the piece in small, overlapping sections. I was surprised at how well I learned the piece and how much more confident my memory was in performance.

An analytic approach to memory does not work alone. If a piece is only played slowly or in small sections, the student will not develop the tactile memory needed to succeed in performance. Tactile, visual, and aural memory all eventually work in connection with the analytic memory in order for a performance to be technically comfortable and musically pleasing.

## Memorization Using Tactile/Kinesthetic Skills

Regardless of what type of memory skill is strongest in a student, every performance is strengthened by tactile memory. A strong tactile memory contributes to comfort at the keyboard. Many pieces are far too fast or complex for the mind to give conscious signals for each note. Tactile memory directs the hands and provides a sense of security at the keyboard.

A word of caution needs to be given to students who rely primarily on tactile memory. Tactile or muscular memory works fine as long as the fingers go where they should. If any notes are missed, however, the finger motion is interrupted and there may be trouble getting back to the correct finger patterns. To compound the issue, if the brain has not developed a deep enough understanding of the piece, or the ear has not developed a strong aural sense of the musical movement, the student may be unable to continue. Too much time may have been spent repeating the piece in order to get it in the fingers, and not enough time supporting that memory with cognitive, aural, and visual memories.

### The role of fingering in tactile memory

There are at least two schools of thought with regard to memorizing fingerings:

1) One fixed and carefully planned set of fingerings should be memorized. Many times memory mistakes are not really lapses in memory at all, but rather strange fingering choices that throw the fingers off-course. If a student uses multiple fingerings while learning a piece, none of them becomes strongly ingrained, and an unexpected fingering that occurs in performance leaves the student short a finger in a run or unable to reach a chord. Multiple fingerings weaken the tactile sense and lead to unanticipated and unusable surprise fingerings in performance.

2) It is valuable to plan and execute more than one set of fingerings. By being able to use multiple fingerings (which must nonetheless be well-planned), the performer is less likely to depend on a single tactile approach to the music. The ability to perform with multiple choices for fingerings also means that the musical content has been solidly memorized.

Regardless of which of these approaches is chosen, the main point of both is that fingering is never random, but rather must be well-planned and intelligently conceived. Strong fingering habits aid tactile memory.

## Memorization Using Aural Skills

Developing a strong aural sense of a piece is essential for a secure performance. Students who hear the music before it is to be played receive strong aural cues that trigger properly memorized music. Aural memory provides a strong tool for overcoming a memory slip, should one occur, as the student "hears" what music should come next and can move forward and away from the slip.

Teachers wishing to reinforce aural memory can start by introducing ear-training and aural skills to students at a young age and continuing such exposure throughout their musical study. The more the ear is developed, the more it will aid with the memory process.

The student who couples an aural memory of the melodic and harmonic structure of the piece with the memory of musical interpretations is engaged on a deep level with the sounds she is making. This student focuses on listening when playing from memory and is able to concentrate on playing musically rather than on concerns about missing a note or an upcoming difficult passage.

As with other forms of memory, aural memory cannot stand alone, but is aided by a strong cognitive understanding of the piece, a secure tactile sense, and the support of visual memory.

## Memorization Using Visual Skills

Some students have such a strong visual sense of memory that they actually "see" the score, as if by photographic memory. A strong visual memory also aids with security at the keyboard. The visual learner sees not only how the printed patterns of the page look, but also how the hands move at the keyboard.

PART VII

ırner may easily be thrown off-guard if the eyes travel differently than their normal
ing a performance. Mistakes can occur if a visual person normally looks at the right hand
passage and for some reason looks at the left hand or looks up during a performance.

o assist students with visual memory is to have them learn to recognize patterns in the
music. When the eye learns to quickly see a melodic, harmonic, or rhythmic pattern as a unit, that
recognition serves as a foundation for visual memory. Having the student describe what they see
when they first look at a piece helps them to realize that they can respond to strong visual cues
before they ever hear the music or develop a tactile sense of the piece.

Developing each student's ability to "see" the music is a strong aid to accurate memorization, especially when used in tandem with the other forms of memory.

## Memorization Assists

To assist with memorization, a number of proven memorization "tricks" have been utilized for years.

- Memorize in small overlapping sections.

- Memorize sections in varying order. Sections can be learned by moving backward from
  the end, in random order, from the beginning, by musical phrases, or with similarities of
  form or structure.

- Look for patterns within the music to assist with memory. Rebecca Shockley's *Mapping
  Music: For Faster Learning and Secure Memory* provides a helpful guide for recognizing
  patterns, mapping those patterns, and developing a roadmap for successfully study and
  memorization.

- Repeat sections until they are securely learned. This usually takes longer than most
  students realize. Be sure that repetition is mindful, focused, thoughtful, and engaged.

- Do daily review of previously memorized sections.

- Play the piece extremely slowly in order to check memory, taking away the perpetual
  motion of the fingers and relying more on knowledge in the brain giving directions for
  what to play next. This often points out weak spots that need extra attention.

- Play one hand on the keys and one hand on the wood above the keys, to see how well
  each part is actually learned. This is especially valuable when testing the harmony hand,
  since most pianists are more likely to have a slip in a harmony line than a melody line.

- Change something about the playing, such as making legato passages staccato, or forte
  passages piano.

- Make a copy of the piece and cut the copy into measures. Place all the cut-up pieces
  into a bag and them pull them at random from the bag, playing the piece from that
  particular measure onward.

## The Ultimate Goal

Total security is the ultimate goal of careful memorization. If a student is secure with only 90% of the memorization, she will feel an uncomfortable sense of insecurity during 10% of her performance. This does not mean that the teacher should demand 100% accuracy in a performance; after all, unexpected mistakes can happen. It only means that walking onstage with a piece that has been memorized with 10% insecurity guarantees an uncomfortable performance experience.

If having a piece 100% securely memorized seems unattainable or overly demanding, remember that it is a goal, not a decree. When students have been taught to memorize well and when standards are set high, they will be more likely to feel positive about their memorization experience, especially when they have been given the tools to succeed. Their memory can be better trusted because their analytic/cognitive, tactic/kinesthetic, aural, and visual memories are all working together.

Teachers who explore research in the area of memorization will discover even more varied and useful approaches to memorization. Additional resources are listed in Chapter 23.

## Resource

Shockley, Rebecca Payne. *Mapping Music: For Faster Learning and Secure Memory, A Guide for Piano Teachers and Students.* Middleton: A-R Editions, 1997, 2001.

> As an aid for reading and memorizing music, Shockley outlines a system allowing teachers and students to quickly recognize and "map" patterns in music. Students are encouraged to review the score away from the piano and draw a map of the basic musical content of the piece. By using graphic notation and harmonic indicators, the outline of the piece can be presented in a clear, straightforward manner. Shockley emphasizes the value of functional skills such as sight-reading, harmonization, transposition, playing by ear, and improvising, and maintains that strengthening these skills reinforces good reading and memorization. The book is full of clear examples of mapping, from early level repertoire through advanced repertoire, plus special applications, such as mapping problem passages. A section for using mapping in teaching includes suggestions for private and group lessons.

**PART VII**

# Chapter 23

# THE ART OF PERFORMANCE

Teaching our students to practice correctly and to memorize proficiently is not enough. If we expect them to perform well, whether in the family living room or a national competition, we must first teach them to perform with poise and confidence. Performance is actually a skill that we must nurture and teach all on its own.

## Performance Anxiety

Performance anxiety affects many, if not all, pianists at some point in their musical careers, and students certainly may feel anxious before or during a recital. Hands may sweat, the heart may race, and a feeling of uneasiness or fear pays an unpleasant visit. The adrenaline rush that many students feel as a result of performance anxiety is unexpected and powerful.

What happens when students have not been properly coached in the art of performance?

- They may stop when there is a mistake or start the piece over.

- They may need to fix the mistake before being able to continue.

- They may be so surprised by an unexpected mistake that the security of the remaining performance is sabotaged.

- Their insecurity may diminish the musicality of their performance.

- Their anxiety and negative performing experiences may overcome their enjoyment of performing to the point that some may even refuse to perform again.

## Teaching Students to Perform

A critical step in helping deal with performance anxiety is to teach students the skills they need to perform successfully in public, which is quite different from performing for oneself or in a lesson. Just as teachers cannot assume that students know how to practice or memorize, they must never assume students know how to perform. Suggestions for successful performing include the following:

### Focus on musical issues

Teachers can build students' confidence in their performance abilities by teaching them to focus on musical issues. By focusing on musical elements such as dynamics, phrasing, articulations, and rubato, students will be less likely to worry about note accuracy or memory slips.

### "Perfection" can be elusive

There are no guarantees of a flawless performance, no matter how many times a piece has been played flawlessly prior to a performance. Like the gifted ice skater who falls in the Olympics during a difficult or even a routine jump, a student can experience an unexpected slip when performing. Teachers need to let students know that although they expect them to learn pieces with accuracy, that goal is not the same as demanding that they perform them with total accuracy. After all, we are all human. Teaching students to strive for the most polished and musical performance possible, without letting them feel they have failed should they fall short of a "perfect" performance, is a vital part of succeeding in a performance setting.

### Do not repeat, fix, or stop

Fixing a mistake onstage interrupts the rhythm of the piece and does not fix anything, as the error has already occurred. Not stopping or fixing during a performance is a skill that must be practiced. Repeating tough spots many times until they are securely learned is wise practice advice, but it does not serve as performance advice. Understanding the difference is the key, and knowing when to shift back to *practicing* an insecure passage is crucial.

Students who must start over when a mistake occurs are on autopilot. They do not have enough mental or aural mastery of the piece to comfortably accommodate a memory slip or a less-than-perfect passage. This is definitely a scary place to be. All students can be taught to continue playing without stopping, fixing, or restarting for any reasons as they practice the performance phase of learning a piece.

### Learn to cover

Should a slip occur, the mishap needs to be absorbed into the performance so that the audience is unaware it occurred. This covering is part thinking-on-one's-feet and part improvising within the musical content of the piece, and it is an essential performance skill that must be taught and practiced at lessons. By practicing covering prior to performance, students can learn that this skill will help them to come out of the trouble spot and back to a more secure passage with poise and confidence. The more students practice the art of covering, the more skilled they will be at successfully camouflaging mishaps onstage, should they occur.

### Practice performing in performance classes

An excellent place to practice performing is during a performance class for students only. Performance classes give students the opportunity to experience the sensations felt when performing in front of others, but in the company of peers who are all facing the same experience. Students may feel nervousness similar to that felt in a recital, but these jitters feel less threatening in the more comfortable environment of the studio. Performance classes also give students the opportunity to find weak spots before they occur in a recital, festival, or competition. Home practice won't always identify such a weakness, but performance in front of others often does. It is far better to discover that a passage isn't secure during a performance class than when performing in recital.

## Final Tips

Below are some final tips to help students take control of their performance anxiety:

- Precede the student's performance with a system of careful practice, thorough learning, and meticulous memorization.

- Contribute to the student's sense of self-confidence and relaxation by reinforcing the positive thinking necessary for a secure performance.

**PART VII**

- Coach the student to avoid negative thoughts during a performance as well as distracting or irrelevant thoughts.

- Encourage the student to focus on the present moment—what is being performed and the musical sounds being created.

- Help the student to use imagery before a recital to assist a confident performance. By visualizing the external performance setting and the internal physical process of performing successfully, the student will anticipate a positive performance experience. Imagery includes visualizing feeling calm, confident, and secure while performing.

- Teach relaxation techniques, breathing techniques, and biofeedback to help the student relax the muscles as well as the mind. For more information on such techniques, check the resources listed below.

Today's teachers are fortunate to have an abundance of reference books on the subject of performance that go far beyond general memorization issues, addressing emotional, behavioral, or physical causes of anxiety. They serve as excellent resources for self-help techniques such as biofeedback, imagery exercises, and desensitization to stress.

# Resources

Caldwell, Robert. *The Performer Prepares.* Dallas: Pst. Inc, 1990.

Stating that "your performance begins in your imagination," this book offers guided exercises and questions to help develop imagination, skill, and comfort with performing. Stressing that many different and unique approaches are possible, the reader is directed to seek a personal method of performing by asking and answering directed questions about the actions and outcomes faced when preparing for a performance. The book is easy to read and includes performers (Sally, Shirley, Richard, et al) who face challenges with performing or stagefright.

Chase, Mildred Portney. *Just Being at the Piano.* Berkeley: Creative Arts Book Co., 1985.

Chase offers her personal insights into achieving a meaningful experience at the piano, describing time spent at the instrument as an "ego-less" focus on the sound being produced. This is a self-help book for pianists, centered on developing a positive attitude at the piano while becoming aware of one's body and movements. Chase offers helpful tips on technique, practice, reading, rhythm, listening, and tone production. The book is flavored with a spiritual and encouraging approach to the piano.

Corragio, Peter, with Jon J. Murakami, illustrator. *The Art of Piano Performance: Imagery In Music.* San Diego: Neil A. Kjos Music Co., 2000.

Written in a comic-book format with cartoon characters, this book serves as a mini-dictionary of essential Italian terms of tempo, character, and spirit. It uses humorous pictures to demonstrate differences in terms, such as the difference between *forte* ($f$), *fortissimo* ($ff$), and *fortississimo* ($fff$).

Elson, Margret. *Passionate Practice: The Musician's Guide to Learning, Memorizing and Performing.* Oakland: Regent Press, 2002.

Using biofeedback techniques first employed to diminish migraine headaches, the author speaks of learning to practice, memorize, and perform with less stress and more relaxation. Focusing on learning as an auditory, visual, and kinesthetic experience, this short book is packed with helpful exercises meant to take the musician from learning, to memorizing, to performing with security and confidence.

Green, Barry. *The Mastery of Music.* New York: Broadway Books, 2003.

Green interviewed musicians from all walks of the profession for this practical insight into mastering musical performance: jazz musicians, classical musicians, virtuoso soloists, conductors, orchestral musicians, and even orchestra management. The results brought Green to what he calls, "Ten Pathways to True Artistry": Communication, Courage, Discipline, Fun, Passion, Tolerance, Concentration, Confidence, Ego and Humility, and Creativity. These serve as the titles for the chapters of the book, each filled with insights offered by the various musicians, and interwoven into a well-paced and well-organized summary by Green. Any performing musician cannot help but find personally meaningful inspiration from amongst the many conversations related in this book.

Green, Barry, and Timothy Gallwey. *The Inner Game of Music.* New York: Doubleday, 1986.

The basic principle behind *The Inner Game of Music* is that a performance is influenced not just by potential (innate ability), but also by the interferences one allows to undermine potential. The book offers suggestions on ways to control such inner influences. Words such as trust, power, experience, focus, feelings, awareness, listening, goals, understanding, acceptance, and choice all appear often in this book, and give the reader an insight into its positive nature. One chapter, "Letting Go," offers helpful insights on how to allow oneself to experience playing in ways never dreamt possible. Suggestions are offered for heightening one's experience, both while performing and while practicing. The book offers a mixture of practical advice and inspiration, with helpful exercises throughout. An *Inner Game of Music* video and workbook are also available.

Hagberg, Karen A. *Stage Presence from Head to Toe: A Manual for Musicians.* Lanham: The Scarecrow Press, Inc., 2003.

This 109-page manual lives up to its name and covers numerous details of stage presence, from proper dress to proper bowing. The author encourages performers to project respect for the music, the audience, other musicians, and themselves through the use of proper stage presence. Some of the many areas covered include raising expectations with an entrance, overcoming annoying physical habits, not reacting to mistakes, the challenges of playing from memory, and acknowledging applause. Chapters address the issues relevant to the soloist, the page-turner, the small ensemble, the large vocal ensemble, and the orchestra, as well as auditions and competitions. A final chapter gives helpful advice on how to teach stage presence.

Provost, Richard. *The Art and Technique of Performance.* San Francisco: Guitar Solo Publications, 1992.

Similar to *The Art and Technique of Practice*, this short and practical book serves as an excellent summary of performance issues. Chapters include "Pre-Concert Preparation," "Performance Anxiety," "Reducing and Controlling Performance Anxiety," "Techniques for Minimizing Performance Anxiety," "Practicing to Perform," and "Teaching Techniques to Lessen Performance Anxiety." Designed for performers on any instrument, this book covers the basic areas related to controlling performance anxiety.

Ristad, Eloise. *A Soprano on Her Head: Right-Side-Up Reflections on Life and Other Performances.* Moab: Real People Press, 1982.

Ristad offers a fresh approach to dealing with the challenges of music, from taming those inner judges to freeing oneself to the "joyous intensity and unselfconscious spontaneity" that is possible through music. She encourages each musician to experience the inner clown by letting go of impossible demands and seeing humor in any situation instead. Understanding that there are many "right" answers to technique and other music-related issues, she encourages musicians to find their own ever-changing personal truths. Chapters offer humorous titles such as "Maybe I Should Just Keep Bees," "Maybe I Like My Problems," and "So You Were a Flop" while addressing significant issues.

**PART VII**

## Resources (cont.)

Triplett, Robert. *Stagefright: Letting It Work for You.* Lanham: Rowman & Littlefield Publishers, Inc., 1983.

This text offers insight into why performers are affected by stagefright and how to deal with it when it occurs. One particularly helpful chapter, "Voices from the Other Side," describes certain personalities such as The Critic, The Weakling, and The Doubter, and offers suggestions on how to transform those personalities into The Mentor, The Discoverer, and the Truster. The second part of the book deals with the practice of overcoming stagefright and offers helpful exercises and suggestions on nutrition for performers.

Wesney, William. *The Perfect Wrong Note: Learning to Trust Your Musical Self.* New York: Amadeus Press, 2003; Milwaukee: Hal Leonard Corporation, 2006.

William Westney focuses on ways to rediscover one's own path to the natural, transcendent fulfillment of making music. The book is geared toward teachers, professionals, and students of any instrument, as well as parents and music lovers of all ages. Westney offers healthy alternatives for lifelong learning and suggests significant change in the way music is taught.

# Chapter 24

# STUDIO RECITALS

Most teachers offer studio recitals once or twice a year, sometimes more frequently. Some choose to offer informal recitals in their homes if the studio allows enough room for seating. This is similar to a performance class, except that family and friends are invited to attend. In this setting, teachers may ask students to announce the title and composer of their pieces rather than have a printed program, and students may be allowed to use their music. Teachers may also choose to hold recitals in a more formal setting such as a recital hall or church, using printed programs and requiring students to memorize all pieces. Whether casual or formal, teachers should be sure that these events provide students with a positive performance experience.

## Recital Repertoire

There is an art to choosing recital pieces.

- **Pick a piece the student likes:** A decision to stick with a piece because it is "a good choice" and the student will "learn to like it" may be regretted as the recital approaches and the student has yet to demonstrate the necessary enthusiasm or commitment.

- **Avoid excessively challenging pieces:** Although all teachers hope to challenge their students, a piece that is too difficult creates undue stress in a recital.

- **Take advantage of ensemble music:** If students seem hesitant about performing, they might feel more confident playing duets or trios in the recital setting. Ensembles also take away from the solitude of recital preparation by adding an element of social music making.

- **Alternate repertoire:** Avoid featuring the same pieces year after year; repeating pieces only once every three to four years keeps the recital interesting to students and parents alike.

- **Incorporate less familiar pieces and composers into the program:** The most famous compositions should be included only sparingly, if at all. Each performance of "Für Elise" is doomed to a flood of unspoken critiques from members of the audience, who through the years have become "Für Elise" aficionados. Performing new or less familiar repertoire allows each student's performance to be accepted on its own terms while providing fresh, new material to be enjoyed by the listeners.

### Themed Recitals

Themed recitals offer another approach to a varied recital experience, especially when students are allowed to pick the theme. Themed recitals can be planned around a multitude of topics, and could be the culmination of a semester's focus on that topic. If each year included one themed semester of study accompanied by a themed recital, imagine the gratification teachers and students would experience as they explored new realms of music together! (It is not necessary that all work for a particular semester centers on the theme. Rather, the theme represents a special focus area for a given time period.)

The possibilities for themes are endless:

- American composers

- Jazz

- Seasonal music (culminating in a seasonal party)

- Broadway hits

- Contemporary music

- Baroque music (or any historical period)

- Original student compositions

- Mozart (or any composer)

- World music

- Dance music

- Movie/TV music

Themed recitals open the doors to additional educational activities. For example, a recital on dances could include research into period dances from historical eras, as well as less familiar ethnic dances from around the world. To add to the recital, students might give a description or demonstration of their dance, sharing a bit of its history and of the composer's approach to the dance. Foods related to the ethnic origins of the music performed could be prepared for the recital reception, and students might even dress in the national costume of their dance's country.

## Required vs. Optional Recitals

At one point in time, participation in recitals was expected; students taking piano lessons naturally participated in the studio recital. In more recent years, there has been a relaxation of this require-ment. Some teachers allow recital participation to be optional while others still expect that all students will participate in studio recitals.

I have heard of students refusing to perform in a recital at the last moment. My hope would be that those students who have been given pieces they love and who have been well prepared by their teacher will take pride in participating in a studio recital.

## Memorization in Recitals

As stated in Chapter 22, it is difficult to predict which student will end up loving piano so much that she may someday perform in competition or in a solo recital. If memorization is never required in recital, students will be at a real disadvantage should they major in music. Although my voice was one of the many moaning about the need to memorize during my college years, I wholeheartedly recom-mend that students have the opportunity to perform from memory in recital.

## Preparation Timeline

Students need a timeline for recital preparation. Too many students will delay completing memorization or polishing a piece until the very last week before a recital, which is just too late. The whole process of memorizing and polishing needs to be completed well in advance of the recital in order to ensure success in performance. Teachers should set specific benchmarks for students to follow that lead toward a goal of having recital pieces memorized a minimum of three weeks in advance for elementary/intermediate-level pieces. Advanced students should be required to complete memorization even earlier.

## Performance Classes

Holding regular performance classes in advance of a recital provides students with a valuable tool for comfort and security in recital. As mentioned in Chapter 23, regular performance classes (attended by the teacher and students only) have numerous benefits:

- Performance classes provide students with the opportunity to experience the sensations felt during a performance in front of a group.

- Students become familiar with how an adrenaline rush feels and learn to use it to their advantage.

- Weak spots are discovered and dealt with while there is still time.

- Students can practice performing without stopping or fixing.

- Students can develop the skill of covering errors.

- The informal, supportive environment gives students opportunities to develop into comfortable and confident performers before the recital date.

## Stage Presence

### Basic Etiquette

Students must be taught good stage presence. In competitions, I am often amazed to see a student who has been obviously well-taught, performs beautifully, and yet has no sense of proper stage etiquette. Regardless of whether a recital is casual or formal, students need to look and act professionally. The following is a list of stage etiquette tips to go over with each student prior to the recital:

- Walk confidently to the piano, always approaching it from the keyboard side rather than the back end of the instrument.

- Smile as you walk to the piano. Regardless of how serious the piece is, look enthusiastic about being onstage.

- Stop at the front edge of the piano, turn to the audience, and bow.

- Bow with your arms at your sides and feet together. (Girls: Curtseys belong in the 18th century or ballet recitals. Boys: Do not hold your stomach as you bow, as this looks like you are about to throw up.)

- When performing duets, decide ahead of time how to approach the bench to sit.

**PART VII**

- Adjust the bench if necessary (up or down, and forward or backward).

- Place your feet on the pedals if pedal will be used.

- Put your hands in your lap and wait about five seconds before putting them on the keys.

- Put your hands on the keys and wait another five seconds. (This serves two functions: it keeps a student from plunging in before she is mentally ready, and prevents accidental starts in the wrong place on the keyboard.)

- At the end of a piece, keep your hands on the keys for the full value of the last note of the final selection.

- Put your hands back in your lap between pieces.

- Repeat the steps above, waiting five seconds with your hands in your lap, and then place them on the keys before starting the next piece.

- Put your hands back in your lap before standing, smiling, and bowing.

- Walk confidently away from the piano, with a pleased expression on your face.

## Facial Expression and Body Language

During a performance, facial expressions that reflect the involvement the student feels with the music are appropriate, but students need to be taught to avoid any sort of facial expression or physical motion that gives anything away if an error occurs.

### STORY ONE

I remember being at a recital where the pianist was playing a difficult Liszt piece. Suddenly the pianist's eyes grew large and startled. Nothing else changed; he kept on playing without the slightest hesitation, and after about a line or two of music, his eyes returned to their former look of concentration. But his eyes during those two lines gave away a temporary sense of panic.

Any physical indication of distress, such as head shaking, deep sighing, or emitting an audible sound of annoyance, is a dead giveaway that something is amiss. Students must instead be taught how to keep a good poker face if something is incorrect in a performance.

### STORY TWO

I attended a recital at the Kennedy Center where the performer gave a concert of 20th century music. The first piece was *L'Isle joyeaux* by Claude Debussy, a difficult and impressive piece. She soon experienced some major problems with memory and since I had performed the piece, I knew that about half of her performance was improvised.

I was sweating for her by the time the piece was over, but her facial expression never revealed that she was experiencing trouble. Instead she presented a fabulous smile with a glorious bow at the end of the piece. I was surprised at how much the audience seemed to enjoy her version of the Debussy and realized that her performance was smooth enough that if one hadn't known the piece, it would have been hard to discern the errors. The rest of her 20th century selections went by without a hitch—or at least I think they did. Since I didn't know the other pieces, how could I be sure? Her magnificent smiles certainly never gave anything away.

Teaching students the importance of body language cannot be overstressed. A student who storms off after a performance with a scowl sends a strong and undeniable message. The exact same performance followed by a brilliant smile and a confident exit with head held high, sends a very different message. The audience will respond to the clear signals being sent by body language and will interpret what they have seen and heard accordingly. I tell my students, "If you perform well, smile happily because you did such a good job; and if you are not happy with your performance, smile because you are done, but smile!"

This does not in any way imply that it is okay for a student to play poorly onstage as long as she pulls the wool over the audience's eyes. No one is trying to dupe the audience, but if a problem occurs, body language need not send out distress sirens either! It is imperative to walk onstage with a successfully learned and memorized piece. But we are all human—errors can happen, and students need to be taught how to handle them so they won't be devastated. The more they "practice performing" the better able they will be to think on their feet, respond creatively to challenges, and get out of even the toughest scrapes, all the while looking professional and confident.

## Recital Attire

Although casual dress is appropriate for casual recitals, more professional dress lends dignity and importance to students' efforts in more formal recitals. Students do not instinctively know the best way to dress for such a recital and will need guidance. Dress should be more formal than school wear without being overly dressy.

Teachers need to keep the financial means of students' families in mind when recommending recital attire, as some students cannot afford what might be considered proper recital attire. One year a mother called me to say her daughter was worried because I had said jeans would not be acceptable for the recital. Jeans were all that her daughter owned and they couldn't afford a dressier outfit. Naturally I modified my policy to include the following suggestions, with the understanding that students can dress within their financial means:

Suggestions for recital attire for girls:

- Appropriate-length skirts or nice pants

- Outfits that do not expose bellies, backs, or cleavage

- No overly high heels

- Clean jeans and an appropriate top for those who do not own skirts or dress pants

Suggestions for recital attire for boys:

- Dress pants and shirt

- Dress shoes

- Clean jeans, an appropriate top, and clean sneakers for those who do not own dressier attire

Suggestions for recital attire for boys *and* girls:

- Bring dry shoes if it is raining or snowing, especially if the soles are rubber, as wet soles will squeak on the pedals.

- If shoes are new, practice walking and pedaling in them in advance.

- No jewelry should be worn on the wrists or fingers.

- Chewing gum is never an appropriate accessory when performing.

- Hair needs to be pinned back away from the face or in a pony tail so that the audience can see who is performing.

- Practice performing in the outfit before the recital to ensure arms can move comfortably, fabric does not cling, and clothing is appropriately modest.

## Recitals as Significant Events

Recital time is not only a time to perform, but also a time to honor students' efforts and achievements throughout the year. One option is to alternate recitals between a more relaxed setting and a more formal environment. This allows a teacher and her students to benefit from both types of recital settings: to have fun in informal recitals and concerts, and to stress the significance and importance of a more formal recital experience.

Although each teacher can decide exactly how she wants her recitals to be conducted and presented, my own preference is to make each recital—whether informal or formal—important.

Recitals can have an air of importance without appearing formidable by considering a few basic steps:

- **Hold the recital away from the studio,** but in a room that is not overwhelming in size. Most towns and cities have a small church, public library, or service club that would be appropriate.

- **Print programs of the recital.** Printed programs serve as valuable reminders of students' achievements, and offer a helpful guide during the recital itself. As a compromise to printed programs, teachers may ask students to announce the title and composer of their repertoire before they perform. This adds to a student's self-confidence while speaking in front of a group, especially when the announcements have been rehearsed in front of a performance class.

- **Require students to dress nicely** as this lends an air of importance to the recital.

- **Offer a warm welcome** to the entire group before the recital to help promote a comfortable atmosphere.

- **Allow students to sit with their families or friends**, rather than backstage or in a front row, as this often helps them to feel more comfortable.

- **Encourage proper audience etiquette.** A brief announcement at the start of each recital can remind the audience of proper recital etiquette:
    - Turn off cell phones and pagers.
    - Families and students should stay for the full recital.
    - Avoid whispering or excessive coughing, and take crying babies outside the room if necessary.

– Enter or leave the room only between pieces, never during a performance.

– Applaud enthusiastically as each student walks to the piano and again after each student has finished performing.

- **Offer a reception after the recital** to add to the importance and festiveness of the recital. To cut back on the teacher's expenses and work, a letter can be sent in advance asking each family to bring a plate of homemade treats for the reception. The teacher can provide punch and paper goods, or an overly busy family could provide these items rather than bake. If the teacher prefers to provide the whole reception, a store-bought sheet cake, a can of nuts, and a can of mints are far easier than hours of baking.

To be sure students and parents are aware of the suggestions for the recital, I send a letter to parents before each recital reminding them of recital date, time, location, suggestions for attire, and guidelines for audience etiquette.

Recitals are indeed significant events, and as such are worthy of a teacher's best effort to make them successful and enjoyable for everyone involved. It takes discipline, patience, and confidence to execute a musical and secure recital performance, and students deserve to have these efforts honored by a well-planned recital.

# Resource

Marlais, Helen. *In Recital Throughout the Year® (with Performance Strategies)*. Volume One, Books 1–6 and Volume Two, Books 1–6. Fort Lauderdale: The FJH Music Company, Inc., 2004, 2005.

Each volume in this series contains six books, ranging in level from early elementary to late intermediate. The unique quality of this series is found in the suggestions and guidance given in each book pertaining to practice and performance strategies. Topics include Recital Preparation Tips for the Teacher and A Note to Students; the latter includes a checklist of practice suggestions for the student to follow when preparing for a performance. Steps for a Winning Performance, suggestions for During and After the Recital, tips for Practicing With the Metronome, and Managing Performance Jitters are just a few of the other topics included in this series. Each book clearly states the concepts covered in each level. The books include original solos and duets as well as arrangements of famous classical themes and seasonal repertoire, appropriate for themed recitals at Halloween, Christmas, and the Fourth of July.

**PART VII**

# Chapter 25

# ADDITIONAL PERFORMANCE, ASSESSMENT, AND TESTING OPPORTUNITIES

As a child I experienced a number of different approaches to performance when moving from state to state and teacher to teacher. Some of my teachers held recitals, and some did not. Some of the teachers encouraged participation in local performance opportunities such as festivals, guild auditions, and competitions, while others never participated in activities outside the studio. As a young piano student who loved to play, I must admit, I enjoyed the teachers who offered a variety of performance opportunities.

Today there are many different ways to widen a student's opportunities, both in performance and in the testing of musical skills. Outside opportunities for performing and testing skills exist at every level of study and for every degree of talent. While recognizing the many possible approaches to competitions, festivals, assessment, and testing, each teacher will make her own personal choices concerning activities outside the studio. Some regularly enter students in national competitions; others prefer to stay closer to home. As teachers, it is important to know about some of the options available. Perhaps entering a student in a new event will offer that student (and the teacher) a fresh and exciting challenge.

## Music Teachers National Association (MTNA)

### MTNA Performance Competitions

Music Teachers National Association sponsors some of the most prestigious competitions available to students. They are highly competitive, and students must be extremely skilled to place on the state, divisional, or national level. The description of the competitions on the website states:

> The purpose of the Music Teachers National Association Performance competitions is to provide educational experiences for students and teachers and to recognize exceptionally talented young artists and their teachers in their pursuit of musical excellence. The state competitions are considered the primary educational level, with the division and national levels showcasing outstanding performance and honoring significant pedagogical achievement.

> **MTNA Junior Performance Competitions**
> **MTNA Senior Performance Competitions**
> **MTNA Young Artist Performance Competitions**
> **MTNA Chamber Music Performance Competition**

### MTNA Music Achievement Award Program

Students who do not wish to compete, but who may be motivated to work for structured goals may find MTNA's Music Achievement Award Program attractive. As stated on the website:

The purpose of MTNA's Music Achievement Award Program is to help encourage ALL the students in the teacher's studio, especially the "everyday" students, to continue their music study and to strive to achieve goals that will not only help them become better musicians, but will also enhance their love and appreciation of music.

The teacher sets goals that are both realistic and attainable for each individual student according to the student's needs, ability, and motivational level.

The student achieves the goals over a specified period of time.

Students completing the program are rewarded for this achievement with a special MTNA pin. While the true reward is your students' musical achievements and enhanced love of musicianship, a beautiful pin especially designed for this program will be a fitting symbol of the accomplishment.

The following are included in the free implementation packet:

- Program description

- Program implementation suggestions

- Achievement goals suggestions

- Goals list suggestions

- Order form for MTNA award pins/free stickers

- Suggested press release and directions

- Suggested notice to parent(s)/guardian(s) with tear-off return form

## MTNA Music Study Award Program
Designed to motivate students by acknowledging their commitment to music lessons, the Music Study Award Program offers certificates from MTNA that recognize years of study completed in two-year increments for up to 12 years of study.

## MTNA Studio Festival Program
The Studio Festival Program offers teachers and students the opportunity to create their own mini-festival. The judge is a musician chosen and hired by the teacher to critique the teacher's students in the teacher's studio as they perform in this non-competitive event. There are no set rules or regulations, and the event can be tailor-made to the teacher's needs. The program is open to students of all ages and levels, and provides motivation for progress within the studio.

MTNA provides all materials free, including:

- Organizational checklist/timeline

- Budget worksheet

- Judge's guideline sheet

- Judge's comment sheet (may be duplicated)

PART VII

- Sample letter to parents (may be duplicated)

- Festival performance schedule (to be completed by teacher)

- Order form for student certification and medals

- Press release and information about publicizing a studio festival

The four MTNA programs listed above, and all related materials, can be found at www.mtna.org/HLtext.

## National Federation of Music Clubs (NFMC) Festival Programs

The National Federation of Music Clubs (NFMC) is perhaps best known for its Junior Festival programs, which are designed to promote study, stimulate interest in American and world music literature, and encourage each participant to reach a high standard of musical achievement. Junior Festival participants do not compete against each other, but rather perform for a judge who gives each participant a personal evaluation and a rating. The ratings convert to gold-cup points, which are accumulated from year to year, and eventually result in earning gold cups of varying sizes. In most piano categories, one repertoire choice for the Junior Festival is from a NFMC Festivals Bulletin, and a second piece is of the student's choice.

The Junior Festival categories appropriate for piano are:

- Piano Solo Event

- The Lynn Freeman Olson Piano Solo Event

- Piano Concerto Event

- Piano Duet Event (one piano, four hands)

- Piano Trio Event (one piano, six hands)

- Piano Duo Event (two pianos, four hands)

- Piano Quartet Event (two pianos, eight hands)

- Piano Accompanist Event

- Hymn Playing Event

- Piano Trio Event I (piano-violin-cello)

- Piano Trio Event II (piano-flute-cello)

- Piano Trio Event III (piano-clarinet-viola)

- Musicianship through Classical Improvisation Event

- Musicianship Theory Event

### NFMC Awards and Competitions

The National Federation of Music Clubs also sponsors a number of awards, as well as competitions, that offer generous cash awards. Some of the annual and biennial competitions offered for varying age groups include:

- Young Artist

- Duo Piano

- Student Auditions

- Junior Special

- Music for the Blind Performance Awards

National Federation of Music Clubs website: www.nfmc-music.org

## The National Guild of Piano Teachers

The National Guild of Piano Teachers is a division of the American College of Musicians and offers annual testing for students of all levels of performance and keyboard skills. This is a non-competitive event, and students are rated solely on their own merits. The following description of the Piano Guild is taken from their web page at www.pianoguild.com.

> Our primary function is to establish definite goals and awards—in noncompetitive auditions—for students of all levels, from the earliest beginner to the gifted prodigy. With the exception of our "special" programs, teachers have the flexibility to choose all repertoire for student auditions. Students are judged on individual merit, by a well-qualified music professional, in the areas of accuracy, continuity, phrasing, pedaling, dynamics, rhythm, tempo, tone, interpretation, style, and technique. Our purpose is to encourage growth and enjoyment through the study of piano.

> Yearly auditions are held in over 863 U.S. cities and 17 foreign countries. Students are adjudicated by national/international judges and receive report cards, certificates, and fraternity pins. Programs are diversified to meet the needs of both students and teachers. Programs are flexible and include repertoire as well as technical goals (musicianship phases). A variety of programs is available in which students can enroll:

> **Memorized Programs**
> Students of all levels may perform anywhere from one to 20 pieces.

> **Hobbyist**
> Unmemorized programs: students of all levels may perform anywhere from one to eight pieces.

> **Jazz Programs**
> Students of all levels may perform anywhere from one to 20 pieces memorized, or one to eight pieces unmemorized.

> **Duet/Duo Programs**
> Students of all levels may perform anywhere from one to three pieces.

> **Ensemble Programs**
> Students of all levels may perform one piece.

**PART VII**

**Social Music**

**Special Medal Programs**
Sonatina, Sonata, Early Bach, Advanced Bach

**Diploma Programs**
High School, Collegiate, and Young Artist

**International Composition Contest**
Beginning composers through advanced levels compete for cash awards.

American College of Musicians/National Guild of Piano Teachers website: www.pianoguild.com

## The National Music Certificate Program Examinations

The National Music Certificate Program Examinations provide a systemized approach to curriculum and assessment in piano study. Based on the curriculum of The Royal Conservatory of Music (RCM) in Canada, a consistent assessment for curriculum provides students and teachers with a solid framework for musical and professional growth.

The *Piano Syllabus*, 2008 Edition, is available for examination requirements in repertoire, and is supported by a *Theory Syllabus*, which lists the appropriate requirements for each level of testing.

The Certificate Program offers the following:

- 12 Practical Certificates

- 7 Theory Certificates

- 3 Achievement Certificates

- 2 Associate of the Royal Conservatory of Music in Toronto (ARCT) Diplomas

The Practical Syllabus includes information on:

- Repertoire

- Etudes

- Technique

- Sight-reading

- Ear-training

Theory includes:

- Rudiments (4 levels)

- Harmony (4 levels)

- Counterpoint

- Analysis

- History (3 levels)

The National Music Certificate Program provides each teacher with an organized, sequential program from which to teach, along with well-matched theory, music history, keyboard skills, sight-reading and ear-training goals for each level.

The *National Music Certification Program* website: www.nationalmusiccertificate.org

## Royal Conservatory of Music Examinations

The Royal Conservatory of Music (RCM) exams consist of performance of pieces, performance of studies and technical tests, sight-playing, and aural tests. There are ten grades of examination, each with theory co-requisites and in the higher grades there are also tests for history, harmony, and analysis. Students can actually get high school credit for piano examinations if they complete both the corresponding grades of practical and theory requirements.

Students perform from a recommended syllabus of materials, progressing from grade to grade, but may study other materials as well. Although many students take annual examinations, they are not required to take the examinations, nor are they required to take the examinations in every grade level; they may take examinations at various grade levels as they choose.

One of the main benefits of progressing through the RCM materials is that students advance at a systemized pace. The *Piano Syllabus*, 2008 Edition, helps guide teachers through progressive ear tests, sight-playing, repertoire, history, harmony, and analysis.

*Royal Conservatory of Music Examinations* website: www.rcmexaminations.org

## Associated Board of the Royal Schools of Music (ABRSM) Examinations

The Associated Board of the Royal Schools of Music (ABRSM) is the world's leading music examining board. ABRSM provides a system of examinations for over 620,000 student candidates annually in more than 90 countries around the world, including the United States.

Associated Board practical exams provide a progressive system of assessments beginning with the Prep Test and moving up through eight grades to diplomas. They are designed to motivate pupils and students at all levels by providing clear attainable goals. The grades are recognized as international benchmarks and the examinations are valued by teachers and institutions all over the world.

All information for the practical exams can be found on the ABRSM website: www.abrsm.org

   – Select "Exams"

## Other Opportunities

In addition to the numerous national competitions, which are often designed for the most exceptional students, a number of more inclusive opportunities are also available:

- Competitions and recitals sponsored by local music teacher organizations
- Area events sponsored by a local music teacher association, such as a Bach Festival, Chamber Music Festival, or Monster Concert

PART VII

- Solo and ensemble festivals sponsored by state music organizations

- Piano competitions sponsored by local music stores

- Piano events/competitions sponsored by high schools, universities, symphony orchestras, and private arts agencies

- Performances in senior citizen centers and retirement communities

- Performances in malls or other locations arranged by the teacher

- School talent shows

- Places of worship

# Resources

RCM Examinations. *Piano Syllabus*, 2008 Edition. Mississauga, Ontario: Frederick Harris Music Co., 2008.

The *Piano Syllabus* is essential for teachers preparing students for RCM Examinations (Canada) and the National Music Certificate Program (USA). The Piano Syllabus outlines the piano curriculum for Preparatory to ARCT levels, including requirements for repertoire, technique, ear-training, and sight-playing. Information is included for examination registration and regulations. There is a helpful section on resources, listing a number of excellent general and keyboard resources.

RCM Examinations. *Theory Syllabus*, 2009 Edition. Mississauga, Ontario: Frederick Harris Music Co., 2009.

The *Theory Syllabus* is used jointly for theory examinations offered by RCM Examinations and the National Music Certificate Program Theory Examinations. Even if a teacher is not entering students in either of those programs, this syllabus provides an excellent outline for the study of theory. Section 1 has general information on RCM exams; Section 2 covers graded theory examination, including levels for Preliminary Rudiments, Rudiments, Harmony, Counterpoint, Analysis, Keyboard Harmony, History, and Musicianship Examinations. Section 3 covers requirements for the ARCT exams; Section 4 lists musical terms, a description of scores, chord symbols, and non-chord tones; and Section 5 is an extensive bibliography.

# PART VIII

## TEACHING SKILLS – NOT PIECES

Being a piano teacher involves more than teaching pieces; students need to be taught the many skills involved in becoming an independent, disciplined, and creative pianist. In Part VIII, a number of skills involved in piano study will be addressed. Tackling the challenges of timing, technique, sight-playing, fingering, pedaling, developing the ear, improvisation, and harmonization all contribute to students becoming well-rounded pianists, capable of lifelong and independent learning at the piano.

When less time is spent teaching individual pieces and more time is devoted to teaching important skills, students actually learn all pieces faster and better. Students who have been taught to plan careful fingerings or tap the timing of a piece before starting will need less time devoted to these issues in the lesson. Such skills allow lesson time to be focused more on the expressive aspects of a piece and less on the details that are ultimately the student's responsibility.

# Chapter 26

# TIMING AND RHYTHM

When I was in high school I finally studied with a teacher who was a real stickler on timing. Whereas former teachers had overlooked my timing deficiencies or had given instructions such as "Play it like this…" I finally studied with a teacher who insisted that I develop an impeccable sense of timing. His particularly strict regimen seemed like torture at the time, but how grateful I am now for that teacher!

Far too many piano students on every level require help with timing. The last thing any teacher wants to encourage is dependence on the teacher to clarify the counting of every new piece or difficult passage. Instead, we must teach students to decipher timing with reliable accuracy and independence.

## Movement and Rhythm

Although the terms "timing" and "rhythm" are often used interchangeably, they may also be viewed as slightly different. The timing of a piece is sometimes thought of as the actual beats and note values of the music. Patterns of beats produce rhythm, the motion or flow of the piece through time. Clearly understanding timing (beats, note values) is a necessary step toward expressing the rhythmic energy and structure of a piece. The ultimate goal of good timing then becomes internalizing rhythm and actually sensing rhythmic motion from within. Rhythmic accuracy and expressiveness rank among the most important skills needed by any musician.

On the most basic level, internalizing rhythm starts with learning to move rhythmically to a beat. On a more advanced level, it means incorporating a rhythmic vibrancy into the interpretation of each piece.

Many educators believe the best way to initially introduce rhythm is through full body motions, such as the rhythmic swaying of the arms, or through rhythmic walking. The feel of the rhythm becomes a physical sensation which the student internalizes and later reproduces at the keyboard. Coordinated movements supply a kinesthetic understanding of rhythms before the cognitive understanding of note values is attempted. Three music educators have contributed to this concept during the last century:

- Émile Jaques-Dalcroze (1865–1950)

- Zoltán Kodály (1882–1967)

- Carl Orff (1895–1982)

Dalcroze, Kodály, and Orff each stressed various aspects of singing, solfege, improvisation, ear-training, and rhythmic responses through the use of physical motion. Today, classes and workshops offer the independent teacher the opportunity to learn the innovative, well-balanced approaches these educators have pioneered. Early childhood music programs, which will be discussed in Chapter 41, owe a great deal to these three innovators in music education.

## Methods of Counting

Even if an approach of large, physical motions is used initially, students must eventually be taught to count and understand time values. An important initial goal is to teach students how to count out loud and tap rhythms by themselves, without the need of a teacher to count for them. There are multiple systems for teaching early counting, including unit counting, metric counting, nominative counting, and syllabic counting.

### Unit Counting

This method involves speaking the number of beats a note receives.

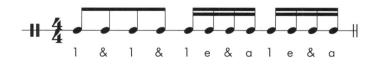

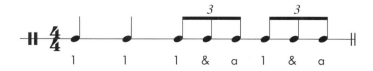

**Pros**

- The student develops a solid understanding of the value of each type of note.

- The relationship between various note values is evident.

**Cons**

- The system gets confusing and cumbersome when note values in RH and LH are different.

- The counting does not give the student a sense of where she is within the measure.

- The system does not accommodate changing meter (4/4 to 6/8, etc.).

## Metric Counting

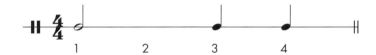

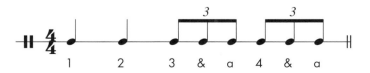

Some teachers prefer to establish a set way of subdividing that is not altered by the types of notes in the measure. Different note values are then placed within the predetermined method of subdividing. Taking the last three examples listed under metric counting, this method of subdividing would appear as follows:

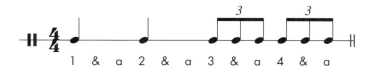

**Pros**

- The student understands the basic beat.

- The numbers can be used when different time values are played in RH and LH.

- The student is clear about where she is within the measure.

- The system accommodates changing time signature (4/4 to 6/8).

**Cons**

- Young students may confuse counting numbers with finger numbers.

- Discussions about this note being worth half of that note or only a quarter of another note may get confusing, especially to students who do not understand fractions.

- Students may grow to depend on saying something for every type of note, feeling uncomfortable playing rhythms without accompanying words (such as "e-and-a") on each note, which becomes impossible with 32nd and 64th notes.

- Rhythmic groupings may be difficult to internalize, and playing can be bogged down with the awkwardness of too many words.

## Nominative Counting

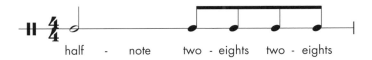

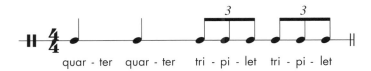

**Pros**

- Students become secure with types of notes.

- Students say an audible pattern for note types, without needing to understand concepts such as fractions.

**Cons**

- The rhythm of the words doesn't necessarily match the rhythm of the notes (quar-ter).

- Once the student has differing rhythms in RH and LH, this system becomes less effective.

- This counting does not give the student a sense of where she is within the measure.

- Students may grow to depend on saying something for every type of note, feeling uncomfortable playing rhythms without accompanying words on each note, which becomes impossible with 32nd and 64th notes.

## Syllabic Counting

There are several methods of syllabic counting that are based on Kodály. I have listed two possible types:

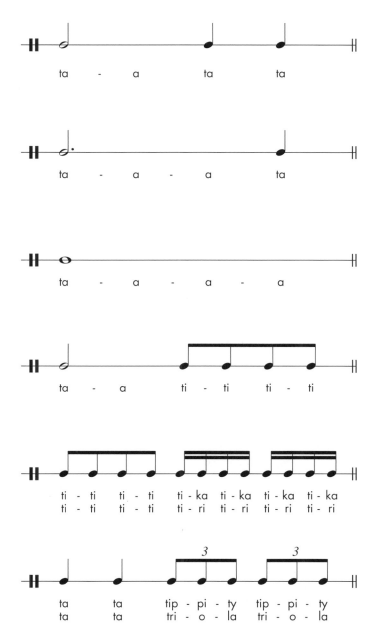

Syllabic counting, such as in this Indian style, is also used in other countries:

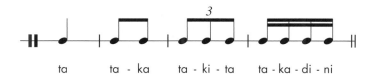

**Pros**

- Students internalize rhythmic groupings and the sound of rhythms.

- Rhythms of words match the rhythms of the notes.

- Finger numbers are not confused with counting numbers.

- Complex rhythms can be played accurately before they are understood mathematically.

**Cons**

- Once the student has differing rhythms in RH and LH, this counting becomes less effective.

- The counting does not give the student a sense of where she is within the measure.

Many teachers use a form of syllabic counting that offers students an easily remembered and executed set of words, such as "Miss-is-si-pi mud pie" for four sixteenths and two eighths, or "bum-ble-bee-bum-ble-bee" to demonstrate triplets or 6/8 time. A variety of rhythmic word groupings is possible, and teachers and students can create their own word groupings within the lesson.

Recently I was reviewing a tape of a young student who was studying with one of my college pedagogy students. The eight-year-old played beautifully, but had one major problem. In a piece in 6/8 time with constant groupings of three eighth notes, her rhythm was played like two eighths and a quarter rather than three equal eighths. When I pointed this out to my pedagogy student, she lamented, "I know, but she won't count, and when I play it for her she gets it, but then she forgets." I made suggestions for my pedagogy student, but she insisted that she had tried it all, and nothing worked.

I volunteered to help, and in the next lesson the eight year-old played her piece for me with her incorrect timing. I suggested she try counting "1 + a 2 + a." She cried. I switched gears and said, "Why don't you try 'but-ter-fly but-ter-fly,' or would you like to pick some other word with three syllables?" She thought for a moment before responding, "How about my name?" We all agreed that was a great idea, and in the recital she played with perfect timing, rhythmically whispering "E-mi-ly E-mi-ly" in every measure throughout the piece. She will of course need to learn more about other methods of counting, but this was a first step, and got her over her discomfort with counting.

Students usually progress from one system such as "ta - ta - " to another, such as "one - two." The main goal is for students to decipher note values accurately, to eventually internalize rhythmic groupings, and ultimately to become rhythmic musicians who do not need a teacher to clarify timing for them. Remembering to have the student read the piece before hearing the teacher or parent play it, as mentioned in Chapter 21, ensures that the student's efforts to develop rhythmic independence will not be handicapped by prematurely "hearing how the timing goes." Parents may need to be reminded not to show the student the correct way to play a rhythmically challenging piece or passage, no matter how well-intentioned that assistance may be.

Even as the rhythms in their pieces become increasingly complex, the student's independence should never be compromised by premature showing, but rather enhanced by directed discovery.

Directed discovery is a way to ask questions and guide learning, without actually resorting to, "Play it like this." Questions may include: How will you count this piece? Do you see any repeated rhythmic patterns? Will you please tap the first four lines for me before starting this piece at home?

Books that focus on rhythm can serve as a valuable tool to help strengthen the important skills of being able to read, count, and play rhythms. *Winning Rhythms* by Edward Ayola, for instance, presents rhythms starting with basic patterns, and continuing through those of increasing difficulty. The logical progressions provide excellent practice for students, allowing them to focus completely on the challenge of rhythmic accuracy.

One way to approach the exercises in *Winning Rhythms* is to have students tap the rhythms while counting "1 - 2 - 3 - 4 - " without saying anything on the notes between the beat, no matter how complex the subdivisions become. Learning to count metrically, but without subdividing, develops a more intrinsic understanding of rhythmic units such as triplets, or combinations of sixteenths, rests, and eighths. The need to always say "1 e + a" when there are sixteenths fosters a dependence on words that actually detracts from rhythmic energy. Although I am a strong believer in being able to count with and without subdivisions, an even larger goal is to have rhythmic units understood, internalized, and automatically reproducible.

From the beginning lessons, students can be encouraged to tap and count a piece before playing it, isolating the timing and securing a strong understanding of the rhythm. If a student has a problem with note values in a certain passage, tapping the confusing section while counting out loud provides clarity. If the timing can't be tapped correctly, it surely will not be played correctly. By extracting difficult passages and focusing on counting apart from note playing, total attention can be focused on solving the timing challenges, without being distracted by confusing notes or demanding technique.

For students who are visual learners or who have difficulty understanding the concept of "this note being equal to two of those notes," there is a helpful product called "NoteBlocks." Each set is color coordinated and sized by height for note value. For example, two of the quarter-note blocks (which are the exact shape of a quarter note) stack up to equal the exact height of the half-note block, and two half-note blocks stack up to the height of the whole-note block. The set comes with whole, half, quarter, and eighth blocks for notes and rests, time-signatures, bar lines, dots for dotted notes, and twelve-beat mats. This is a hands-on tool for students who benefit from seeing or touching as they learn.

## The Metronome

The metronome is an invaluable tool that unfortunately is often underused. Teachers do their students a great disservice if they ignore the metronome, or introduce it late in study. The later the metronome is introduced, the more potential there is for frustration when learning to match its steady ticks. A student who is unable to hear or execute steady beats has a major weakness to overcome. Conversely, students who can play with the metronome are able to place beats exactly in time. This is somewhat like being able to perform exactly in sync with a very strict duet partner.

It is understood that most repertoire is not metronomic, but even music that has rhythmic freedom through the use of rubato must be grounded in an understanding of a steady beat. Once a solid understanding of the timing has been achieved, students can focus on the rhythmic pulsing of phrasing and the stylistic elements affecting rhythm. This more polished, refined formula can be thought of as:

Correct timing + musical understanding of pulse, phrase shape, and style = rhythmic energy.

The ability to read, understand, count, and execute note values, coupled with a sense of rhythmic vibrancy, is essential to any musician. Teachers serve their students well by teaching them the skills needed for rhythmic independence.

# Resources

## DRILLS, EXERCISES, AND WORKBOOKS

Ayola, Edward L. *Winning Rhythms.* San Diego: Neil A.Kjos Music Company, 1985.

> An excellent tool for teaching rhythms, this book offers pages of rhythm patterns, starting with quarter notes and advancing to complex combinations of triplets, 16th notes, and syncopated rests. The patterns develop in a logical and systematic fashion, allowing the student to tap or play increasingly more advanced patterns with ease.

Berlin, Boris, and Andrew Markow. *Ear Training for Practical Examinations: Rhythm Clapback/Singback.* Mississauga, Ontario, Canada: The Frederick Harris Music Co., Ltd., 1989–1991.

> There are three volumes in this series, which covers Levels one through seven in examination systems such as RCM Examinations and National Music Certificate Program Examinations. Each book offers a series of rhythms designed to improve rhythmic accuracy and reading.

Hale, Charlotte, and Constance Preston. *Rhythm Without the Blues*, Volumes 1 & 2. Milwaukee: Hal Leonard Corporation, 2007, 2008.

> *Rhythm Without the Blues* presents a comprehensive rhythm course with listening, writing, dictation, and tapping exercises. A self-assessment is included at the end of each book. The series includes two volumes to date, books with CDs, and is designed to give students an in-depth perception of rhythm.

Haroutounian, Joanne. *Rhythm Antics.* San Diego: Neil A. Kjos Music Company, 1988.

> Using a combination of approaches to counting (such as "ti-di-ti-di" and "huck-le-ber-ry" to teach groupings of four 16th notes), *Rhythm Antics* is in a workbook format, starting with an introduction to the metronome and including creative exercises for developing rhythmic skills.

Marlais, Helen, with Kevin Olson. *Sight Reading & Rhythm Every Day*®, Books 1A, 1B, 2A, 2B, 3A, 3B, 4A, 4B, & 5. (The entire series will include Books 6, 7, and 8.) Fort Lauderdale: The FJH Music Company, Inc., 2005–2007.

> This is a carefully leveled curriculum designed to develop a student's sense of rhythm, key recognition, time signature recognition, pattern identification, interval recognition, and response to articulation and dynamics. Students will learn the concept of playing a piece from beginning to end without stopping. The exercises and drills will guide students in a simple and straightforward approach to sight-reading with ease, accuracy, and musicality.

McArthur, Victoria, with Edwin McLean. *Making Rhythm Easy*, Books 1 & 2. Fort Lauderdale: The FJH Music Company, Inc., 1998, 2001.

> Designed to help students understand and perform basic rhythms, these workbooks offer rhythm examples to tap and count (with teacher duet), games, written examples that reinforce correct counting, ear-training activities, review pages, and rhythm evaluations to help pinpoint areas that need work.

Small, Allan. Basic *Timing for the Pianist.* Van Nuys: Alfred Publishing Co., Inc., 1970.

> Using a five-finger C major position in every exercise, the book focuses on rhythm and includes 105 short exercises of increasing difficulty.

Starer, Robert. **Basic Rhythmic Training.** Milwaukee: Hal Leonard Corporation, 1986.

> This book assumes no prior musical knowledge and begins with elementary rhythm notation. It provides a comprehensive understanding of basic rhythm and its components: the beat, pulse, time signatures, notes, rests, and syncopation. The book is written for general music classes as well as private instruction and assures better, quicker sight-playing, ear-training, and rhythmic proficiency.

Whaley, Garwood. **Basics in Rhythm.** Galesville: Meredith Music Publications, 2003. Distributed by Hal Leonard Corporation.

> This collection of short, graduated studies is designed for teaching or learning to read rhythms. Exercises cover all fundamental rhythms, meters, and mixed meters. Each of the 75 exercises focuses on a specific set of rhythm patterns. The book may be purchased with or without a CD that features the examples in the book.

## VIDEOS, GAMES, AND ACTIVITIES

Abramson, Robert. **Feel It.** Van Nuys: Alfred Publishing Co., Inc., 1998.

> Written by Robert Abramson, a leading figure in the applications of the Dalcorze Method, *Feel It* is an activity book highlighting various listening skills and body motions. Accompanied by two CDs of musical accompaniment, there are seven chapters in the book: Games of Beat, Games of Measure, Games of Duration, Games of Pattern, Games of Ensemble, Games of Sub-Division, and Games of Legato and Staccato.

Cresswell, Luke, and Steve McNicholas. **Stomp Out Loud.** Brighton, England: Yes/No Productions Ltd., 1997.

> As stated on the cover, this video features an "explosive mix of music and dance, created by drumming, shaking, rattling and rolling anything that makes a sound from the obvious, to the unexpected." The Stomp artists use energy and enthusiasm in this percussive exploration of rhythm in everyday things. *Stomp Out Loud* is an excellent video to show students when demonstrating that music and rhythm are all around us. *Stomp Out Loud* is also available as a DVD.

Masala, Kenya. **Rhythm Play! Rhythm Activities and Initiatives for Adults, Facilitators, Teachers and Kids!** Austin: FUNdoing and Kenya Masala, 2004.

> Confirming the benefits of rhythmic play, this book includes a number of activities designed to explore the often-overlooked inner sense of rhythm. Each activity includes a suggestion for group size, challenge level (0–5), time needed for the activity, instruments used, type of formation required (various formations are described at the beginning of the book), and variations on the activity. A helpful resource section at the back of the book includes suggestions for developing a percussion ensemble using items from a hardware store. CD included. Visit **www.rhythm-play.com** for more information.

Schnebly-Black, Julia, and Stephen Moore. **Rhythm: One on One – Dalcroze Activities in the Private Music Lesson.** Van Nuys: Alfred Publishing Co., Inc. 2004.

> This book transfers Dalcroze activities from a group setting to the private music lesson. These one-on-one activities are applicable for studios where space is ample or limited. Sample lessons are included.

**PART VIII**

## Resources (cont.)

### BOOKS

Choksy, Lois. *The Kodaly Method I: Comprehensive Music Education*, 3rd Edition. Upper Saddle River: Prentice Hall, 1998.

> This book serves as an excellent tool for those wishing to organize a comprehensive music program for K–6 students. The material is presented in a sequential fashion and includes over 200 songs, grade-by-grade guidance, and suggested materials. The approach includes singing, moving, listening, musical reading and writing, improvising, and composing. Although the book is expensive, it is an excellent tool for teachers wishing to improve their students' understanding of musical skills.

Goodkin, Doug. *Play, Sing, and Dance: An Introduction to Orff Schulwerk.* Mainz, Germany: Schott, 2002.

> Doug Goodkin has been described as a strong advocate for the innovative ideas presented by Carl Orff. This book starts with an introduction to Orff Schulwerk and goes on to present a sequential approach to teaching using the Orff Schulwerk approach to music and movement. Chapters address games, musical poetica, singing, movement, dance, body percussion, play, drama, rhythm vocalization, solfege, and music intended for children.

Schnebly-Black, Julia and Stephan F. Moore. *Rhythm: One on One, Dalcroze Activities in the Private Music Lesson.* Van Nuys: Alfred Publishing Co., Inc., 2004.

> Designed specifically for the private music teacher, this brief book uses eurhythmics to increase a student's musicality. Movement is stressed, as is the use of instruments and games. The book covers activities for students from beginning to advanced levels and includes practical applications of the material for the independent studio.

Schnebly-Black, Julia, and Stephen Moore. *The Rhythm Inside: Connecting Body, Mind and Spirit Through Music.* Van Nuys: Alfred Publishing Co., Inc., 2003.

> A short, readable guide into the world of eurhythmics, *The Rhythm Inside* is based on the research of Émile Jaques-Dalcroze. Celebrating the senses of sound, motion, and touch that are inherent in each of us, the book offers insight into musical responses that may have been forgotten as we age. The authors discuss Dalcroze's goal: allowing our bodies and minds to respond to music with a multitude of rich possibilities, while developing a better sense of self-awareness.

### WEBSITES

*American Orff-Schulwerk Association*
> www.aosa2.org

*Dalcroze Society of America*
> www.dalcrozeusa.org

*Latin Percussion*
> www.lpmusic.com
> > – "Play Like a Pro" produces a pull-down menu
> > – Select "Lessons for Kids"

*NoteLogic*
> www.notelogic.com
> > – Select "NoteBlocks Stacking Notes"

*Organization of American Kodály Educators*
> www.oake.org

*Rhythm Play*
> www.rhythm-play.com

*STOMP*
> www.stomponline.com
> > – Select "percussion for kids"
> > – For lesson plans, select "younger students"
> > – Select "lessons"
> > – For a PDF file of the STOMP study guide, select "percussion for kids" and then "STOMP study guide."

# Chapter 27

# TECHNIQUE

———————————

**N**o two teachers approach technique in the exact same way. I know this since my father was in the military and our frequent moves resulted in 11 different piano teachers before I went to college. I was exposed to more varied approaches to technique than any person should experience in her formative years! I heard everything: wrists up, wrists down, elbows out, elbows in, sit closer, sit back, don't raise your fingers, raise them high, keep your wrists still, rotate those wrists! Somehow they all agreed that I should sit up straight.

When discussing technique, perhaps the easiest thing to do first is to identify what not to do. One would hope all teachers would be in agreement about avoiding the following:

- Flat fingers

- Floppy, weak fingers

- Stiff, rigid fingers

- Fingers that cannot play independently

- Sitting too close to the keyboard

- Sitting too far from the keyboard

- Tension in fingers

- Tension in wrists

- Curled fingers

- Raised, tense shoulders

- Elbows too close to the body

- Slumped posture

- Wrists too high

- Wrists too low

From there, things get sticky. Forming opinions about technique is somewhat like forming opinions about politics. Everyone sees things differently, often becoming quite adamant about their own personal beliefs. With that in mind, only the most basic of thoughts about the fundamentals of technique will be offered here.

## Historical Overview

The approach to keyboard technique was far different 300 years ago than it is today. In the early 1700s, with the birth of the pianoforte, the action of the keys was not much stiffer than that of the clavichord or harpsichord. Finger technique was the key approach taught by teachers of the day, with a great deal of emphasis on repetitive exercises and rapid execution of notes. The arm and wrist were kept as free from motion as possible. Technique was not necessarily connected with musical goals, but rather with clean, fast, and articulate playing.

By the early to mid 1800s, music became more technically challenging, and performers such as Beethoven performed with a more impassioned approach to technique. Piano builders responded to the increased demands of the repertoire and the newer performance styles by building instruments with larger frames and stronger strings. The increased possibilities in dynamics coupled with improvements in piano action served the advances in technique well.

Eventually pianists focused more on arm weight, rotation of the wrist, and interaction between shoulders, arms, wrists, and fingers. Distinctly varied schools of thought on technique flourished. Some teachers continued to focus on finger motion while others stressed movement of the whole body. Some incorporated the two approaches together. At this point, teachers started to impress upon students the expressive goals of technique, rather than insisting solely on repetitive exercises.

*The Great Pianists: From Mozart to the Present*, by Harold C Schonberg, gives a historical summary of the varied approaches to technique and performance of keyboard players such as Mozart, Beethoven, Chopin, Liszt, and Rachmaninoff, as well as famous pianists of the 20th century. The approach of "greats" toward technique, improvisation, and memorization are discussed, as is how each perceived the art of performing. The book is easy to read and provides an insightful look into the lives of composers and performers of the past, and into the varied approaches to piano technique that have existed through the centuries.

## Modern Day Practices

Today, mind-boggling extremes exist when it comes to the teaching of technique. At one end are those who believe the only thing that should be taught in the first two years of piano study is technique. In this school of thought, absolutely no repertoire or note-reading is to be taught as the student lays a strong technical foundation for later development. At the opposite extreme is the teacher who never comments on any element of technique at all, allowing poor hand position, tense shoulders, and other physical problems to go uncorrected.

In the 21st century, teachers often stress that the ultimate goal of good technique is a good sound. Although some may present technique and musicianship as separate elements, many teachers view technical study ultimately as defined by a musical goal. A beginning student can be encouraged to feel the music right from the start. She can describe what the music means to her or make up a story about the piece that fits the way she wants it to sound. As she listens to her own playing, she then decides how well she is projecting her story. This is technique—being able to project the sounds one wishes to create.

This early guidance in projecting a personal interpretation helps develop a student's ability to combine musicianship and technique. Focusing on technique is, therefore, another example of goal-oriented practicing. The goal may be to play steady 16th notes and clean octave passages, maintain a beautiful balance between melody and harmony, or employ lyrical legato phrasing. In all cases, the technical and musical elements are intertwined.

Besides increasing the ability to play musically, the other main goal of technique is to allow the student to play increasingly more difficult repertoire with comfort and ease. If pain is experienced when playing, something is wrong and the alarms need to go off. Any approach to the keyboard that causes pain will ultimately cause injury. A player with good technique is relaxed, yet in control of the sounds being produced.

In order to teach relaxation and a tension-free approach to playing the piano, current readings on technique include opinions regarding each of the following:

## Hand position

Many early-level books start by asking the student to stand with arms and hands relaxed at the side. This relaxation allows the hand to form a natural curve that, when placed on the keyboard, results in a natural and effective hand position. Placing all five fingers on the keys gives the early student a natural feel of the keyboard and allows the complete hand to rest in a proper position.

## Finger motion

The degree and type of finger motion taught varies from teacher to teacher (and sometimes from piece to piece), but most teachers agree that the fingers are to stay curved and relaxed. Fingers cannot be floppy or flat, and need a firm distal joint (the joint closest to the fingertip). The energy used is often guided by a combination of finger motion, finger strength, and weight. Finger motion does not include any tense pushing or over-exaggerated lifting.

## Wrist

When discussing technique, the wrist is probably the source of greatest controversy. Some teachers feel the wrist should have relatively little motion, while staying aligned with the arm and hand. Some feel that a slight rotation in the wrist allows the pianist to remain relaxed. Others see lateral side-to-side motion as essential in certain passagework. Certainly different passages (and different students) require different motions in the wrist. How and when to use wrist motion should be carefully researched in order to avoid injury. The one overriding truth is that the wrist needs to be relaxed and tension-free.

## Head, neck, shoulders, and face

Alignment of the head, neck, and shoulders has been stressed more in recent years. Any tension in the shoulders results in difficulty when playing. Tension may also appear in the face with a tense jaw, clenched teeth, or flared nostrils. Students need to be reminded to relax, lower the shoulders, and keep the face and neck area relaxed. Relaxation and stretching exercises provide a good prelude to practice.

## Motion of upper arm, lower arm, and elbow

Although at one time students were taught to keep the arm completely still, modern-day technique more often includes discussion on why, how, and when to move the arm. Many motions at the piano originate in the upper arm. Motion can include in-and-out motion, lateral motion, or a rotating motion, and is determined by what is being played: octaves, scale passages, arpeggios, chords, etc. Motion is also used as a means of aligning the arm with the notes being played. One problem younger students often have is playing with their elbows glued to their sides. This closeness of the elbows to the body acts as an inhibitor of motion and fluidity. I remind my students that baseball players don't hug their bodies when at bat and swimmers let their arms move away from the body.

## Arm weight

Too many students push hard on the keys rather than use natural weight to produce a rich, full sound. The weight of the arm, along with upper body weight, provides a sufficiently full sound. Pushing past the point of sound is unnecessary and is not needed to produce an impressive fortissimo.

## Posture at the keyboard

Because teachers often sit beside students, watching fingers and hands, they sometimes miss the big picture. Moving away from the piano and looking at the student's complete body offers a different picture than is available when sitting close. Some students naturally slump… badly. If neither their grandmothers nor an English finishing school corrected this bad habit, the teacher must take over and explain why good posture is important at the keyboard. Sitting straight, while feeling totally relaxed in the upper body, allows the student to feel relaxed and tension-free while executing any technical challenges at the keyboard more effectively. A slumped posture, on the other hand, does not allow for maximum control and energy at the piano.

## Distance from the piano

Students will often make the mistake of sitting too close or too far from the piano—usually too close. Sitting too close can lead to poor hand position, tension, and the inability to move effectively at the keyboard. When reaching for high or low notes, they will be forced to get out of their own way by leaning backward, basically centering their weight toward the back of the room rather than toward the keys.

Students often sit at the given height of the bench, even when it is set too high or too low for their physique. If a bench with adjustable height is not owned, it would be wise to include such a purchase in the next studio budget. An even better option might be to purchase an adjustable duet bench to better serve the studio needs. Until such a purchase is made, substitute an adjustable bench with items that raise the height of the seat for shorter students. Possibilities include multiple padded bench covers (bench covers also come in a variety of thicknesses) or a favorite item the student brings from home.

Footstools are another tool to help smaller students with proper posture at the piano. Stackable footrests are available as are footstools that also serve as pedal extenders. Parents should be encouraged to buy an adjustable bench and a foot stool/pedal extender if their home bench does not accommodate their child's height.

## Whole body

The use of the whole body is crucial in producing a beautiful tone; no single part of the body can do it all alone. Finger action alone, for instance, will most likely result in a percussive sound. The complete body—head, neck, spine, shoulders, upper arms, elbow, forearms, wrists, and fingers—are interrelated and all contribute to a musical, injury-free approach to the keyboard.

## Relaxation

Relaxation does not mean weakness. Teaching students how to be relaxed as they focus their energy requires that they understand the physiology of the whole upper body. Relaxation does not apply only to the body; it is also a state of mind. Tension can be generated from inner sources, and teachers need to be on the lookout for any inward causes for emotional stress, mental stress, or physical tension that students may be experiencing.

### Breathing

Some students take very shallow breaths while playing. They need to be encouraged to find places to breathe (physically) and to be aware of their breathing at the keyboard. Places to breath—both physically and musically—can be conditioned into the student's approach to phrasing.

### Listening

Listening is one of the most important elements of good technique. If students do not listen to the tone being produced, they will be unable to judge if their physical motions are achieving the desired musical goals. How will a certain wrist motion contribute to a lovely legato if students are not judging the effect their technique has on legato playing? Students need to be continually engaged in active listening.

I have touched on each area only minimally, with the understanding that the study of technique requires far more than can be covered here. Ultimately each teacher should decide how to ensure that students develop a musical, relaxed, and tension-free approach to the keyboard. Three good ways for a teacher to improve her ability to teach technique effectively are:

- **Read:** Teachers learn from the experts by absorbing information from books, magazine articles, journals, and the Internet.

- **Actively seek knowledge:** Teachers who attend conferences, workshops, and presentations where technique is discussed are able to learn from successful teachers.

- **Study:** By taking lessons, especially with an accomplished teacher, teachers are able to ask questions specifically related to the teaching of technique.

Students realize direct benefits from any improvement in technique experienced by their teacher. A teacher is never too old or too accomplished for continued dedication to improving technique.

## Types of Resources

An abundance of resources for improving technique are available for teachers and students alike. In my studio, I have organized student technique books into four categories, plus a category for books that cover more than one of the four major areas of technique:

- Scales, arpeggios, cadences, chords

- Technical studies

- Musical studies centered on technical challenges

- Repertoire that is taught with technique as an important focus (which means just about everything else)

- Combinations of techniques

## Scales, arpeggios, cadences, chords

Teachers differ on how to incorporate items such as scales, arpeggios, and chords into the weekly lesson. Although some teachers see them as functional keyboard skills more related to theory, others see them as an excellent tool for improving technique.

During scale and arpeggio practice, students have the opportunity to work on their physical approach to the keyboard, including finger motion, wrist rotation, posture, and the use of the arm, without being distracted by complicated notes or rhythms. Scales and arpeggios also assist with the following:

- The ability to perform with steadiness
- An increased dynamic range
- Greater facility with the left hand
- Ease with fast tempi
- Improved strength at the keyboard
- Increased finger independence
- Improved evenness of tone
- A broader use of articulations (scales can be practiced with multiple touches)
- Standardized fingerings when such passages occur within repertoire
- Familiarity with key signatures and comfort playing in all keys

Beginning students share in these benefits at an early age by preparing for scale-like practice with five-finger patterns.

At some point, serious music students will be required to know all of the major and minor scales and arpeggios, and will have been well served if they have developed ease and skill in these areas. Studying cadence patterns and chords in inversions also provides a more grounded facility at the keyboard.

## Resources

*The Brown Scale Book: Scales, Chords, and Arpeggios for Piano.* Mississauga, Ontario: The Frederick Harris Music Co., Ltd., 1948, revised 2002.

> *The Brown Scale Book* has served generations of pianists, and includes scales in parallel motion, contrary motion, thirds, sixths, and double thirds. Triads are presented in solid and broken form, chords appear in four-note format and in inversions, and arpeggios are presented for triads and dominant seventh chords.

Faber, Nancy, and Randall Faber, with Jeanne Weisman. *Achievement Skill Sheets.* Fort Lauderdale: The FJH Music Company, Inc., 1995–1997.

Each of these brief foldouts offers the basics in an "all-at-a-glance" format, and focuses on one specific area of technique:

**No. 1** Major 5-Finger Patterns

**No. 2** Minor 5-Finger Patterns

**No. 3** One-Octave Major Scales & Arpeggios

**No. 4** One-Octave Minor Scales & Arpeggios

**No. 5** Two-Octave Major Scales & Arpeggios

**No. 6** Two-Octave Minor Scales & Arpeggios

**No. 7** I-V-I Cadences

**No. 8** Cadence Booklet

McArthur, Victoria, and Edwin McLean. *The FJH Classic First Scale Book.* Fort Lauderdale: The FJH Music Company, Inc., 2001.

Providing an introduction to scales, chords, arpeggios, and cadences, this book is specifically designed to be accessible to students after the first few weeks of lessons. Each key of the circle of fifths is represented with a page consisting of easy-to-read pentachords, a cross-hand arpeggio, the tonic chord broken and blocked, and two versions of the authentic cadence. A similar page based on the parallel minor follows the major keys. One-octave white-key major scales and commonly used minor scales are also included.

McArthur, Victoria, and Edwin McLean. *The FJH Classic Scale Book.* Fort Lauderdale: The FJH Music Company, Inc., 1996.

Beginning with an explanation of major and minor scale structure, this book goes on to include checklists with metronome speeds for scales, triads, arpeggios, and cadences. Each major key is presented with scales in parallel and contrary motion as well as in thirds and sixths. Triads and dominant seventh chords are presented in blocked and broken format in all inversions, and arpeggios are given in all inversions. Three cadence patterns are included per key. Minor keys include the natural, harmonic, and melodic scales followed by triads, arpeggios, and cadences. The end of the book includes fingerings for chromatic scales, pentatonic scales, and whole-tone scales, as well as convenient quick guides to scale and arpeggio fingerings.

Palmer, Willard A., Morton Manus, and Amanda Vick Lethco. *The Complete Book of Scales, Chords, Arpeggios & Cadences.* Van Nuys: Alfred Publishing Co., Inc., 1994.

Scales, chords, arpeggios, and cadences are presented by key, with all material for each key appearing on two pages. The format is clearly written and easy to understand.

Pollei, Paul. *Essential Technique for the Pianist: An Organized and Systematic Method of Teaching Piano Technique.* Van Nuys: Alfred Publishing Co., Inc., 1996.

Subscribing to the premise that those who have the best technical skills are able to sight-read and perform with the most agile facility and confidence, this volume is presented as a tool for the understanding and drill of technique.

Ramsey, Ross. *Piano Essentials: Scales, Chords, Arpeggios, and Cadences for the Contemporary Pianist* (with CD). Boston: Berklee Press, 2006. Distributed by Hal Leonard Corporation.

This is designed to guide students through the most common chord progressions in pop, rock, and jazz. The book, well-suited to older students, progresses along a natural presentation of scales, arpeggios, and cadences, and includes related theory study.

**PART VIII**

## Resources (cont.)

Rossi, Wynn-Anne, and Lucy Wilde Warren. *Get Ready for Chord and Arpeggio Duets!*, Books 1 & 2. Fort Lauderdale: The FJH Music Company, Inc., 2002, 2003.

> These books pair the student's cadences and arpeggios with a pleasing teacher duet. The books also include theory games, review activities, and practice flashcards.

Rossi, Wynn-Anne, and Victoria McArthur. *Get Ready for Major Scale Duets!, Get Ready for Pentascale Duets!, Get Ready for Minor Scale Duets!* Fort Lauderdale: The FJH Music Company, Inc 1999, 2001, 2001.

> These books add attractive teacher duet parts to the student's scale study. Each volume includes additional games and activities such as ear-training activities, fingering guidelines, scale technical warm-ups, and theory games.

## Technical Studies

Experts divide into two camps when it comes to the value of practicing technical studies such as Hanon:

**Those in favor:**

- There is value in addressing technique separately in exercises and then applying the skills learned to musical settings.

- Exercises such as Hanon are essential tools for developing technique, much like an athlete would do strength-building or speed-building exercises when training for a sport.

**Those opposed:**

- Practicing exercises such as Hanon do not serve the purpose that is intended.

- Practicing such exercises will not improve the student's ability to play Mozart; practicing Mozart is the best tool for conquering the technical challenges of playing Mozart.

- Practicing a similar pattern over and over actually increases the risk of strain or injury.

Each teacher ultimately decides this issue individually. For those choosing to use technical exercises, a number of books of technical studies exist, some more famous than others. For example, there are multiple editions of Hanon's *The Virtuoso Pianist* and Czerny's *The Art of Finger Dexterity*.

Most piano methods include a technique book at each level. When a teacher reviews a method series, the approach to technique should be high on the list of important elements to evaluate.

# Resources

Burman, Edna Mae. *Dozen a Day Technical Exercises for Piano.* Florence: Willis Music Company, 1950, 1953, 1956, 1957, 1964, 1974, 2002. Distributed by Hal Leonard Corporation.

> An older set of technique books that retains its popularity, this series includes the Preparatory Level through Level Four. Each book contains short warm-up exercises to be played at the beginning of the student's practice session. The series has been updated and now includes a CD accompaniment.

*Czerny for the Developing Pianist.* New York: G. Schirmer, Inc., 2003. Distributed by Hal Leonard Corporation.

> The 29 etudes in this book are taken from Carl Czerny's *The Little Pianist, Opus 823.* The editors have made adjustments in slurs, articulations, dynamics, and fingerings. Tempo markings are added at the start of each piece to correspond to the CD or General MIDI accompaniment disks that are available for the book. Each etude is preceded by a worksheet divided into three sections: Practice Tips, Quick Quiz, and Creative Corner.

*Hanon for the Developing Pianist.* New York: G. Schirmer, Inc., 2001. Distributed by Hal Leonard Corporation.

> This collection of Hanon studies is made more accessible to younger students by substituting eighth notes for 16th notes, shortening the exercises, and placing the RH and LH two octaves apart for comfort at the keyboard. A worksheet precedes each exercise and includes Practice Tips, a Quick Quiz, and Virtuoso Variations. An accompanying CD or MIDI disk includes orchestrated accompaniments for each exercise.

Rollin, Catherine. *Pathways to Artistry – Technique*, Volumes 1–3. Van Nuys: Alfred Publishing Co., Inc., 2003–2005.

> Written to accompany the *Pathways to Artistry Repertoire* books, the Technique books, Vols. 1–3, are an excellent supplement to any method. Rollin offers clear directions for a number of technical skills such as strong fingers, wrist rotation, two-note slurs, finger independence, wrist staccato, trills, voicing, balanced arpeggios, pedal technique, and much more.

Schultz, Robert. *Accelerando*, Levels 1–7. Fort Lauderdale: The FJH Music Company, Inc., 2003–2007.

> The exercises in this series progress sequentially from beginner to intermediate level. The series focuses on developing touch, finger independence, contrasting articulations, and steady rhythm as well as the ability to play at a wide range of tempi.

## RESOURCES WITH A VARIETY OF STYLES

Deneff, Peter. *Blues Hanon: 50 Exercises for the Beginning to Professional Blues Pianist.* Milwaukee: Hal Leonard Corporation/Musician's Institute Press, 2002.

> Although this book is centered on blues licks, it can be a useful technique tool for students of any medium of piano playing. Deneff has based the studies in the book on Hanon, and offers a variety of blues exercises, including major and minor blues modes; workouts for the right and left hand; building fluency in all 12 keys; suggested fingerings; practice tips; and soul, gospel, boogie woogie, R&B, and rock styles.

Other books in this series by Peter Deneff include:

> Deneff, Peter. *Jazz Hanon: 50 Exercises for the Beginning to Professional Jazz Pianist.* Milwaukee: Hal Leonard Corporation/Musician's Institute Press, 2001.
>
> Deneff, Peter. *Rock Hanon: 70 Essential Exercises for the Beginning to Professional Pianist.* Milwaukee: Hal Leonard Corporation/Musician's Institute Press, 2003.
>
> Deneff, Peter. *Salsa Hanon: 50 Essential Exercises for Latin Piano-Musicians.* Milwaukee: Hal Leonard Corporation/Musician's Institute Press, 1997.
>
> Deneff, Peter. *Samba Hanon: 50 Exercises for the Beginning to Professional Pianist.* Milwaukee: Hal Leonard Corporation/Musician's Institute Press, 2007.
>
> Deneff, Peter. *Stride Hanon: 50 Exercises for the Beginning to Professional Pianist.* Milwaukee: Hal Leonard Corporation/Musician's Institute Press, 2006.

**PART VIII**

## Resources (cont.)

Konowitz, Bert. *From Hanon to Jazz: Skills, Etudes & Performance Pieces.* Fort Lauderdale: The FJH Music Company, Inc., 2003.

> Written with classical piano students in mind, this is more than a technique book based on Hanon. Allowing classically trained students to enter the world of jazz with ease, each piece comes with performance directions in areas such as touch, accents, rhythm, chord progressions, etc. Information is included on reading chord symbols and lead sheets, learning to read seventh-chord symbols, and much more. The final section of the book includes suggestions for improvising on a few standards such as "When the Saints Go Marching In." A CD accompanies the book.

## Musical studies centered on technical challenges

For teachers who prefer to incorporate the learning of technique into the learning of repertoire, collections of musical studies are available. Understanding that part of developing a good technique is developing a musical approach to the keyboard, a number of books focus on improving technique through expressive playing. The following list offers just a few of the musical etude books currently available.

## Resources

Burgmüller, Friedrich. *25 Progressive Pieces, Opus 100.* New York: G. Schirmer, Inc., 2004. Distributed by Hal Leonard Corporation.

> Well suited for younger pianists, these etudes never exceed the reach of the interval of a seventh. Titles such as "Tender Blossom" and "Innocence" offer a descriptive window into each piece. Although there are numerous editions of these etudes, this edition offers insightful interpretative suggestions, pertinent fingerings, and historical and stylistic commentary.

Guy, Suzanne, ed. *Expressive Etudes: Traditional Studies for Artistic Development at the Piano*, Primer plus Levels 1–6. Fort Lauderdale: The FJH Music Company, Inc., 2002–2006.

> Written as a sequenced approach to technique from four centuries, this series covers early elementary to advanced literature. A short description of technical elements is listed below the title of each etude. The pieces selected cover a variety of composers, styles, keys, and tempi. This series serves students of all ages, including adults.

Heller, Stephen. *Selected Studies Opus 45 and 46.* New York: G. Schirmer, Inc., 2005. Distributed by Hal Leonard Corporation.

> Both the Opus 45 and 46 etudes were written with musical as well as technical interests in mind. This edition, as with other selections in the G. Schirmer Performance Editions series, presents each piece with interpretative suggestions as well as historical and stylistic commentary.

McArthur, Victoria, ed. *Beautiful Etudes*, Levels 1–4. Van Nuys: Alfred Publishing Co. 2001, 2002.

> Designed to make the best use of limited practice time, each etude is preceded by a page that includes a brief biography of the composer and the following sections: *Before You Play*—offering tips for practice preparation; *As You Play*—with suggestions for focus during practice; *Transpose*—suggesting a possible key for transposition; and *Create*—offering a creative activity related to the piece.

Moszkowski, Moritz, edited by Maurice Hinson. *20 Short Studies, Op. 91.* Van Nuys: Alfred Publishing Co., 2002.

Although designed to address a specific technical challenge, each etude focuses on a musical issue as well. A written introduction to the book includes a brief description of the technical challenges of each piece.

## Repertoire that is taught with technique as an important focus

Every repertoire piece worth its salt has a technical challenge. If technique is viewed as the foundation for producing a musical tone, the discussion of every repertoire selection will in some way focus on technique.

## Resource

Hinson, Maurice, ed. *Essential Keyboard Repertoire, Volume 6: 75 Early/Late Intermediate Selections to Develop Technique and Musicianship.* Van Nuys: Alfred Publishing Co., Inc., 1995.

The foreword to this excellent collection states: "Each piece is an effective and expressive work that presents a specific facet of keyboard technique while developing musicianship. Each piece is an etude and each etude is a piece." Contents are conveniently listed in a number of categories:

- By technical categories: Broken Chords, Crossing Hands, Double Notes and Chords, Finger Action, Legato, Loose Wrist, Perfect Coordination, Repeated Notes, Staccato, and Two- and Three- Note Slurs
- By composer
- By title
- By level

**PART VIII**

## Combinations of Techniques

There are many books that cover multiple areas of technique. The following resources reflect more than one of the four categories of technique books.

## Resources

Cisler, Valerie, and Maurice Hinson. *Technique for the Advancing Pianist.* Van Nuys: Alfred Publishing Co., Inc., 2004.

Written to provide instruction in technical skills for advancing piano students, this book has 11 sections, each centering on a specific issue. Sections include scales, chord and arpeggio playing, finger independence, evenness in tone between the hands, double notes, trills, repeated notes, rotation, hand alteration, and chromatic patterns.

# Resources (cont.)

Clarfield, Ingrid Jacobson. *Burgmüller, Czerny & Hanon – Piano Studies Selected for Technique and Musicality*, Books 1–3. Van Nuys: Alfred Publishing Co, Inc., 2001, 2005, 2006.

> Focusing on the etudes of Burgmüller, Czerny, and Hanon, these books include units that focus on a specific technical skill. Some of the musical and technical issues addressed by the etudes include finger strength, velocity and independence, melody over accompaniment, slurs, double notes, voicing, trills, scales, repeated notes, wrist rotation, hand crossing, and broken chords.

*Technical Requirements for Piano*, Preparatory Volume – Volume 8. Mississauga, Ontario: The Frederick Harris Music Co., Ltd., 2008.

> This series conveniently divides scales, chords, and arpeggios, as well as sight-reading and ear-training exercises into progressive levels from beginner to early advanced. Each level corresponds to the grade levels of the curriculum of RCM and Royal American Conservatory Examinations.

## ADDITIONAL RESOURSES

Bernstein, Seymour. *Twenty Lessons in Keyboard Choreography.* Portland: Manduca Music Publications, 1991.

> A good basic guide for technique, this book is divided into two main sections. Book I discusses the *Piano Mechanism* by giving a historical overview of the piano's development as well as a description of the inner workings of the piano. Book II discusses the *Human Mechanism* and includes chapters on sitting height at the piano, distance from the keyboard, body posture, hand position, flat and curved fingers, and a number of chapters discussing finger, arm, and wrist motion while playing. Besides including pictures to reinforce each suggestion for hand and arm position, symbols are used to represent motions, offering a helpful visual aid to understanding the application of each movement. A series of lessons is included and are helpful for piano teachers who wish to improve their students' technique.

Coraggio, Peter, illustrated by Jon J. Murakami. *The Spectrum of Expressive Touches.* San Diego: Neil A. Kjos Company, 1997.

> Using a comic book format and the comic characters Maestro Profondo, Musabella, and Agitato, the book offers students helpful insights into the technique required for good tone production.

Fink, Seymour. *Mastering Piano Technique: A Guide for Students, Teachers, and Performers* (DVD). Pompton Plains: Amadeus Press, 2005. Distributed by Hal Leonard Corporation.

> This DVD was produced as a companion for Seymour Fink's book, *Mastering Piano Technique*. The advantage to the DVD is that one can see the exact motions being produced as each is described, and listen to musical examples demonstrating the application of each technique. Fink discusses the parts of the body and large motions involved in piano technique before going into more specialized motions. The DVD is easy to navigate, and would be an excellent tool for a group setting, camp on technique, music teachers meeting, or to demonstrate individual techniques to individual students in lessons.

Gerig, Reginald. *Famous Pianists and Their Technique.* Bloomington: Indiana University Press, 2007.

> With over 500 pages of reading, this text provides an in-depth study of the technique of famous pianists. A valuable resource for the advanced student or serious teacher, the book offers a wealth of information on numerous aspects of technique. The historical context of the book provides a rewarding insight into the evolution of piano technique. The text is comprehensive and the serious pianist will find it well worth reading.

Schonberg, Harold. *The Great Pianists: From Mozart to Present.* New York: Simon & Schuster, 1987.

> Although this book covers far more than technique, it gives valuable insight into the evolution of piano technique through the centuries. It reads well, and gives a glimpse into famous composers and pianists seldom covered in standard music history texts.

## Injury and Stress Prevention

The prevention of performance-related injuries requires that pianists learn about their own anatomy. Books written by scientists, hand specialists, surgeons, neurologists, concert pianists, and musicians recovering from injuries provide insight into the pianist's physical and psychological structure.

Some books discuss pre-injury issues such as injury prevention, relaxation techniques, mental imagery, avoidance of fatigue, and proper warm-ups. Other authors address what to do once a music-related injury such as carpal tunnel syndrome is experienced, with sections often centered on the physical details of the body, hand, wrist, arm, shoulders, back, and neck, and their related tendons, nerves, muscles, and bones.

Overusing any muscle or using the body incorrectly can easily cause injury. Pain is one indicator of such a problem; having incomplete or inadequate control of the hands is another. Fortunately, a number of modern doctors specialize in the area of music injuries. Today, injuries are more likely to be diagnosed correctly, and more treatments are available for those suffering or unable to play their instrument.

Damage to the arm, back, or wrist is not the only injury musicians might suffer. Loss of hearing can also be experienced, with the potential to adversely impact a musician's career. Psychological problems can develop relating to the stress of performing. Numerous articles and books address music-related challenges to mental wellness such as performance anxiety and stress at the keyboard. Chapter 23 lists additional readings to help musicians remain stress-free at the piano.

Fortunately, teachers can learn from experts and need not feel alone if they are suffering from music-related injury or anxiety. Below are only a few of the many resources available to today's piano teacher.

# Resources

Brill, Peggy, with Susan Suffes. *Instant Relief: Tell Me Where It Hurts and I'll Tell You What to Do.* New York: Bantam Dell, A Division of Random House, Inc., 2003.

> Although not written specifically for musicians, the book gives helpful advice on ways to prevent and manage pain. One hundred easy exercises (demonstrated with pictures and written descriptions) provide relief for pain in the head, neck, shoulders, elbows, hands, mid-back, lower back, hips, knees, calves, and feet.

Butler, Sharon J. *Conquering Carpal Tunnel Syndrome and Other Repetitive Strain Injuries: A Self-Care Program.* Oakland: New Harbinger Publications, 1996.

> This self-care book is targeted for those who have the potential to develop repetitive strain injuries as well as those who have already developed them. Written for the lay person, the book includes charts with suggestions targeting specific professions. It describes repetitive movement patterns used within these professions, and suggests exercises to assist with those movements The second half of the book includes diagrams of the exercises (upper body, forearm, wrist, finger, and thumb) with descriptions on how to perform them, and the value of each. The book also includes information on self-care success and trouble-shooting.

**PART VIII**

# Resources (cont.)

Culf, Nicola. *Musicians' Injuries: A Guide to their Understanding and Prevention.* Tunbridge Wells, UK: Parapress Ltd., 1998.

> This 101-page book provides easy to understand information about musicians' injuries. The five chapters include: What is an Overuse Injury?; Causes of Overuse Injury; Ways of Preventing Overuse Injury (with sections on Healthy Practice Habits, Early Management of Pain, General Health and Fitness, and Natural Technique); Which Instrumentalists are Affected?; and Healing a Chronic Overuse Injury. There is a helpful appendix listing Book References/Suggested Further Reading. The book also includes helpful diagrams and drawings to assist with a deeper understanding of muscles, joints, and suggested exercises.

Mark, Thomas. *What Every Pianist Needs to Know About the Body.* Chicago: GIA Publications, Inc., 2003.

> Based on *What Every Musician Needs to Know About the Body*, this book is meant specifically for pianists, and includes supplementary material for organists written by Roberta Gary and Thom Miles. The author outlines how to map the various parts of the body for playing a keyboard instrument. It is clearly written, accompanied by pictures and descriptions of the hand, arm, shoulder, spine, etc. An excellent cross between the musical and the medical, the final chapter has helpful information on injuries and retraining.

## WEBSITES

*Carpal Tunnel Syndrome*

> www.carpaltunnel.com

*CPS Imports*

> www.cpsimports.com
>
> - Select "Our Products"
> - Scroll down to "Adjustable Foot-Pedal Stool"
> *or*
> - Scroll down to "Duet Size Leather Adjustable Artist Concert Piano Bench with Storage/Skirt"

*Music and Health*

> www.musicandhealth.co.uk

*Music Teachers National Association Wellness Bibliography*

> www.mtna.org/HLtext
>
> This is an excellent resource for books pertaining to wellness, each with a thorough description written by Linda Cockey.

*Piano Maps: A Resource for Pianists*

> www.pianomap.com

*Work Safe BC Safety at Work Center for the Performing Arts & Film*

> http://www2.worksafebc.com/Portals/ArtsAndFilm/Music.asp

*Young Musicians*

> www.ymonline.com
>
> - From list of links on left, select Piano Accessories
> - Select Piano Footrest
> - Select Nested Piano Foot Rest
> *or*
> - From Piano Accessories, select Piano Pedal Assistant

# Chapter 28

# SIGHT-PLAYING

At one point in my life, I felt that being a good sight-player was pre-determined, like being six feet tall; you either were or you weren't. Fortunately someone taught me several good sight-playing tips and I soon realized that sight-playing skills can be improved by observing important steps. By guiding students in the process, their sight-playing skills will improve and they will experience the benefits of being strong readers.

## Developing Sight-Playing Skills

The ability to sight-read, now often referred to as sight-playing, is a valuable skill to develop. Good sight-players:

- Spend far less time learning assigned pieces

- Are more readily able to play favorite music just for fun

- Are more likely to become skilled and sought-after accompanists

- Are more likely to be lifelong learners at the piano

On the other hand, poor sight-players:

- Spend a painstaking amount of time learning each piece

- May feel that the process of learning new pieces is so arduous that they quit lessons

- Are less likely to sit at the piano and play through new pieces for fun

- Are less likely to accompany

- Are less likely to be lifelong learners: the frustration level is just too high

The skill of sight-playing is first addressed when students are taught to recognize patterns and repetitions in music. At first, pattern recognition is easily taught away from the piano, through singing, clapping, and movement. These tools allow students to internalize basic musical concepts without concern for note accuracy.

The next step applies pattern recognition to written music. As pieces are first introduced, students can be taught to identify rhythmic patterns, melodic patterns, harmonic patterns, and repetitions in form. Reinforcing pattern recognition with sight-singing as well as sight-playing, strengthens students' ability to internalize the music as they read.

Although it is desirable for students to strive for complete note accuracy when learning assigned pieces, as they are taught to sight-play, accurate rhythm becomes the most important indicator of success. The good sight-player is able to read without stopping or delaying beats, even if notes are missed.

## Tips for Solid Sight-Playing

The accomplished sight-player is able to play with rhythmic accuracy while responding to the majority of the notes and musical elements. The following steps help students in the process of sight-playing.

### Look over the piece before playing it.

Looking over the piece should be done with a quick eye to all details: time signature, key signature, key changes, leaps, accidentals, form, etc. It is especially helpful to notice any patterns within the music, such as a sequenced melody line or the repeat of an A section.

### Accept rhythmic accuracy as the single most important element to good sight-playing.

If a flawless sense of rhythm has not already been developed, the student will need to count out loud when sight-playing. She cannot get behind or ahead by even one beat; each beat must be counted accurately, even if notes are missed. If subdivisions within the beat are too complex to be read precisely, the student can leave them out, but must still be on the correct beat. If the notes are suddenly too difficult to play, counting out loud allows the student to leave out a few beats (or measures), jump back in at a more manageable point, and continue without losing her place in the music.

A student, especially one with poor rhythmic skills, will sometimes argue, "I am counting; I'm counting in my head!" When a student counts to herself, she uses only one process, the process of thinking. Counting out loud uses at least three processes:

- Thinking

- Speaking

- Hearing

When a student executes a rhythm incorrectly, she may only be aware of the fact that she is counting the numbers. When this same student is encouraged to count out loud, the incorrect or syncopated counting is suddenly heard, and the student becomes aware of why the rhythm was inaccurate.

Unlike singers or trumpet players who have only a single line to observe, pianists often have multiple rhythms. Counting out loud (using the metric system at this point) establishes a steady context for executing complex rhythms accurately. Once the student has developed rhythmic accuracy to a completely dependable level, the counting can be internalized.

### Keep going, no matter what.

The luxury of stopping and fixing notes, rhythms, or fingerings does not exist when sight-playing. Although teachers may train students to fix all errors and not let mistakes go uncorrected when practicing repertoire, this is actually a deterrent to good sight-playing. No one who stops to correct notes will be able to collaborate with a duet partner or accompany a choir.

Playing without stopping to correct mistakes, regardless of what surprises may appear in the music, is a learned skill that must be practiced.

## Edit difficult passages as needed.

When the notes are too challenging to sight-play with total accuracy, choices must be made in order to play with reasonable accuracy. For example, have the student play:

- Only the most important melodic notes rather than attempting a fast passage or complex rhythms

- Only half the chords rather than attempting every chord in a measure

- Just enough of the tones within thick chords to allow the rhythm and harmony to move forward

- With the metronome, so that the metronome acts like a steady partner

Learning what to leave out and still have an effective rendition of the piece allows students to sight-play increasingly complex music. Paradoxically, the more the skill of choosing what to play and what to leave out is practiced, the more the accuracy level increases. If, on the other hand, students stop and fix errors, improving accuracy in sight-playing on any substantive level will remain elusive.

## Keep eyes reading ahead of fingers.

This will avoid being surprised by upcoming changes in the music. If a student has not developed the ability to read ahead, she may stare at the beat being played too long; by the time her eyes move to the next beat, it is too late to grasp the material in time to play it. The brain did not have time to take in what should be played by the intended beat, making it difficult to continue.

Studies have been made of eye movement during sight-playing suggesting that the best readers' eyes quickly move back and forth while reading. Even if eye movement is not continually moving forward, but occasionally jumps backward, one thing is certain: the ability to look ahead is crucial to avoid being surprised by the material to come.

The human brain is like a wonderful computer with a limitless capacity for memory. Students are capable of looking at a measure, storing that information in a memory chip as it is played, all the while looking ahead to the next measure. By looking ahead, the next few beats will not come as a paralyzing shock. The more skilled students become at sight-playing, the farther ahead they will look as they play, and the better they will be able to recall data with increasing accuracy. Although memory is involved to a certain degree, the information needs to be stored only for the briefest of moments, far different than when music is memorized for a performance.

When a teacher watches a student's eyes as she reads, it is possible to judge how far ahead she is looking. If the last beat of the line is played before the eyes move to the next line, the student needs additional training on forward eye motion. By taking a book and covering the measure a student is playing, she will be forced to look to the next measure and keep her eyes ahead of her hands. Although my students sometimes feel flustered the first time I do this, they are always surprised at how much better they read when they are forced to look ahead. Their improved success when looking ahead inspires them to develop the skill further.

**PART VIII**

## Keep looking at the music.

When reading, the eyes should be on the music rather than on the keyboard. I have seen beginning students, whose hands never need to leave a five-finger position, look down to find every note! It is important to teach students early on that they do not need to look at the keys in order to play them. Visually impaired pianists prove this point effectively. By insisting that students not look at their hands, teachers ensure that their tactile sense continually improves. As the feel of the keyboard improves, so does their ability to play increasingly challenging leaps, chords, scales, and arpeggios accurately, without looking at the keyboard.

When eyes are kept on the music rather than on the hands, the brain stays focused on what is changing (the music on the page) rather than what is not changing (the piano keys). Every time students look down from the music they lose their place on the page, even if only briefly. This is especially dangerous in sight-playing when the eyes are not familiar with the score, making it even more challenging to look back to the music and find one's place. The choice was made to look at the keys in the hope of finding notes that would be far better located by touch alone.

If students continue to look at their hands, the keyboard can be covered with a piece of sheet music so that they will not benefit from looking down. Just like covering the notes on the page, covering the keys often surprises students with how well they can play by redirecting their eyes.

Practicing scales, arpeggios, and chord progressions without looking at the hands helps to develop familiarity with the keyboard as well as ease with pattern recognition on the page.

## Read hands-together.

Even though reading two staves is more challenging than reading one, always sight-play with hands together. Students who are not comfortable with sight-playing will sometimes let one hand drop out, especially if they normally learn their pieces one hand at a time. Although some teachers prefer that their students learn pieces one hand at a time, this is not a good approach for sight-playing. Sight-playing, by its very nature, means playing a piece as accurately as possible at sight. Unless it is a one-handed piece, that accuracy means playing the piece as it is intended—for two hands. If students struggle with reading hands together, an easier level of reading will allow them to feel more successful. The level of difficulty then increases as the skill of reading hands-together increases.

If the student leaves out one hand briefly, and jumps right back in after a beat or two, that may be a good choice in maintaining forward motion. Students who leave out one hand consistently, however, need to improve their reading with both hands.

## Learn to read intervallically.

Most modern methods introduce intervals fairly early. Steps and skips are soon renamed seconds and thirds and are followed by larger intervals. Learning to read intervallically provides a parallel system of reading that reinforces note reading.

If students do not recognize intervals, they will struggle with large intervals or notes written above or below the staff. If, on the other hand, students immediately recognize a high note as part of an octave, they will not need to count lines and spaces to name that higher note. If a note is written on the bottom line of the bass clef followed by a note a fifth below, the lower note will immediately be recognizable as C.

As the complexity of music increases, interval recognition becomes an even greater tool in confident sight-playing. Students whose hands move to the feel of a fifth will automatically read faster and more accurately than students who rely solely on the names of the notes.

### View chords as a single unit; put theory to use.

This is done in order to read chords quickly and accurately. If a C major chord is viewed as four separate notes, the brain needs to recognize each note: C-E-G-C. But when that chord is seen as a single unit rather than as individual notes, the brain needs to give only one fast cue—C major. The faster chords are recognized, the quicker the sight-playing.

Just as intervals are introduced in the earliest method books, so are I, IV, and V chords. The more music theory is emphasized, the more effortlessly students will be able to recognize chord inversions and identify harmonic progressions. A solid grounding in theory gives students a better understanding of the musical content of their pieces, and also allows them to use that knowledge to their advantage when sight-playing or memorizing music.

### Develop good fingering habits.

Students who develop good fingering habits will be far better sight-players than those who ignore fingerings. The student who responds well to written fingering will be able to execute a long scalar passage, reach a large interval, or play a thick chord. Instilling good fingering habits in repertoire pieces lays the groundwork for good fingering habits in sight-playing, while poor fingering habits cause road blocks such as difficulty with arpeggios or scales. Students who learn good fingering habits will also make better choices on their own when no fingerings are given.

## Sight-Playing in the Lesson

One of the best gifts a teacher can give to students is the ability to sight-play with ease. Sight-playing in the lesson can be approached in a number of creative ways. One teacher I know purchases a roll of theater tickets at an office supply store. She gives students five tickets at the beginning of each lesson's sight-playing session: one each for correct rhythm, correct notes, correct fingering, not stopping, and not fixing. If students achieve all five, they keep all five tickets. If an error is made, one ticket is taken away (per category). At the end of the year, the students may exchange tickets for items from a music catalog that has been affixed with a ticket price. This creative and motivational tool, along with the attention given to sight-playing, has helped her students to excel at sight-playing.

Other approaches to sight-playing in the lesson include:

- Setting aside a certain amount of every lesson for sight-playing

- Giving weekly assignment in sight-playing

- Having a grab bag of used or loaner books for sight-playing

- Using overlapping lesson times to allow students to sight-play pieces with a student partner

- Arranging time for students who are in multi-keyboard ensembles to sight-play

- Choosing highly patterned selections to assist students who are not yet comfortable with sight-playing

- Taking advantage of supplementary materials on sight-playing in a method series

- Devising a motivational system for sight-playing, such as the theater tickets mentioned above or the "one-week" piece mentioned in Chapter 17

- Playing teacher-student duets so that the student must sight-play without fixing in order to keep up

- Using accompaniment CDs or GM disks so that the student can better enjoy the process of staying on track (An increasing number of methods and collections come with digital accompaniments.)

# Resources

Costley, Kevin, edited by Helen Marlais. *Intervallic Reading Series.* Fort Lauderdale: The FJH Music Company, Inc., 2005–2007.

Books in the *Intervallic Reading Series* include *Be A Star!* Books 1–3, *Be A Star at Christmas!* and *On Stage!* Books 1 & 2. *Be A Star!* provides short, early elementary to mid-intermediate level pieces that encourage students to read intervals and patterns in the music rather than note by note. Understanding that pattern recognition is a fundamental skill necessary for sight-reading, these short patterned pieces offer interesting repertoire while strengthening reading skills. The books include practice strategies by Helen Marlais that focus on blocking, interval reading, finger placement, and directional reading. *Be A Star at Christmas* is designed to assist elementary to late elementary students with interval and pattern recognition through the use of familiar Christmas repertoire. *On Stage!* Book 1 focuses on playing on the black keys and Book 2 includes concepts such as blocking intervals and identifying whole-tone scales, melodic and harmonic intervals, and triads.

Covello, Stephen. *Step, Skip & Repeat: Basic Patterns for Note Reading*, Books 1 & 2. Fort Lauderdale: The FJH Music Company, Inc., 1997, 1998.

Designed to enable students to read music using the three basic music patterns of steps, skips, and repeated notes, these books contain over 100 melodic etudes that progress by a series of small, carefully planned learning tasks. Book 1 is meant for early elementary students, and Book 2 is designed for elementary students.

Faber, Nancy, and Randall Faber. *I Can Read Music*, Books 1–3. Fort Lauderdale: The FJH Music Company, Inc., 1992, 1994, 1999.

Designed to supplement any method, these books include written note-speller assignments as well as short exercises to sight-read. Book 1 starts with basic five-finger positions, Book 2 explores intervals up to a sixth, and Book 3 continues with sevenths, octaves, and upper and lower ledger lines.

Marlais, Helen, with Kevin Olson. *Sight Reading & Rhythm Every Day*®. Books 1A, 1B, 2A, 2B, 3A, 3B, 4A, 4B & 5. (The entire series will include Books 6, 7, and 8). Fort Lauderdale: The FJH Music Company, 2005–2007.

This series of student workbooks is designed to develop a student's sense of rhythm, key recognition, time signature recognition, pattern identification, interval recognition, and response to articulation and dynamics.

### Books for examination preparation:

The following may be helpful in preparing for The Royal Conservatory of Music or National Music Certificate Program examinations and may be used by any teacher to strengthen sight-playing skills.

## Resources

Bennett, Elsie, and Hilda Capp. *Complete Series of Sight Reading and Ear Tests*. Books 1–10. Mississauga, Ontario: The Frederick Harris Music Co., Ltd., 1968–1970.

This progressive series consists of various exercises to help students develop skills in sight-reading and ear-training. Effective for examination preparation, each book corresponds to the curriculum of both RCM Examinations and National Music Certificate Program.

Berlin, Boris, and Andrew Markow, edited by Scott McBride Smith. *Four Star Sight Reading and Ear Tests*, Introductory–Book 10. Mississauga, Ontario: The Frederick Harris Co., Ltd., 2002.

This series is designed to correspond to the levels of the curriculum of RCM Examinations and National Music Certificate Program Examinations, and provides exercises in sight-reading as well as ear tests and written exercises. Guidelines are given for incorporating these skills into piano lessons and daily practice. The series addresses visual, tactile, aural, and analytical skills in a thorough and systematic progression.

**PART VIII**

Chapter 29

# FINGERING

In my early years of teaching, I did not focus much on correct fingerings. Far more concerned with what I considered to be important musical concepts, I highlighted phrasing, dynamics, articulation, pedaling, stylistic elements, etc. After all, playing musically is the ultimate goal, right? How I wish I could call each of those early students and apologize for my lack of attention to fingerings!

As my teaching years progressed, I realized that it is not possible to play musically with poor fingering habits. Scale passages will not be seamless but rather will include unexpected hiccups as the hand runs out of fingers. Large melodic intervals cannot be connected within a phrase when proper fingering has not been planned in advance. A legato execution of the phrase becomes impossible. Poor fingering choices have musical, or rather unmusical, consequences. They impact technique as well, making chords awkward to play or fast passages cumbersome. Often, difficult passages are not a technique problem at all, but rather a fingering problem.

## Fingering Problems and Fixes

One poor fingering habit can generally cause additional problems when it comes to fingering. There are three major problems that may arise, with the second and third often arising as a direct result of the first.

1) Ignoring fingerings on the page

2) Inconsistent fingering choices

3) A lack of a personal inventory of intelligent fingering choices

### Ignoring fingerings on the page
**Problem:** Fingerings on the page are ignored out of habit, virtually guaranteeing that the student will experience difficulties with fingerings.

**Fix:** In the kindest of ways, insist on correct fingerings. Left to their own devices, too many students ignore fingerings, and when questioned about this lack of concern, reply that they want to "get the notes" first. Allowing them to learn notes with incorrect fingerings and then learn the fingering later is like allowing them to bake a cake and add the eggs after it is baked. It doesn't work. It is too late. Too much will need to be unlearned, if that is even possible. It is far better to be firm about correct fingerings right from the start.

If a teacher has not insisted on correct fingerings in the past, it may now seem overwhelming to start such a regimen. A few suggestions might help ease the process and keep the student from feeling flustered:

• Temporarily assign easier pieces, to be played with accurate fingerings.

• Assign shorter pieces; accuracy will seem more manageable.

- Decide that for a few weeks, the main focus of lessons will be on fingerings. Let the student know that, for those few weeks, correct fingering will be the number-one goal.

- Choose pieces that have a particular need for careful fingering.

- Establish a motivation or reward system, such as points for correctly learned fingerings, or rewards from a goodie-jar.

- Increase attention to fingering by having students practice scales and arpeggios. These fingerings become the groundwork for an intelligent and automatic approach to similar passages while sight-playing and learning repertoire.

## Inconsistent fingering choices

**Problem:** The student who does not observe careful fingerings tends to use multiple, random choices, thus diminishing the tactile sense of the piece. This can have a huge impact when performing a piece, especially from memory.

**Fix:** In order for fingerings to become solidly learned in a new piece, students must be taught to use a well-thought-out set of fingerings: the fingerings on the page. It is never wise to ignore the fingering on the page, as this only reinforces the bad habit of ignoring fingerings in general. I tell my students, "You must only and always use the fingerings written in the music."

Before the reader's eyes open too wide at that statement, this does not mean the fingerings the editor or composer has listed will work for everyone. What it does mean is that if the student truly feels the written fingerings are not workable or a different option will work better for her, then she must mark out the editor's fingerings, and mark in her own. Once the student has marked in her own fingerings, she must "only and always use the fingerings written in the music," in this case, her own.

If the teacher has the student learn more than one set of fingerings as a memory tool (as stated in the discussion of memorization in Chapter 22), the fingering choices must still be planned and intelligent, avoiding any sense of randomness.

Students who do not learn a piece with a planned set of fingerings will not play the piece as fluidly. Random choices are frequently poorer choices, and the hands do not develop the tactile memory of the keys needed to execute the piece with confidence. Often in performance, a memory slip is not a memory slip at all, but rather an unexpected poor choice of fingering that throws off the tactile sense of the piece or interrupts the flow of a phrase.

## A lack of a personal inventory of intelligent fingering choices

**Problem:** Because the student has a habit of ignoring written fingerings, she has not developed a personal inventory of intelligent fingering choices. This lack of experience with workable fingerings inhibits the ability to develop effective fingering choices when none are given.

**Fix:** Students need to make many fingering choices on their own. Editors do not always mark all the fingerings needed, and teachers should not spoon-feed workable fingerings to students. When students have a background of observing careful fingerings, they will have developed a more intuitive sense of what works based on past memories of successful choices.

Students must learn to make intelligent decisions when refingering music or writing in fingerings where none are given. Suggestions for fingering choices include:

- **Plan ahead.** Many students will think of fingering based on where they have been, but not necessarily where they are going. It may seem logical to play E-D-C-D-E-F-G in the right hand with fingers 3-2-1-2-3-4-5, but not if the next note in the phrase is A.

- **Decide on the musical repercussions to fingering choices.** Will a certain fingering assist with the musical shape of a phrase?

- **Plan fingering choices to provide the most effective means for executing techncally challenging passages.** Students must know that if a passage is difficult, fingerings provide a crucial key to success. If a challenging passage remains difficult, they may need to reconsider the fingering choices that have been made. Sometimes it is better to refinger a difficult passage, even after it has been learned, than to stay wedded to a poor choice.

- **Realize the impact that fingerings have on articulation.** Fingering choices impact the sound of certain articulations. Notes within a phrase must be fingered to allow for legato playing while a series of two-note phrases over the exact same pitches might be fingered differently.

- **Plan fingerings consistent with scale and arpeggio fingerings** of the key whenever possible.

- **Choose fingerings that minimize strain on the hand and wrist.** Some fingerings, such as those that result in continued over-extension, cause strain on the hand and wrist and should be reconsidered.

As students observe the fingerings on the page—intelligently reassigning the given fingering choices when necessary, and adding necessary fingerings where none are given—they strengthen their ability to think for themselves and learn independently. Above all else, students need to be convinced of the musical and technical advantages of careful fingering.

## Fingerings for Small Hands

Young students or adults with small hands face unique challenges when deciding on fingerings. A few of the many possibilities for accommodating small hands include:

- Avoid fingering octave passages 1-4, 1-5, 1-4, 1-5 in order to play the octaves legato. A small hand just cannot do this, and should not even attempt such a fingering.

- Use pedal to help connect passages of notes that others could connect with a legato fingering.

- Leave out some inner notes from particularly thick chords or a series of thick chords.

- Refinger standard arpeggio fingerings to accommodate the small hand.

- Avoid "reaching" as much as possible; certain passages need to be given fingerings that allow for a more natural positioning of the hand, even though more position changes may be required.

Pianists with small hands are now able to perform on a piano that accommodates their hand size. One example is the 7/8 keyboard, with a key area approximately seven inches shorter than its standard-size cousin. The diminished size allows pianists with small hands to play with less stress. The fingering challenges they face on this instrument are made similar to the challenges felt by most other pianists on a standard-size keyboard. In addition to purchasing a piano with a reduced-size keyboard, it is possible to retrofit a standard grand piano to serve the same purpose.

## Resource

### REPERTOIRE FOR SMALL HANDS

Hinson, Maurice, ed. *Essential Keyboard Repertoire, Volume 5: 83, Early/Late Intermediate Selections Requiring a Hand Span of an Octave or Less.* Van Nuys: Alfred Publishing Co., Inc., 1995.

A welcome collection for intermediate students with small hands, this book is carefully edited to include fingerings adapted to the limitations of a smaller hand. The pieces are organized by level: Early Intermediate, Intermediate, and Late Intermediate. The repertoire chosen for the collection helps students avoid the need for excessive stretching.

PART VIII

# Chapter 30

# PEDALING

---

Just like never assuming that our students know how to practice or memorize, we cannot assume they know how to pedal. Students need far more specific instructions than "Now add the pedal." We must first explain how the pedals function, followed by clear lessons on the varied uses for the pedals. Explaining historical approaches to pedaling gives our students the deeper understanding necessary as they develop a wise and musical approach to pedaling. We need to present pedaling as an extremely sophisticated art requiring a great deal of training. That training begins the very first time our students use the pedal.

## Explaining Pedal Mechanisms

Pianists are notorious for knowing little or nothing about their instrument. How many piano players, from professional performers to teachers, were actually taught about the inner workings of a piano, including the pedals, as young students? Current students can be shown the inside of the piano, how the hammers and dampers work, and the reasons all three pedals function as they do. Using a picture diagram of the inner workings of the piano and the pedals can assist with the explanation; several of the popular piano methods include just such a diagram. Students are more able to use the pedals well when they first understand how and why they function as they do.

## The Damper Pedal

The pedal that needs the majority of attention is the damper pedal. There is not just one use for the damper pedal, but several, including:

- Assisting with a legato line

- Connecting chords or melodic leaps that cannot be connected with the fingers

- Blending sonorities

- Prolonging sound

- Adding to tone color

- Contributing to dynamic shape

## WHAT IF STUDENTS DO NOT OWN AN ACOUSTIC PIANO?

Before going further into discussion of the damper pedal, it is important to note that some students may own a digital piano (or worse yet, only a keyboard). Some newer digital pianos offer simulated damper pedal resonance, but many do not. Students who have only a digital piano may not have the opportunity to hear the tone color and resonance variations that the damper pedal provides. They may experiment with tone color variations in the weekly lesson, but cannot practice any subtle expressive uses for the pedal at home. Teachers need to know what kind of instrument (and pedals) each student works with when practicing.

The damper pedal is one of the most misused parts of the piano. Students often pedal music more as a means of covering errors than as a musical choice. In reality, pedaling is an extremely sophisticated art.

### Ten biggest mistakes when using the damper pedal

(Please keep in mind that some of these problems will be difficult to address on a digital piano or keyboard.)

**1) I don't know when the piece was written.**

Students who are not aware of the stylistic elements of the various periods of music may choose to pedal Bach the exact same way as Chopin, or Ravel like Beethoven. Students need to be taught that different periods of music incorporate different approaches to pedal use, as do various composers within each period. For instance, students must learn that Bach wrote for the harpsichord, the clavichord, and the organ—instruments that do not possess the damper pedal—and that the pedal, although not forbidden, must be used with great discretion. One such use may be in providing some assistance with connecting two notes within a legato line that the fingers cannot reach.

There are no absolutes. The temptation might be to tell students never to pedal a Baroque piece, but in reality there are careful approaches to pedaling Baroque music on a modern day instrument. If, for instance, the student is playing an accompaniment that is a reduction of legato string parts, she may need to pedal to connect the chords that were initially made up of individual legato string lines.

Mozart is different from Debussy, not just because they are two different people, but because of when and where they lived, the instruments for which they wrote, and the stylistic qualities that led to their development. It is important that students are taught when a piece was written, by whom, and the significance of the pedal during that period and for that composer.

**2) It's all or nothing. (Part 1)**

Students will tend to depress the pedal all the way down as if that were the only option when pedaling. They can be taught to do much more. There are shades of gray: one-half pedal, one-quarter pedal, and everything in between.

PART VIII

The following exercise explores the many levels of pedaling:

1) Have the student sit at the keyboard playing a gently repeated detached note, with no pressure on the damper pedal.

2) Slowly have the student apply minimally increasing amounts of pressure to the damper pedal, listening all the while to any changes in the sound of the gently repeated detached notes.

3) When the pedal first starts to "catch" the notes as they are repeated, a somewhat detached echo will be produced.

4) As the damper pedal is gradually depressed more and more, the tone changes to more of a shimmer and the repeated notes sound less detached.

5) The sound continues to change as the pedal is ever-so-gradually depressed further.

6) Eventually the notes no longer sound detached, but rather legato, with an increasingly full sound.

This exercise allows the student to hear the varying degrees of legato and the many changes in color that can occur when using the damper pedal.

### 3) It's all or nothing. (Part 2)

Students tend to lift the pedal all the way as if that were their only choice. Teaching them to "flutter pedal," or release some but not all of the sound, introduces a new realm of possibilities. Sound can be lightened, while maintaining a shimmer of sound that would be lost if the pedal were completely cleared. Gradual release of the pedal aids with dynamic color, such as assisting in the diminuendo of a rich chord.

### 4) Bad footing

Sometimes a young student will lift the whole foot, heel and all, when changing the pedal. Each student must learn to keep the heel of the foot on the floor and the ball of the foot on the pedal. Also, the pedal is not a percussion instrument in and of itself. Generally, the audience does not wish to hear the sound of the pedal hitting against the wood as it is released or a performance marred by the rhythmic thudding of the foot crashing down on the pedal from on high.

### 5) Right idea, wrong time

Students may understand which beat requires a change of the pedal, but lift slightly too soon or too late. If the pedal is changed at the exact same moment that the hands lift, a legato phrase will be interrupted by an audible break in sound. If a pedal change occurs too soon or too late, a muddy sound will be produced as beats blend that should not.

### 6) Wrong idea

Some students will change the pedal "just because." There seems to be no rhyme or reason as to why it is being changed. They need to decide why they are pedaling. The pedal does not change only on beat one, for instance, just because it is beat one. There may be the need to change three times during the measure if there have been three distinct changes of harmony in the measure. Or perhaps there should be no change for three full measures. If all three measures are a G major arpeggio played up and down the keyboard, keeping the damper pedal depressed blends the high and low sounds into a sonority far richer than if the pedal were changed in each measure.

**7) If a tree falls in the forest and no one is listening....**

Besides knowing why to pedal, it is important to listen in order to hear if the desired effect is actually being achieved. Are the chords sounding rich and sonorous? Are harmonies being blended that should not be? Is a lush legato being produced or are too many conflicting sounds accumulating on the pedal? Are pedal changes clean? Is the pedal assisting with a warm tone color? If the pianist isn't listening to the sounds created by her pedaling, who knows what sound is being created? If a piece is pedaled in a practice session but no one is listening....

**8) My way is the right way.**

There is more than one way to pedal correctly. Students sometimes feel flustered when they are first introduced to a new pedal technique such as delayed pedaling or syncopated pedaling. "That's not how I do it..." The last thing students should feel is that they are married to only one way of doing things, and that any other suggestion feels impossible.

**9) I'll do the pedal later; right now I'm doing the dynamics.**

The pedal serves as an excellent tool for expanding dynamic color. It can help with an especially rich *ff* chord, assist with a diminuendo, and it can add punch to accents. The pedal need not be viewed as separate from dynamics, but rather as a contributing factor to dynamic color.

**10) I'll do the pedal later; right now I'm learning the piece.**

As a piece is practiced, pedaling need not be delayed until notes and rhythms are learned. Students should start pedaling early in the learning stage, and then be open to modifying pedaling as their musical understanding of the piece develops and they enter the polishing stage.

## The Soft Pedal and Sostenuto Pedal

Students often know very little, if anything, about the soft pedal and sostenuto pedal. Explanations about the pedals should always include a description of the mechanism of each as well as how and why they are used.

**The soft pedal:** On a grand piano, when the soft pedal (the pedal furthest to the left) is depressed, the hammers shift and instead of hitting three strings, they hit two. On earlier pianos, the dampers shifted over and hit one, thus the indication for the soft pedal evolved: *una corda*, or one string. To release the soft pedal, the indication is now *tres corde* (or "three strings"), allowing the hammers to hit all three strings tuned to the same pitch.

(As the strings get larger, the hammer shifts to hit one instead of two strings tuned to the same pitch, and part of the very large single strings in the bass instead of the full string.)

The soft pedal on an upright piano functions differently than on a grand. On an upright the hammers are moved closer to the strings and thus produce less force (and a softer sound) when they strike the strings. Some pianos have what is sometimes called a "moderator pedal," which allows a piece of cloth to come between the dampers and hammers, thus diminishing the sound and altering the tone color produced. This pedal was common on earlier pianos, such as in Beethoven's time, but is less common now.

Depressing the soft pedal not only softens the sound, but also changes the tone color being produced. Accomplished pianists, those who are more than capable of playing $pp$ with their fingers, often use the damper pedal to alter tone color as much as to diminish dynamics. Students need to be warned that this is not a pedal to use just to play softer; decisions need to be made about the desired tone color that goes along with the softened sound.

**The sostenuto pedal:** The middle pedal is called the sostenuto pedal, or sustaining pedal. The sostenuto pedal on a grand piano allows certain bass notes to be sustained while others are not. For example, if two low-octave Cs appear in the music and are tied for three measures, the pianist can play that low octave, hold both notes, and depress the sostenuto pedal. The hammers on only those low Cs will be lifted, allowing those notes to be treated as a pedal point; those pitches will be sustained without other bass notes being sustained. If the damper pedal were used in this same instance, all bass notes would be sustained, potentially resulting in three measures of overlapping and conflicting harmonies.

When using the sostenuto pedal, it is important to keep it depressed for as long as one wishes the bass notes to continue sounding. It should always be used with care (there are not too many instances when the composer intended its use). In addition, the sostenuto pedal functions differently on different pianos, and students must be warned of this before attempting its use on an unknown piano. For example, the sostenuto on an upright often lifts the hammers of all of the bass notes, not just the ones being lifted at the time the pedal is engaged.

One unit of *Artistic Pedal Technique* by Katherine Faricy is devoted to the use of the soft pedal, including information on the history of the soft pedal, its use in a modern grand piano and in upright pianos, current uses of soft pedal, notation, and a few exercises. A unit on the sostenuto pedal covers many of the same topics. Faricy also discusses the use of all three pedals by various composers, and her book is a valuable resource for current piano teachers. In addition, she goes into more detail than is possible here for a number of pedal techniques, including:

- Control of the Depth of Damper Pedal

- Syncopated Pedal

- Simultaneous Pedal

- Flutter Pedal

- Gradual Pedal Release

# Resources

Banowetz, Joseph. *The Pianist's Guide to Pedaling.* Bloomington: Indiana Press, 1985.

A valuable guide for every piano teacher, this thorough text starts with The History of the Piano's Pedal. Part One covers Pedaling Techniques: The Right Pedal; The Middle Pedal; and The Left Pedal. Part Two includes chapters written by four additional contributors, and covers Pedaling Works of Selected Composers and Styles: Using the Pedals When Playing Bach; Using the Pedals When Playing Haydn and Mozart; Beethoven's Uses of the Pedals by William S. Newman; Executing Beethoven's Long Pedals on the Modern Piano; Pedaling the Piano Works of Chopin by Maurice Hinson; Using the Pedals When Playing Schumann; Using the Pedals When Playing Liszt; The Catalan School of Pedaling by Mark Hansen; Gieseking's Pedaling in Debussy and Ravel by Dean Elder.

Corragio, Peter, with Jon J. Murakami, illustrator. *The Art of Piano Performance: Pedaling – "The Soul of the Piano."* San Diego: Neil A. Kjos Music Co., 1997.

Written in a comic book format with cartoon characters, the book offers practical guidance to intermediate students for establishing good pedaling habits. The characters Maestro Profondo, Musabella, and Agitato demonstrate a wide spectrum of valuable information on the pedal.

Faricy, Katherine. *Artistic Pedal Technique: Lessons for Intermediate and Advanced Pianists.* Mississauga, Ontario: The Frederick Harris Music Co., Ltd., 2004.

Offering specific information about all three pedals, the book also contains a section called Stylistic Principles of Pedaling, which includes excerpts of pieces from the masters, including Bach, Mozart, Beethoven, Schubert, Liszt, Debussy, and Ravel. The scores are marked with a kind of graphic notation for the pedaling, giving readers a visual understanding of when and how to press and release the pedal. This book is an excellent resource for piano teachers of intermediate and advanced students.

Lew, Gail, ed. *Selections from Samuel Maykapar: Pedal Preludes.* Van Nuys: Alfred Publishing Co., Inc., 1974, 2000.

Selected compositions by Samuel Maykapar are included, with each piece using a specific type of pedaling: rhythmic pedal, delayed pedal, syncopated pedal, quickly syncopated pedal, chain of delayed pedals, and staccato pedal, with distinct pedal markings for each. Pieces include challenges such as pedaling an unaccompanied melody, pedaling notes and chords with grace notes, pedaling melodies with accompaniment, una corda or soft-pedal, and the use of the left pedal and damper pedal together. At the end of the book are specific comments on the pedaling execution for each piece. For those who may not have thought about the pedal in such distinct terms, this book is an excellent starting point to teaching pedal with a thoughtful, musical approach.

Rossi, Wynn-Anne. *Pedal Technique*, Volumes 1 & 2. Fort Lauderdale: The FJH Music Company, Inc., 2004, 2007.

Designed for the late elementary student, *Pedal Technique* introduces a step-by-step method of pedal instruction. Starting with a unit on the various pedal mechanics, this systematic approach to teaching pedaling helps students avoid learning bad habits in the early stages. Simple pieces and a workbook format allow the student to practice specific techniques such as keeping the heel on the floor, changing the pedal silently, and working on timing for depressing and releasing the pedal. Volume Two takes the early intermediate/ intermediate student further into the world of artistic pedaling, encouraging the student to develop a musical ear when pedaling. The soft pedal and sostenuto pedals are addressed, as are varying pedal styles for different musical eras.

**PART VIII**

# Chapter 31

# DEVELOPING THE EAR

If any of my teachers mentioned ear-training when I was a young piano student, I certainly have no recollection of any such instruction. Either the topic was completely overlooked, or very marginally taught. After all, I was a piano student incapable of playing in tune or out of tune on my own, so why develop the ear?

## Ear-Training and the Ability to Listen

Although the great pianists of centuries past received training in aural skills and solfege during their musical studies, by the mid 20th century, relatively little was said about ear-training in piano lessons. With increased research on memorization, effective practicing, improvisation, musical interpretation, and comfort in performance in recent years, a greater value is now placed on improving aural skills. Pianists are no longer perceived as playing an instrument that is either in tune or not, with no need to develop their ear.

Ear-training begins in the very first lesson as the teacher plays notes and asks the student to identify them as high or low. As lessons progress, increasingly complex challenges are set, including hearing major and minor chords, recognizing cadence patterns, describing intervals, and identifying melodic patterns. Workbooks with CDs or GM disks assist with teaching aural skills as do computer-lab assignments. When solfege is included in aural training, students strengthen their ability to identify intervals and apply ear-training skills to repertoire.

As a student's listening ability improves, other abilities naturally progress as well:

- A student who recognizes the sounds of chords and chord progressions is more able to improvise and harmonize with ease.

- Interval recognition reinforces the student's understanding of a melodic line.

- Memorization skills improve:
  - Having an aural understanding of patterns assists with the memorization process.
  - Once a piece is memorized, the student's facility in playing from memory is reinforced, as she will "hear" the music in her head as she performs.
  - Memory slips will be more easily overcome, as the inner ear reminds the brain of the direction of the melodic line or the harmonic pattern.

- The ability to "listen" to musical content is strengthened.

- Students are more able to play expressively.

The ear is developed, not only from solfege and ear-training exercises, but also by example. Teachers help strengthen aural skills by demonstrating musical sounds in a lesson. Although caution was given in an earlier chapter against playing students' pieces for them before they have had a chance to decipher the fundamentals of timing, this in no way negates the need to model the desired sounds at some point. When a teacher models musical playing, students are able to aspire to a higher level of musical sophistication.

Students also benefit from listening to recordings:

- Playing recordings by great concert artists provides students with a better understanding of varied styles of performance. Exposing them to multiple recordings of a single work develops critical listening skills. Asking students which recording is preferred and why increases their ability to assess what they hear.

- Asking for a verbal or written description of the musical qualities of a performance compels students to become more actively engaged while listening.

The ultimate goal of developing a good ear is to play musically, an ability all students should attain. Chapter 21 (The Art of Practice) included recommendations for developing a plan for an aural approach to practicing. Chapter 43 (Studio Uses for Technology) includes a list of software programs designed to assist with aural skills.

## Resources

Braaten, Brenda, and Crystal Wiksyk, edited by Laura Beauchamp-Williamson. *Sound Advice: Theory and Ear Training*. Levels 1–8. Mississauga, Ontario: The Frederick Harris Music Co., Ltd., 2006–2007.

*Sound Advice* offers an innovative approach to integrating ear-training and theory into music study. The books and recordings can be used both at home and during lessons, allowing students to expand their understanding and appreciation of music. The materials work well in individual lessons as well as a studio or group setting. This series serves as effective preparation for the ear-training and theory components of examination systems such as RCM Examinations and National Music Certificate Program Examinations. All of the listening exercises referred to throughout the series can be downloaded from the *Sound Advice* website at **www.soundadvicedirect.com** (Online audio tracks are on the website).

Harrison, Mark. *Contemporary Eartraining, Level One: A Modern Approach to Help You Hear & Transcribe Melodies, Rhythms, Intervals, Bass Lines and Chords.* Milwaukee: Hal Leonard Corporation/Harrison Music Education Systems, 1994.

Harrison, Mark. *Contemporary Eartraining, Level Two: A Modern Approach to Help You Hear & Transcribe Chord Progressions, Modal Scales and Key Changes.* Milwaukee: Hal Leonard Corporation/Harrison Music Education Systems, 1994.

Ear-training enables musicians to "hear ahead" in their playing and writing. *Contemporary Eartraining* uses solfege to apply techniques within a key-center-based "relative pitch" framework. Level One works on hearing and transcribing melodies, rhythms, intervals, and bass lines, and moves on to identify triads and simple progressions. Level Two covers hearing and transcribing triad and four-part chord progressions, key changes, chromatic tones, modal scales, and the combining of melodic and harmonic dictation. Both levels include vocal drills and exercises.

# Resources (cont.)

Lavender, Cheryl. *Solfege Bingo.* Milwaukee: Hal Leonard Corporation, 2003.

> *Solfege Bingo* is a game designed to help students hear, read, perform, and identify solfege melody patterns. It develops ear-training and sight-reading skills essential for music literacy and overall musicianship. Level A includes melodic patterns based on the C pentatonic scale, and Level B uses the C major scale. The accompanying CD includes eight different sound sequences ranging from easy to challenging, so the game can be played again and again. The Game/CD Package includes 30 player cards, a helpful educator's guide, cutout caller cards, a Kodály hand sign poster, and CD recording.

Prosser, Steve. *Essential Ear Training for Today's Musician.* Boston: Berklee Press Publications, 2000. Distributed by Hal Leonard Corporation.

> This method assumes a basic understanding of theory on the part of the user. The book features text and studies centered on four areas: rhythm, sight recognition, solfege, and melody. Part I offers a brief series of lessons that serve as the basis for the main focus of the book: the studies listed in Part II.

Schroeder, Carl, Joe Elliott, and Keith Wyatt. *Ear Training for the Contemporary Musician.* Milwaukee: Hal Leonard Corporation, 2005.

> This book focuses on training the ear to understand patterns of contemporary popular music, including rock, R&B, blues, country, and pop. A double CD pack is included with multiple examples of exercises based on basic pitch matching, singing major and minor scales, identifying intervals, transcribing melodies and rhythm, identifying chords and progressions, seventh chords and the blues, modal interchange, chromaticism, modulation, and much more.

## Books for examination preparation:

The following may be helpful in preparing for The Royal Conservatory of Music or National Music Certificate Program examinations and may be used by any teacher to strengthen ear-training skills.

# Resources

Bennett, Elsie, and Hilda Capp. *Complete Series of Sight Reading and Ear Tests.* Books 1–10. Mississauga, Ontario: The Frederick Harris Music Co., Ltd., 1968–1970.

> This progressive series consists of various exercises to develop skills in sight-reading and ear-training. Effective for examination preparation, each book corresponds to the curriculum of both RCM Examinations and National Music Certificate Program.

Berlin, Boris, and Andrew Markow. *Ear Training for Practical Examinations: Melody Playback/Singback.* Mississauga, Ontario: The Frederick Harris Music Co., Ltd,. 1989–1991.

> There are four volumes in this series, which covers levels 1–11 in examination systems such as RCM Examinations and National Music Certificate Program. Each book offers 100 graded melodies designed to improve aural skills.

Berlin, Boris, and Andrew Markow. *Ear Training for Practical Examinations: Rhythm Claback/Singback.* Levels 1–7. Mississauga, Ontario: The Frederick Harris Music Co., Ltd., 1989–1991.

> *Rhythm Clapback/Singback* helps students develop the essential skills of musical memory and aural recognition, and gain an awareness of rhythmic patterns. This series is designed to be used along with the Melody Playback/Singback series to help prepare students for practical examinations.

Berlin, Boris, and Andrew Markow, edited by Scott McBride Smith. *Four Star Sight Reading and Ear Tests,* Introductory–Book 10. Mississauga, Ontario: The Frederick Harris Music Co., Ltd., 2002.

> This series is designed to correspond to the levels of the curriculum of RCM Examinations and the National Music Certificate Program, and provides exercises in sight-reading as well as ear-training tests and written exercises. Guidelines are given on incorporating these skills into piano lessons and daily practice. The series addresses visual, tactile, aural, and analytical skills.

Hale, Charlotte, and Constance Preston. *Ear Without Fear.* Milwaukee: Hal Leonard Corporation, multi-volume set, 2007.

> *Ear Without Fear* offers a comprehensive ear-training course with listening, writing, dictation, and tapping exercises. A self-assessment is included at the end of each book. The series offers students an in-depth training in aural skills.

Kowalchyk, Gayle, and E.L. Lancaster. *Basic Piano Library Ear Training Books*, Levels 1A-6. Van Nuys: Alfred, 1990–1996.

> Designed to be used with Alfred's Basic Piano Library, this series of ear-training books can be used with any method. Suitable for private lessons, group lessons, classes, or camps, the books reinforce an aural understanding of theoretical elements such as intervals, chords, scales, and rhythm.

Schlosar, Carol. *Comprehensive Ear Training, Professional Series: Exercises Based on the Examination Requirements of The Royal Conservatory of Music and National Music Certificate Program.* 10 vols. (Levels 1–ARCT, book with CD or MIDI.) Mississauga, Ontario: The Frederick Harris Music Co., Ltd. First published Sicamous, BC: Keystroke Publishing, 1993.

Schlosar, Carol. *Comprehensive Ear Training: Student Series.* 11 compact discs (Levels 1–ARCT). Mississauga, Ontario: The Frederick Harris Music Co., Ltd. First published Sicamous, BC: Keystroke Publishing, 1998.

> These graded series effectively prepare students for the ear-training components of major examination systems, including RCM Examinations and the National Music Certificate Program. *Comprehensive Ear Training* is available in two series: *The Student Series* is designed for home use by the student. Each level consists of recorded practice sessions on one CD and a fully notated answer booklet. *The Professional Series* is ideal for use by both student and teacher, either in the lesson or for home practice. Each level consists of a book with notated examples that can be purchased alone or with CD or MIDI recordings. The Professional Series features twice as many practice sessions as the Student Series.

## WEBSITES

*Easy Music Theory*

> www.EasyMusicTheory.com

*Good Ear*

> www.good-ear.com

## HARMONIZATION AND TRANSPOSITION

Kern, Alice M. *Harmonization–Transposition at the Keyboard.* Van Nuys: Alfred Publishing Co., Inc., 1963, 1968.

> This timeless volume includes 549 short melodies presented for harmonization and transposition in a group setting or private lesson. The melodies are grouped in sections that progress from tonic and dominant seventh harmonies through I, IV, and V in various positions, passing tones and changing harmonies, the natural minor , secondary triads in major keys, secondary dominants, and modulation.

**PART VIII**

# Part IX
## UNIQUE CURRICULUM

Much more is expected of the present day piano teacher than merely teaching pieces. Today the diverse resources available allow teachers to develop a more creative curriculum in the studio. Part IX presents a variety of content areas for study, either within the structure of the lesson or through special programs designed to augment lesson time and embrace national teaching standards. Potential focus areas include music history, music theory and harmony, collaborative arts (including chamber music), composition, jazz, blues, improvisation, world music, music camps, workstations, and additional teaching options such as early childhood music, group or partner lessons, and adult instruction.

Various chapters of this book address ways for the independent teacher to embrace standards of excellence. Personal standards of excellence can be augmented by an awareness of the National Standards developed by the *National Association for Music Educators*. The piano skills mentioned in Part VIII combined with the curriculum areas of Part IX reflect these standards and contribute to an enriched course of study, one that offers students a more complete understanding and appreciation of the world of music.

Chapter 32

# EMBRACING NATIONAL STANDARDS IN STUDIO TEACHING

How do we, as independent teachers, know we are on the right track with our students? Is there any way to compare our students' progress with any sort of national standard? Fortunately, we do not need to feel totally alone when it comes to standards within our studio. National standards have been developed that can help us all when setting curriculum and measuring student progress.

National standards have been developed in four arts disciplines: music, visual arts, theatre, and dance. These standards include an outline of expectations for levels of achievement in grades one to twelve. They were developed by a partnership of organizations, including the Music Educators National Conference (which is now MENC–The National Association for Music Education), the Consortium of National Arts Education Associations, the U.S. Department of Education, the National Endowment for the Arts, and the National Endowment for the Humanities.

The goal of the standards is to ensure that students in public schools receive an acceptable level of education in the arts. Within the independent studio, these standards provide valuable benchmarks when making decisions concerning curriculum areas outside of repertoire. As such, they serve as a natural bridge between the skills outlined in Part VIII and the curriculum areas discussed in Part IX.

## National Association for Music Education (MENC)

The following National Standards can be found on the MENC website at www.menc.org. Type "Standards" into the search box and select "National Standards for Music Education." Essentially, these standards ask that students be capable of the following by the time they have completed secondary school:

1) Singing, alone and with others, a varied repertoire of music.
2) Performing on instruments, alone and with others, a varied repertoire of music.
3) Improvising melodies, variations, and accompaniments.
4) Composing and arranging music within specified guidelines.
5) Reading and notating music.
6) Listening to, analyzing, and describing music.
7) Evaluating music and music performances.
8) Understanding relationships between music, the other arts, and disciplines outside the arts.
9) Understanding music in relation to history and culture.

The role piano teachers potentially play in implementing these standards is clear. It is in the best interest of all piano students that piano teachers support these standards as they teach performance, improvisation, composition, harmonization, listening, analysis, self-evaluation, and music history.

Perhaps one of the most beneficial elements of the national standards is the structured goals for learning that are set for each grade. These goals serve as an outline for the independent studio and can help ensure that appropriate material is taught and that it will be matched to students' levels of learning.

## Music Teachers National Association

MTNA has developed a set of standards suitable for the independent music teacher. Entitled *Essential Skills for Promoting a Lifelong Love of Music and Music Making*, these standards serve as a guide for curriculum content, although they are not broken down by level or age group:

- Ability to internalize basic rhythms and pulse

- Ability to read: musical literacy

- Ability to perform with physical ease and technical efficiency

- Ability to hear the notes on the page

- Ability to work creatively: improvise, compose, harmonize, and play by ear

- Ability to understand basic elements of theory, form, harmony, etc.

- Ability to respond to the interpretive elements of the composition to express the emotional character of the music

- Ability to conceptualize and transfer musical ideas

- Ability to work independently and to problem-solve

- Ability to perform comfortably individually and with others in a variety of settings

The MTNA abilities listed above provide worthy guidelines for planning teaching curriculum and, when followed, ensure a well-rounded approach to teaching. *Essential Skills* can be found at www.mtna.org/HLtext.

**PART IX**

# Chapter 33

# MUSIC HISTORY AND PERFORMANCE STYLES

Involving my students in the world of music history is a real pleasure for me. Students seem genuinely interested in learning about a composer's life and in understanding the different periods of history. They immediately grasp the importance of learning to perform music with stylistic accuracy and are often eager to read or do research about composers on their own.

An abundance of music history-related materials exists to aid today's piano teacher. During lessons repertoire books can provide descriptions of composers and stylistic periods of composition, including information on form, ornamentation, pedaling, and other stylistic elements. Music history videos, DVDs, and CDs are available for use in group lessons, workstations, and camps. Student-level reading books and workbooks can be used for assignments outside the lesson.

Even if a teacher does not feel proficient in the field of music history, there need not be concern about introducing history into the curriculum. With the many resources now available, teachers can easily find valuable information about composers, types of compositions, and periods.

## Performance Styles and Periods

Students need to understand stylistic elements if they are to perform music effectively. Students should always know the composer of their piece and the period of the composition, and yet it is surprising how often they do not know even this most basic information! Piano students will have a far better understanding of how to perform Bach if they have been taught about the Baroque period, Baroque dances, the importance of articulation, Bach's approach to ornamentation, and the do's and don'ts of pedaling in Baroque music.

Steps for assisting students with stylistic interpretation include the following:

- Teach students about the major periods of music and the stylistic qualities of each, including approaches to articulations, dynamics, pedaling, and rhythmic interpretation.

- Discuss individual composers, their approaches to composition, and the impact this information has on stylistic playing.

- Have students listen to several recordings of the same work and compare the stylistic interpretations of each performance.

- Hold classes, camps, or group lessons where students listen to recordings of a variety of repertoire from various periods, such as a Bach partita, a Brahms piano concerto, and a Debussy prelude. Discuss the differing stylistic characteristics in each.

Every piano student can be taught the basics of stylistic playing, even in the first few years of study. Discussing the periods of music proves essential if students are to understand why Bach is different from Schumann. Although a thorough explanation of stylistic elements goes beyond the scope of this book, a quick summary of important stylistic elements is offered here.

# Baroque

## General

Baroque music reflects the highly ornamented, extravagant style displayed in the art and architecture of the time. Music often portrayed a generalized emotion or "affection," such as joy.

## Texture/Harmony

The music often has a complex texture, as in the many-faceted layering of contrapuntal lines in a fugue. Major and minor keys (as opposed to earlier modes) have become the dominant form of tonality, and chords serve functions such as tonic and dominant. Harmonic progressions can be complex, displaying a wide range of harmonies and dissonances, with chromaticism often used to express intensity in the music.

## Ornamentation

Baroque music may or may not have ornaments included in the score. Even if symbols are used, the possibility exists for varied interpretations depending on the composer and his country of origin. Since ornamentation is such an important element, charts on Baroque ornaments are available to ensure that pianists interpret symbols stylistically. Students can be encouraged to add their own ornaments within the music as well, a common Baroque practice.

## Articulation

When performing Baroque music, articulations are extremely important, as color is often created by a variety of touches. Detached notes are not as short as a modern day staccato, but often are more of a *portato* touch. Slight emphasis at the start of short phrases, lifting at the ends, and a variety of detached notes add to the rhythmic pulsing of the musical line.

## Pedal

Pedaling is used sparingly, as stated in Chapter 30. Most legato playing is executed with the use of the fingers. Although the harpsichord and organ do not have the equivalent of a modern damper pedal, there are times when the pedal can be used judiciously. The damper pedal might be used to connect large intervals within a legato line and thus compensate for the challenge of the wider keys of a modern piano. In accompaniments that are orchestral reductions, it may be necessary to pedal a series of chords that cannot be played legato with the fingers, but which represent the legato lines of a string orchestra. Occasionally the pedal can be used for dynamic emphasis as well.

## Dynamics

Since the organ and harpsichord were the main keyboard instruments, dynamics were not created as they are on the modern piano. Crescendos and diminuendos were not possible with the use of the fingers alone, and a terraced approach to dynamics was common. Terraced dynamics produce immediate changes from one dynamic level to another (such as $f$ to $p$). On Baroque keyboard instruments, this would have been achieved by changing from one manual to another or by the use of various stops to add or subtract from the dynamic level.

## Rhythm

Baroque composers normally used a steady approach to rhythm, but some types of music have a free, recitative-like tempo. A toccata-like section may have an improvisatory feel to it, while a fugue would be executed in strict tempo. Understanding dance rhythms helps to facilitate the rhythmic feel of Baroque compositions based on dances. Students should avoid rubato as it is executed in Romantic music.

### Composers' Role

Composers of this period often served patrons, such as ecclesiastical institutions or a prince. These patrons determined a great deal about the type and quantity of the composer's output.

## Classical

### General

The Classical period is known for its noble simplicity. Composers strove to imitate the perfection of form of the early Greeks, as was often displayed in architecture of the time. The music was meant to be readily understood and enjoyed. It is often said that Classical music, art, and architecture stands the test of time. Emotion, although more restrained than in Baroque music, was expressed elegantly, especially in slow movements. The piano replaced the harpsichord as the favored keyboard instrument during the Classical period, but the early fortepiano was quite different from today's instrument. The touch of the keys was closer to a harpsichord than that of a modern grand piano.

### Texture/Harmony

Unlike the complexity of Baroque music, Classical music was often built on short "periods" of balanced music, such as four-measure phrases with clearly defined themes. When modern players execute these phrases, great attention must be given to performing them as interconnected musical units. The texture frequently consists of a melodic line supported by simple harmonic structure, often executed in an Alberti bass pattern of broken chords. The harmonies are simple, especially in the early Classical period, often centering on the I-IV-V chords, and modulating to strongly related keys such as the dominant or relative minor.

### Ornamentation

As in Baroque music, ornamentation was extremely important. During this period, ornaments tended to be written on the page more than in earlier years. The practice of improvising ornaments during performance continued, and ornaments were similar in style to those of the Baroque period. Books on ornamentation can assist student and teacher alike with stylistic interpretations of ornaments in Classical music.

### Articulation

Articulation is also extremely important in Classical music, offering color and adding to the rhythmic energy of a piece. A clean, articulate approach to technique is essential. Students who ignore articulation in Classical music will diminish the success of their performance ten-fold.

### Pedal

The pedal can be used in classical music, although it is still used sparingly in early Classical music. An over-pedaled piece from the Classical period loses its crisp, clean sound. The pedal begins to be used more in compositions of the late Classical period.

## Dynamics

Although the dynamic levels of current pianos far surpass the dynamic capabilities of early instruments, dynamics in Classical music have moved past terraced dynamics to include markings such as crescendo and diminuendo. Dynamic color expanded greatly by the latter part of the period.

## Rhythm

Mozart referred to rubato in his writings, but on the whole, Classical music is played with a steady approach to rhythm. The rubato of the Romantic period is hinted at in Classical music.

## Composers' Role

The patronage system was still in place, but some composers, such as Mozart and Beethoven, worked with a number of individual patrons rather than one exclusive employer.

# Romantic

## General

In some ways music from the Romantic period is similar to music from the Classical period, but on a grander scale: expanded form, more expressive dynamics, larger orchestras, longer works, and a broader harmonic palate. The restraint and control of the Classical period gives way to more freedom, and the performer is challenged to express that freedom while still being true to the composer's intentions. The piano grew in size with a stronger frame, stronger strings, and a new action allowing for faster, louder, more dramatic playing. Composers responded by writing increasingly virtuosic music. Many pieces in Romantic style tell a story, with descriptive titles such as "The Happy Farmer." The performer has the obligation to tell the story as well. Romantic music is generally more dramatic than Classical music. Performers are faced with the challenge and the joy of expressing a wide array of emotions as they perform.

## Texture/Harmony

Composers use a variety of textures, from homophonic to polyphonic, and from simple to complex. Harmonic color expanded during this period to include denser chords, an expanded use of non-harmonic tones, and a wider range of unrelated keys or distantly related keys when modulating. Understanding these more complex harmonies assists students with learning, interpreting, and memorizing Romantic music.

## Ornaments

Although some improvisation of ornaments was done by Romantic performers, most Romantic composers gave clear directions for how they wished their ornaments to be performed. Some composers—such as Chopin and Field—even wrote ornament-like, improvisatory passages directly into their scores.

## Articulation

Romantic music uses a variety of articulations, often illustrating extremes, from legato to crisp detached notes. Observing articulation is crucial to the overall color of the piece.

## Pedal

Pedal is used for a variety of purposes in Romantic music. Students need to understand why to use the pedal (richness of tone, legato, blending, dynamic emphasis), and not overuse or misuse it.

**PART IX**

### Dynamics

The dynamic range of Romantic music expanded to include dramatic crescendos, diminuendos, and everything from *ppp* to *fff*.

### Rhythm

Rubato is frequently employed, allowing the performer to color the interpretation of a piece with a slight intensifying or relaxing of the rhythm. Although the use of rubato is common, the amount of rubato used may be affected by the tempo of the piece.

### Composers' Role

Romantic composers started to express their own personal emotions, rather than the affections of the Baroque period or the generalized emotions of the Classical period. They saw themselves more as artists and less as servants, and were not usually employed by one patron.

## Contemporary

### General

By the end of the Romantic period, the traditional boundaries of music expanded to the point of breaking. A variety of new instruments came into use, including natural objects, found objects, man-made instruments, and electronic instruments, thus widening the timbres available to composers. Graphic notation (using symbols other than notes) evolved as a means to indicate nontraditional sounds. Contemporary music sometimes looked to the past and incorporated counterpoint, modes, older forms, and other stylistic elements from previous centuries.

### Styles within the Contemporary period

The Contemporary period opened the door to a variety of styles: impressionism, expressionism, serialism (twelve-tone), aleatory or chance music, neo-classical, neo-romantic, jazz, folk music, musique concrète, and other approaches to electronic music. Understanding these different types of music helps students understand how to interpret a contemporary piece.

### Texture/Harmony

The texture of contemporary music can be hugely varied, from a simple monophonic texture to a highly complex, multi-layered texture. Anything is possible! Contemporary approaches to harmony have changed from strictly tonal music (with one key center) to include music that is atonal (no key center), bi-tonal (two key centers), or polytonal (many key centers).

### Ornaments

Ornamentation is highly individualized in Contemporary music, and composers often write out the exact notes they wish to have performed.

### Pedal/Dynamics/Rhythm

Stylistic interpretation can vary from one extreme to another: use pedal/don't use pedal; use a broad range of dynamics/use a limited range of dynamics; use rubato/stay in strict tempo. A variety of approaches to rhythm has been used, including polyrhythms, mixed meters, and unmetered music. Each piece requires an understanding of the composer's intentions in order to be well executed.

**Composers' Role**

Individualism and experimentation are important to Contemporary composers, who do not follow one overriding style as much as any number of more individual paths.

## Stylistic Ornamentation

Ornaments must be interpreted according to the stylistic practices of the historical period of each composition. Deciding on the interpretation of an ornament is rarely a simple decision; many a doctoral dissertation has been written on the topic. Very few students (or for that matter teachers) will become experts in this field, but with some basic study, students can be taught to ornament their pieces with appropriate stylistic consideration.

It is of the utmost importance to choose editions that are judiciously ornamented. Scholarly editions are extremely beneficial to teachers and students alike. Explanations of ornaments are presented in a variety of ways:

- In the introduction to the book

- With a spelled-out (or "realized") version written above the ornament's symbol

- At the bottom of a page

- By printing the edited realizations in gray rather than black, so that teacher and student are able to discern between the composer's symbol and the editor's explanation

There is no single interpretation of an ornament symbol. One symbol can be interpreted four different ways by four different Baroque composers who all lived in France during the same century. That same symbol can have a different interpretation in the Classical or Romantic period. To be confident about ornamentation, teachers can supplement careful editions by purchasing a basic guide to ornamentation.

## Resources

**BOOKS ON ORNAMENTATION**

Earle, Eugenia. *Baroque Ornamentation 18th Century Dances: How to Add Melodic Ornamentation.* New York: Lee Roberts Music Publications, 1973. Distributed by Hal Leonard Corporation.

> Meant to help piano students understand how ornaments were improvised in the 18th century, this book provides a logical, systematic approach to improvising ornaments within a melodic line. Short musical examples are given, with suggestions for adding ornaments to each included at the bottom of the page.

Lloyd-Watts, Valery, and Carole A Bigler. *Ornamentation: A Question and Answer Manual.* Van Nuys: Alfred Music Co., 1995.

> This brief guide to ornamentation can serve as a basic text for students and a handy reference for teachers, with sections offering suggestions for ornamentation by musical period. Although sometimes the material is oversimplified, the book is a short, easy, and affordable reference for piano students interested in a historical perspective on ornamentation.

## Music History in the Curriculum

Although music history can be a part of every lesson, additional possibilities for incorporating music history into the studio curriculum include the following:

- Develop a board game based on a music history topic, as mentioned in Chapter 17, and have students receive points each time they complete a music history activity.

- Purchase music history teaching aids at a music store, through vendors at a music conference, on the Internet, or by ordering through a catalog.

- Take advantage of the numerous books, videos, DVDs, and games intended for classroom teaching and adapt them to group settings within the studio.

- Use music history in a workstation by purchasing books, workbooks, and CDs for a non-computer workstation, or music history software for a computer lab.

- Keep a student computer powered up and available during lessons so that students can search the Internet for answers to history-related questions, teaching them that they can easily find important information when at home.

- Have students develop individual presentations using studio resources, the library, magazines, and the Internet. Topics may include composers, periods of music, the history of music in other countries, or the history of a particular type of music such as jazz or opera.

- Have students create a group presentation as a studio project, thus providing an opportunity for collaboration while learning about the assigned topic; they could then give their presentation at recital time or on a parent night.

- Hold a camp on any history-related topic.

- Hold special workshops or weekend classes on topics related to music history.

- Develop a "Composer of the Month" program.

- Center student research and repertoire study on a particular composer, allowing students to choose their own individual composer.

Some expenses for resources can be passed directly to the student (individual workbooks) and others, like software or a video on Beethoven, are a tax-deductible studio expense and can be reused from year to year.

# Resources

## REPERTOIRE BOOKS WITH A HISTORICAL PERSPECTIVE

Bachus, Nancy. *The Spirit Series.* Van Nuys: Alfred Publishing Co., 1998–2004.

Designed to give students a broader understanding of master composers and musical styles, this series includes historical background on eras, composers, and individual pieces. Book One, for the early intermediate to intermediate levels, presents an overview of the era, related art, and the role music played in society. Book Two, for intermediate to early advanced students, features music by the major composers of the period and shows connections to the next style period. Books contain some analysis of form and key schemes (fugue, binary, rounded-binary, sonata-allegro), as well as maps, images of composers, and related art. Both familiar and lesser-known works are presented and the accompanying CD includes recorded performances of each. The series is available in two formats: eight individual books with CD and a Library Edition consisting of each style period presented in a single volume with two CDs.

> *The Baroque Spirit, Books 1 & 2 – Library Edition: The Baroque Piano*
>
> *The Classic Spirit, Books 1 & 2 – Library Edition: The Classic Piano*
>
> *The Romantic Spirit, Books 1 & 2 – Library Edition: The Romantic Piano*
>
> *Beyond the Romantic Spirit, Books 1 & 2 – Library Edition: The Modern Piano*

*Celebration Series®, The Piano Odyssey®.* Mississauga, Ontario: The Frederick Harris Music Co., Ltd., 2001.

*Celebration Series®, Perspectives®.* Mississauga, Ontario: The Frederick Harris Music Co., Ltd., 2008.

These series provide a carefully graded selection of repertoire pieces and supporting materials. The Perspectives Preparatory level through level eight has three books available per level:

> *Piano Repertoire*
>
> *Piano Studies/Etudes*
>
> *Student Workbooks*

Levels nine and ten include the repertoire and etude books only.

*Piano Odyssey* has similar books and levels, except the Introductory Level does not have a workbook. CDs are available at each level and a *Handbook for Teachers* is available for the complete series. The student workbook is of particular value, providing historical facts about the composer, format of the composition, and musical style of each piece. A number of questions are posed to help students analyze each piece, allowing for a thorough study and understanding of the repertoire. An *Answer Book for Student Workbooks* is also available to assist teachers and parents in monitoring the progress of students using the workbooks.

Marlais, Helen, ed. *Succeeding with the Masters®.* Fort Lauderdale: The FJH Music Company, Inc., 2004–2007.

As stated in the introduction, "This series provides a complete and easily accessible method for learning and performing the works of the masters. Each book presents the works in historical perspective for the student, and provides the means and the motivation to play these pieces in the correct stylistic, musical, and technical manner." The books come with CDs, and include Volume One for Early Intermediate/Intermediate Repertoire, and Volume Two for Intermediate/Advanced Repertoire. Books in the series include:

> *Baroque Era*, Vol. 1 & 2, *A Guide to Practicing and Performing the Works of Bach, Handel, and Scarlatti.*
>
> *Classical Era*, Vol. 1 & 2, *A Guide to Practicing and Performing the Works of Haydn, Mozart, and Beethoven.* Classical Era Vol. 1 & 2 each comes with a *Student Activities Book* with numerous puzzles, games and activities and a *Teacher's Handbook* that includes the answers to the student activities as well as additional ideas for group activities and a suggested music listening list.
>
> *Romantic Era*, Vol. 1 & 2, *A Guide to Practicing and Performing the Works of Schubert, Schumann, and Tchaikovsky.* Chopin is included in Vol. 2. (20th Century volumes are forthcoming.)

# Resources (cont.)

*Schirmer Performance Editions.* New York: G. Schirmer, Inc., 2004–2008. Distributed by Hal Leonard Corporation.

*Schirmer Performance Editions* are designed for piano students and their teachers as well as for professional pianists. Pedagogical in nature, these editions offer insightful interpretative suggestions and historical and stylistic commentary. Prepared by artists/teachers, these publications provide an accurate, well-informed score resource for pianists. Each book comes with a companion CD. The series includes representative works by numerous composers, including J.S. Bach, Beethoven, Burgmüller, Chopin, Clementi, Gurlitt, Heller, Kabalevsky, Kuhlau, Mozart, and Schumann.

## CLASSROOM AND OTHER RESOURCES THAT CAN BE ADAPTED INTO GROUP SETTINGS WITHIN THE INDEPENDENT STUDIO

Althouse, Jay, and Judith O'Reilly. *Accent on Composers.* Van Nuys: Alfred Publishing Co., Inc., 2001.

A complete music appreciation course is contained in this 120-page, reproducible book/CD package. For each of the 22 featured composers there is a biography focusing on his or her personal life, a portrait, a listing of the types of music he or she composed, composer factoids, and a timeline. The CD contains a listening example for each composer. The reproducible listening guide includes information about each listening example and what to listen for in the music. Also included are reviews (tests) for each composer, plus more than two-dozen pages of supplementary material. Composers include Bach, Beethoven, Brahms, Copland, Debussy, Handel, Joplin, Felix and Fanny Mendelssohn, Mozart, Stravinsky, Tchaikovsky, Verdi, and more.

Atkin, Henrietta. *Famous Composers and Their Music*, Books 1 & 2. Pittsburgh: Hayes School Publishing Co., Inc., 2001, 2004.

Designed for music teachers, these workbooks offer a two- to three-page biography and three to four pages of worksheets on composers from Bach to Debussy. The copyright allows the teacher to reproduce the activity sheets once the book has been purchased.

Gibbons, Jacqueline Wollan. *Great Composers of the 20th Century.* New York: Cherry Lane Music, 2000. Distributed by Hal Leonard Corporation.

Easily adapted to group settings within an independent piano studio, this handy all-in-one resource collection allows teachers to introduce upper elementary and middle school students to the great masterworks of the 20th century. Developed by *Music Alive!* magazine, each section features a specific composer and includes a reproducible student article (written at an age-appropriate level), reproducible student sheets (including games, activities, and listening maps keyed to the selected composition for that composer), and a detailed National Standard-based lesson plan. All the musical examples are on the accompanying CD. Featured composers include Claude Debussy, Arnold Schoenberg, Béla Bartók, Igor Stravinsky, Dmitri Shostakovich, Aaron Copland, John Cage, and Leonard Bernstein.

Henderson, Betsy. *The Composers' Specials Teacher's Guide.* Milwaukee: Hal Leonard Corporation, 2000.

Although this series was developed with the elementary and middle school music class in mind, it is well suited to group classes in the independent studio. The teacher's guide includes a thoroughly designed curriculum, complete with lesson plans for studying the lives of Bach, Handel, Rossini, Liszt, Strauss, and Bizet. Intended to accompany the Composers' Specials Video Series, the book offers numerous creative activities, including listening examples on each of the soundtrack CDs.

**Videos:** The Composers' Specials Video Series (from Devine Entertainment) includes *Bach's Fight for Freedom, Handel's Last Chance, Rossini's Ghost, Liszt's Rhapsody, Strauss: The King of Three-Quarter Time,* and *Bizet's Dream.*

Montgomery, June, and Maurice Hinson. *Meet the Great Composers*, Books 1 & 2. Van Nuys: Alfred Publishing Co., Inc., 1995, 1997.

> These books provide an excellent introduction into music history and include biographies and historical facts on 17 different composers in each book. They may be purchased with or without listening CDs. The activity sheets are reproducible, and class kits may also be purchased.

Wilmeth, Ellen. *Classical Connections to United States History.* Milwaukee: Hal Leonard Corporation, 2002.

> This all-in-one resource explores United States history and its connections to Western Music. Designed for upper elementary through high school students, it is well suited for group settings within the independent piano studio. Along with a historical timeline, each section includes a reproducible student article, activity sheets, games, and listening maps for 16 composers spanning five centuries. Full-length National Standards-based lesson plans accompany each section, and all musical listening selections are included on the CD. Historical periods and composers include The New World (DePrez, Palestrina), The Colonial Period (Bach, Vivaldi), Mid-1700s (Scarlatti, Gluck), the American War of Independence (Haydn, Mozart), the War of 1812 (Beethoven, Schubert), the Civil War (Liszt, Brahms), the Industrial Revolution (Ravel, Elgar), and the early 20th Century (Holst, Prokofiev).

## BOOKS ON MUSIC HISTORY, SUITABLE FOR STUDENT-LEVEL READING IN A WAITING AREA, AT A WORKSTATION, OR FOR HOME ASSIGNMENTS

Barbers, David W. *Bach, Beethoven, and the Boys: Music History As It Ought To Be Taught.* Illustrated by Dave Donald. Toronto, Canada: Sound & Vision Publishing, Ltd., 1986.

> This book provides a brief and humorous approach to teaching music history. Chapters display the author's tongue-in-cheek approach: *Those Romantic Types*; *The Russians Are Coming, The Russians Are Coming*; *A Ridiculously Short History of Opera*; and *The Mess We're In Now*. The chapters are short enough to provide students with an easy reading assignment at a workstation or at home, and although the book is humorous, it is based on factual information.

Barbers, David W. *When the Fat Lady Sings: Opera History As It Ought to Be Taught.* Illustrated by Dave Donald. Toronto, Canada: Sound & Vision Publishing, Ltd., 1990.

> Similar in format to *Bach, Beethoven, and the Boys*, this easy-to-read history of opera is a great starter for students who have not yet learned about this important art form. The book covers all of the greatest composers of opera in short, entertaining chapters.

Bye, L. Dean. *Student's Guide to the Great Composers.* Pacific: Mel Bay Publications, Inc., 1988.

> With only 74 pages of text, this is a starter book on the lives of great composers. Ideal for short reading assignments, it could be used at a workstation or in a waiting room.

Comeau, Gilles, and Rosemary Covert. *An Illustrated History of Music for Young Musicians.* Van Nuys: Alfred Publishing Co., Inc. 1999–2000.

> The *An Illustrated History of Music for Young Musicians* series includes separate books for the Middle Ages and Renaissance Period, the Baroque period, the Classical period, the Romantic period, and the Contemporary period. The series is written in a student-level format and includes valuable illustrations and informative descriptions of the art, composers, and musical life of each era.

Kidd, Leonice Thomspon. *They All Sat Down: Pianists in Profile.* Florence: Willis, 1989. Distributed by Hal Leonard Corporation.

> This short and easily read book centers on the lives of famous pianists/musicians. Originally intended for junior high and high school age pianists, the book includes brief, interesting facts about some of history's most famous pianists.

**PART IX**

# Resources (cont.)

## BOOKS ON WOMEN COMPOSERS, SUITABLE FOR TEACHER READING

Ammer, Christine. *Unsung: A History of Women in American Music*, 2nd Edition. New York: Amadeus Press, 2001. Distributed by Hal Leonard Corporation.

> Written in 1980 and updated in 2001, this thorough text on women in music includes bibliographies of hundreds of women in music. The book is well-organized, including chapters such as: The First Flowering— At the Organ; The "Lady Violinists" and Other String Players; Seated at the Keyboard; The First "Lady Composers"; Apartheid—The All-Women's Orchestras; American Composers in European Idioms; Grass Roots—Composers in American Idioms; Opera Composers and Conductors; Contemporary and Postmodern Idioms—After 1950; Electronic Music, Mixed Media, Film, Performance Art; and Today's Orchestras, Conductors, and Instrumentalists.

Bowers, Jane, and Judith Tick, ed. *Women Making Music: The Western Art Tradition, 1150-1950.* Urbana-Champaign: University of Illinois Press, 1986.

> An historical text on women in music, starting with The Cloistered Musician in the Middle Ages, this book progresses through secular musicians in medieval France, women in 15th and 16th century Italy, women and lied, Barbara Strozzi, Clara Schumann, composers in late 19th century Germany, British women composers, American musical life, and women orchestras in the United States in the early part of the 20th century. Biographies of outstanding women performers and composers are included and material is presented within the historical context affecting each artist.

Pendle, Karen, ed. *Women and Music: A History*, 2nd Edition. Bloomington: Indiana University Press, 1991, 2001.

> True to its title, this text is a comprehensive history of women in music, starting from the early Greeks and Romans and going throughout history to modern times. The religious and political beliefs affecting women's role in music are discussed and numerous biographies of women musicians are given. The second edition features more women composers, performers, and patrons, and an expanded view of women outside of Europe and North America.

## WEBSITE ON WOMEN COMPOSERS

*The Kapalova Society*

> www.kapralova.org
>
> > – Scroll down and choose desired link at the bottom of page

## SUPPLEMENTARY MATERIALS ON STYLISTIC ELEMENTS AND MUSIC HISTORY

Corragio, Peter, with Jon J. Murakami, illustrator. *The Art of Piano Performance: Musical Style.* San Diego: Neil A. Kjos Music Co., 2003.

> Written in a comic-book format with cartoon characters, this book serves as an introduction to the Baroque, Classical, and Romantic eras. Stylistic elements of each period are covered in an easily accessible format.

*Discover the Great Composers: 24 Posters and Fun Facts.* Milwaukee: Hal Leonard Corporation, 2002.

> These full-color 9"x12" laminated posters present 24 composers from the Baroque era to the 20th century. Each poster comes complete with a photo or illustration on the front and a short biography on the back, including a list of representative works and interesting "fun facts." The posters can be used for studio display, bulletin boards, class discussions, group activities, and summer camps. Featured composers include Bach, Beach, Beethoven, Brahms, Chavez, Chopin, Copland, Debussy, Grieg, Handel, Haydn, Liszt, Mendelssohn, Mozart, Palestrina, Rossini, Schubert, Still, J. Strauss, Stravinsky, Tchaikovsky, Villa-Lobos, Vivaldi, and Wagner.

Hammond, Susan. *Classical Kids® Teaching Edition.* Pickering, Ontario: The Children's Group, 2008.

Susan Hammond's *Classical Kids®* uses storytelling and recorded music to bring alive the life, times, and music of Bach, Vivaldi, Handel, Beethoven, Mozart, and Tchaikovsky. The series also explores the Merlin legend in *Song of the Unicorn* and children's poetry and singing in *Daydreams and Lullabies*. The Teacher's Edition is designed for students in grades K–8, and would be ideal for group music history classes in the independent studio. The Teacher's Resource CD-ROM includes printable material, including:

- Comprehensive Teacher's Notes: background information, discussion topics, musical scores, age-appropriate activities, music appreciation and worksheets.
- Scripts for each CD: print-off sections for read along, ESL programs, and drama.
- Slideshow Discussion Points: guidance to move students from passive watching to active discussion and art activities.
- Slideshow DVD: hundreds of pictures of art, architecture, and fashion from the times of the great composers.
- Music-only CD: useful for musical analysis, drama, or ambient music.

Hinson, Maurice, and Stewart Gordon. *Performance Practices.* (DVD). Van Nuys: Alfred Publishing Company, Inc., 2003–2004.

Maurice Hinson has made a series of DVDs devoted to performance practices in various periods of music, including Baroque, Classical, Romantic, and Impressionistic. Stewart Gordon presents music of the Late 20th Century. Each DVD is easy to navigate and the set is useful for independent teachers, classes within the studio, camps, and local music teacher association libraries.

Kirby, F.E. *Music for Piano: A Short History.* Portland: Amadeus Press, 1995, corrected reprint 1997, 2000. Distributed by Hal Leonard Corporation.

This historical survey focuses on music for piano solo, but also includes important compositions for piano duet and two pianos. Scholarly yet readable, it covers the entire repertoire from the Renaissance to the late 20th century and incorporates a bibliography of 1,100 sources for further study.

Koch, Karen. *My Own Music History.* Trenton: The Music Studio, 1989.

By associating a color with each major period of music history, this set of materials reinforces music history as students learn repertoire. Students keep color-coded lists of repertoire by era and learn which composers belong in which period. The student kit contains six timelines of musical periods ready to be completed with color-coding and labels of composer name, dates, and images (included). All materials fit in a standard three-ring binder (optional), which can serve as an assignment notebook. The Teacher Packet provides reproducible documents, reference pages, highlighting pens for color-coding, and a 15-minute video or DVD that introduces music history in the *My Own Music History* format. Colored repertoire sheets and other materials are available individually.

Lavender, Cheryl. *Music Listening Bingo.* Milwaukee: Hal Leonard Corporation, 1996.

This game comes with a large reproducible Music History Timeline chart that shows the five periods of music history: Renaissance, Baroque, Classical, Romantic, and Contemporary. Five reproducible Listening Smart pages are included (one for each period); 30 playing cards, a Composer's Listening Guide, and two CDs. Directions are included for playing four games: Composer Connection, Music Listening Bingo Level 1, Music Listening Bingo Level 2, and Composer Identification. The professionally produced CDs have listening examples of the music of 24 composers, including Palestrina, Praetorius, Vivaldi, Bach, Scarlatti, Haydn, Mozart, Beethoven, Schubert, Brahms, Debussy, and Gershwin.

**PART IX**

# Resources (cont.)

Lavender, Cheryl. *Music Styles Bingo.* Milwaukee: Hal Leonard Corporation, 2002.

This collection (with CD) of hands-on activities is designed to help students in grades 4–8 identify, describe, and compare 24 different styles of music—from folk to classical, from heavy metal to new age. While playing the game, students can be guided to learn the origins of musical styles, investigate cultural and historic influences, discover how music styles evolve, and make meaningful connections among different styles of music.

McLean, Edwin. *Music Crossword Puzzles and Games* and *Christmas Crossword Puzzles and Games.* Fort Lauderdale: The FJH Music Company, 2006, 2007.

Handy to have in a waiting room or to give as a gift to students, these fun books include crossword puzzles, matching games, word scrambles, and word searches. The puzzles and games progress in difficulty from very easy to advanced.

Mertens, Michael, *Discover Music History & Culture: 24 Posters and Fun Facts.* Milwaukee: Hal Leonard Corporation, 2005.

These attractive full-color laminated posters present a multitude of images relating music, historic events, visual arts, and architecture from the Middle Ages to the present. Posters come complete with photos, illustrations, and a short summary of historic information covering the Middle Ages, Renaissance, Baroque, Classical, Romantic and 20th Century eras. The posters can be displayed in a studio, and referred to in private lessons, group lessons, or camp settings. A variety of interesting "fun facts" are included with the posters.

Rathnau, Heather. *Composers in Time.* Missouri City: Theory Time Partners, 2002.

This convenient, 28-page booklet serves as a brief but valuable reference manual on composers and stylistic periods of music. Each section centers on a period of music history, and offers two items:

1) A bulleted list of each period's major musical elements

2) A chart of each period's main composers' names, country of origin, date of birth, and date of death

The periods covered include Medieval, Renaissance, Pre-Baroque, Baroque, Rococo, Classical, Romantic, Impressionistic, and Contemporary.

## WEBSITES

*Indiana University Libraries*

http://library.music.indiana.edu

– Scroll down; under "References and Instruction" select "Worldwide Internet Music Resources"

(**One word of caution:** If the site is too busy, you will receive a message that states "Too many connections." If this message appears, try again later as the site is well worth visiting.)

Issued by the William and Gayle Cook Music Library at the Indiana University School of Music, this site has helpful links to composers and professional journals as well as hundreds of links to other music-related sites. It is well-organized and easy to navigate.

*Naxos.com*

www.naxos.com

– Select "Composers"

This site lists an introduction to hundreds of composers, an A–Z glossary of musical terms, an introduction to classical music and opera, a thorough list of related links, and much more.

*Yahoo! Entertainment*

 http://dir.yahoo.com

  – Select "Arts & Humanities"; select "Performing Arts"; select "Music"; select "Genres"; select "Classical"

 This is a huge website with references to classical composers, women composers, ethnic music, opera, ancient music, and much, much more.

## OTHER WEB RESOURCES FOR MUSIC HISTORY RESEARCH

*The Classical Music Navigator*

 www.wku.edu/~smithch/music

*Classics for Kids*

 http://classicsforkids.com

*CMEA Bay Section, an Affiliation of the California Association for Music Education*

 www.cmeabaysection.org/resources.html

*Empire Union School District*

 www.empire.k12.ca.us

  – Select "Capistrana"; select "The Music Room"

*Essentials of Music*

 http://essentialsofmusic.com

*The Internet Public Library*

 www.ipl.org/div/mushist

PART IX

# Chapter 34

# MUSIC THEORY AND HARMONY

When I took freshman theory I felt quite indignant to have this course forced upon me. Why did I need to take theory? After all, I was a performer, not a composer! I also must say that I thoroughly disliked the class and struggled mightily the whole year. Fortunately, after taking additional classes, I grew to appreciate and understand music theory. Now I am a firm believer in teaching students as much theory as possible, and as early as possible.

I have taught music theory in lessons, in classes, and at workstations, both with and without a computer. One of my favorite methods of teaching theory involved Saturday classes offered every other week, with students divided by levels. My students looked forward to the theory games as well as the fun workbooks. It amazed me that students were disappointed when it was an off-week, and looked forward to the next time they would attend theory class. I was thrilled that they enjoyed the subject that was so unpleasant to me during my freshman year of college!

## The Importance of Studying Theory

In order to help students become more engaged in music theory, teachers must first be committed to the many benefits that a foundation in theory brings:

- Students who analyze or identify the harmonic and structural elements of a composition will learn pieces with added security and ease.

- Those who study theory are more able to understand and describe musical content using words. Verbal descriptions demonstrate a deeper understanding than, "I know what it is; I just don't know how to describe it."

- Understanding theory helps to interpret pieces. Those who recognize a modulation or unusual chord progression may be influenced to use dynamics or rubato differently than those who are unaware of the musical content of the piece.

- The abilities to analyze, describe, understand, and interpret music all lead to added retention when learning repertoire.

- Memorization is improved when chords, harmonic progressions, melodic patterns, key changes, etc. can be identified.

- Sight-playing ability improves dramatically with a more complete understanding of musical patterns and a more highly developed vocabulary of intervals, chords, cadences, and form.

- Understanding theory provides a solid foundation for skills such as improvisation, harmonization, and composition.

Restated on the student level, "Studying theory will help you to learn and memorize music more easily, play more beautifully, sight-play more comfortably, and be more creative at the piano."

From the most casual learner to the most serious performer, all students benefit from the study of theory. Conversely, all students will have a diminished understanding and ease with piano study if they are not taught theory. More serious students will be at an added disadvantage; college-bound music majors suffer from a past teacher's negligence if they have not studied theory.

No teacher knows which young student may choose to become a professional musician. Teachers owe it to all students to prepare them for any eventuality, and to enhance their appreciation of music by improving their understanding of theory—the musical nuts and bolts that hold a composition together.

## Types of Resources

Fortunately, a number of creative resources exist for teaching theory. Some are best suited to individual lessons, while others provide excellent activities for group classes, workshops, workstations, and camps. Possible resources include:

- Theory books that are part of a method series

- Theory and harmony workbooks not associated with a method

- Music theory software

- Internet websites for theory

- Teacher websites with theory-related lesson plans

- Music theory games

- Books intended for teachers that describe music theory games and activities

- Activity books for students

- Theory lesson plans and books developed for the public school music teacher

## Theory Testing

A number of organizations offer standardized testing in music theory and keyboard skills. These tests present an outline for the systematic teaching of theory. Levels are clearly defined, allowing teaching to be geared toward well-conceived yearly goals. Some of the many outside sources for theory testing include:

- **State Music Teacher Associations:** numerous state syllabi and theory and keyboard skills exams

- **National Federation of Music Clubs:** Junior Festival Musicianship Theory Event

- **National Music Certificate Program (USA):** theory syllabus and exams

- **Royal Conservatory of Music Examinations:** theory syllabus and exams

# Resources

RCM Examinations. **Official Examination Papers.** 15 volumes. Mississauga, Ontario: The Frederick Harris Music Co., Ltd., published annually.

> This series of test books is based on recent examination papers in subject areas such as rudiments, history, harmony, counterpoint, analysis, and piano pedagogy. *RCM Examinations: Official Examination Papers* serve as excellent practice tests for students preparing for examinations in these areas.

RCM Examinations. **The Royal Conservatory of Music Theory Syllabus**, 2009 Edition. Mississauga, Ontario: The Frederick Harris Music Co., Ltd., 2009.

> This syllabus is used jointly for theory examinations offered by RCM Examinations and the National Music Certificate Program Theory Examinations. Even if a teacher is not entering students in either of those programs, this syllabus provides an excellent outline for the study of theory. Section 1 has general information on RCM exams; Section 2 covers graded theory examination, including levels for Preliminary Rudiments, Rudiments, Harmony, Counterpoint, Analysis, Keyboard Harmony, History, and Musicianship Examinations. Section 3 covers requirements for the ARCT exams; Section 4 lists musical terms, a description of scores, chord symbols, and non-chord tones; and Section 5 is an extensive bibliography.

## BOOKS

Adair, Audrey. **Ready-to-use Music Activities Kit.** Boston: Family Education Network, 1984.

> Although worksheets may not be the favorite activity for many independent music teachers, this book contains 200 reproducible worksheets on music theory, singing, composing, listening, ear-training, and instruments. The sheets can be used as straightforward theory assignments in a workstation, group setting, or as take-home assignments.

Clough, John, Joyce Conley and Boge Claire. **Scales, Intervals, Keys, Triads, Rhythm, and Meter: A Programmed Course in Elementary Music Theory, With an Introduction to Partwriting**, 3rd Edition. New York: W.W. Norton & Co., 1999.

> The 3rd Edition covers the basics of music theory and part-writing in a well-organized format ideal for self-paced study. Each section builds progressively on the information already given and tests are included at the end of each part. All tests include an answer key allowing students to self-check their work and proceed from week to week independently. The companion CD offers valuable aural reinforcement of concepts presented in the book. This book is somewhat expensive, but well worth the purchase due to the accessible and organized presentation of concepts. The book could also serve as the foundation for theory classes within the private studio.

Fleser, Jim. **The Chord Wheel.** Milwaukee: Hal Leonard Corporation, 2000.

> Valuable for students who are composing, transposing, or studying music theory, *The Chord Wheel* simplifies the basics of chord identification and chord progressions. By turning a transparent wheel, the user can identify chords by Roman numeral in any key, analyze chord progressions in any key, and transpose a chord progression to any key.

Harrison, Mark. **All About Music Theory.** Milwaukee: Hal Leonard Corporation, 2008.

> This book/CD package provides a fun and engaging way to help students understand the fundamentals of music. Topics include learning to read music, understanding chords and scales, musical forms, improvisation, and composition. Students learn about music theory through many popular songs from artists such as Elton John, Coldplay, Steely Dan, the Beatles, Duke Ellington, Nirvana, Ray Charles, and classical composers, including Johann Strauss, Bartók, Beethoven, and Chopin. The accompanying CD includes many of the examples from the book.

Harrison, Mark. *Contemporary Music Theory: A Complete Harmony and Theory Method for the Pop & Jazz Musician.* Milwaukee: Hal Leonard Corporation/Harrison Music Education Systems; Levels 1 & 2, 1995; Level 3, 2001.

> Intended for the pop or jazz musician, *Contemporary Music Theory* adopts a slightly different format than traditional theory courses. Presented from the viewpoint of the contemporary musician, the book goes well with *Contemporary Eartraining*, and reinforces aural skills while learning theory. Each chapter includes instructions, workbook questions, and workbook answers. A helpful glossary of terms is included in the back of each volume. All levels cover a comprehensive amount of material. A student who completes all three levels will have gained an expansive knowledge of harmony and theory.

Hawn, Carol, and Dorothy Munz. *Chord Construction: Learning Through Shapes and Forms.* Milwaukee: Hal Leonard Corporation, 1997.

> This book is ideal for visual learners or anyone who wants to study chords in a clear, logical presentation. The authors use pictures, such as notes marked on the keyboard coupled with the chord written on a staff, to clearly identify the notes in a chord. Chord shapes are illustrated with black and white symbols to represent black and white keys. The organization of the book allows the student to see the big picture. For example, in the section explaining major chords, all major chords appear together on one page and are organized in groupings of similar white-black shapes on the keyboard. The page also includes a keyboard picture of each chord along with each chord written on the staff. Also discussed are the circle of fifths, various forms of triads, harmonization, inversions of chords, chord progressions, and seventh chords.

Lopez, Barbara. *Music Notes: The Quick and Easy Guide to Music Basics.* Fort Lauderdale: The FJH Music Company, Inc., 2004.

> This six-page cardboard foldout includes a brief introduction to a number of topics and serves as quick and handy reference material within the studio. Areas presented include: What is Music?, The Grand Staff, Bass Clef, Treble Clef, Rhythm, Note Values and Time Signatures, Melody, Note Names, Sharps and Flats, The Major Scale, The Minor Scale, Circle of Fifths, Harmony, Intervals, and Chords.

McLean, Edwin, with Derek Richard. *The FJH Keyboard Chord Encyclopedia.* Fort Lauderdale: The FJH Music Company, Inc., 2004.

> An introductory section covers the basics of constructing simple triads, 7th chords, chords with suspended tones, and dominant 7th chords with altered or added tones. Naming 7th, 9th, 11th, and 13th chords, inverting voices, and alternate notations are presented next, followed by a thorough encyclopedia of chords. Each page includes nine chords in one key, written in the treble clef and demonstrated on a drawing of a keyboard.

*Picture Chord Encyclopedia.* Milwaukee: Hal Leonard Corporation, 2002.

> This 363-page encyclopedia of chords offers a thorough representation of chords and inversions. Following the initial introduction to chords and chord types, each page includes chords represented in three ways: on the staff, with a drawing of the keyboard with keys highlighted and individual pitch names written, and in a picture of real hands playing the chord on a real keyboard. The encyclopedia is so thorough that pages 16–44 cover the chords based on C alone!

Pinksterboer, Hugo. *Music on Paper: Basic Theory.* Heemstede, the Netherlands: The Tipbook Company, 2002, 2004. Distributed by Hal Leonard Corporation.

> This fact-filled manual serves well as a supplement to other theory materials, or as a self-help book for older students to use as a study guide. Geared toward musicians in all styles, the clearly worded explanations cover basic information such as dynamics, rhythm, time and meter, major and minor keys, and intervals, as well as less commonly covered areas such as articulation and ornamentation. A valuable addition to the book is the use of *Tipcodes*, which allow the reader to access soundtracks and other additional information at www.tipbook.com.

PART IX

## Resources (cont.)

Sarnecki, Mark. *Elementary Music Rudiments.* Preliminary, Grades 1 & 2. Mississauga, Ontario: The Frederick Harris Music Co., Ltd., 2001.

> This series covers notation, pitch, rhythm, meter, key signature, major and minor scales, intervals, chords, modal scales, melody writing, the keyboard, and beginning harmony. Frequent review sections, practice tests, and hands-on exercises accompany concise and systematic explanations of music theory.

Sarnecki, Mark. *Harmony.* Books 1–3. Mississauga, Ontario: The Frederick Harris Music Co., Ltd., 2002, 2003, 2005.

> Sarnecki adopts a clear, straightforward approach to harmony in these three volumes. An effective course of music study for basic, intermediate, and advanced harmony, each book gradually and systematically expands the student's harmonic vocabulary through the use of carefully selected music examples and exercises.

Surmani, Andrew, Karen Farnum Surmani, and Morton Manus. *Essentials of Music Theory.* Van Nuys: Alfred Publishing Company, Inc., 1998.

> *Essentials of Music Theory* can be purchased in four books: Book 1, Book 2, and Book 3, or as one "Complete Book" that includes all three levels. Companion software can also be purchased to allow the instructor to test and drill students, keep track of student progress, and make use of interactive instruction in the classroom. These books cover the basics of music theory: treble and bass clef, note values, time signatures, dynamics, ear-training, and more.

Vandendool, Grace. *The Basics of Harmony: A comprehensive introduction to harmony.* Mississauga, Ontario: The Frederick Harris Music Co., Ltd., 2006.

> This well-organized, comprehensive workbook offers an introduction to basic harmony: chords and cadences, nonharmonic tones, resolution of the 7th chord, the six-four chord, common errors in voice leading, modulation, melody writing, transposition for orchestral instruments, analysis, popular chord symbols and harmony, and Classical era ornaments. Other books in this series include:
>
> *The Basics of Harmony Answer Book,* 1997
>
> *The Intermediate Harmony,* 2002
>
> *The Intermediate Harmony Answer Book,* 2002

Vandendool, Grace. *Keyboard Theory Preparatory Series.* Books A–E. Mississauga, Ontario: The Frederick Harris Music Co., Ltd., 1995.

> *Keyboard Theory* is a progressive series of workbooks written to provide the young student (ages 6–8) with a thorough knowledge of the fundamentals of music theory. The five-volume series teaches theory in the simplest form; graphic illustrations are used to relate written notes to the keyboard. Wide-spaced staves, large print, games, and illustrations all make this an appealing series for young students.

### THEORY-RELATED ACTIVITIES

Cox, Maureen, edited by Victoria McArthur. *Blast Off with Music Theory!* Books 1–5. Fort Lauderdale: The FJH Music Company, Inc., 1998–2000.

> Although these are basically workbooks, the exercises are presented in a game format with an outer-space theme. The appealing format presents theory in an accessible fashion to young students while covering all of the basics. Word searches, crossword puzzles, and brainteasers are just some of the techniques used to teach everything from note values to key signatures.

Elliott, Katie. **Theory Fun Factory.** London: Boosey and Hawkes, 1995, 1996. Distributed by Hal Leonard Corporation.

> This series presents theory for early grades using puzzles and games, and is in a child-friendly format. Although the pages are a little busy looking, students may enjoy working on the puzzles at a workstation or while waiting for lessons. All areas are presented sequentially. Books in the series include:
>
> > *Theory Fun Factory 1,* 1995: Pre-grade
> >
> > *Theory Fun Factory 2,* 1995: Grade 1
> >
> > *Theory Fun Factory 3,* 1995: Grade 2
> >
> > *Theory Fun Factory Complete,* 1996: Collection of Books 1–3

Matz, Carol, with Victoria McArthur. **All About Music: Elementary Activities, Games, and Listening to Teach Music Appreciation and Theory.** Fort Lauderdale: The FJH Music Company, Inc., 1998.

> *All About Music* has been written to serve the busy teacher as a flexible teaching "assistant." The materials can be used in private lessons, group lessons, summer lessons, workstations, theory classes, or summer music camps.

## WEBSITES

*Ababasoft*

> www.ababasoft.com
>
> > – Select from "Online music games"

*Boowa & Kwala*

> www.boowakwala.com
>
> > – Select "All the games"
> >
> > – Select "Musical games"

*CMEA Bay Section, an Affiliation of the California Association for Music Education*

> www.cmeabaysection.org/resources.html
>
> > – Select "Music Theory Lines"

*FlashMusicGames*

> www.flashmusicgames.com

*MTNA Websites for Kids*

> www.mtna.org/HLtext

*New York Philharmonic Kidzone*

> www.nyphilkids.org
>
> > – Select "Game Room"

*PBS Kids*

> www.pbskids.org

*Piano Technician's Guild*

> www.ptg.org
>
> > – Select "Learning Center"

*Quia*

> www.quia.com/web
>
> > – Select "Music"

*Ricci Adams' musictheory.net*

> www.musictheory.net

*Teoria Music Theory Web*

> *www.teoria.com*

**PART IX**

# Chapter 35

# COLLABORATIVE ARTS

My early years of piano lessons provided hours of solitary work. I sat alone, rarely experiencing the joy of playing with others. I have very few memories of even playing a duet, much less accompanying another student, accompanying a choir, or playing in a chamber music ensemble. Perhaps because of our frequent moves from state to state, I had fewer opportunities to develop collaborative skills, but I now see those years of study as unnecessarily isolated.

While band or choir members feel the excitement of musical interaction, piano study too often remains a solitary activity. Sometimes this aloneness causes students to stop lessons altogether. They may yearn for the fun of interacting with peers and dislike the hours of lonely work. In reality, pianists need not spend all their time alone, as literature exists for keyboard ensembles, accompanying, and chamber music at every level of study.

## Opportunities to Collaborate

All students' musical experiences will be enriched when they take part in varied and rewarding collaboration. Teachers can foster collaboration with others from the earliest stages of learning. Some possibilities include:

- Perform student/teacher duets in early lessons

- Assign duets, duos, and trios to student partners

- Organize ensembles for multiple keyboards

- Organize Monster Concerts for students at multiple keyboards

- Have students of all ages accompany other students

- Encourage more experienced students to accompany ensembles

- Involve the complete studio in chamber music

## Duets, Duos, and Keyboard Ensembles

Most method books include teacher duets right from the start. Students light up as they play those first duets. The teacher's part, when joined with the young student's efforts, offers a sophisticated sound far beyond what the student could produce alone. That joy in working together can be fostered through a variety of future experiences.

Playing in a keyboard ensemble provides a number of benefits:

- Piano students enjoy the challenge of playing with others, especially friends.

- The aloneness of practicing is balanced by music-making with peers.

- Listening skills are improved as students respond to a partner's music-making.

- Rhythm skills improve.

- Sight-playing skills improve as students read new pieces together.

- The ability to "think on one's feet" is strengthened as students respond to the musical cues (and sometimes surprises) provided by their partners.

- Collaborative skills improve as students plan dynamics, discuss tempi, and work out technical challenges together.

With the advent of electronic keyboards, CDs, and MIDI accompaniment disks, students have a broader range of collaborative options than was once available. MIDI keyboard patches produce rich, orchestral sounds (discussed further in Part X, "Technology") and multiple students can play together along with additional pre-recorded/electronic accompaniments.

One popular form of ensemble experience is a Monster Concert, consisting of students performing at multiple keyboards. Large groups of students, often from a number of different teachers, rotate throughout the concert. When such concerts are arranged by music teacher organizations, they can have the added benefit of serving as a fund-raiser, often raising substantial amounts of money with only a minimal entry fee.

## Resource

Weekley & Arganbright. *The Piano Duet: A Learning Guide.* San Diego: Neil A. Kjos Music Co., 1996.

This text by renowned piano duet artists Weekley & Arganbright addresses fundamental ensemble issues. A practical guide for teachers as well as students, the text includes topics such as pedaling for another person, balance unique to one piano, four-hand performance, signaling your partner, and other pedagogical concerns.

## Accompanying

Opportunities for the solo pianist do not abound in our culture, but skilled accompanists are in high demand. Practicing piano for personal gratification is important, but many students want more out of all of those years of practice, and accompanying can fulfill that desire.

Unfortunately, many piano students are not given early opportunities to accompany. When they are finally asked to accompany (as high school or college students, or even adults), they arrive untrained and unskilled in the art of collaboration.

Students can begin accompanying at an early age. A number of children's songbooks include accompaniments that are quite easy. *150 Easy Piano Children's Songs* includes popular songs such as "Old MacDonald" and "Mary Had a Little Lamb." The accompaniments to these popular tunes are quite easy, and early-level students could learn them without difficulty. Once a piece has been learned, the chance to accompany could be arranged in a studio performance class, with the young student playing the accompaniment while other students sing the familiar tunes.

## Accompanying Soloists

Another option is to partner with vocal or instrumental teachers and pair their students with more advanced piano students. Care must be given to choose accompaniments wisely, so that students do not feel overwhelmed by accompaniments that are too difficult. Teachers can assist with the process if they are able to sing or play a secondary instrument in the lessons while the student accompanies.

Certain guidelines help students when accompanying singers or instrumentalist soloists:

- Listen, listen, listen!

- Know how each instrumentalist wishes to tune, using the correct pitch in the correct register.

- Insist on rhythmic accuracy. It is far preferable to play in time but miss some notes than it is to play all of the correct notes but get a beat behind the soloist.

- Plan dynamics together and respond to each other's dynamic choices during performance.

- Work for appropriate balance. Although accompanists should not overpower the soloist, neither should they play so softly that they do not provide adequate support.

- Know the style of the piece, and interpret it accordingly. If it is a Baroque piece, for instance, be sure that articulations are stylistically accurate.

- Bring out the piano parts meant to be prominent, such as introductions or interludes.

- Discuss the use of rubato, ritards, and breaths. Constantly listen to and respond to the soloist for rhythmic alterations due to breathing and interpretation.

- Agree on musical choices. If, for example, the soloist starts an ornament on the main note, the accompanist should not start that same ornament on the upper note. Making good choices that do not match are not good choices at all.

- Take care with the use of the pedal. Many accompanists over-pedal, either blurring the sound or using an inappropriate amount of pedal for the period of music. Accompaniments need to sound clean, and the pedal must be used judiciously and appropriately.

- Learn to cover for the soloist. If the soloist leaves out a measure or comes in a beat early, the accompanist must be trained to hear this, and accommodate the error smoothly. It is the accompanist's job to make the soloist look good and to cover for any errors that occur.

- Keep going no matter what. If the singer stops mid-sentence, the pianist cannot stop with her, but must continue to play, giving cues that will bring the singer back, such as seamlessly switching from the piano's melodic line to the singer's melodic line.

- Understand the mood of the piece. In vocal selections, ask the soloist to translate the words or explain the text, so that the words can be conveyed in the piano part as well as the vocal part.

- Learn how to edit difficult accompaniments. Orchestral reductions can be especially thick or unpianistic, and students need to learn to edit intelligently by reducing awkward chords, changing 16th-note accompaniment patterns to eighths, substituting single notes for octaves, or avoiding large leaps by changing the register.

## Accompanying Ensembles

Besides accompanying soloists, students may be offered the opportunity to accompany a small ensemble, the high school choir, or a group in a religious setting. Encouraging students to play in an ensemble setting shows them their skills are needed and appreciated in their community. Not only will students gain self-confidence by accompanying, but they will provide a valuable service to a choir director who may be struggling with multiple duties.

Preparation for accompanying ensembles includes:

- Explaining conducting patterns if the student has never played in a conducted ensemble (If a pianist has never played under a conductor before, the teacher may wish to conduct the student's accompaniments, using conducting motions to express changes in tempo or dynamics to work on the student's ability to follow.)

- Teaching an effective method for counting measures during long passages of inactivity

- Including ensemble accompaniments as a regular part of the lesson, thus placing importance on accompaniments while assisting with details

- Reading separate SATB lines from a score, first one at a time, then two at a time, etc., when reading choral parts

- Remembering to read the tenor part of a choral score in the treble clef but an octave lower than written

- Playing with the same dedication to rhythmic and stylistic accuracy that was mentioned when accompanying a soloist

- Emphasizing the need to "keep going no matter what," with no fixing or falling behind

Organizing a summer camp around accompanying provides an enjoyable tool for getting all students involved, while allowing the time needed for coaching collaborative skills. Music camps will be discussed further in Chapter 39.

# Resources

Grill, Joyce. *Accompanying Basics.* San Diego: Neil A. Kjos Company, 1987.

This short, practical guide offers suggestions for teaching the basics of accompanying. Chapters include information on why we accompany, who should accompany, required training, preparation and practice, choral accompanying, the art song, orchestral reductions, instrumental accompanying, chamber music, dance accompanying, stage presence, page turning, and general tips for the pianist.

Nielsen Price, Deon. *Accompanying Skills for Pianists*, 2nd Edition. Culver City: Culver Crest Publication, 1991, 2005.

This excellent book can be used as a guide for teachers or students, or as a text on accompanying. Numerous areas of interest are mentioned: musical textures, responsive playing skills (with sections for each type of accompanying: vocal, vocal groups, string, wind, chamber), improving pianistic skills, efficient rehearsals, and preparing for and executing performances, to name a few. The sections of special interest are Chapter 4: Sightplay with Skillful Eyes, and Chapters 6–9, each dealing with performing a different period of music stylistically. The book ends with an epilogue: Reflections on a Career as a Collaborative Pianist, which would prove of interest to anyone considering such a career.

# Resources (cont.)

Rizzo, Gene. *Accompanying the Jazz/Pop Vocalist: A Practical Guide for Pianists.* Milwaukee: Hal Leonard Corporation, 2002.

> Gene Rizzo covers topics including exploring song forms, intros and endings, writing a lead sheet, accompanying different vocal styles, descriptive accompaniment, tempo rubato, transposition, and more. The book includes two complete songs, and the CD contains both full-version tracks and tracks with the piano part deleted for play-along practice. This is appropriate for both solo piano accompanists and players who are part of a combo.

## VOCAL BOOKS WITH STUDENT-LEVEL ACCOMPANIMENTS

Boytim, Joan Frey, comp. *Easy Songs for the Beginning Mezzo-Soprano/Alto.* New York: G. Schirmer, Inc., Distributed by Hal Leonard, 2000.

> This series was designed to supplement traditional vocal instruction. Each piece is in English and has a limited vocal range as well as a piano accompaniment playable by a student pianist. The pieces include art songs, folksongs, humorous songs, and suitable vintage popular songs, and all are appropriate for contest solos. The accompanying CD includes professionally-recorded accompaniments.

*Kid's Broadway Song Book.* Milwaukee: MPL Communications, Inc. and Hal Leonard Corporation, 1993.

> This collection features songs originally sung onstage by children. The book comes with a companion CD of piano accompaniments, and provides accompanists at the intermediate level with many favorite tunes, including "It's the Hard-Knock Life," "Tomorrow," "I Whistle a Happy Tune," and "Gary, Indiana."

*150 Easy Piano Children's Songs.* Milwaukee: Hal Leonard Corporation, 2001.

> It is often lamented that young students no longer know the nursery rhymes and folk tunes that have been such a part of our culture. Designed for young singers, this book has 150 children's songs, with easy piano accompaniments that are well suited to the early-level piano student. Useful for young singers, the book also provides an excellent introduction to accompaniment with such favorite children's songs as "Eensy Weensy Spider," "London Bridge," "Oh! Susanna," "On Top of Old Smoky," "She'll Be Comin' 'Round the Mountain," and "This Old Man."

## Chamber Music

My first opportunity to perform chamber music came in college and I was immediately hooked. I loved the experience of playing with other musicians in a small, intimate ensemble, and the level of musical collaboration that this afforded. As a teacher, I have found that chamber music is a powerful addition to the independent studio. The joys of performing chamber music can be given to even the youngest students.

One method of incorporating chamber music into a piano studio is to collaborate with other teachers of strings, woodwinds, or brass. The collaborating teachers work together to form well-matched chamber groups, assign repertoire, and develop a system for coaching. Tuition is established for regular chamber music lessons in a similar fashion to setting fees for other types of group lessons. Weekly chamber music lessons focus on the intricacies of ensemble playing while the details of the repertoire are being perfected. Many piano students, accustomed to playing alone, find such collaboration to be truly rewarding.

Once the members of a chamber ensemble feel comfortable with the repertoire, they can perform for studio performance classes or in a group chamber music class. From there, opportunities for chamber performances might include regular studio recitals, chamber music recitals, chamber music festivals, and even jobs within the community, such as concerts at the mall, background music at restaurants, holiday parties, and weddings.

Piano students interested in chamber music who do not have the time for a weekly chamber music lesson could be invited to participate in a monthly chamber music rehearsal. Such a rehearsal could serve two purposes:

- Rehearsing current chamber music assignments
- Sight-playing music as an ensemble to improve sight-playing skills in an enjoyable and meaningful environment

In communities with an abundance of string players (the most frequently used partners in chamber music), it should be possible to find string students and teachers willing to work together on chamber music. In smaller, rural communities, a different approach may be needed. If string players are not available in a small community, creative approaches to finding and funding collaborators may be necessary.

- Hire advanced high school students or college students from a neighboring community.
- Hire college professors from a neighboring college.
- Hire professional musicians.
- Charge piano students either tuition or a chamber music fee to cover the cost of hiring outside musicians.
- Seek outside sources of income to cover costs.

When I decided to start a Chamber Music Festival in my small town in North Dakota, there were no string players in town with whom to collaborate. I wanted area piano students to have the opportunity to play trios, so I contacted a college 60 miles away that had a nationally recognized music department. The orchestra director was happy to recommend students he felt would be good collaborators in such a festival. For the first three years of the festival, the four members of a college string quartet served as the string players. They were paid to come to town, rehearse with piano students in the recital hall, perform in concert with the young pianists, and finish the concert with a quartet performance of their own.

The local piano students were well-prepared before the college students arrived to rehearse. They had all learned their pieces in advance and each student's teacher had played the string parts on a second piano in order to familiarize the students with the string parts. Students had been coached in performance techniques and how to play in an ensemble and they had performed their pieces in studio classes before the rehearsal day.

The day the college students arrived, each piano student was assigned a 20-minute rehearsal time, during which they practiced not only their piece, but also walking on and off as an ensemble, starting and stopping together, and bowing as a group. In those first years, this 20-minute rehearsal offered the piano students their only chance to perform with string players before the evening's concert. The students then performed in concert that same night in the same recital hall.

**PART IX**

This may not sound like the optimal way to experience chamber music. Where is the opportunity for an evolving interpretation of the repertoire or for the musical growth of the ensemble? Although the opportunity to develop a group voice over time did not exist with only one rehearsal, what did exist was an exciting opportunity for collaboration that was otherwise unavailable.

In this small, rural community, the early chamber music festivals provided the only option for piano students to perform with string players, and they loved it! Each year, 100% of the piano students involved left the experience completely exhilarated, with glowing parents expressing their gratitude for the opportunity their children had been given.

Because the college string players were more advanced than the elementary school, junior high, and high school piano students, the piano students also had the benefit of performing with musicians who were more skilled than they. The college students treated the pianists with respect and did not intimidate the younger musicians. Like playing tennis with a better tennis partner, these more advanced string players brought out the best in each piano student.

I soon set my sights even higher. If I could hire excellent college students, why couldn't I hire professional string players? When I heard that the Chiara String Quartet, a professional group of Juilliard graduates from New York City, was doing a Chamber Music America residency in North Dakota, I invited them to be a part of our Chamber Music Festival. I wrote a grant through our state arts council to help cover costs, and got local businesses to donate the food and lodging needed for the members of the quartet.

Over a three-day span, the Chiara String Quartet members conducted and performed with the local orchestra and gave a presentation/concert at two elementary schools and the high school. They rehearsed with a select group of students one afternoon, and then performed that same night in a chamber music recital with the students. The following night they gave a full quartet concert of their own.

The three days were immensely inspiring to the students at the schools, the orchestra members, and the students in the chamber recital. Members of the community enjoyed the student recital as well as the quartet recital given by the group. Not many music students in the country, much less in a small town in North Dakota, will ever have the opportunity to collaborate with musicians on a par with the members of the Chiara String Quartet. This group returned each year to participate in the chamber music festival during the years of their residency in North Dakota.

Because of a growing string program, the town eventually had enough string students to form trios and quartets for chamber music study throughout the year. String teachers and piano teachers worked together to organize a curriculum for the regular study of chamber music. Even so, I continued to hire professional string players to come to town and perform with the students in the recital. Not only were the students exhilarated by the experience, but so were the professional musicians. Year after year, the professional musicians felt the contagious excitement of the students, and left the stage with comments like, "This is what true music making is all about. Thank you for the opportunity to play with your students!"

If chamber music can be presented at this level in a small farming community with no pre-existing chamber music resources, it can become a part of any studio. Whether hiring string students, performing with professional musicians, or collaborating with other teachers, any teacher can devise a workable chamber music program for her studio.

Years ago it might have been difficult to find music for all levels within a studio. Today, a growing number of chamber music books are written for student performers at the elementary, intermediate, and advanced levels.

# Resources

## CHAMBER MUSIC COLLECTIONS AND PIECES

Breth, Nancy, and Jean Goberman, arr. *The Beggar's Opera*. Milwaukee: Hal Leonard Corporation, 2005.

> This trio arrangement (violin, cello, piano) of six songs from the 1728 *The Beggar's Opera* by John Gay gives young musicians an early introduction into the world of chamber music. In the introduction, Breth outlines helpful suggestions for starting a chamber music program in an independent studio, including how to match students according to age, level of advancement, instrumentation, available times, and geography. A timeline takes the teacher from the first rehearsal through the first recital, and into a longer view of the possibilities for incorporating chamber music into a studio curriculum.

Haroutounian, Joanne, ed. *Chamber Music Sampler*, Books 1, 2, & 3. San Diego: Neil A. Kjos Music Co., 1992.

> These carefully edited works have well-thought-out fingerings and articulation marks, and include works in graded difficulty by Clementi, Köhler, Klengel, Haydn, Mozart, Beethoven, and Schubert. Included in each volume are tips for cues, rehearsals, performance, and helpful definitions of string markings for the student pianist. These three volumes are an excellent purchase for any teacher wishing to incorporate chamber music into a studio curriculum.

Various composers. *The Miniature Trios Series and Miniatures Series*. London: Stainer & Bell (ECS Publishing).

> Composers such as Adam Carse, Peter Martin, and Frank Bridge contribute to these chamber works, ideal for intermediate-level piano students. Selections are of varying degrees of difficulty. Even the simpler pieces exhibit sophistication worthy of a chamber music or studio recital.

## WEBSITES

*ACMP – The Chamber Music Network*
> www.acmp.net

*Chamber Music America*
> www.chamber-music.org

*MTNA Intermediate Chamber Music Repertoire Database*
> www.mtna.org/HLtext

*National Federation of Music Clubs*
> www.nfmc-music.org
>
> (Junior Festival has Chamber Music categories)

**PART IX**

# Chapter 36

# COMPOSITION

---

When I decided to include composition in my studio, I started by hiring a local composer to present a composition workshop to my students. The workshop was offered in place of that month's performance class and all of my students attended. To cover the cost, I partnered with another piano teacher and each of our students paid $10 for the workshop. Even though neither I nor the other teacher had a strong background in composition, our students were so inspired by the presenter that composition became a regular part of both studios.

I realized that a degree in composition was not necessary to make composition a rewarding component of lessons. I would have missed out on years of creativity, fun, and enthusiasm in my studio had I not gone outside of my comfort zone and included composition in the curriculum. My students would not have experienced the empowering feeling of creating music that was truly their own. A few of my students demonstrated real talent in composition, even going on to win composition competitions. This talent would never have been discovered had that local composer not come to my studio and gotten us all started.

## Approaches to Teaching Composition

I have attended a number of presentations on teaching composition, and the process generally falls into two categories:

- Composition following formal guidelines of theory

- Composition following general suggestions for sound and ideas, with theory-related guidelines coming later

### Composition following formal guidelines of theory

The first approach uses the knowledge that students gain in the earliest method books, such as five-finger patterns and I–V chord progressions, as the basis of early compositions. As the student's musical knowledge increases, so does the level and complexity of the compositions. Form is discussed, as are key signatures, and the music theory that students learn is successfully reinforced through composition right from the start.

When choosing this approach it is important to offer specific guidelines that do not overwhelm the student. A suggestion such as, "Compose a piece and use all the chords you can and watch the form," is too vague and overwhelming. A better suggestion might be, "Compose a melody using C-D-E-F-G." The next week the student can add harmony using C chords and G chords. During week three, the student could add dynamics and articulations and maybe title the piece. From there the student can lengthen the composition to include additional phrases, chords, and melody, all in a manageable, step-by-step process.

Each week's composition time can focus on elements such as understanding form, improving a melodic line, and learning how to use new chords. A balance must be struck between introducing new elements and allowing time to feel comfortable with earlier concepts. By relating composition to concepts and information presented in the method books, the student can better understand the inter-connectedness of what is being taught. Certain method series include composition within the method, and teachers interested in composition would be wise to use such a series.

## Composition following general suggestions for sound and ideas

In the second method, students are first shown how to make pleasing or unique sounds on the piano, without an initial regard for tonality, form, or melodic line. Instead, sound exploration might show that soft high notes on the piano sound like rain drops, and low fast clusters of notes sound like the rumble of thunder. From there, a student could be asked to come to the piano and play a piece about a storm.

The presenter who came to my studio stressed that since anything is acceptable, there can be no right or wrong notes. This important statement is quite liberating, as it frees the students from concern that they will do the wrong thing or write a composition that won't be "good enough."

A story with two characters can be read, while two students sit at the piano, becoming the two characters. One may be a shy, quiet bunny, and the other a loud, clumsy elephant. As the teacher tells what the bunny and the elephant say or do, the children create the story at the piano. This is fun to do and gets them to realize that they can make stories at the piano; they can compose.

Offering guidelines, such as "Let's compose a piece using only the black notes" gives the students a manageable framework from which to start and helps keep them from feeling overwhelmed by choices. Helping them to create a beginning, middle, and ending to their composition starts them on the basics of form.

As students bring their compositions to the lesson, the teacher's role becomes one of encouragement, giving minimal guidance such as, "What do you want the puppy to do next?" or "After the rain starts, does the storm get bigger?" Since sounds are the initial focal point, the students can experiment with a plethora of sounds, often incorporating programmatic elements into the composition.

When a student is comfortable with composition, the teacher's comments may expand to suggestions such as, "What about repeating that sound an octave higher?" Initially, however, the teacher's role should be to provide a manageable framework from which to begin, acknowledge the student's success, and encourage continued efforts.

It was amazing to observe the results of such a free approach and rewarding to see how my students loved composing. Any concern that I had that this would turn into just a lot of fiddling around on the piano was soon assuaged. Without restrictions for "correct" choices, student compositions became more and more sophisticated, with increasing attention to form, tonality, and melodic line.

**PART IX**

### Notating compositions

Learning to write their compositions on staff paper or through a computer program was a goal for all of my students. In the early stages, however, students often composed pieces with intricate rhythms or complex harmonies that were too difficult to notate on their own. Such students were encouraged to draw pictures of their compositions using symbols to represent sounds. This early journey into graphic notation reflected different sections, techniques, and moods. Traditional dynamics and phrase markings were added to the score, which became a basic map of the piece. Eventually, all of my students worked on notating their own compositions, an important tool for understanding and documenting their efforts.

### Student compositions in recitals

Two things surprised me about my students' efforts at composition: the level of enjoyment experienced by the students kept many of them enthusiastic about lessons in general, and their efforts were amazingly creative and sophisticated. My June recitals were a high point of each year, as students performed one piece by a known composer and one or two of their own compositions. Everyone attending the recitals thoroughly enjoyed the student compositions, perhaps even more than the pieces composed by the masters!

## Incorporating Composition into the Curriculum

Introducing students to composition exposes them to a creative process that is enjoyable, inspiring, and educational. There are several ways to open the doors to composition, including:

- Hiring a local teacher who successfully teaches composition, or a local composer, to come to the studio and give a presentation on getting started with composition

- Hiring a composer to give masterclasses on composition in the studio

- Initiating an adopt-a-composer program where a living composer works with students (by e-mail or in person), critiquing student composition and offering advise

- Holding recitals of student compositions

The adopt-a-composer option is particularly enjoyable for students. A composer, hopefully one within the local area, can be invited to act as a special studio mentor for composition. The composer may be invited to serve in a number of functions:

- Give presentations or masterclasses on composition to the studio

- Critique student compositions in person or through e-mail

- Give students 15-minute lessons on their compositions

In return, a recital can be held highlighting the compositions that the students and composer worked on together, as well as pieces written by the mentor/composer.

In a session on composition given at a state conference, teachers shared their suggestions for successfully incorporating composition into the curriculum:

- Include guidelines in any composition assignment. Saying "Go home and compose a piece" is too general and will feel daunting to the student.

- Give opportunities to improvise before starting structured composition.

- Make a sound recording of each student's yearly compositions, with the student announcing the name and date of each composition. Keep a binder of all written compositions. The recording and the binder will provide valuable memories in future years.

- Have students write a composition using only the black notes of the piano.

- Use the rhythm of the student's full name as the rhythmic foundation of a composition (Ma-ry El-len Tark-ing-ton).

- Assign each letter in the alphabet a musical pitch and have students compose a piece based on the letters of their name.

- Put pitch names into a hat and have students draw the first four pitches of a composition.

- Suggest that students go on a "sound walk" and write down all the sounds they hear. Have the students recreate those sounds at the piano.

- Have students compose a rhythm based on fun words of their own choosing ("I'm not eating liver." "Choc-o-late, choc-o-late, where are you, choc-o-late?").

- Have students compose a simple melody and then change the composition by altering a single element such as rhythm or register.

- Let them experiment by adding harmony to their melody, using three or four different chords in the same spot to hear how each affects the sound.

- Have students compose a short three- to five-note melody, put their compositions in a basket, and then have students draw from the basket, using the melody as the start of a new composition.

- Use graphic notation (symbols rather than notes) for non-traditional sounds.

- Have students compose using found objects, non-traditional instruments, traditional instruments used/played in non-traditional ways, or percussion instruments.

- Continually point out compositional tools in the repertoire the students are studying. "Did you notice that the melody is inverted here?" "See how the composer does the same thing one octave higher?" "What key does the composer modulate to in this section?"

PART IX

# Resources

Balodis, Frances. *Young Composer's Notebook: A Student's Guide to Composing.* Volumes 1–3. Mississauga, Ontario: The Frederick Harris Music Co., Ltd., 2001.

> This series of three workbooks gives young music students a practical introduction to the theory of composition. Students come to understand composition through simple visual concepts; teachers and parents will benefit from the insights of the accompanying notes. These books offer excellent supplementary theory material for young students.

Cisler, Valerie, and Deanna Walker-Tipps. *Composition Book*, Levels 1A, 1B, & 2. Van Nuys: Alfred Publishing Company, Inc., 1996–1997.

> Designed to be used with *Alfred's Basic Piano Library*, this series of books can be used by any student in any method. Exploring composition from the most basic elements of improvisation, the series reviews areas such as melodic and harmonic intervals, form, parallel phrases, primary triads, and blocked and broken chords.

Lavender, Cheryl. *The Song Writing Kit.* Milwaukee: Hal Leonard Corporation, 1986.

> Designed with the early elementary classroom in mind, the activities in this book can be used in a large group, small group, or as individual projects, including writing songs with given lyrics and original lyric-writing. Concepts such as beat, rhythm, meter, lyrics, and melody are included. Each lesson plan covers materials, setup, concept statement, objective, and vocabulary, along with step-by-step directions for the lesson.

Olson, Kevin. *Keys to Success*, Books 1–3. Fort Lauderdale: The FJH Music Company, Inc., 2003–2005.

> Serving a number of functions, this series addresses composition as well as technique, improvisation, transposition, and note-reading. Each book centers on a specific area: Book 1 – Major Pentascales, Book 2 – Minor Pentascales, and Book 3 – Major Scales. Each unit covers a new key following the order of the circle of fifths. The assignments in each unit include four sections: Basic Training, Detective Work, Jam Session, and World Premiere.

Olson, Kevin, and Wynn-Anne Rossi. *Music by Me: A Composition Workbook*, Books 1–5. Fort Lauderdale: The FJH Music Company, Inc., 2004–2007.

> These workbooks offer an introduction to composition. The seven sections include composing with rhythm; composing with melody; composing with harmony; learn a special tool: repetition; using a musical form; modern music; and time for review.

Russo, William, with Jeffrey Ainis and David Stevenson. *Composing Music: A New Approach.* Chicago and London: The University of Chicago Press, 1983.

> By offering clear guidelines accompanied by exercises for every new concept, this book serves as a tool for "learning composition by doing." The exercises teach the aspiring composer to dig right in, beginning with a first, brief example, and then proceeding gradually to develop increasing competence. Each exercise provides specific and limited resources with which to work. These limitations help to guide the user in an initial direction, without being overwhelmed with too many choices. Teachers who wish to incorporate composition into the curriculum will appreciate the focused and detailed information. Some of the chapters include The Cell, the Row, and Some Scales; Harmony; Transformation; The Small Theme and the Large Theme; Accompanying Procedures; Counterpoint; Imitation: A Useful Game; Words and Music; and Picture Music.

Wiggins, Jackie. *Composition in the Classroom: A Tool for Teaching.* Reston: MENC – The National Association for Music Educators, 1990.

> Published by MENC and designed for classroom teachers, this short guide to teaching composition offers valuable information for the independent teacher as well. In less than 40 pages a number of helpful tips are given for initiating teacher-guided composition, small-group composition, and free composition. Any independent piano teacher who is considering composition in the studio would benefit from the suggestions offered in this short, readable booklet.

## Composition competitions and projects

For students with a keen interest in composition, a number of composition competitions exist on the state and national levels, as well as in many local music teacher organizations. Just a few of the many competitions and festivals available include the following:

# Resources

*From the Top*

### From the Top Young Composer Project

In addition to appearing on NPR's radio show *From the Top*, hosted by Christopher O'Riley, composers selected for the *Young Composer Project* will be prominently featured on *From the Top's* website. Each honoree of the *Young Composer Project* is also paired with a professional composer for a unique one-on-one mentoring session. Honored young composers also participate in community outreach performances through *From the Top's* Cultural Leadership Program.

**www.fromthetop.org**

– Go to "Education" and select "Young Composer Project" from the pull-down menu.

*MTNA Student Composition Competitions*

Levels: Elementary, Junior, Senior, and Young Artist

**www.mtna.org/HLtext**

*National Federation of Music Clubs*

### The NFMC Junior Composer Contest

Levels I–IV, ages 9 and under, 10–12, 13–15, and 16–18

### Lynn Freeman Olson Composition Awards

**www.nfmc-music.org**

– Select "Competitions & Awards"

*National Guild of Piano Teachers*

### International Composition Contest

Elementary, Intermediate, Preparatory, College/Young Artist, Special Categories, Gifted Students, Adult Student Division, Teacher Division

**www.pianoguild.com**

– Select "Composition Contest" from the sidebar

*National School Boards Association and The National Association of Music Education*

### NSBA/MENC Student Electronic Music Composition Talent Search

Co-sponsored by National School Boards Association (NSBA), the winners are spotlighted annually at the NSBA Technology + Learning (T + L) Conference

**www.menc.org**

– Type "Electronic Music Composition" into the search box

# Resources (cont.)

**ADDITIONAL WEBSITES**

The following websites include lists with links to numerous composition competitions.

*The Center for the Promotion of Contemporary Composers*

www.under.org

- Select "Opportunities;" select "Competitions"

*dmoz Open Directory Project*

http://dmoz.org

- Select "Arts;" select "Music;" select "Compositions;" select "Competitions;" select "Cash or Performing Awards"

**LOCAL AND STATE ASSOCIATIONS**

A number of local and state music associations and organizations host composition competitions and festivals

# Chapter 37

# JAZZ, BLUES, AND IMPROVISATION

My first real exposure to jazz study came in graduate school when I took a class in improvisation. I was amazed to learn that the mysteries of jazz improvisation were less mysterious than I had thought! There were specific tools that I could use when learning improvisation and I no longer viewed jazz as a foreign language that I would never be able to speak. I understood that without a real effort, I would never speak the language of jazz fluently, but I also gained my first insights into approaching jazz in my piano studio.

## Removing the "vs." from "Classical vs. Jazz"

Too often jazz and classical music have been perceived as worlds apart, with practitioners of one knowing little about the other. Instead of being limited by this separation, classically trained students can benefit in all areas of their piano playing by exposure to jazz and blues. Students who study jazz (and all references to jazz in this chapter imply a reference to blues) have the potential to:

- Develop a better understanding of theory

- Become more creative in improvising and musical expression

- Improve their rhythmic skills

- Gain more confidence as performers

- Develop a keener sense of technique

Those who become proficient in jazz also have the opportunity to work in a number of collaborative settings such as the school jazz band or in small jazz ensembles. An increased potential exists for students to love and create music throughout their lives. They usually respond so well to jazz that they are not aware that their rhythm is improving or that they are understanding theory better— they are just having fun!

A teacher with a strong background in jazz or blues need not be shy about sharing that skill with students who have been classically trained or who retain a classical focus. If, on the other hand, a teacher has a limited background in jazz, today's resources provide opportunities for teacher and student to learn together. Jazz and blues resources include:

- Jazz/blues method books

- Books explaining chord symbols

- Jazz/blues theory books

- Jazz/blues technique books

- Jazz/blues texts

- Online resources and web pages

- Jazz/blues repertoire for students of all ages and levels of ability

- Educational jazz/blues CDs, DVDs, and videos

- Books about great jazz or blues legends and various jazz styles

- Jazz/blues camps

## Getting Started

There are a number of ways for teachers to improve their skills and to incorporate jazz into the curriculum:

- Take lessons with an area jazz pianist.

- Take a jazz studies class at an area university or college.

- Have a guest artist come to the studio and present a session on jazz or blues.

- Teach chords and chord progressions in all keys.

- Incorporate jazz and blues elements into the teaching of theory.

- Review jazz teaching books for use in the studio.

- Partner with other teachers to create student ensembles/performance experiences.

- Offer jazz/blues camps (Preparing the camp will expand the teacher's knowledge.)

- Use some lesson time to comp (improvise a harmonic background) as students improvise a melody or to improvise a melody as students comp.

- Include jazz/blues history in the curriculum.

- Give students jazz/blues listening assignments.

- Include jazz/blues in workstation time (using CDs, workbooks, Internet).

Although all piano teachers have the potential to develop jazz skills by using the many available resources, their level of ability may not be sufficient for all students. If a piano student is serious about jazz and wishes to be a professional jazz pianist, studying with a master jazz pianist is essential. If the current piano teacher is not an expert jazz pianist, research should be done to find an instructor who is able to teach jazz piano on a professional level. Any student who is serious about jazz will have been well served when their technique and ability to perform musically have been enhanced through previous classical study.

## Improvisation

Improvisation is the defining element of jazz. Many jazz enthusiasts would argue that, even with pieces exhibiting a jazz flavor through their use of blues-scale-based licks, extended harmony, swing feel, and form, the music is not really jazz unless improvisation plays a major role.

Fortunately for today's teachers and students, there is a rekindling of interest in improvisation. In earlier eras, much music was improvised, and as late as the Baroque, Classical, and even Romantic periods, improvisation was an essential skill taught and nurtured by music instructors. Many famous composers were also famous improvisers; Mozart was known for his improvisations in concert, Beethoven often improvised in parlor competitions with other composers, and numerous organists improvised preludes on the spot. Somewhere in the last 100 years, the art of improvisation lost its prominence. The one exception to this is in the world of jazz, which holds improvisation as its primary defining characteristic.

Modern-day teachers once again realize the benefits of improvisation in developing a well-rounded musician:

- When students are encouraged to improvise, they are freed from the limits of performing only currently learned repertoire.

- They are taught that their knowledge of music is dynamic, fluid, and personal.

- Improvisation gives them the confidence to express their creativity outside of interpreting a written page.

- Students who improvise inevitably take great pleasure from this skill and often develop a deeper love and commitment to music.

- When students become comfortable with improvisation, additional areas of music may open up, such as playing with the school jazz band, a small ensemble, or a garage band.

- Not many classical musicians make a living solely by performing, but the ability to earn an income from performing increases if students are comfortable with improvising in a variety of musical styles.

In order for students to feel comfortable with improvising, an environment that allows for experimentation needs to be nurtured in the studio. If students' early efforts are criticized or too many suggestions for change are offered, their desire to create will be hindered. They need to feel that the process allows for experimentation and that the teacher is supportive of their efforts.

If the teacher's background in improvisation is limited, by making improvisation a regular part of the studio, teacher and student can grow together. Fortunately, a number of resources are currently available to assist with this goal.

Students may take great pleasure from creating improvisations on pieces from their repertoire books. Inverting a melody, filling in a rest, altering a rhythm, ornamenting a melody, changing an octave, and adding an inner voice are all ways to experiment with improvisation using the student's current pieces.

**PART IX**

Many current method books include improvisation exercises, and improvising can continue long after students graduate from method books. Improvisation can be discussed in lessons, taught in group activities, or presented through the use of computer programs, recordings, and workbooks. Chapter 43 includes a list of software programs designed to assist with improvisation and harmonization, as well as more information on how to teach improvisation in a lesson.

For improvising skills to progress past an elementary level, a study of harmony is essential. A solid understanding of harmony includes the basics of theory, chords types, chord symbols, chord voicings, chord progressions, and key relationships. A sequential well-planned course of study for improvisation can be greatly aided by the numerous resources that are currently available. Activities might include experimentation with any of the following:

- Improvising a melodic line

- Rhythmically altering a melodic line

- Breaking up the melodic line

- Combining varied accents in melody and harmony

- Combining varied attacks (legato vs. staccato)

- Learning chords derived from scale degrees in all major and minor keys

- Executing multiple voicings of chords

- Harmonizing a melodic line

- Transposing the melody and harmonization to new keys

- Playing blues scales in all keys

- Playing pentatonic scales in all keys

- Using walking bass note patterns in all keys

The study of harmony not only improves students' ability to improvise and harmonize, but also aids with reading, learning, and memorizing standard repertoire. Learning to transpose expands the student's library of musical choices when improvising.

For students who are serious about improvisation, who show great talent, and who see improvising as part of their life's work, studying with a master improviser is essential. If any of these students' current piano teachers are not expert at improvisation, research should be done to find an instructor who is able to teach these skills on a professional level.

The following resources include a wide variety of instructional aids on jazz, blues, and improvisation.

# Resources

## TUTORIAL BOOKS

Alldis, Dominic. *A Classical Approach to Jazz Improvisation.* Milwaukee: Hal Leonard Corporation, 2003.

> This improvisation instruction book is designed for the person who was trained classically but wants to expand into the world of jazz improvisation. Author Dominic Alldis provides clear, easy-to-follow explanations and musical examples of pentatonic improvisation, the blues, rock piano, rhythmic placement, scale theory, major, minor, and pentatonic scale theory applications, melodic syntax, the language of bebop, and left-hand accompaniment.

Baumgartner, Eric. *Jazzabilities*, Books 1–3 and *Jazz Connections*, Books 1–3. Florence: Willis, Books 1 & 2, 2002; Book 3, 2003. Distributed by Hal Leonard Corporation.

> *Jazzabilities* allows teachers, including those who are inexperienced with jazz, to present a solid introduction to jazz studies. In this series, "the emphasis is on developing rhythmic control through short, jazzy exercises—in essence, building a jazz vocabulary." Manageable exercises introduce concepts that are then reinforced by the *Jazz Connections* repertoire books.

Beale, Charles. *Jazz Piano: The Complete Method*, Levels 1–5. Hal Leonard Corporation in association with ABRSM Publishing, 2002.

> *Jazz Piano* is a comprehensive introduction to the world of jazz. Five levels of graded pieces contain a wide range of styles: funky jazz, up-tempo swing, calypso, Latin, jazz waltz, modal, bebop, gospel, ragtime, free jazz, and more. There are classic tunes by Duke Ellington, Miles Davis, Bill Evans, and Thelonious Monk. Within each level there are 15 pieces, aural tests, quick studies, scales, arpeggios, and a CD. The 15 pieces are presented in three categories: blues, standards, and contemporary jazz.

Beale, Charles. *Jazz Piano from Scratch: A How-To Guide for Students and Teachers.* Hal Leonard Corporation in Association with ABRSM Publishing, 1998.

> *Jazz Piano from Scratch* is a complete step-by-step guide to playing jazz with confidence and style. Designed for a beginner in jazz with some pre-existing musical experience, it breaks down the process into simple activities, with many musical examples to illustrate the points made. The accompanying CD provides examples, activities, and samples of trio playing to use as a backdrop/accompaniment to the student's own work.

Berg, Shelton G. *Essentials of Jazz Theory.* Van Nuys, CA: Alfred Publishing Co., Inc. 2004.

> Offered as a foundation for learning the basic theoretical elements necessary to improvise and create jazz, *Essentials of Jazz Theory* can be purchased in four books: Book 1, Book 2, and Book 3, or as one Complete Book that includes all three books as well as answers to all ear-training activities. All books come with a CD that includes tests for listening skills, and musical examples played by a variety of instruments. The books are well-paced and include clear definitions of all new concepts.

Boyd, Bill. *Exploring Basic Blues for Keyboard.* Milwaukee: Hal Leonard Corporation, 1993.

> This book introduces the blues in a systematic and easy-to-understand format. Chapter topics include Blues Accompaniments, Basic Material for Improvisation, Starting to Improvise, Twelve-Measure Improvisation, Devices to Enhance the Melodic Line, The Minor Blues Scale, and Boogie and Rock Blues, as well as borrowing and chords. Two helpful appendixes list the complete major and minor blues scales in all keys. The material is organized in an accessible, step-by-step sequence to best serve those new to the blues.

> Bill Boyd has a number of other jazz and blues instructional books, also published by Hal Leonard Corporation, which are of value to beginner and intermediate students:

| | |
|---|---|
| *A Jazz Method – Early Intermediate Level* | *Jazz Chord Progressions* |
| *Exploring Jazz Scales for Keyboard* | *Jazz Keyboard Basics* |
| *Exploring Traditional Scales and Chords for Jazz Keyboard* | *Jazz Piano: A Complete Guide to Jazz Theory and Improvisation* |
| *Intermediate Jazz Chord Voicing for Keyboard* | |

**PART IX**

# Resources (cont.)

Caramia, Tony. *A Guide For Jazz Piano Harmonization.* San Diego: Neil A. Kjos Music Co., 1983.

This brief text of jazz harmonization techniques and traditions is in an easy-to-understand format for the beginning jazz player. Topics include chord analysis, diatonic extensions, altered tones, chords, and tritone substitutes. Additional supplementary sections on jazz pianists, jazz repertoire, and developing an individual style are included.

Chung, Brian, and Dennis Thurmond. *Improvisation at the Piano: A Systematic Approach for the Classically Trained Pianist.* Los Angeles: Alfred Publishing Company, Inc., 2007.

The introduction to this book states, "If you can talk, you can improvise," and the authors do not fall short of their claim that improvisation is a learnable skill. The text is designed for students with a background in theory and classical music who often have felt hesitant to enter the world of improvisation. It progresses from the most basic steps of improvisation through increasingly advanced material, all in a logical and accessible format. The pages are easy to read as new categories and exercises are highlighted in bold text. Each chapter ends with a box addressing the "Key Points from This Chapter." Various styles of improvisation are addressed and the book ends with a chapter on Improvisation Through the Ages, which highlights improvisational styles from the Medieval through the Romantic periods. This is an excellent text for teachers who wish to expose their students to the world of improvisation.

Collins, Ann. *Jazz Works.* Van Nuys: Alfred Publishing Co., Inc., 2000.

*Jazz Works* is a beginning jazz piano method created for the classically trained pianist who plays and reads on the intermediate level. Concepts and skills are presented through examples and explanations in each chapter. Practice exercises prepare the player to apply the new skills to the tunes included in each chapter. Pieces are presented in lead-sheet format, with melody lines and alphabet chord symbols. Accompaniment tracks are available for most exercises and all tunes are recorded on the two CDs included, but are also available separately in GM disk format.

Denke, Debbie. *Amazing Phrasing – Keyboard: 50 Ways to Improve Your Improvisational Skills.* Milwaukee: Hal Leonard Corporation, 2002.

*Amazing Phrasing* is for keyboard players interested in learning to improvise and improve creative phrasing. This method is divided into three parts:

- Melody: scales, arpeggios, using licks, riffs, and runs
- Harmony: progressions, voicings, bass line, comping, combo playing
- Rhythm & Style: swing, laying back, shaping phrases with accents

The companion CD contains 44 full-band demos for listening, as well as many play-along examples for practicing improvising over various musical styles and progressions.

Evans, Lee. *Beginning Jazz Improvisation.* Milwaukee: Hal Leonard Corporation, 1984.

Starting with the basics, the student becomes actively involved in creating improvised melodies based on blues progressions, walking bass, boogie-woogie, and other patterns.

(It should be noted that Lee Evans has a number of books for teaching jazz, including jazz method books, jazz technique books, and graded repertoire books—all worth investigating.)

Evans, Lee. *Discovering Blues Improvisation*, Books 1 & 2. Milwaukee: Piano Plus, Inc., 2006. Distributed by Hal Leonard Corporation.

Featuring several original blues compositions by Evans, *Discovering Blues Improvisation* encourages students to study jazz improvisation through notation. After learning pieces in the style of masters such as Jelly Roll Morton, Louis Armstrong, and Duke Ellington, students are encouraged to write out their own riffs, as well as compose their own 12-bar blues. Each book includes biographies of the jazz greats, as well as a CD of performances by the author.

Faber, Nancy, and Randall Faber, with Edwin McLean. *Discover Beginning Improvisation.* Fort Lauderdale: The FJH Music Company, Inc., 1992.

> Designed for students of all ages who have had no previous experience improvising, this primer lays the foundation for composition and improvisation using the simplest possible exercises in imaginative settings. The book features solo and duet improvisations, written assignments, theory review, and teacher accompaniments.

Faber, Nancy, and Randall Faber, with Edwin McLean. *Discover Blues Improvisation: An Introduction to Blues Piano.* Fort Lauderdale: The FJH Music Company, Inc., 1997.

> This book provides a comprehensive approach for the beginning blues player, featuring instruction in improvisation and theory, appealing pieces with improvisation options, blues technique, and blues ear-training. The book can be purchased with or without CD.

Hill, Willie L. *Approaching the Standards*, Volumes 1–3, Van Nuys: Alfred Publishing Company, Inc., 2000.

> Volumes 1, 2, and 3 of this set each include eight jazz standards such as "I Got Rhythm" and "Satin Doll." The books present written melodies and chord symbols, and the accompanying CD includes two tracks per title: one with the selection being performed by a full band, and the second with rhythm section only. The first track per title allows the student to hear and imitate a professional improvisation, and the second track allows students to improvise on their own along with the rhythm section. The book includes a box with written information, including "Composer Insight," "Licks and Tricks," and "Scales and Chords" for each of the selections included.

LaPorta, John. *A Guide to Jazz Improvisation.* Boston: Berklee Press Publications, 2000. Distributed by Hal Leonard Corporation.

> First published in 1968 and now thoroughly updated and revised, this method provides a practical and intuitive approach to teaching basic jazz improvisation through 12 lessons and an accompanying CD. It also features information on jazz theory, rhythm training, performance, ear-training, and much more.

Marlais, Helen. *In Recital® with Jazz, Blues, & Rags.* Fort Lauderdale: The FJH Music Company, Inc., 2008.

> This series includes arrangements and original compositions intended for early elementary to late intermediate piano students. The series is sequential and can serve as a supplement to any method, giving students additional exposure to the world of jazz. Each book comes with a CD to assist students with understanding the different styles of the pieces.

Myette, Willie. *JazzKids*, Levels 1–4. Providence: JazzKids, 2005–2006.

> *JazzKids* easily integrates into a teacher's pedagogy by providing simple, step-by-step improvisation pieces (jazz and other styles) and exercises. The books develop the student's aural skills with ear-training and vocalization of straight and swing rhythms. CDs and DVDs provide another level of assistance for the teacher and student, ensuring that those with little or no improvisation experience can get started quickly. For more information, visit www.jazzkids.com.

Paparelli, Frank. *Boogie Woogie for Beginners.* Milwaukee: Hal Leonard Corporation, 1943, 1988.

> This short, easy method for learning to play Boogie Woogie is designed with the "beginning and average" pianist in mind. The material is at a level comparable to early intermediate method books, and gives clear and simple examples for bass figures, rhythm and dynamics, and Boogie Woogie effects. Boogie Woogie exercises and solos are also included.

**PART IX**

# Resources (cont.)

Rizzo, Gene. *Best of Jazz Piano.* Milwaukee: Hal Leonard Corporation, 2005.

> A tool for studying the piano styles and techniques of great jazz pianists, this book offers a step-by-step breakdown of the piano styles and techniques of jazz artists such as Nat "King" Cole, Bill Evans, Oscar Peterson, Billy Taylor, and more. All selections are heard on the accompanying CD.

Simpson, Joel. *Blues – By You: The Direct Route to Piano Improvisation.* New York: Cherry Lane Music, 1997. Distributed by Hal Leonard Corporation.

> In the introduction to this book, the author claims, "If you take one step at a time and master it thoroughly, you can be playing a good-sounding blues in an astonishingly short time—usually in about a month or two—with 30 to 60 minutes of practice each day. In another couple of months, at the same rate, you should be producing interesting improvisations." The book is so logically written, and the accompanying CD has such good examples, that this claim seems entirely possible. Students using the book would need to have prior basic knowledge of theory, but the clear format and understandable directions allow upper-intermediate to lower-advanced students to learn to play the blues.

## JAZZ AND BLUES HISTORY

Anderson, Tom, and Bradley Shank. *Exploring the Blues.* New York: Cherry Lane Music Company, 2001. Distributed by Hal Leonard Corporation.

> An all-in-one resource, this book is designed to introduce students to the great American art form of the Blues. Originally developed for *Music Alive* magazine, each topic includes a reproducible student article, reproducible activity pages (including listening maps, worksheets, and other enrichment ideas), and a detailed National Standards-based lesson plan. All musical examples are included on the enclosed CD. Topics include: Birth of the Blues (W.C. Handy), Early Blues Guitarists (Charlie Patton, Robert Johnson, and others), Women and the Blues, Now and Then ("Ma" Rainey, Dinah Washington, Aretha Franklin, and others), The Blues Begin to Rock (Chuck Berry, Elvis Presley, Eric Clapton, and others), Blues Across America, and a special section on blues greats Bessie Smith, John Lee Hooker, and B.B. King.

McCurdy, Ronald C., *Meet the Great Jazz Legends.* Van Nuys: Alfred Publishing Co., Inc., 2004.

> Ideal for junior high or high school students, the 17 chapters in this book introduce 17 of the greatest jazz musicians ever to live, including Louis Armstrong, Duke Ellington, Count Bassie, Ella Fitzgerlad, Billie Holiday, Charlie Parker, Dizzie Gillespie among others. Each chapter includes a short biography of the featured composer as well as activities. The book may be purchased with or without reproducible activity sheets for a group setting such as a jazz camp or jazz history group lesson.

## ADDITIONAL RESOURCES

- Technique books with a jazz focus are listed in Chapter 27.
- Theory books with a jazz focus are listed in Chapter 34.

### The *Jazz For Young People™ Curriculum*

> This learning program includes 17 lessons narrated by Wynton Marsalis. The program comes with a teacher's guide, 30 student guides, a video, and ten CDs that include numerous jazz performances by the Lincoln Center Jazz Orchestra and special guests. This set would also be ideal in a music camp centered on jazz. The curriculum is designed for fourth through ninth grade students and can be ordered via e-mail: curriculum@jalc.org; phone 212-258-9800; or online at www.jazzforyoungpeople.org.

**WEBSITES**

*Classics for Kids*

   www.classicsforkids.com

   – Select "On the Radio"

   – Select "Past Shows"

   – Select "Collections of Music by Period"

   – Select "Jazz"

*Hornplace*

   www.hornplace.com

   This site includes a list of improvisation materials with links to descriptions of each.

   – Select "Improvisation"

*PBS Kids*

   www.pbskids.org/jazz

*Smithsonian Jazz*

   www.smithsonianjazz.org

*ThinkQuest*

   library.thinkquest.org/library

   – Select Arts & Education

   – Select "Music"

   – Select "Jazz"

**PART IX**

# Chapter 38

# MUSIC OF MANY CULTURES

When I was 13, my family moved to Europe for a few years. We lived in Verona, Italy, which has a beautiful 2000-year-old outdoor amphitheater. The ancient amphitheater is much like the Coliseum in Rome, but in better shape. Every summer, all of my teenage friends and I would go as often as we could to the amphitheater for some amazing nights of opera. Because of their love of opera, the Italians sang along and when they yelled "Encore!" they meant it; they wanted to hear the aria again. The costumes and scenery were spectacular (complete with live donkeys and horses, light shows, and huge sets), and even American teenagers who didn't normally have any connection with classical music loved the operas in Verona.

The operas of Italy are loved throughout Western civilization and are far more familiar than the music of a small island tribe or an Asian village. Nonetheless, opera seems to be perceived quite differently in the Italian culture than in the American culture, and it was a real joy for me to experience opera as it is experienced in Italy.

As teachers, we may not be able to take our students to experience live music in Italy, India, Korea, Pakistan, Vietnam, Zimbabwe, Jamaica, or Mexico, but we can certainly expose them to the music of many cultures. Such exposure teaches students that music is a universal language, understandable by all.

## World Music

### Incorporating into the curriculum

The study of world music offers students an opportunity to become more diversified in their musical tastes as well as to learn and appreciate the beauty of other cultures.

A number of ways exist for a teacher to incorporate world music into the curriculum:

- Introduce students to repertoire centered on world music.

- Highlight world music in a themed recital with students playing pieces from other cultures, dressing in native costumes, giving a short presentation on another culture, or preparing ethnic food for a reception.

- Make use of world music materials developed for the classroom; numerous catalogs for K-12 music include excellent resources.

- Develop a world music camp.

- Hire artists from other cultures to sing, dance, or play the instruments of their culture.

- Invite individuals from other cultures to talk about their country's history and current events.

- Create projects for students centered on world music.

- Research world music on the Internet, including teacher websites for lesson plans on world music.

- Create a board game centered on the cultures of other countries.

- Develop workstation or class assignments centered on world music (CDs, DVDs, workbooks, Internet).

- Purchase world instruments, such as African drums, for use in the studio. Research music catalog companies for world music materials and instruments.

- Create ensembles for students using world instruments.

- Develop a world music festival with other area teachers, musicians, and artists.

## Organizing a world music festival

*Music of Our World* by John Higgins was developed with the elementary classroom in mind, and could serve as a foundation for a world music festival. The book centers around the music of eight cultures: Japan, Hawaii, India, Sweden, Brazil, Laos, South Africa, and Mexico. Each chapter includes a brief history of the music as well as descriptions of a festival celebrated in that region. A song is included, as is a phonetic guide to singing the words and information about the song and its significance. A lesson plan, activities, and a written accompaniment are included in each chapter. An accompanying CD has two tracks for each song: one with vocals, and one with accompaniment only.

Although some may think that *Music of Our World* seems more suited to a children's choir or to a vocal studio, piano students benefit from singing and developing aural skills. By learning the songs of other cultures, the students' love and appreciation of all music can be increased. This book can then be supplemented with piano repertoire or other activities and used to present a creative end-of- the-year program, parent's night, or recital.

Repertoire books and pieces with a world music theme are too plentiful to mention here, but one particularly delightful book is *20 Little Piano Pieces from Around the World* by David Patterson. This book provides an excellent first exposure to world music for any beginning pianist.

The following are only a few of the many resources now available that can be used to broaden students' horizons and add a unique flair to a studio. Anyone interested in world music will find that a minimum amount of research produces many resource materials and helpful websites, including those that were originally intended for classroom teaching or singing.

**PART IX**

# Resources

### GAMES

Lavender, Cheryl. *World Instrument Bingo.* Milwaukee: Hal Leonard Corporation, 1999.

*World Instrument Bingo* is a collection of five collaborative learning games students can play to discover and identify folk instruments from around the world, such as timbales, mbira, and shofar. The games help students identify tone colors, explore sound production, and compare cultural influences on music. The kit comes complete with 30 Bingo play cards, an instruction booklet with game directions and world instrument fun facts, a CD with sound samples of 24 world instruments recorded on six separate sound sequences, a world instrument poster, and one page of 24 cut-out caller cards.

### BOOKS

The following are centered on singing, and can be used in the independent piano studio to reinforce world music, improve aural skills, or serve as the foundation for a summer camp.

Higgins, John. *More Music of Our World: Multicultural Festivals, Songs, and Activities.* Milwaukee: Hal Leonard Corporation, 2005.

A global collection of songs, articles, and activities, this Book/CD Pak is ideal for a group setting such as a summer camp. Authentic folksongs, children's songs, and work songs demonstrate the music of Cuba, Zimbabwe, Jamaica, the Philippines, Mexico, Lebanon, the Caribbean, and Chile.

Higgins, John. *Music of Our World: Multicultural Festivals, Songs, and Activities.* Milwaukee: Hal Leonard Corporation, 2003.

This multicultural collection celebrates music cultures and traditions as they happen around the world. Festivals, songs, and activities are included that enhance global awareness and provide rich musical experiences. This all-in-one Book/CD Pak provides background on each festival, step-by-step instruction for each song based on the National Standards, piano/vocal accompaniments, song translations, reproducible song sheets, expanded activities, and a CD recording of each song, with vocals and accompaniment tracks only. The book centers around eight cultures: Japan, Hawaii, India, Sweden, Brazil, Laos, South Africa, and Mexico.

### REPERTOIRE BOOKS

O'Grady, Amy, arr. *World Gems: International Folksongs for Piano Ensemble.* Milwaukee: Hal Leonard Corporation, 2004.

These six arrangements of familiar international folksongs create sonorities for electronic keyboards and/or pianos. Titles include: African Noël, Choucounne, El Condor Pasa, Jasmine Flower Song, Mexican Hat Dance (Jarabe Tapatío), and Sakura (Cherry Blossoms).

Patterson, David. *20 Little Piano Pieces from Around the World.* Milwaukee: Hal Leonard Corporation, 1998.

These easy and delightful pieces reflect cultures and instruments from around the world. As stated in the introduction, "In this collection we have gathered and adapted 20 traditional songs and dances from six continents, along with translations and information about the music and the people who perform it. There are illustrations of some of the instruments associated with the music, and we've included a guide to assist in the pronunciation of difficult words."

Ranson, Jana. *Keyboard Cookbook: Recipes for Playing More Than 40 Styles.* Milwaukee: Hal Leonard Corporation, 2004.

Celebrating the music of the American culture, this book is presented in cookbook style. Each piece is preceded by a recipe page that includes Time, Yield, Ingredients, For Best Results, Spice It Up, and Sample the Recipes of These Leading Chefs of the Style. Seven main areas are covered: blues, country, jazz, Latin, popular, R&B, and traditional, with a number of categories in each. For example, the jazz area includes bebop, cool jazz, Dixieland, hard bop, ragtime, and stride. The format of the book is creative and the book provides an excellent introduction into the musical styles of the Unites States.

## Folk Music, Children's Songs, and Patriotic Music

When world music is presented, our own culture should not be forgotten. Many of today's young students do not know the numerous children's songs and folksongs that were a staple of past generations. Fewer and fewer people know the words to our national anthem, or even recognize which piece *is* our national anthem.

In an early childhood class that I taught, only one of the three-year olds had ever sung "Eensy Weensy (Itsy Bitsy) Spider" and knew how to do the hand gestures that accompany the song. At one point, the song was a standard children's tune, sung with gestures by parents and children together.

Our country, young as it is, has a rich heritage of folksongs, children's songs, and patriotic music that is not being passed along to younger generations. Piano teachers can help to keep music alive by doing the following:

- Point out folksongs when they appear in method books, as students may not know the difference between these pieces and other pieces in the method.

- Emphasize the importance of our culture's music by including folk or patriotic pieces in each student's repertoire.

- Teach folksongs by ear.

- Offer a summer camp on America's music.

- Perform a "musical" of folk tunes, children's tunes, or patriotic music at the end of the year or in the summer.

- Explore the vast number of publications of patriotic music that are available at every level and in a variety of styles.

## Resources

### FOLKSONG COLLECTIONS

*Golden Encyclopedia of Folk Music.* Milwaukee: Hal Leonard Corporation/Lewis Publishing Company, 1969.

Including over 180 folksongs, this book is dedicated to the rebirth of folk music. Words are included for multiple verses, and the piano parts are at an early intermediate level. Chord names appear throughout, allowing the accompaniments to be accessible to guitarists as well. Not to be confused with children's songs (although some are included), the book contains a mixture of well-known and little-known folksongs.

*150 Easy Piano Children's Songs.* Milwaukee: Hal Leonard Corporation, 2001.

It is often lamented that young students no longer know the nursery rhymes and folk tunes that have been such a part of our culture. Designed for young singers, this book has 150 children's songs, with easy piano accompaniments that are well suited to the early-level piano student. Useful for young singers, the book also provides an excellent introduction to accompaniment with such favorite children's songs as "Eensy Weensy Spider," "London Bridge," "Oh! Susanna," "On Top of Old Smoky," "She'll Be Comin' 'Round the Mountain," and "This Old Man."

PART IX

## Resources (cont.)

Seeger, Ruth Crawford. *American Folksongs for Children.* New York, London, Paris, Sydney, Copenhagen, Madrid: Oak Publications. 1948, 1975, 2002.

This collection of over 90 songs is far more than a book of children's folksongs. Seeger, well-known for her dedication to folk music, offers a 35-page guide to using the book in a group teaching setting. Many songs are accompanied by Seeger's suggestions for improvisation and rhythmic or dramatic play. Helpful indexes in the back of the book include a subject index, a rhythmic index, and indexes organized around tone play, name play, games, finger play, small dramas, and quiet songs. The songs include multiple verses, and the piano accompaniments are playable by intermediate-level students.

# Chapter 39

# MUSIC CAMPS

My piano pedagogy students must each develop a summer music camp, including the curriculum, budget, list of materials, lesson plans, marketing strategy, and timeline for activities. Although this project is originally met with a certain amount of uneasy groaning, the students inevitably get excited as they work on their camps. All the students learn a great deal about their chosen topic and inevitably say, "I didn't think I would have enough material, but now I have more than I need!" Sometimes students get so excited by the projects they have to hold themselves in check, "I realize I need to spend more time on my other homework, but this is so much fun!"

What is particularly gratifying to me is that the students realize they have the skills to develop a camp on any topic, just by doing the necessary research and understanding the organization that is required.

## Benefits

Summer music programs are not new: programs such as Tanglewood, Interlochen, and university-sponsored programs have long existed for the talented or serious music student. Such options are now even more abundant and are supplemented with many innovative programs developed by independent piano teachers for students of all ages and levels of achievement. Any teacher can organize a music camp on any appealing topic, offering students a gratifying and educational musical experience.

A music camp gives students in-depth exposure to a topic that cannot be covered thoroughly during a private lesson. Within this group setting, students are able to learn together and experience the peer interaction often missing from private piano lessons, while expanding their understanding of the focal point of the camp.

The students will not be the only ones who grow. The teacher's horizons will also broaden, as organizing a camp allows a teacher to expand her own knowledge in a given area. Teachers need not be experts on a topic in order to present a camp. There are numerous resources to use when organizing the camp, and with some basic research, abundant information can be gathered on any topic, allowing for a camp to be presented with ease and confidence.

## Length of the Camp

A music camp can be any length, from a few hours a day for a few days to full days over a number of weeks. Summertime offers the best option for offering the camp over consecutive days, while a camp organized during school months might be best suited to a weekend, consecutive weekends, or a choice such as four Wednesday evenings. If offering a camp is a new experience within a studio, a shorter camp can provide a good starting point for teachers and students.

## Themes, Activities, and Resources

### Themes

When planning a camp, an appealing theme provides an important starting point. Any area of interest can be pursued, including:

- Opera

- Jazz

- Schubert (or any great composer)

- Contemporary music (or any period of music)

- Dance influences in piano music

- Patriotic music

- Disney favorites

- Folk music

- Musical theater

- The music of Africa

- Native American music (or any culture)

- Ensemble music

- Chamber music

- Composition (including composing a musical or opera)

- Technique

- Music theory

- Improvisation

- Memorization

- Sight-playing

- Ear-training

- Rhythm

- Accompanying

- Music technology

- Religious music

- World instruments

- Adult beginners

A camp could even be developed on an interdisciplinary theme such as:

- The Art and Music of Italy

- Religion and Music

- Politics and Music

- Wars and Their Influence on Music

- Great Love Stories and Music

## Activities

Time flies when activities are numerous and varied; a camp's activities might include:

- Sharing of information

- Topic discussions

- Art or project time (such as making an African drum, doing an Aboriginal bark painting, etc.)

- Snack or cooking time

- Movie time (a movie on Beethoven, an opera, or a jazz great)

- Research time (on the Internet or in resources collected for the camp)

- Listening to recordings (symphony, chamber music, etc).

A final concert program for parents provides a fulfilling close to a camp. Students can give a presentation, demonstrate their homemade instruments, perform pieces from the era studied, do the play they wrote on a composer's life, perform in a mini-musical, etc.

In other words, there are a number of activities from which to choose when planning a camp curriculum. Standing in front of students, lecturing, and "being the expert" are not the best options; educational, enjoyable, hands-on activities serve a far better purpose. As new topics are developed, a library of activities, resources, and camp curriculums can be built for future use.

## Finding Resources

A multitude of resources is available for camp activities. Publishers have produced books designed for the school classroom that can easily be adapted to a summer camp format.

- Check your local music retailer and the many publishers and catalogs that offer games, videos, books, CDs, and DVDs suitable for use in a camp curriculum.

- Free lesson plans exist on Internet teacher websites, outlining the materials needed, the appropriate age group, and a step-by-step guide to the activity.

- Local or state music teacher organizations can be asked to give sessions on summer camps to aid with further ideas for curriculum and resources.

Many elementary school resource books and lesson plans provide activities appropriate for the group setting of a camp. Some include vocal selections that offer piano students the opportunity to further develop their listening and singing skills.

**PART IX**

# Resources

**MUSIC EDUCATORS MARKETPLACE** (www.musicedmarket.com)

A free outline (not a complete packet) for a Music History camp can be found by going to the Music Educator's Marketplace website and selecting "Free Offerings" in the left column. This outline can be supplemented with helpful products found at the "Music History" link.

The following fully developed camps can be purchased at the Music Educator's Marketplace website, by selecting "Our Store" and then selecting "Games, Camps, and Groups."

- Patriotic Camp
- Adventures in Music
- Christmas Camp

**THEORY TIME** (www.theorytime.com)

If anyone is hesitant to develop a camp from scratch, complete camp formats can be purchased. These camps can be presented with no further research or they can be personalized by adding supplemental activities. For example, *Theory Time* offers reproducible summer camp curriculum packets, already developed, in a ready-to-use format. The packets contain all that is needed for a self-contained camp, including:

- Reproducible student booklets
- Lesson plans
- Listening exercises
- Suggested hands-on art projects and activities
- Games
- Sample schedule
- Checklist for advanced preparation
- Business materials such as a sample flier, registration form, and parent letter

The camp packets available from *Theory Time* are:

- Great Composers from Bach to Bartók
- Ancient Egypt
- Hansel and Gretel
- Cinderella, Then and Now
- Have a Blast with the Past
- Hit a Home Run with Theory – Game Pack
- Hit a Home Run with Theory – Lesson Plans and Worksheets
- Musical Stories and Suites

**OTHER WEBSITES**

As mentioned earlier, the Internet has an abundance of teacher sites that offer free lesson plans. These sites usually have links to lesson plans for specific topics (such as music), and give the appropriate grade level for all activities. Some Internet sites that focus on lesson plans, many with multiple links to other good sites, include:

*A to Z Teacher Stuff*

www.atozteacherstuff.com

- Type "music lesson plans" into the search box

*The Classical Archives*

www.classicalarchives.com

- – Type "Learning Center" into the search box; many good links will show.
- – From that page, scroll down and select "Sitemap" from the "Quick Searches" box for additional links.

*Discovery Education*

http://school.discoveryeducation.com

- – From menu, select "Lesson Plans Library"
- – Scroll down and select "Fine Arts"

*Hot Chalk's Lesson Plans Page*

www.lessonplanspage.com/music.htm

*Ricci Adams' musictheory.net*

www.musictheory.net

Internet sites, catalogs, and additional resources listed in other chapters of this book (such as music history, music theory, jazz, etc.) will be helpful in researching materials for music camps on a multitude of subjects.

## Budgets

When first planning a camp, a projected budget must be developed listing all anticipated expenses and income. Itemizing and estimating costs helps to focus on the optimum number of students as well as the charge-per-student necessary to cover all costs. If cost cannot be covered from tuition alone, outside sources of income need to be sought.

When working on the budget, certain questions must be asked:

- • What supplies will be necessary?
- • What administrative costs will be incurred?
- • What are the marketing costs?
- • How much will be paid for salaries and rent?
- • What is the estimated enrollment of the camp?
- • How much would each student need to be charged for tuition in order to cover the costs of the camp?
- • Are there any grants or donations available to assist with costs?
- • Will there be any in-kind expenses or income?

### Expenses and Income

When figuring a camp budget, a few basic principles must be followed. First, the expenses and income amounts must be equal. A budget should not be planned where the income is listed as $1000 more than the expenses. That extra income should go into some category: increased wages, additional supplies, annual savings, etc. This is especially important when seeking outside funding. What agency would give us $1000 if the budget shows the camp will make $1000 over its expenses already? Even more clearly, no budget should reflect a cost of $1000 more than the camp will earn unless the planner is very rich or very reckless.

### Salaries

Those running the camp also need to be paid a salary, not only for the actual hours spent teaching the camp, but also for camp preparation and for administrative duties, such as marketing, mailings, and registrations.

### In-kind Expenses

Understanding and including in-kind expenses (anything offered without charge) is essential to an accurate budget. If, for example, the camp will be held in a church but the church is not charging rent, the cost of using the space would be listed in the in-kind column, along with all other items that are used without charge. Other possible in-kind items include:

- The use of utilities

- Janitorial services

- A copy machine

- Mailings

- Any facilities or equipment used for the camp

- Volunteer time

Even though there are no charges for in-kind items, they must always be figured into a budget's income and expenses in the in-kind column, as this gives a more accurate view of the true cost of the camp. It is also necessary to list in-kind items when seeking a grant. In-kind income can usually be used to meet part of the matching funds if such are required.

An example of a budget follows. In this make-believe budget, there is no charge for the use of the facility. The rent is being donated, so its cost, $250, is listed under in-kind expenses (the cost to rent) and income (the amount of the donation).

## PROJECTED BUDGET OF INCOME AND EXPENSES:

| EXPENSES | ACTUAL | IN-KIND |
|---|---|---|
| Rent | — | 250 |
| Wages | 700 | — |
| Insurance | 100 | — |
| Food/snacks | 250 | — |
| Supplies | 450 | — |
| Postage | — | 50 |
| Printing | 100 | — |
| Marketing | 100 | — |
| **Total expenses:** | **$1750** | **$300** |

| INCOME | ACTUAL | IN-KIND |
|---|---|---|
| Tuition | 1000 | — |
| Grants | 450 | — |
| Donations | 300 | — |
| In-kind | — | 300 |
| **Total income:** | **$1750** | **$300** |

### Supplies

Supplies include any books, CDs, DVDs, games, craft items, etc., that will be bought for use in the camp. The cost of these items should be recuperated through the income received and often supplies can be reused in future camps. An expensive DVD can be viewed as an investment that will continue to have value in the studio. Expenses such as copying reproducible worksheets, printing posters, postage for letters, etc., should be included in the camp budget.

### Grants

Local or state arts agencies usually offer grants only to organizations with a 501c3 (non-profit) status. Camp organizers can partner with a non-profit organization if they wish to apply for such a grant. Grants and contributions may also be obtained from a visitor's bureau or local chamber of commerce, and will be discussed further in Chapter 49.

At the end of the camp, the actual income and expenses are then calculated. If the planning has been done carefully, these figures should be close to the original budget. If grant money was received, a final report including a final budget with actual income and expenses figures will need to be sent to the funding agency. At tax time, tax-deductible expenses will need to be reported as well as income, so all receipts for income and expenses must be kept and well-documented.

## Marketing

Camps can be organized for one's own students, or they may be made available to students outside of the studio. For example, a world music camp or a camp on Brahms need not be restricted to piano students. Camps can be organized for any special group, such as adults, at-risk youth, home-schooled students, or individuals with special needs.

If the camp is meant to appeal to clientele from outside the studio, a number of options for marketing are available:

**PART IX**

- Local papers sometimes print articles about new arts programs, but this may depend on the size of the newspaper. If the paper will not print an article on the camp, paying for an ad is another way to market through the paper.

- Many local radio stations will advertise arts events, or may even do an interview about a new program. Some local radio and TV stations do several Public Service Announcements without charge, or may advertise events with a minimal fee.

- One of the easiest ways to advertise is by distributing posters and fliers with the main information about the camp. Fliers can be sent home in school bags with students. Posters or fliers can be put on counters or on public bulletin boards in malls, grocery stores, libraries, places of worship, YMCAs, Parks and Recreation Centers, and willing businesses.

- Mass mailings can also get the word out about the camp. Letters can be sent to other music teachers, public school teachers, Parks and Recreation, Social Services, or anyone who might show an interest.

- Professional newsletters provide an additional source for marketing. An article could be sent to local or state arts councils, local or state music teachers' organizations, or the Chamber of Commerce for inclusion in their newsletters.

For more information on marketing, see Chapter 7.

## Location

Independent studios provide an excellent location for a camp as long as local zoning laws allow for the desired number of participants. Zoning laws may put an unworkable restriction on the number of students a teacher can have at any one time, or the studio space itself may be too small. In either of these situations, other possible locations exist that may be suitable for the camp, usually for a fee:

- Places of worship

- Universities

- Area clubs (such as the Eagle's Club or the YMCA)

- Music stores

- Community schools of the arts

If an outside site is used, insurance issues need to be discussed to determine if the camp will be covered under site insurance, or if separate insurance must be purchased for the camp. A word of caution: if the rent to use an outside facility is exorbitant, it may be difficult for the camp income to cover all expenses. Teaching and administrative salaries inevitably suffer in such a case.

## Collaboration

When organizing a camp, a teacher may wish to partner with others rather than organize the whole camp alone. The section on Networking and Partnerships in Chapter 19 can serve as a guideline when seeking partners. One excellent option includes several piano teachers building a camp together.

The theme of the camp may offer added ideas for collaborating. A camp on Baroque dances may provide an opportunity to partner with a dance instructor, while a string teacher might be interested in a camp on chamber music. A jazz musician or a composer is a good choice for a camp on improvisation or composing, while a voice teacher would contribute to a camp on opera or accompanying.

## Sample Curriculum

Although an endless supply of topics exists from which to choose, suggestions are included here on two topics—contemporary music and world music—to show how easy it is to develop a personalized music camp.

### Contemporary Music Camp

Many music history textbooks can assist a teacher with reviewing and understanding contemporary music. When developing camp curriculum, one book, *Great Composers of the 20th Century* (by Jacqueline Wollan Gibbons. New York: Cherry Lane Music, 2000. Distributed by Hal Leonard Corporation), could serve as the basis for a camp outline. This book, based on articles and lesson plans from the general music education magazine, *MUSIC ALIVE!* covers eight 20th century composers: Claude Debussy, Arnold Schoenberg, Béla Bartók, Igor Stravinsky, Dmitri Shostakovich, Aaron Copland, John Cage, and Leonard Bernstein.

Because the book was intended for a classroom setting, it provides organized lesson plans on each composer, along with reproducible articles and activity sheets. The chapter on Schoenberg, for instance, includes the following sections: Reviewing Tonality; Introducing Atonality; Listening to Schoenberg's Music; Creating Atonal Music; and Reviewing Concepts and Terms. A section called "Extending the Lesson" supplies suggestions for further study and dialogue. A CD accompanies the book with a number of listening examples for each composer and guidelines for discussion. Additional CDs can be purchased that further demonstrate Impressionism, expressionism, minimalism, 12-tone music, neo-Classicism, and more.

If desired, individual projects can be designed to further enhance the curriculum of the camp:

**Graphic notation project:** One contemporary music project my students love is introduced when we study graphic notation:

1) The students divide into Group A and Group B.

2) Each group composes a piece using graphic notation (drawings to indicate the sound patterns) instead of traditional notation.

3) Instructions for the composition include composing for found objects such as plastic containers, oatmeal containers, plastic bags, sticks, whistles, etc.—anything capable of making a sound.

4) A chart or key must be included with the composition that explains the graphic notation symbols used to produce the desired sounds.

5) Once the composition is complete, the groups swap the charts that explain their graphics, as well as copies of their composition.

6) Each group goes off and learns the other group's composition according to the explanation for the graphic notation they have been given.

PART IX

7) When the groups come back together, Group A performs Group B's piece, and Group B performs Group A's piece.

8) The composers of each work then perform their own original composition as they had intended it to sound.

9) The two performances of each composition are then compared: How well was each group able to convey its intentions to the other group?

The students enjoy composing, performing, and comparing the two performances, as well as discussing the challenges of notation, composition, indeterminate (unplanned) elements in composition, and the nature of music. Lively discussion often follows on what is "real" music!

**12-tone grid project:** When learning about 12-tone music my students compose a 12-tone row. They then draw a complete grid (matrix) of the row with all of its transpositions, inversions, retrogrades, and retrograde-inversions. Students have a much better appreciation for 12-tone (dodecaphonic, or serial) music when they have composed their own 12-tone row and explored all of the possibilities of the series. Students then create a short composition incorporating at least four different versions of the row.

**Impressionist project:** Using the Internet, a favorite Impressionist piece is paired with an Impressionist painting that the student feels projects a similar mood. The student puts both examples into a PowerPoint® presentation, which includes a written comparison of the artistic elements of both works (such as the approach to color, form, texture, and motion).

**A broader perspective:** Included in the Contemporary Music Camp are many discussions on what makes music good. Students are encouraged to be open to a variety of sounds, not just those that consist of a pretty melody. Pieces with shocking or unconventional sounds are shared in order to generate discussion.

**Composition:** Students compose their own pieces based on what they have learned about contemporary styles. Included in this project is a written description of the student's intentions and the musical elements chosen to project those intentions.

**Parent's Night:** The camp concludes with a number of activities presented to the parents:

- Performance of the individual compositions
- Performances of the graphic notation group projects
- A presentation of the PowerPoints® on Impressionism
- A display of the 12-tone grids, graphic notation charts, and any completed worksheets
- A viewing of video clips taken of the students during camp

If any area of contemporary music sounds a bit foreign, a small amount of research is all that is needed to learn (or relearn) the information necessary for presenting a camp. If a student asks a question the teacher cannot answer, a simple, "That is a great question, and I am not sure of the answer. Let's look that up," shows students that instructors, too, are lifelong learners.

## World Music Camp

A number of my pedagogy students choose to do camps on different aspects of world music to fulfill the summer camp assignment mentioned at the beginning of this chapter. One student put together a camp on the music of Australia. Once she got started, she realized:

- She couldn't talk about the music of Australia without discussing the art.

- She couldn't cover the art without mentioning the history.

- She couldn't speak of the history without talking about the geography.

- She couldn't speak of the geography without referring to the animals.

The project ended up being a multi-disciplinary camp, rich in information on many aspects of Australian culture.

One student chose to do his camp on Native American Music. Although he knew relatively little about the subject when he first started the project, he developed a summer camp using resources such as the library, the Internet, CDs, teacher catalogs, resources at the North Dakota state capitol, and interviews with Native American musicians.

Each day's curriculum included four lessons: one on the history of native tribes; a lesson on Native American music; an art project; and a cooking project. His students made masks, drums, dream-catchers, dance sticks, and "eagle" feather art. He taught the students in his camp native dancing, drumming, and singing. His camp included numerous history lessons and pictures, and above all, he learned that he can indeed research a topic, no matter how little he knew initially, and develop an educational camp that his students will enjoy.

Multicultural resources are listed in Chapter 38, all offering a starting point for a camp on world music. From presenting native folksongs to studying the customs and instruments of other cultures, an abundance of material exists to help organize a world music camp. Developing a camp on any topic takes time, but with the resources available it may take less time than one thinks. Camps can be reused and augmented in future years, and students and teachers alike will benefit from the new knowledge gained in each camp.

**PART IX**

# Chapter 40

# WORKSTATIONS

The first time I saw a workstation with computers, MIDI keyboards, and sequencers, I was overwhelmed. This was many years ago, and the whole area seemed baffling to my untrained eye. I couldn't imagine how the teacher could keep everything straight, or why she would want to include all of this technology in her studio in the first place.

Since then, I have become a technology convert. I have written grants to acquire computers, MIDI keyboards, and software for a computer lab, and have gotten excited by the possibilities that technology brings to a workstation.

I sometimes call workstations with computers a "computer lab" and those without computers or keyboards simply a "workstation," but in reality, both are types of workstations. I have used both types in my teaching, and regardless of the complexities of the equipment, I have found that one of the best ways to successfully integrate a broad curriculum and expand instruction time within the studio is by incorporating a workstation.

## Uses

Since a workstation can be simple or elaborate, low-tech or high-tech, each teacher has to decide on the type of workstation she wants in accordance with the elements she wishes to reinforce through its use. Some of the uses for a workstation include:

- To improve theory skills

- To increase knowledge of composers and music history

- To improve aural and rhythmic skills

- To compose and improvise

- To gain exposure to world music

- To develop sight-playing skills

- To improve keyboard skills

- To function as a listening station for all types of music

Using a workstation produces important studio benefits:

- A workstation allows the teacher to cover more areas than are possible in a private lesson alone.

- Areas of study can be covered more thoroughly.

- A more creative curriculum increases students' enjoyment and varies their learning opportunities.

- Students often look forward to their workstation experience with enthusiasm due to its "break in routine" nature.

- Additional income can be earned.

# Low-Tech Workstation

### Basic

Some misconceptions about a workstation are that it is expensive, it requires high-tech equipment, and it requires sophisticated skills. In actuality, an extremely functional workstation can be built with only three pieces of furniture:

- Table
- Chair
- System for organizing student folders and books, such as a file cabinet, cubbies, or shelf with dividers for folders and books

Each student can sit at the table and work from an individualized folder, with the assignment for the day included. Perhaps a music theory workbook would be kept in each folder, or a reading assignment for music history. Although certain books may need to be purchased, the cost of individual workbooks could be charged directly to the students.

### Listening Station

Add to this basic setup just a few more items, and the workstation becomes a listening station:

- CD player, MP3, or iPod
- Headset
- CD collection

A listening station can be used for assignments on a number of topics:

- Music from each historical period
- Musical genres: concertos, symphonies, operas, chamber music, and solo repertoire on all instruments
- A composer the student is currently studying
- Stories about the great composers or about periods of history
- Other musical styles: jazz, world music, pop/rock, Broadway, movie, etc.
- Listening organized around a theme such as scary music, sad music, fast pieces, technically challenging pieces, pieces for children, holiday music, etc.

All of the above listening assignments could be accompanied with a workbook assignment or written assignment, such as "Describe the Romantic elements you heard in this composition" or "Describe what you liked best about this style of music, and why you found it appealing."

Many teachers already have a number of reference books and a large CD library, but even if materials must be purchased, they will be a business expenses, a tax deduction, and a great asset to the studio.

# High-Tech Workstation

### Basic

The possibilities for a high-tech workstation are limited only by money and space, with a multitude of potential uses. The most basic equipment includes:

- Computer

- Headsets

- Basic software programs

### Basic Add-ons

The potential for varied assignments increases with two important additions:

- MIDI keyboard (and appropriate cables)

- Internet connection

This type of workstation requires the space needed for a table for the computer and keyboard, a chair, and a system for organizing folders and workbooks as mentioned above.

### Advanced

Software programs expand the capabilities of the computer and are available for:

- Music theory in all levels, from basic note recognition to advanced harmony

- Music history, including information on composers and periods

- Aural skills, including melodic dictation and harmonic dictation

- World music

- Composition

- Notation

- Rhythm drills

- Practice partner for keyboard skills, sight-playing, or improvising

These programs assist with areas that cannot be covered completely in lessons. Take composition, for instance; notation packages aid with composing music and sequencing programs help students write multi-layered compositions, combining string sounds with flute or trumpet sounds, etc.

Often, software programs can be tailored to a desired age and level, with many covering a wide range of levels. Some programs include tests, and reports on student progress can be saved within the program. It is important to give the student specific assignments and to check progress regularly. Mixing assignments between different programs or types of activities also helps hold a student's interest. Software programs will be discussed further in Chapter 43.

With access to the Internet, students can research material related to their repertoire, a composer, a type of piece, or a period of music—they can actually help develop a studio catalog of helpful Internet sites. By conducting a search such as "Baroque music," "Robert Schumann," or "opera," the Internet will provide a number of educational sites, complete with pictures and often with links to musical examples. Students can then report verbally on their research, do a written report, or prepare a presentation for extra studio credit. Never fear that students will be unable to use the technology. Usually they are more technologically savvy than the adults in their lives!

When the workstation consists of multiple keyboards and computers, potential activities include ensemble playing, group research on the Internet, and interactive learning. Another piece of equipment to consider for a workstation, especially if it is in a separate room, is a television with VCR and/or DVD capability for large group viewing. (Keep in mind that most computers, and all of those made within the last few years, include DVD-playing capability. When selecting a computer for your workstation, consider getting one with a large enough monitor for small group viewing of DVDs.) A number of videos and DVDs on music-related topics can be incorporated into a planned curriculum of study before or after lesson time, in group settings, or during music camps.

## Teacher Time and Increased Income

In order to maintain a workstation, it helps to put aside part of each month's budget for workstation materials. Building a functional library of materials does not take long, and they can be used and reused through the years. In addition to the extra expense of maintaining a workstation, running one requires that the teacher set aside time to:

- Research new materials (workbooks, software, CDs)

- Learn new software programs before using them

- Plan curriculum

- Prepare individual assignments

- Read written assignments

- Correct workbooks and check progress within software programs (unless a self-correcting text or software program is used)

Increased work and expenses from the addition of a workstation should result in the addition of a workstation fee or an increase in overall tuition. Studio literature should reflect this special feature of the studio so that parents will understand the reason for any additional fees.

Many teachers charge half of the private lesson fee for an equivalent amount of student time spent at a workstation. Some teachers employ an older student to help with correcting workstation assignments or organizing materials. Often workstation time is arranged as 30–60 minutes before or after the weekly private lesson, adding significantly to student time in the studio. The additional fees help cover the cost of the workstation but also increase the income of the teacher. It is worth remembering that the more a teacher does for her students, the more she should be paid for her services!

PART IX

# ADDITIONAL TEACHING OPTIONS

A traditional independent studio offers lessons to elementary through high school students in the afternoons and early evenings. Many teachers do not feel limited to this option and are able to expand their clientele, teaching hours, and teaching income by offering early childhood music classes, group and partner lessons, and adult instruction.

I have gained a great deal from including all three of these additional teaching options in my studio. Not only has it been enjoyable to work with expanded age groups while increasing my teaching hours and income, but I have also felt invigorated by the wider breadth of the studio offerings.

## Early Childhood Music

One of my favorite alternatives to the traditional piano lesson is offering early childhood music classes. Perhaps my most memorable experience with very young children came the year I wrote and received a grant to teach special-needs pre-schoolers at a local school. This particular class did not have music in the curriculum and the teachers were eager to accept my offer to bring music to their students.

Since the children had varying degrees of physical abilities (some could talk but not walk; some could move, but not talk) and varying levels of cognitive abilities, I chose a curriculum that was designed for very young children and which allowed for a great deal of flexibility. The students in the class loved our time together; those who were able danced around the room while others sang along. The smiles on their faces when I came for music time were truly rewarding.

Perhaps the biggest lesson on the power of this program came from a four-year-old girl. She was unable to move or control her muscles and was always held by a teacher's aide during the class. Cognitively she was at the level of an infant, so she could not sing along. She was unable even to follow motions with her eyes. When I first started, I wondered what she would gain from the class.

Every day when I arrived for class, this young girl would be crying inconsolably. As soon as the music started, the crying would stop, and her face would glow calmly through the whole class. I realized the many levels of appreciation that exist as we listen to music, and the profound impact music can have on us all.

Today's early childhood programs owe a great deal to three innovators in music education: Émile Jaques-Dalcroze, Carl Orff, and Zoltán Kodály. Each played a significant role in developing an approach to music education that includes listening, whole-body movement, singing, rhythm, improvisation, solfege, and the use of instruments.

### Early Childhood Music & Movement Association
The Early Childhood Music & Movement Association (ECMMA) is an established non-profit association uniting music and early childhood professionals, all dedicated toward a similar goal:

as stated on their website, "The Early Childhood Music & Movement Association is an organization of professional educators dedicated to the ideal that all children should be give the advantage of music and movement instruction in their formative years—from birth to age seven. The organization is for all teachers of young children, whether they teach in formal or informal, public or private settings."

*Perspectives* is published quarterly, giving national and regional news and articles for professional development for all members of ECMMA. The organization holds conferences and provides a membership directory. It also offers benefits such as certification of teachers of early childhood music, a group-rate liability insurance plan through the Private Practice Professional Liability Insurance Plan for Educators, and the opportunity to network with other professionals in the field. There are also a growing number of ECMMA chapters for local professional support and periodic workshops.

The ECMMA website states that its focus is to:

- Be an advocate for joyful music and movement experiences vital to the development of the whole child.

- Further the advancement and development of music and movement education for young children.

- Serve the needs and encourage ongoing professional development of educators in music and other areas of early childhood education.

- Support family structure by encouraging positive interaction between parents and children through the sharing of music.

- Foster a free exchange of expertise, ideas, and experiences in the areas of music, movement, and early childhood development.

The ECMMA website includes a "Links" page with a number of excellent links to websites including a number of early childhood music programs, professional organizations, and child-centered music websites. Contact information can be found in Appendix C.

## Early childhood programs

There are numerous early childhood music programs. Anyone interested in pursuing this area within a studio would be wise to do research on a number of programs before deciding which to choose. The following list offers only a few of the programs to consider, and are chosen merely to show varied approaches. Though different, all are geared to similar age groups, centered on their own specially devised curriculum, and involve adult and child in music and movement.

**KINDERMUSIK** (www.kindermusik.com)

With more than 25 years of experience, Kindermusik is one of the oldest early childhood music programs in the world. The program centers on whole child development, with music as the vehicle for learning. Programs are geared toward specific levels of development for each age group, and parents are involved in the classes. Family classes and sign language classes are also available. Teachers are licensed through Kindermusik, which provides a complete curriculum and a number of books, CDs, instruments, and games for purchase. The Kindermusik philosophy is based on the belief that music nurtures a child's cognitive, emotional, social, language, and physical development, and that every child should experience the joy, fun, and learning that music brings to life.

Kindermusik requires yearly licensing fees for educators. Enrolled families are required to purchase materials kits that supplement each level of the curriculum.

### MUSIC TOGETHER (www.musictogether.com)

Priding itself on its innovative, research-based, and developmentally appropriate early childhood music curriculum, Music Together offers family-style classes of mixed ages for infant, toddler, preschool, and kindergarten children and their parents, as well as programs for preschool settings. Music Together encourages young children to experience music and movement at an early age, thus developing their innate basic music competence. Educationally fundamental to the program, the Music Together CDs, songbooks, and parent guide are provided at no extra charge to all enrolled families. In addition, Music Together offers child-friendly instruments at their online store.

Every registered Music Together teacher has successfully completed the Music Together teacher training, and basic teacher-support materials are provided to all active teachers at no charge. There are no annual or added fees beyond the teacher training tuition and the application fee to open a center.

### MUSIKGARTEN (www.musikgarten.org)

Musikgarten provides live, interactive training for teachers who wish to begin a Musikgarten studio or use Musikgarten materials in a school or church setting. Carefully sequenced curricula for children ages newborn to nine feature flexible lesson plans, so that the developmental and musical needs of all children can be met. Musikgarten Certification and Licensing are encouraged, and Musikgarten training can also be used toward ECMMA Certification, as well as collegiate continuing education.

Within the Musikgarten License Program, musical materials are provided at reasonable prices to enrolled families. These family materials include a CD, a parent songbook, and child's manipulative/instrument.

### WIGGLES N' TUNES (www.wigglesntunes.com)

An award-winning curriculum that combines the teachings of Suzuki, Dalcroze, Orff, and Kodaly, Wiggles N' Tunes can be used by teachers with or without formal training. Designed to meet the national music standards, it is a ready-to-use complete curriculum accompanied with high quality CDs and professional marketing materials. The program is designed to be rewarding and educational for children, and complements Suzuki and other early music programs, acting as an ideal program upon which to build future studio enrollment. It fosters meaningful creative experiences while allowing teachers to make a difference in the lives of children and their families.

Wiggles N' Tunes requires only a minimum investment. There are no required workshop fees or yearly licensing fees. Family CDs provide a profit for the educator and are affordable for enrolled students. All start-up costs can be quickly recovered within the first few weeks of teaching.

# Resources

## BOOKS

Connors, Abigail Flesch. *101 Rhythm Instrument Activities for Young Children.* Beltsville: Gryphon House, Inc., 2004.

Centering on the pleasure young children derive from sound, this book offers a variety of activities using simple instruments. It is divided into sections depending on the suggested instruments: rhythm sticks, shakers, jingle bells, and sand blocks. A section includes activities for other instruments such as cymbals, tambourines, and drums, and the final section is for rhythm bands of multiple instruments. The directions for each activity are simple, and often the activities are based on popular tunes with altered words, such as singing "Wake up, Groundhog" to "Good Night, Ladies," thus making the activities easy to learn and teach.

Feierabend, John M., Gary M. Kramer, comp. *Music for Little People: 50 Playful Activities for Preschool and Early Elementary School Children.* New York: Boosey & Hawkes Music Publisher, Inc., 1989. Distributed by Hal Leonard Corporation.

Designed for toddlers to preschoolers, the songs in this book require various degrees of movement, from "Moving Fingers" and "Moving Bodies" to "Moving Around" and "Leading Others." "Moving Voices" and "Taking Turns" are focused on vocal precision. Pictures demonstrate the motions used in each song.

Feierabend, John M., Gary M. Kramer, comp. *Music for Very Little People: 50 Playful Activities for Infants and Toddlers.* New York: Boosey & Hawkes Music Publisher, Inc., 1987. Distributed by Hal Leonard Corporation.

The songs in this book are designed for infants to toddlers with an adult. Pictures show motions and finger plays for the various songs, and words and music are included. The songs are divided into motion categories: wiggles, tapping, circles, bounces, tickles, clapping, and lullabies.

Wirth, Marian, et al. *Musical Games, Fingerplays and Rhythmic Activities for Early Childhood.* West Nyack: Parker Publishing Company, Inc., 1983.

Originally designed for classroom teaching, this book focuses on active learning through physical motion and singing. Each song lists an appropriate age level (the youngest age listed is two and the oldest is ten), the benefits of the activity, the materials needed, and directions followed by a few closing comments from the authors. The book is divided into three main parts, including Part 1: Singing Activities; Part 2: Chants; and Part 3: Games for Auditory and Listening Skills.

## ADDITIONAL WEBSITES

*American Orff-Schulwerk Association*

www.aosa.org

*Dalcroze Society of America*

www.dalcrozeusa.org

*Organization of American Kodály Educators*

www.oake.org

**PART IX**

# Group, Partner, and Overlapping Lessons

Group, partner, and overlapping lessons provide another alternative to independent piano study, as they:

- Provide an interactive, social aspect to music

- Allow students to learn from each other and feel motivated by peers to try their best

- Develop better listening skills

- Improve retention

- Offer an ideal forum for working collaboratively on ensemble music

- Improve sight-playing and rhythm skills

- Increase the student's enjoyment while studying (Students who enjoy performing in a favorite band or youth orchestra can attest to the fact that there is a great deal of satisfaction experienced from working collaboratively.)

- Increase income

Group, partner, and overlapping lessons are an efficient and enjoyable way to present areas of music that are more suited to longer periods of time than the private lesson allows, such as:

- Music theory

- Sight-playing

- Harmonization

- Music history

- Keyboard skills

- Performance in front of a group

- Aural skills

- Rhythm

If a teacher has two acoustic pianos, groups of four can be scheduled with two at each piano. Those who wish to instruct older or larger groups are more likely to use digital keyboards, with one student per keyboard. In such a studio, the teacher takes advantage of headsets and a keyboard controller to monitor activities, as discussed in Chapter 43. When teachers have developed their ability to teach in group settings, their students may prefer the group lesson format and be hesitant to switch to private lessons, even when given the option.

Other teachers provide combinations of group and private lessons. For instance, teachers may offer:

- Private lesson during some weeks, alternating with group lessons in others

- Private lessons every week supplemented with an additional group lesson during certain weeks

- Two lessons a week: one private and one group

There are three main keys to success when developing group lessons in the independent studio:

1) It is essential to organize groups that work well together. Matching age, level of playing ability, and personalities with the time available in students' busy schedules is a real challenge.

2) The dedicated and successful teacher of group lessons develops an intelligent curriculum for the group. Organized lesson plans and materials that are carefully chosen to fit the group are essential to a musically fulfilling environment.

3) The space and equipment of the studio must be sufficient to serve the needs of the class.

## Adult Instruction

Adult beginners generally understand concepts much more quickly than children, but can be frustrated by the physical challenges of learning to play the piano. An adult cannot learn languages as quickly as a child, no one can start gymnastics at age 30 and become an Olympic gymnast, and an adult beginner will most likely not be performing Brahms's 2nd Piano Concerto with the Boston Symphony in this lifetime. This does not mean that the adult beginner should be discouraged in any way. The most successful adult beginners will be those who look forward to lessons without rigid, predetermined indicators for success or failure.

Care must be taken when choosing a method for an adult beginner. A number of method books are written specifically for adults. Within these adult methods, many are meant more as texts for class piano in a university setting. Such methods may not serve adults as well as those written to be accessible to the adult recreational learner.

Some adult students are not beginners, but come to the studio with a strong background in piano, and repertoire must be carefully chosen for them as well. If they want to play Chopin, let them! If they want to play Irving Berlin, let them! Suggesting a particularly rewarding piece outside of their comfort zone will hopefully broaden their horizons, but there is not the same obligation to develop a well-rounded repertoire that exists when taking a younger student through their formative years of study.

Many adult students see piano lessons as a time to indulge themselves, to enjoy an activity away from the stress in their lives. For them, piano becomes a special and personal choice; no one else is insisting they take lessons. These students are a real delight, especially when they take pleasure from the journey regardless of the final destination.

At one point, I had 15 adult students out of a studio of about 40. The adults came one evening a month for a party (we didn't call it a performance class) and the students played for each other, brought food, and sipped wine. They grew to like each other as friends and the camaraderie of the parties increased their enjoyment of lessons while providing me with some much needed adult conversation!

PART IX

# Resources

Kern, Fred, and Phillip Keveren, Barbara Kreader, and Mona Reijino. **Adult Piano Method**, Books 1 & 2. Milwaukee: Hal Leonard Corporation, 2005, 2006.

> The Hal Leonard Student Piano Library *Adult Piano Method* is designed to give adults who are new to piano a challenging but realistic pacing for lessons. Repertoire is taken from classical, folk, pop, rock, and jazz selections, and the pacing of the book is challenging without being overwhelming. Within the series, music theory, technique, stylistic elements, and improvisation are also studied. The books come with CD or GM disks, allowing students to play with appealing orchestral accompaniments. The *Popular Hits* and *Christmas Favorites* books offer supplementary material with enjoyable arrangements of familiar songs, and can also be purchased with CD or GM disks.

Mach, Elyse. **Learning Piano: Piece by Piece.** New York, Oxford: Oxford University Press, 2006.

> This book is intended for a wide range of audiences, including the adult hobby student. It uses a logical, step-by-step approach allowing material to be understood in a progressive and accessible fashion. The book offers a combination of repertoire, theory, improvisation, technique, history, and keyboard skills. Two CDs of orchestrated accompaniments are included with the book, and an Instructor's Manual containing suggested lesson plans is available online.

# PART X

# TECHNOLOGY

Some teachers embrace the use of technology while others are fearful of it, reluctant to change. They may question the value of technology in the piano studio. Part X explores the growing use of music technology in the 21st century. With careful research, teachers can decide what applications appeal to them, and how best to incorporate technology into their teaching.

Technology can improve students' understanding of music theory, music history, aural skills, rhythm, sight-playing, keyboard skills, ensemble work, improvisation, and composition. It enhances lessons, increases opportunities to record performances, and assists with bookkeeping in the studio. Technology serves as an excellent tool to augment all aspects of the independent studio.

# Chapter 42

# EQUIPMENT

---

**P**ersonally, I wanted to live to be 90 and say "I've never touched one of those darned computers and I've done just fine, thank you very much." Instead, I moved to a sleepy little town in rural North Dakota, where they would never even have heard of technology, right? Wrong! The university where I work is the second in the country to go completely laptop, with every faculty member and student being issued a new laptop computer every two years. Faculty members are encouraged to map the use of technology in all class syllabi and include technology-related projects in their course-work. The university is on the cutting edge in all areas of technology, including music. Before taking the job, I knew nothing about technology and had never even used a typewriter! I was embarrassed to ask questions and fearful of getting started.

Technology offers piano teachers an avenue for abundant creativity. Its use in the independent studio can be customized in endless ways, fulfilling the needs of each teacher. Those who hesitate to use technology are well served by starting small and seeking help when needed from colleagues, students, friends, family, workshops, magazines, or conferences. It is far better to ask for help than to give up out of frustration!

Now is the time for anyone who has yet to incorporate technology into the studio to get started. Avoiding technology altogether would put a teacher in the same league as the doctor who refuses to learn about new treatments; not a desirable place to be! Those who are already using technology know that it is a constantly changing field with opportunities for continual growth. All of us can increase our understanding of technology; none of us has the luxury of complacency in this ever-changing and significant addition to the world of music.

## Getting Started, Getting Educated

Although a multitude of high-quality software programs and helpful equipment exists, a costly mistake could be made without first researching any purchase. It may seem obvious, but the most important thing to decide is how one wants to use technology in the studio, and the teacher can start by asking herself some basic questions:

- Should software be used at a workstation where students can practice skills (drill) that have already been presented in a lesson?

- Should tutorial software be used to actually teach musical concepts independently from lesson time with the teacher?

- Should software programs and equipment be used to reinforce areas such as composition or improvisation?

- Will students work independently or in groups?

Other teachers can provide a wealth of information about technology applications. Tech-savvy colleagues are often happy to explain and demonstrate their uses for technology. By talking to a number of teachers, decisions can be made concerning which teaching activities to supplement with technology and which programs or equipment sound manageable.

Another way to learn about technology is by attending music technology presentations. Local and state music organizations, music stores, and the creators of technology equipment and software often give helpful workshops on music technology applications.

## Conferences

Technology sessions are frequently incorporated into national conferences, with presentations often geared toward teachers of applied lessons. New technology equipment and software are showcased and workstations are set up in order for teachers to experiment with the merchandise. Vendors at the conference are able to sell the software or equipment that is demonstrated in the sessions, and experts in the vendor area are available to answer questions and to offer creative ideas for technology uses in the studio.

The Association for Technology in Music Instruction (ATMI) conference is devoted entirely to the use of technology in music education. Presentations at both conferences represent work at all levels of technology expertise, from beginner to advanced user. Technology Institute for Music Educators (TI:ME) offers training for music educators that leads to a certification in the use of music technology. TI:ME is a non-profit corporation whose mission is to assist music educators in applying technology to improve teaching and learning music.

Contact information:

*Association for Technology in Music Instruction (ATMI)*
http://atmionline.org

*Technology Institute for Music Educators (TI:ME)*
www.ti-me.org

## Magazines

There are helpful articles in a number of music magazines. The *American Music Teacher* and *Keyboard Companion* both have a regular technology column with articles that are particularly helpful and accessible to the studio piano teacher. Publications devoted entirely to music technology, such as *Music Education Technology* and *Electronic Musician*, delve even deeper into current technology applications.

Contact information:

*American Music Teacher*
www.mtna.org/HLtext

*Keyboard Companion*
www.keyboardcompanion.com

*Electronic Musician*
www.emusician.com

*Music Education Technology*
http://metmagazine.com

## Books

In addition to magazines, a number of books have been published on technology applications in music, some are more user-friendly for beginners, and some are more in-depth for the experienced teacher.

Sandra Bowen's *Electrify Your Studio* (Fort Lauderdale: The FJH Music Company, Inc., 2000) is full of practical, easy-to-read lists, making this guide to technology ideal for the independent studio. Chapters include information on studio equipment, software, lab stations, keyboard ensembles, sequencing, notation, teaching applications, studio setup, and a helpful section on Internet resources. Bowen is enthusiastic about the possibilities for utilizing technology in the studio, and offers valuable information for independent teachers wishing to expand their use of technology.

Although written with K-12 classes in mind, *Strategies for Teaching Technology* (Compiled and edited by Sam Reese, Kimberly McCord, and Kimberly Walls. Reston: MENC – The National Association for Music Educators, 2001) includes lesson plans that would be appropriate for group lessons, classes, workstations, and individual lessons. Each plan is written to the National Standards, includes appropriate grade/age level, a materials list, and any prior knowledge and experience needed for the lesson.

*Experiencing Music Technology*, 3rd Edition, by David Brian Williams and Peter Richard Webster (Belmont: Thomson/Schirmer, 2006) offers a good compromise between a beginner book that covers only the basics of technology, and a more advanced book, which might be meant for more tech-savvy teachers. Although each area is covered in greater detail than in many books, this book's explanations and charts allow even those new to music technology to follow along and comprehend. The main areas of the book include Musicians and Their Use of Technology, Computer and Internet Concepts for Musicians, Digital Audio Basics, Doing More with Digital Audio, Music Sequencing and MIDI Basics, Doing More with MIDI and Beyond, Music Notation, Computer-Aided Instruction in Music, and Putting It All Together. A free accompanying DVD-ROM provides activities featuring step-by-step tutorials in using such applications as Finale, Sibelius, Cubase, Logic, Band-in-a-Box, Audacity, Auralia, Practica Musica, iTunes, and MiBAC Music Lessons. Links are included to related materials, including worksheets that students can use to track their progress and teachers can use to evaluate students' work.

## Types of Technology

Any list of equipment will naturally be outdated immediately, as new and upgraded items are constantly evolving. The list below does not mention all the technology currently available, but briefly summarizes some of the independent studio's more standard items and their uses:

**CD player and CD library:** CDs provide valuable instruction at a listening station and during lessons.

**MP3 player:** An MP3 is a type of audio file that takes up less computer space than a regular file from a CD track. MP3 players can hold hundreds of hours of music, making music playback and storage much simpler. For example, a standard MP3 player, which is often smaller than the size of a deck of cards, can hold music from hundreds of CDs. This eliminates the need to store and search through a library of CDs, when all the music from a CD library can be contained in one small unit. MP3 players can easily connect to any standard stereo system for playback. Students can bring MP3 files into the lesson from home that can be downloaded to the teacher's MP3 player and/or computer. Many MP3 players also play video.

**CD/DVD burner:** A CD burner or DVD burner can be used to back up data for pedagogical and business purposes. (An MP3 player can also be used for this purpose.) Recordings of student performances or lessons, business records, documents, and more can be backed up by "burning" them on to a CD or DVD. Most present-day computers come with a CD and/or DVD burner built in, and this provides a convenient tool for burning CDs and DVDs from data on the computer.

**CD recorder or Dual Drive CD recorder or Portable CD player and recording system:** Recording and playing systems exist that not only record performances directly to a CD, but can play a CD with a number of musical alterations such as changing key by half-steps, adjusting tempo to slower or faster without impacting pitch, reducing lead vocals, and creating practice loops. Besides recording directly to a CD, the systems provide functions such as copying any CD with a personalized tempo and key preference.

**Computer:** A computer can be used for studio bookwork as well as with music-related software programs. An increasingly important feature is the ability to burn CDs and DVDs mentioned above.

**Digital photo camera:** Photos taken from a digital camera are useful in publicity documents such as a studio brochures, fliers, newsletters, and even recital programs. Digital pictures can easily be transferred to a computer and used for multiple purposes.

**Digital video/DVD video camera:** Videos taken with a digital video camera are easily downloaded onto a computer. Such videos have pedagogical and professional value: students can learn from taped performances or practice, and promotional videos can be made for marketing purposes or submission with grant applications. DVD video cameras record directly to mini DVD-R/RW and mini DVD discs, making downloading and storing of video even easier.

**Digital keyboard(s) or digital piano(s) with MIDI capability:** Digital keyboards and pianos can be used for ensembles as well as musical applications such as composing or improvising. These instruments can be used alone or in conjunction with music software. MIDI stands for Musical Instrument Digital Interface and is a standardized system for ensuring that instruments and programs/computers can communicate with each other. All MIDI devices communicate back and forth by sending data, not sounds, so MIDI files are actually data files. General MIDI is a system where sounds are standardized with the same name and number so that various instruments and programs can "talk to each other." For example, sound 07 is always "Harpsichord" in any General MIDI system, making it easy to compose on one system and recreate the harpsichord sound on any other system that uses General MIDI.

Since not all keyboards are MIDI compatible, it is important to look for the MIDI symbol on the keyboard (or MIDI-cable jack). A MIDI keyboard that is connected to a computer and communicates with it by performing functions such as controlling the sounds inside the computer is known as a keyboard controller. Most computer/MIDI keyboard setups require a MIDI interface that allows the keyboard to both connect to and communicate with the computer via a MIDI cable. In recent years, more and more keyboard controllers are able to be connected to a computer via the Universal Serial Bus (USB) port, not requiring a MIDI interface. Many of these USB keyboard controllers do not require separate power; the keyboard is powered via its connection to the computer.

**PART X**

**Direct recording unit or mobile digital recorder:** Direct recording units allow recorded material to be transferred directly to a computer hard drive using the USB port to attach the recording unit to the computer; the material recorded on the direct recording unit can then be transferred using an easy drag-and-drop method to the computer, where it can be used to create customized CDs, MP3s, and DVDs.

**DVD player/VHS player/television:** DVD players or VHS players are necessary for showing music-related DVDs and videos, but most computers can also play DVDs. In addition, videos can be shown on many MP3 players.

**Keyboard Lab controller:** If multiple computers and keyboards will be in use, a studio system must be planned where the teacher can hear the stations individually or together. For example, a keyboard lab controller can pair groupings of duets, quartets, or even solo keyboards on headsets so that selected performers can hear each other as they practice. By using the keyboard lab controller—a system of "boxes" that are linked to each other—the teacher is able to listen to the full class, one select group, or one student at a time, while the remaining students work using headsets to hear only themselves.

**Printer, copy machine, scanner, fax:** Printers and copy machines provide assistance when developing studio materials and professional correspondences. Scanners are valuable when duplicating a document so that it can then be transferred onto a computer. Fax machines transmit documents to other locations using a phone line. Many printers are printer/scanners/fax all in one unit.

**Sequencer:** A sequencer is a recording device used to record MIDI data, but capable of doing far more than just recording. Once the MIDI data is recorded, it can be edited or altered to fit exact specifications and then played back. Sequencers allow for multiple voices to play against each other, offering numerous options for composition, harmonization, ear-training, improvisation, rehearsing, and ensemble performance. Sequencers can be purchased in three ways:

- As a feature of a digital piano
- As a free-standing unit
- As a software program to be installed on a computer

Software programs offer the most flexibility, including the ability to record audio such as the human voice. Many sequencers can also convert recorded MIDI data into musical notation. Sequencers also have audio recording capabilities, meaning they can record real instruments or voice in addition to MIDI data.

**Software:** Educational software programs can be purchased and downloaded (placed on the computer) to assist with learning music theory and history, or developing skills in areas such as ear-training, harmonization, improvisation, composition, etc.

**Speakers, microphones, jacks, cables, headsets:** When setting up a MIDI lab, it is important to purchase the best speakers for one's needs (sound quality, loudness, size and placement considerations, etc.). Compatible jacks and cables are essential to connect various pieces of equipment, as are headsets (headphones), which will enable students to be heard both individually and together.

## Chapter 43

# STUDIO USES FOR TECHNOLOGY

There are limitless technology choices awaiting those who are willing to experiment. Technology changes quickly and it is understood that new programs/software and equipment/hardware will be marketed each year. For that reason only some of the better-known software programs available today are mentioned here, and no recommendations or references will be made concerning specific types of equipment. Once a decision is made concerning the reasons to use technology, each teacher should conduct further research on the programs and equipment that best suit her needs and budget.

## Software

Many teachers feel it is impossible to cover all necessary areas of study in one weekly lesson. Computer software enhances the time spent with students by reinforcing material covered in the lesson (such as scales) or introducing material that is entirely new (such as an in-depth lesson on a Beethoven sonata).

When researching software packages, a number of questions are worth asking:

- Is the software a tutorial program that will teach the student new skills?
- Is the software a drill program that reinforces skills that have already been presented by the teacher?
- Does the program employ a game format with colorful pictures or cartoon characters?
- Is the format more similar to black and white worksheets?
- What age levels will the program suit?
- How many levels does the program include?
- If students log in individually, does the program test them as they progress and record their scores for the teacher to view later?
- What is the range of skills covered by the program?
- Is the program easy to use? What level of training will students need before they can function on their own?
- At what pace does the program move? Will students be easily bored by a slow-moving program or frustrated by a fast-moving program?
- How much reinforcement of concepts does the program include?
- Can the program be run entirely on a computer, or is a MIDI keyboard required?

In order for software programs to work in the studio, the teacher must study them carefully before giving students assignments. Such study enables the teacher to understand which students will benefit from which programs, and the appropriate level for each.

The software can be presented to students in three ways:

- The instructor teaches the students how to use the program.

- Students learn the program on their own (with adequate directions in the software itself, or left in a folder to help them access the program themselves).

- A tech-savvy student supervises student computer time (if zoning laws allow for an outside employee).

Some of the musical areas covered by software programs available today include:

- Music fundamentals, theory, and harmony

- Music history and appreciation

- Aural skills and rhythm

- Sight-playing and keyboard skills

- Improvisation and composition

If should be noted that some of the software available to help enhance the above areas comes in the form of musical games. Musical computer games can focus on one specific area such as harmony or history, or combine multiple areas, such as aural skills, technique, and composition, all in the same game.

## Music Fundamentals, Theory, and Harmony

Software programs can cover the basic levels of music fundamentals, advanced levels of theory and harmony, and everything in between. Some programs start with the basics of note and rhythm identification and progress to modes, secondary dominants, Neapolitan chords, jazz chords and scales, and augmented sixth chords, covered in the upper levels. A number of programs offer a variety of approaches and levels worth researching.

### *MiDisaurus* – Town4kids, Levels 1–8, plus four additional "Focus" volumes

An entertaining and educational multimedia approach, *MiDisaurus* includes over 500 learning activities, providing a complete introduction to music theory. Starting with the musical alphabet and basic note-values in Level 1, the program progresses to blues and pentatonic scales, basic chord progressions, and major, minor, augmented, and diminished chords in Level 8. The four "focus" volumes (available in a Reference Bundle) offer additional material in the areas of rhythm and notation, and compile the lessons on instruments (including instruments from around the world) and composers such as Bach, Handel, Haydn, Mozart, Beethoven, from Levels 1–8.

**www.town4kids.com**

### *Music Ace* – Harmonic Vision

*Music Ace* contains 24 lessons, each with its own game, and each presenting the fundamentals of music theory to beginner students of music. Lessons cover staff and keyboard relationship, pitch identification, note reading, listening skills, sharps and flats, key signatures, keyboard basics, major scales, octaves, staves, whole and half steps, and more. Student progress can be tracked from lesson to lesson, and a unique music "doodle pad" allows students to compose using instrumental sounds.

**www.harmonicvision.com**

### *Music Ace 2; Music Ace Deluxe; Music Ace Maestro* – Harmonic Vision

*Music Ace 2* is designed for beginning and intermediate students. Featuring 2,000 musical examples, it covers treble, alto, and bass clefs, and lessons on tempo, rhythmic dictation, counting, note and rest values, key signatures, syncopation, rhythmic composition, time signatures, major and minor scales, intervals, harmony, ear-training, composing melodies, and more. As in *Music Ace*, there are 24 comprehensive lessons as well as challenging games and a creative composition tool. *Music Ace Deluxe* has 36 lessons and games; both programs include the popular *Doodle Pad*, for use in creating compositions using instrumental sounds. *Music Ace Maestro* includes all 48 *Music Ace* and *Music Ace 2* lessons, as well as educator tools for customizing the instructional environment.

**www.harmonicvision.com**

### *Music Lessons I Fundamentals* – MiBAC

*Music Lessons I* provides comprehensive music theory and ear-training for ages eight and up. Its interactive drills cover note names, circle of fifths, key signatures, major and minor scales, modes, jazz scales, scale degrees, intervals, note and rest durations, and ear-training for scales and intervals. The program provides instant feedback, on-screen help and scores, multiple skill levels for each drill, choice of clefs, and a built-in music theory reference. Individual progress reports can be printed and saved for unlimited users. MIDI is optional.

**www.mibac.com**

### *Music Lessons II Chords and Harmony* – MiBAC

*Music Lessons II* teaches students to name chords they see, write chords on the music staff, play chords on the built-in piano keyboard and guitar fretboard (or MIDI), and hear and identify chords in the ear-training drills. Topics covered include chord elements, triads, triads ear-training, seventh chords, seventh chords ear-training, Roman numeral chord identification, secondary dominants, Neapolitan chords, and augmented sixth chords. The program's interactive, drill-based format provides instant feedback, on-screen help and scores, multiple skill levels, custom drills, choice of clefs, a built-in theory reference, and individual progress reports for unlimited users.

**www.mibac.com**

### *Musition* – Rising Software

*Musition* is a complete theory and musicianship package, suitable for students of all ages. The program is in an interactive drill format and covers

**PART X**

four main areas: note reading, terms and symbols, key centers, and instruments. A vast amount of material is included within each of these main areas. For example, "key centers" includes drills on intervals, chord/scale relations, jazz scales, key signatures, modulation, scales, scale degrees, and scale home keys. *Musition* gives instant practice on 25 topics, from note reading and rhythm for beginners, to jazz chords and instrument keys and range for experienced students of music theory.

**www.risingsoftware.com**

### *Pianomouse Goes to Preschool* – **Pianomouse**

This entertaining CD-ROM introduces young children to beginning theory, the musical alphabet, notes, musical patterns, and instruments. Preschoolers will also learn about the lives and music of great composers.

**www.pianomouse.com**

### *Pianomouse's Music Theory FUNdamentals Preparatory* – **Pianomouse**

This interactive CD-ROM uses the Pianomouse Story to present the fundamentals of music, including interactive lessons, games and review tests to teach pitch, the musical alphabet, treble/bass clef notes, note and rest values, time signatures, sharps, flats, naturals, and more.

**www.pianomouse.com**

### *Practica Musica* – **Ars Nova**

*Practica Musica* offers drills in over 80 areas. Starting with beginning activities such as understanding whole steps and half steps, reading treble clef, reading bass clef, and reading accidentals, *Practica Musica* progresses to more complex areas such as pitch matching, pitch reading, rhythm matching, rhythm reading, two-part rhythm reading, interval playing, interval ear-training, scales and key signatures, chord spelling, chord ear-training, chord progression ear-training, pitch dictation, rhythm dictation, and much more. This is an excellent program for theory instruction and ear-training, and most activities have multiple levels of difficulty.

**www.ars-nova.com**

### *TimeSketch Editor Pro* – **Electronic Courseware Systems**

This software allows the user to create a map of the form and analysis of any piece. The editing capabilities work with any CD, MP3, WAV, AIFF or MIDI sound file. Users can insert text below sections of a bubble chart that they create to describe the form, key, etc. at any given point of the piece. Clicking on any section of the bubble chart will take the listener directly to that section of the piece.

**www.ecsmedia.com**

# Resources

**WEBSITES**

The following sites offer online study in music theory:

*Ababasoft*

    www.ababasoft.com

        – Select from "Online music."

*Dolmetsch Online*

    www.dolmetsch.com

        – Select "music theory" in the quick links box in the center of the page.

*Google lists a number of sites at:*

    http://directory.google.com/Top/Arts/Music/Theory

*MusicLearningCommunity.com*

    http://musiclearningcommunity.com

*Ricci Adams' musictheory.net*

    www.musictheory.net

*Teoria Music Theory Web*

    www.teoria.com

## Music History and Appreciation

Music history software is increasing in popularity. Programs expose students to eras of music accompanied by pictures, recorded music, and interactive games. Students can learn about the lives of great composers as well as the history of music from the Medieval era through today. The pictures, sound, and interactive quality of many of these programs offer a far more inclusive demonstration of historical concepts than a book alone could provide.

### *Hearing Music* – Viva Media

This musical games program is meant for young students and is designed to train a child's ear to identify changes in patterns, melody, rhythm, and more. The music of famous composers is used throughout and each game moves through progressively more challenging levels. There are 12 music history-related chapters.

**www.viva-media.com**

    – Select "Music"

### *Pianomouse Meets the Great Composers* – Pianomouse

This interactive CD-ROM includes biographies and games centered on the lives of eight great composers and their music: Bach, Handel, Haydn, Mozart, Beethoven, Schubert, Brahms, and Tchaikovsky.

**www.pianomouse.com**

A number of Music History Internet sites that would be suitable for research are listed in Chapter 33. Additional online sites to consider for a Music History workstation include:

### *Carnegie Hall Listening Adventures*

This delightful site offers listening examples while presenting pictures to reinforce what is being heard.

**www.carnegiehall.org**

– Select "Explore & Learn," "Interactive Resources," then "Listening Adventures."

### *The New York Philharmonic Kidzone*

Designed with younger children in mind, this site includes a game room, an instrument lab (that shows homemade instruments), an instrument storage room (that gives a brief history of each instrument stored), a musician's lounge (highlighting members of the NY Philharmonic), a composition workshop, a composer's gallery, and a newsstand.

**www.nyphilkids.org**

### *Play Music*

This website introduces children to the instruments of the orchestra.

**www.playmusic.org**

## Aural Skills and Rhythm

Aural and rhythmic skills are often difficult to cover in limited lesson time. Interactive computer programs drill students in these areas, allowing them to better develop their ear. Some programs include pattern recognition, interval recognition, melodic dictation, and chord progressions. With an increased awareness of the value of ear-training within the study of piano, software that increases students' aural skills proves valuable for students of all levels. Such software is of added significance for those who plan to continue in the field of music in college and as professionals.

### *Aural Skills Trainer* – **Electronic Courseware Systems**

This program develops a student's ability to hear and identify intervals and chords. *Aural Skills Trainer* keeps student records, gives progress reports, and keeps track of completion scores.

**www.ecsmedia.com**

### *Auralia* – **Rising Software**

A highly respected ear-training software programs, *Auralia* offers hundreds of graded exercises in five main content areas: intervals and scales, rhythm, pitch and melody, chords, and harmony and form. The program gives instant feedback and can be used by classical, jazz, and rock/pop students. Teachers of jazz will appreciate the attention to jazz scales and chords.

**www.risingsoftware.com**

### *Ear Training Coach* – **Adventus Software**

Written for ten grades of curriculum and developed in accordance with the RCM syllabus, *Ear Training Coach* contains thousands of exercises. Topics include music dictation, rhythm, melody, intervals, sight-reading, chords, cadences, games, and a personal profile that maintains individual performance records.

**www.adventus.com/products**

### *Interactive Musician* – **Alfred**

Developed for pianists, singers, and instrumentalists, this program has three main areas of study: pitch training, rhythm, and sight-playing. The program can be used with a MIDI keyboard or by entering answers on the computer. There is a student version, an educator version that includes customized tests and printing of class lists, and a network version that includes a database of records for multiple computers. The program can be used in a classroom setting or independent studio. The self-paced exercises include several levels designed to improve sight-playing skills, rhythmic accuracy, and recognition of intervals, chords, and scales.

**www.alfred.com**

– Select "Products"

– Under "Products" pull-down menu, select "School"

– Select "Theory, Reference & Technology"

### *MacGAMUT* – **MacGAMUT Music Software International**

*MacGAMUT* for Mac and Windows is an ear-training drill and practice program with four main components: intervals, scales, and chords; rhythmic dictation; melodic dictation; and harmonic dictation. The program may be used for entry level through advanced level study, and students progress to levels of increasing difficulty only after they demonstrate mastery on each preceding level. Teachers have the option of using the program "as is" or customizing it to fit their own specific needs, using the optional Instructor Disk. (The Instructor Disk includes alternate presets and exercise libraries for beginning students and for specific ear-training texts.) The intervals, scales, and chords component covers melodic and harmonic intervals, all major and minor scales, modes and other scales, and triads, seventh chords, and four-voice chords in inversions. Rhythmic dictation offers more than 1000 exercises, beginning with simple rhythmic patterns and ending with irregular meters. Melodic dictation, again with a library of more than 1000 exercises, starts with easy step-wise melodies and progresses to chromatic, modulatory, and rhythmically challenging melodies. Harmonic dictation has over 1000 four-voice chorale-style progressions, ranging from two to ten chords in length, including chromatic chords (secondary dominants and augmented sixths) in the upper levels. In each component, the student hears an exercise and notates it on-screen (labeling it, if identification is appropriate). The computer scores the student's response, marks errors, and invites the student to correct his/her work, if necessary. Finally, the student may compare his/her response and the correct response both visually and aurally.

**www.macgamut.com**

PART X

### *Practica Musica* – Ars Nova

One of the most comprehensive programs on the market today, *Practica Musica* includes over 80 activities. The program can be used to improve sight-reading, ear-training, or the fundamentals of music theory. Aural skills areas covered include pitch matching, pitch reading, rhythm reading, interval ear-training, scale ear-training, chord ear-training, chord progression ear-training, pitch duration, pitch dictation, rhythm dictation, hearing altered chords, active listening, atonal dictation, transposed pitch reading, and more.

**www.ars-nova.com**

### *Tap-It Rhythm Creator* – Electronic Courseware Systems

A series of rhythm and tapping drills designed to strengthen rhythm skills, the *Tap-It* programs increase in difficulty and include Tap-It I, Tap-It II, and Tap-It III. The Tap-It Creator and Player allow a teacher to create and play back exercises and drills for students.

**www.ecsmedia.com**

## Resources

**WEBSITES**

*Good Ear*

www.good-ear.com

This site includes a web based aural skills program.

– Select " Ear Trainer."

*AbabaSoft*

ababasoft.com

– Select "Online music games."

– Scroll down the complete page.

## Sight-Playing and Keyboard Skills

Software exists that allows students to read along at a computer-driven tempo, thus ensuring that the student's eyes travel forward, without stopping or fixing mistakes. Some programs have timed-reading drills and games, and teachers can use notation programs to compose short sight-playing exercises.

Keyboard skills can be enhanced by the use of a sequencer (a device, either software or hardware-based, that allows for multi-track recording of MIDI and audio) as well. Sequenced accompaniments to keyboard exercises such as scales, arpeggios, and cadences provide a more interesting sound while ensuring that the student plays at a set, steady tempo, adjusted to fit the needs of each student.

An advantage to sequenced sight-playing materials is that the tempo of the material can be altered without altering the pitch, allowing different students to read material at different tempi according to their abilities.

### Electronic Courseware Systems

This company has a number of programs to assist with reading. Far too many to list, a visit to the site will reveal a number of reading programs.

**www.ecsmedia.com**

### *Home Concert 2000* and *Home Concert Xtreme* – Time Warp Technologies

*Home Concert 2000* is an accompaniment program with the option of three performance modes: *Learn Mode* is for someone who is just learning a piece. The program waits for the performer before proceeding with any note of the accompaniment. Notes that need to be played are shown in notation as well as on an on-screen keyboard. In *Jam Mode* the performer need not play the solo part with complete accuracy, and in *Performer Mode*, the program responds to the performer's tempo, dynamics, and even to jumps from section to section within the music. *Home Concert Xtreme* has most of the features of *Home Concert 2000* along with additional features such as more sophisticated score-following, more advanced MIDI options, and the ability to record and save multiple performances.

**www.timewarptech.com**

### *Piano Suite Premier* – Adventus Interactive

This program was designed to be used with a MIDI computer and keyboard. There are six main areas of focus: Piano Player, with over 500 musical pieces to play; Theory Thinker, which provides two years of music theory lessons and exercises; Composers Corner, which helps to create and edit compositions; History Happens, with over 300 biographies of composers and performers, timelines of musical eras, and more; Games, a total of eight games that reinforce the lessons presented in the program; and Evaluation, detailed reports that track each student's progress and activities.

**www.adventus.com**

## Improvisation and Composition

Technology is an excellent supplemental tool when teaching improvisation. A sequencer can provide assistance with creating chord patterns, adding a rhythm section, orchestrating new sounds, and having students improvise along with a harmonic background. Programs such as *Band-in-a-Box* create accompaniment patterns in numerous styles that students can use as a background as they improvise.

Many early method books have students improvise a melody on black notes while the teacher plays an accompaniment in D-flat major; similar sequenced patterns (on black keys, in a mode, or in a major key) in a software program allow students to feel safe enough to "fool around," which is the beginning of improvisation. These sequenced accompaniment patterns provide a more varied and interesting background for the student's efforts, as well as a rhythmic structure from which to progress.

**PART X**

Many keyboards and digital pianos have auto-rhythms that sound like percussion instruments, and can provide a rhythmic framework for the young improviser. Similarly, auto-accompaniments provide a harmonic framework from which to work, often activated by the left hand on the keyboard. The right hand then serves as the basis for melodic improvisation as the student hears the pleasing and full sound of harmony and rhythm. The auto-rhythm and auto-harmony components keep the rhythmic and harmonic progressions moving forward, allowing the student's melody to move forward as well. Where many students have trouble staying with a metronome, the auto features of the keyboard are impossible to ignore, and will keep the student engaged in the ongoing process of improvisation.

Improvisation and composition sometimes overlap, as improvising often leads to composing. As discussed in Chapter 36, when students first attempt composition, they need not feel they must compose something specific such as a melody in C position using two chords in the left hand. They may be allowed to start off with something more abstract, such as simply playing with low notes and the pedal to create thunder. Allowing students to experiment with multiple sounds can be greatly enhanced by the world of possibilities that digital keyboards provide.

Digital keyboards encourage students to experiment with sounds before being concerned with key, melody, or harmony. Rhythm sounds can be added and harmonies can be easily orchestrated, even before the student understands the complexities of harmony. The pleasure that most students feel in these early days of exploration often leads to a desire to become more proficient with concepts such as form, harmony, and tonality.

When purchasing composition software programs, an initial review will demonstrate that some are gamelike, some experiment with sounds, and others serve as sophisticated notation programs. A course of study for composition can be planned that will encourage composers of all ages and levels of ability to use a variety of compositional programs.

Sequencing is a valuable tool when teaching composition, as students can record multiple tracks using multiple sounds. By creating an orchestra of sounds, they can be encouraged to consider issues such as melody, harmony, balance, and timbre, and to think outside the box as they compose at the keyboard.

Compositions can be recorded on a sequencer and later edited and altered to the student's liking. This editing process is in itself a rewarding experience for young composers, as they basically become sound technicians, altering dynamic levels, changing balance, etc.

Pieces composed using MIDI can be e-mailed to the teacher for comments or assessment. Since MIDI files are data files and not sound files, they are not large, and are easy to send using e-mail.

As students become more proficient with composition, they can be taught to use notation packages that produce professional-looking scores. A series of performances of a student's compositions along with the scores can be burned on a CD or DVD as a special commemorative to the student's efforts in composition.

### *Band-in-a-Box* – **PG Music**

>   The popular *Band-in-a-Box* provides a user-friendly approach to improvisa-
>   tion and composition. The user types in the chords for any piece using

standard chord symbols (like C, Fm7, C13♭9), chooses the desired style, and *Band-in-a-Box* does the rest. The program automatically generates a complete professional-quality arrangement of piano, bass, drums, guitar, and strings in a wide variety of popular styles (jazz, pop, country, classical, and more).

**www.band-in-a-box.com**

### *Finale®* – MakeMusic, Inc.

One of the most sophisticated notation packages available, *Finale* allows the user to notate, edit, save, and play back compositions. Notation can be done by a mouse-click method, by playing on a MIDI keyboard, with a computer keyboard, by importing a MIDI file, by playing on an acoustic instrument, or by scanning existing sheet music. The program allows auto harmonization and transposition, and has auto-arrange and rhythm-section generator features. Text, such as lyrics or tempo markings can be added to scores. *Finale* integrates key sequencer features with StudioView™. Integrated controls for each staff now enable the user to set volume, panning, and instrument patch as well as to choose mute, solo, or record. Users can build compositions track by track in Studio View's multi-track recording environment.

**www.makemusic.com**

### *Finale NotePad®* – MakeMusic, Inc.

*NotePad* is an inexpensive version of *Finale* available for download from the Internet. Good for student use and smaller projects, the software is easy to use and covers all the essentials of setting-up, notating, and hearing a score. Teachers who compose with *Finale* can e-mail a file to students who can then open the composition in *NotePad*, listen to it, and print it out for their own use.

**www.makemusic.com**

### *Making Music* – Viva Media

Written for young children, this program allows students to compose using tools as simple as finger-painting, with different colors representing different sounds. Various modules allow students to alter a melody: *The Building Blocks Module* uses animal blocks to represent different phrases that can be arranged and rearranged; the *Mix and Match Module* and the *Melody and Rhythm Maker Module* allow students to create melody and rhythm and then to combine them. *Games Module* has four activities ideal for developing listening skills.

**www.viva-media.com**
– Select "Music"

### *Making More Music* – Viva Media

Written for elementary-age students, this program allows students to compose and edit music, print and save compositions, and play musical games. Modules include the Rhythm Band, Chamber Music, Theme and Variations, and Games.

**www.viva-media.com**
– Select "Music"

**PART X**

### *MiBAC JAZZ* – **MiBAC**

This software generates authentic-sounding jazz accompaniments for piano, bass, and drums in 12 jazz styles, allowing users to practice or improvise along with a professional jazz combo on any tune, in any key, at any tempo, and for as long as they like. *MiBAC JAZZ* features a large jazz chord vocabulary and flexible song forms and playback. Users can export standard MIDI files, opening their pieces in a sequencer to record multiple tracks, or in a notation package to print out parts.

**www.mibac.com**

### *Sheddin' the Basics Jazz Piano* – **RoxMedia**

### *Sheddin' the Basics Latin Jazz* – **RoxMedia**

An introduction to chord-voicing and voice leading, *Sheddin' the Basics Jazz Piano* includes six practice sessions with introductory lessons, listening examples, and practice tools. Twenty-one different tunes with standard jazz progressions are included, each with a standardized accompaniment of piano, vibes, bass, and drums. *Sheddin' the Basics Latin Jazz* provides interactive instruction for Latin jazz enthusiasts of all levels. This comprehensive method provides the basic techniques, rhythms, and styles to learn and play authentic Latin jazz.

**www.roxmedia.com**

### *Sibelius* – **Sibelius**

*Sibelius* is a notation software that allows the user to write, play, print, and publish compositions. Music can even be written to accompany videos, such as a home video, film, or TV score. Teachers can take advantage of the *Worksheet Creator*, which includes a comprehensive range of ready-made teaching materials—over 1700 worksheets, projects, exercises, songs, instrumental pieces, lyrics, posters, reference materials, and other resources. Teachers can also create personalized worksheets in given categories such as rhythm, scales, or sight-reading.

**www.sibelius.com**

## Ensembles

One of the most popular uses for technology is enhancing ensemble playing at the keyboard. A traditional studio usually has one or two pianos, allowing for two to four pianists to perform together, all with the similar sound of a piano. With the advent of digital keyboards, many studios are now equipped with multiple keyboards, and music teachers are able to organize a variety of ensembles.

Not only is the number of players potentially increased, but the sounds produced are vastly more interesting. Digital keyboards have hundreds of potential sounds, including reproductions of traditional instruments like violin or flute, and non-traditional sounds, such as "seashore" or "bird tweet."

Each keyboardist in a large ensemble can be assigned a distinctive sound, thus making the color of the ensemble more orchestral. Individual parts are easier to hear and follow. Students enjoy experimenting with their own sounds as they listen to the balance within the whole group, contributing to their ability to listen and make musical choices as they collaborate with others.

Sequencers can be used to great advantage in an ensemble. When using digital keyboards in ensemble playing, the individual parts can be recorded on a sequencer. (As stated in the last chapter, some keyboards have built-in sequencers.) Each member of a duet can record her own part for her partner, allowing the partner to practice with the recorded part at home. In larger ensembles, when each part is recorded, the individual members can practice their parts with as many or as few of the other parts as desired. When a member of the ensemble cannot make a rehearsal, the recorded part can fill in for the missing student.

Another use for the sequencer in ensemble playing is to have the performance recorded for the students to edit. When using a sequencer to edit the sound file, students alter and manipulate the sound by selecting new instrument assignments or adding effects.

As stated in the last chapter, the use of a lab controller allows the teacher to group various keyboards together. Using headsets, the teacher can listen to one student at a time, a duet team, or multiple students. Students can hear just themselves or any arrangement of keyboards.

# Resources

Carden, Joy, and Kevin Raybuck. *Easy Ensembles for Multiple Keyboards* and *Intermediate Ensembles for Multiple Keyboards*. New York: G. Schirmer, Inc. Distributed by Hal Leonard Corporation, 1989.

> Written specifically for electronic keyboard ensembles, these two books offer a flexible approach to incorporating electronic keyboards into the traditional piano studio. As stated in the composers' preface, "These ensemble pieces are written for acoustic and electronic keyboards. Teachers and students are encouraged to experiment with different settings and combinations of keyboards. The music may be adapted to accommodate the limitations of the instruments being used, and they may be altered to heighten the effectiveness of unique keyboard features."

Keveren, Philllip arr. *Christmas Piano Ensembles*, Levels 1–5. Milwaukee: Hal Leonard Corporation, 2003, 2004.

> These books consist of four-part student ensembles, arranged for two or more pianos by Phillip Keveren. These ensembles feature favorite Christmas carols and hymns in graded books that correspond directly to the *Hal Leonard Piano Method* levels. CD and GM disk accompaniments are available for all levels. Included are a conductor's score with optional teacher accompaniment, performance configurations for two or more pianos, and suggested instrumentation for digital keyboards.

Keveren, Phillip, arr. *Piano Ensembles*, Levels 1–5. Milwaukee: Hal Leonard Corporation, 1998, 1999.

> Four-part student ensembles arranged for two or more pianos make up this series. These ensembles feature student favorites from the Hal Leonard Student Piano Library. Suggested instrumentation for electronic keyboards is included. Fully orchestrated CD and GM accompaniment disks are available separately.

**PART X**

# Recording

Students can use any number of recording devices to evaluate their practicing, lessons, or performances. Practice can be recorded on a digital keyboard, an instrument such as a Diskclavier, a sequencing program, or any number of new recording devices.

If a portable CD player/recording system is used in the studio, CD recordings of live performances can be burned directly onto a CD. Such a device allows a CD recording to immediately be given to the student. A direct recording unit allows sound to be recorded, which can then be transferred directly to a computer using the USB port. Imagine the value of these devices as they allow the teacher to:

- Document a lesson for home review

- Record recitals or other performances

- Make CDs for college auditions

- Demonstrate practice skills

If recitals were once taped using a VHS camera, equipment and software exists that allows you to transfer old VHS videos of recitals and burn them onto a DVD. If the teacher now uses a digital video camera rather than a VHS camera, the video can easily be transferred directly onto a computer. Since most current computers come with the capability of burning a CD or DVD, a disc of recital performances can then be created from the file on the computer. Newer cameras will even let you save the video directly to a DVD.

It is also possible to make customized CDs for students by including a number of their own performances on a single CD or DVD as a graduation gift. Years ago, I had my students make a recording of their recital pieces using a tape recorder in my studio. They added to their own individual tape from year to year, and when they finally graduated, they had a tape with up to 12 years of recital performances included. It was a wonderful testament to their progress and dedication over the years. How much better would it be to do the same thing with actual video captured on a DVD? Current technologies allow such a DVD to be easily produced.

## Portable handheld recorders

Portable handheld recording devices have become increasingly popular in recent years. Teachers can use them to record lessons and recitals at professional quality. The handheld recorders have two microphones and record in WAV and or MP3 formats, and are small enough to move and store anywhere. Music recorded on these portable devices can be uploaded into a computer and edited as well as burned onto a CD or DVD. The quality, price, and portability of these recorders make them ideal for any independent studio.

For more information on types of handheld recorders, visit your local music retailer. You may also search the Internet by typing "portable recorder" into your favorite search engine.

## Audio recording software

A number of software programs can be used for producing professional quality CDs, DVDs, and movies in a home studio. These programs basically turn a home computer into a recording studio, allowing the user to perform functions such as record, edit, cut, paste, mix, and delete when working with audio files. Although it is not possible to list all of the available programs, the following list offers some possible choices.

*SONAR* – **Cakewalk**

    **www.cakewalk.com**

*Sound Forge®* – **Sony**

    **www.sonycreativesoftware.com**

*Logic Pro* and *Logic Express* – **Apple**

    **www.apple.com/logicstudio**
    **www.apple.com/logicexpress**

*Cubase Studio 4* and *Cubase Essential 4* – **Steinberg**

    **www.steinberg.net**

*Pro Tools* – **Digidesign**

    **www.digidesign.com**

*Digital Performer* – **Mark of the Unicorn (MOTU)**

    **www.motu.com**

*GarageBand*

    **www.apple.com/ilife/garageband**

## Video editing software

Video editing software allows the user to create and edit personal movies on a home computer. Files can be converted to a CD or DVD and shared on the Internet. High-quality home video of studio recitals, individual student performances, and college auditions can be created. Special effects such as titles and transitions can easily be added to the video. The following list represents some of the many options available. All those interested in video editing can search the Internet for further information.

*Pinnacle Studio* – **Pinnacle Systems**

    **www.pinnaclesys.com**
      – Select "Products"
      – From the drop down menu, select "Video editing"

*Final Cut Express* and *Final Cut Pro* – **Apple**

    **www.apple.com/finalcutexpress**
    **www.apple.com/finalcutstudio/finalcutpro**

*iMovie* – **Apple**

    **www.apple.com/ilife/imovie**

*iDVD* – **Apple**

    **www.apple.com/ilife/idvd**

I do not wish to enter the Mac/PC debate, having used both and liked both. Nonetheless, it is worth mentioning that all Mac computers currently purchased come with audio editing and video editing programs pre-installed:

- *GarageBand* (audio recording and editing program as well as MIDI sequencer)
- *iMovie* and *iDVD* (video editing and slide show creation)

All three programs are easy to use and are recommended for teachers who may not be technologically savvy, as well as for young students.

## Internet Lessons

Although it may seem like teaching lessons over the Internet is a scene out of *The Jetsons* and not for this lifetime, such lessons are already possible. Distance lessons can be organized using a computer, a small computer camera, a microphone, speakers, and free downloadable video conferencing software. It is also important to have a broadband Internet connection wide enough to send the amount of data needed for effective, delay-free communication. We have already reached the point where lessons missed due to a blizzard can be taught over the Internet from our house to theirs!

# Resources

### ADDITIONAL TECHNOLOGY RESOURCES

Bowen, Sandra. *Electrify Your Studio*. Fort Lauderdale: The FJH Music Company, Inc., 2000.

> Full of practical, easy-to-read lists, this guide to technology is ideal for the independent studio. Chapters include information on studio equipment, software, lab stations, keyboard ensembles, sequencing, notation, teaching applications and studio setup, and a helpful section on Internet resources. Bowen is enthusiastic about the possibilities for technology in the studio, and offers valuable information for any teacher wishing to expand the use of technology in the independent studio.

Pinksterboer, Hugo. *Keyboard & Digital Piano*. Heemestede, the Netherlands: The Tipbook Company, 2004. Distributed by Hal Leonard.

> This thorough guide assists with the purchase of keyboards and digital pianos, understanding their various working components, producing the desired sounds, tips for maintaining the instruments, and using additional equipment and features such as a sequencer, speakers, headsets, and even a computer with a keyboard or digital piano. It is a small but thorough manual that allows those playing keyboards and digital pianos to get the most out of their instrument.

Souvignier, Todd, and Gary Hustwit. *The Musician's Guide to the Internet*, 2nd Edition. Milwaukee: Hal Leonard Corporation, 2002.

> This book would be ideal for a beginner to technology, yet contains enough information to be valuable to more skilled users as well. Instructions are given for areas as basic as getting online or using e-mail, or more advanced processes such as creating MP3s, creating a web page, and streaming audio. This book is short and can serve as a manageable guide to using the Internet within an independent studio.

Weldon, Craig. *101 Keyboard Tips: Stuff All the Pros Know and Use*. Milwaukee: Hal Leonard Corporation, 2003.

> Written as a guide for aspiring keyboardists, this book offers practical tips on technique, improvising, equipment, practicing, performance, and more. Tips on playing with a band, sound checks, and using a "post-gig" analysis offer guidance to the keyboard player just venturing into the world of group performance.

## We Have Nothing to Fear but Fear Itself...

Younger teachers often feel comfortable with technology and have been exposed to music technology in their college training. Yet even some younger teachers are hesitant to try new programs and equipment. In the ever-changing world of technology, all teachers, whether they are comfortable with technology or not, can count on constant change.

Regardless of one's age or prior experience, music technology is worthy of every teacher's attention. In order to feel comfortable with technology, a few helpful tips are offered:

- Allow time to develop familiarity with new technology tools. Any software program, keyboard, or sequencer can become second nature, just like DVD players, television remotes, and cell phones.

- Explore one or two new areas of technology each year. Eventually, a wealth of technology choices will exist within the studio.

- Don't feel complacent with current knowledge. There will always be new and exciting innovations in technology.

- Remember it is never too late to get started and never too late to expand one's current skills.

- Rather than feel frustrated, seek outside help if it is needed. Offer piano lessons to a tech-savvy student at half price in exchange for technology lessons. Seek assistance from a relative or colleague. Take classes.

- Subscribe to a music technology-related magazine. *Keyboard Companion* and *Electronic Musician* are two useful resources that regularly introduce, review, and describe new products.

- Admit "I don't understand" rather than being embarrassed by it. Such an admission is actually liberating.

- Do not worry that technology is taking over the private piano studio. It will not replace traditional areas of instruction.

- View technology as a tool which enhances a teacher's time with students while creatively reinforcing all areas of instruction.

Reviews of a number of software programs that are listed in this chapter, including downloadable shareware, can be accessed at the Piano Education website:

**Piano Education**

    **www.pianoeducation.org/pnosoftr.html**

Another good site for reviewing music software can be found at:

**Educational Software Directory**

    **www.educational-software-directory.net**

        – Select "Music"

# PART XI

## CAREERS IN MUSIC

As those in the music profession know, music is not for the faint of heart. Most musicians have extremely busy schedules, work in a variety of musical disciplines, and perform a multitude of tasks. This makes the job both demanding and rewarding. Any student choosing music as a future career needs to be committed to the profession in order to succeed. As the famous teacher and pianist Nadia Boulanger once said, "Do not take up music unless you would rather die than not do so." Perhaps Boulanger overstated the case, but for those who choose music as a profession, a lifetime of dedication can reap a lifetime of rewards.

Students deserve guidance on career opportunities should they choose to pursue music as their life's work. At first glance, it may seem as though there are precious few viable career options for a piano student; in reality, there are a number of choices. Students deserve to be informed of the skills required, the education that should be pursued, and the financial outlook and general availability of any job they may be considering. As they contemplate a career in music, they must first ask some important questions:

- What degrees, skills, or training are required?

- How crowded is the field they wish to pursue?

- Will their career choice necessitate supplementary sources of income?

Part XI lists a number of careers in music with a brief summary addressing the questions above.

## Resources

*Berklee College of Music*

This college has a helpful website, listing a number of careers in music with brief descriptions of each.

**www.berklee.edu**

– On the pull-down menu for "Admissions" select "Careers in Music"

*National Association for Music Education (formerly Music Educator's National Conference)*

The MENC website has a link offering information on careers in music, including salaries, educational requirements, job descriptions, links, and more.

**www.menc.org/careers**

# Chapter 44

# PERFORMANCE

---

Since none of my college professors (both undergraduate and graduate) ever asked me what my career goals were, it seemed understood that the goal of degrees in piano performance was to become the best piano performer that I could. Period. What I planned to do after receiving the degrees was never mentioned.

High school students often see career choice in music as limited to either becoming a teacher or a performer. Students who do not want an education degree are too often encouraged to receive piano performance degrees, with no explanation given of the career options such a degree does or does not bring. If a student feels that degrees in piano performance will lead her to a career as a concert pianist, we need to have a serious talk with her.

Too many talented piano students, the best in their town or maybe even their state, have visions of making a living performing regularly in the world's great concert halls. Very few pianists actually will do that. It is somewhat like saying, "I want to go to law school so that I can be a Supreme Court Justice." Most lawyers will not get to that level; even most talented lawyers; even most phenomenal, highly successful, talented lawyers. It is not that we want to discourage talented pianists from considering a career in performance, but we need to be realistic with them. We need to explain how that career might actually take shape.

I would like to share a story that highlights the feeling some students have about a career as a concert pianist. During my years on the East coast, I often went to a well-known conservatory of music and spoke with the piano pedagogy class on the business side of running an independent studio. These students did not want to be taking piano pedagogy because none of them planned on teaching piano, but the class was required. I usually started by asking, "Before I begin, I just want to go around the class and have you each share your career goals." Almost every one of them would say her goal was to be a concert pianist. All certainly were capable of such a dream; they had the technique, the repertoire, the training, the dedication, and the musicality. Nonetheless I would then ask, "Well, hypothetically… just in case that didn't work out, what would you do?" To which most would reply that they would go on and get a doctoral degree and teach in a university. "Which university might you consider?" "Oh, maybe Indiana University or Oberlin."

Most of these students had high expectations, based on the fact that they had truly excelled in all of their piano training. Unfortunately, their expectations were also unrealistic. The missing ingredient, unfortunately, was that no one had talked to them about the market for the jobs they were antici-pating. Each year, thousands of top-notch pianists graduate from undergraduate and graduate school programs around the world, eager to fill the few slots that are available for concert pianists. The laws of supply and demand are not in their favor. When I asked the pedagogy class, "How many of you actually know someone who is making a living 100% as a concert pianist?" very few knew anyone who fit the bill. If they did know someone, that person had had only a brief career as a concert pianist, never a lifelong career doing nothing but performing classical music.

In the 2004 *New York Times* article, "The Juilliard Effect: Ten Years Later," written by Daniel J. Wakin, the author wrote of the 1994 graduating class of Juilliard and the career paths their top-notch training afforded them. Wakin attempted to trace 44 instrumentalists who graduated in 1994 (including pianists) and found that only 36 could be traced. He assumed that the other eight were no longer in music, as they could not be tracked through Google or the Juilliard alumni office. Although 11 of the 36 traced graduates had professional, full-time orchestra jobs, others were freelancers, and still others supplemented freelance performing with teaching.

It can be assumed that the 1994 Juilliard graduates were highly trained in performance and were among the most talented and technically skilled music graduates coming out of universities and conservatories in that year. Nonetheless, 12 are no longer in performance. Wakin lists their professions as "English teacher in Japan, fitness trainer, stay-at-home mother, art museum bookkeeper, software engineer, music therapist, saleswoman at Tiffany's, public relations assistant, insurance underwriter, public school music teacher, and network engineer for the Federal Reserve Bank in San Francisco." The article describes the despair that some of these talented musicians felt at their inability to find the level of performing job they sought, and the frustration felt at approaching their early 30s without establishing a financially secure occupation.

So how do we encourage students who want to be performers while staying realistic? There are many opportunities for students to perform, but they must understand that they most likely will need to derive a good portion of their income from other areas in music. Yes, they may go on to teach in a university or conservatory, but again, they must realize that the competition for those piano jobs is fierce as well. Perhaps they will not end up at Indiana University, but in an excellent music department in a smaller college and community.

We can best encourage students by recognizing and fostering their talents and skills while being honest about their career goals and options. We can expose them to the many career choices in music that supplement a career in performing. We can help them to be realistic as they pursue their dreams by explaining the necessary education and skills their career choice requires.

If a student chooses a life as a performer, several options are open to pianists. Most of these professions will require some form of additional income.

## Resource

Wakin, Daniel. "The Juilliard Effect: Ten Years Later." *The New York Times*, December 12, 2004. Also available online.

## Classical: Solo

If a student chooses to pursue a career performing classical music as a solo artist, she will need to have excellent musical ability and training. Studying with a master teacher is extremely advantageous. Performance skills and technique at the highest level are essential, as is the ability to memorize music solidly. Musical training needs to include a thorough understanding of music theory, music history, and the stylistic elements of each period of music. A large range of repertoire, including concertos, needs to cover all style periods and could include a specialty area such as contemporary music or the music of Liszt.

A performer will either need an agent or good business skills of her own. Traveling on the road or by air and being away from home for extended periods of time will be necessary. If she wishes to continue with a career in performance, a lifetime of practice and dedication to musical growth will be required. The most helpful degrees are in Piano Performance, and could include bachelor's, master's, and doctoral degrees.

## Classical: Chamber

Everything that is listed for the solo performer applies to the pianist who wishes to pursue a career performing chamber music. In addition, the chamber player must learn a large repertoire of chamber works and have the ability to practice, listen, respond, and perform well within the chamber ensemble. Excellent sight-playing skills are highly beneficial. It is not necessary to memorize music, although there are some chamber players who do memorize their repertoire. The degrees to pursue are in piano performance or chamber music. Universities now offer bachelor's, master's, and doctoral degrees in chamber music.

## Resource

*Chamber Music America*
    www.chamber-music.org

## Collaborative Artist/Accompanist/Coach

Accompanists are increasingly referred to as collaborative artists. Excellent collaborative artists are highly sought, and talented pianists should be made aware of this attractive career option. There are more paid positions for collaborative pianists than there are for solo performing, making this a promising career choice.

Within the junior high and high school system, an accompanist may play for the choir, vocalists, or vocal or instrumental festivals. Some schools pay their staff accompanists quite well. On the college level, accompanists serve choirs, lessons, solo recitals, competitions, and practice sessions with college soloists. The college pay is sometimes by the hour and sometimes paid by semester in the form of a contracted salary. Graduate assistantships are available to pianists willing to accompany. Accompanists may also be hired to accompany church services or professional concerts.

In the world of professional musicians, the paid collaborative artist usually leads a life full of scheduling challenges. The collaborative artist may be lucky enough to accompany one concert artist and travel with that person from concert to concert, but will more likely be in the position of accompanying a number of artists or ensembles. Jobs may be set on a steady, predetermined schedule, but often are scheduled randomly and unpredictably. Collaborative pianists must have good business skills, know how to negotiate contracts, and be 100% dependable in meeting all engagements and rehearsals.

Pianists need to put to rest any preconceptions that accompanying is a step down from solo performing. In fact, the collaborative pianist must have technique on a par with the solo pianist. In addition, she must have an excellent sense of rhythm and the ability to listen and follow. The professional accompanist must have top-notch sight-playing skills and be able to transpose at sight. (The singer may say, "I can't get that high note today, please take it down a half-step.") A good accompanist can realize a figured bass and improvise stylistically when performing compositions written in an earlier period. Top vocal accompanists are familiar with multiple languages (Italian, French, and German) and have expert coaching skills.

The life of a collaborative artist usually requires being able to handle unexpected, urgent, last-minute requests. Many collaborative artists thrive on this excitement, somewhat like the emergency room doctor who likes the intensity of the night shift. Degrees might include an undergraduate degree in piano performance and an advanced degree in accompanying or collaborative arts.

## Orchestra/Opera Company/Ballet Company/Band

If a pianist has dreams of being the pianist in an orchestra (not a soloist with the orchestra) it must be understood that there is usually one keyboardist per orchestra. Only in major orchestras is this job a paid, full-time position. Since much of the orchestral repertoire does not require keyboard, smaller orchestras often pay only a part-time salary, covering the few concerts when the keyboardist is used. Orchestral keyboardists must be able to play piano, harpsichord, and celeste; professional organists are usually hired to cover organ parts. Sight-playing skills become increasingly important when playing with a large professional ensemble. When employed by an opera or ballet company, the pianist often serves as a rehearsal pianist.

Positions are available for a keyboardist in bands, including community bands, big bands, and jazz bands, although most would not provide a full-time salary. Military bands employ top-notch musicians and do provide a steady income as well as a steady schedule of performances, but opportunities for keyboardists are limited and highly competitive. Helpful degrees are piano performance, collaborative arts, jazz piano, or accompanying degrees.

## Jazz

A few years ago one of my most talented high school piano students decided he wanted to be a jazz pianist. He wanted to stop his lessons with me and start lessons in jazz. I called a fine jazz pianist who teaches at a nearby university and asked her if she would take him as a student. She recommended some jazz method books and concluded with, "If he wants to be a good jazz pianist, tell him to continue his classical lessons and become the absolute best pianist he can be before he gets to college."

Indeed, the top jazz pianists have technique on a par with the best classical artists. A jazz pianist must understand and read all jazz/chord symbols and have a strong background in music theory. She will need to be able to improvise and be at ease with performing with other musicians, including improvising within a group. An understanding of the various jazz idioms must be developed along with the ability to improvise in a number of jazz styles. Studying with a master jazz artist is highly beneficial. As with classical music, good business skills are important. The ability to travel and spend time away from home may be required. A top jazz artist develops a unique, individual style and devotes herself to a lifetime of dedication to her art. The field is highly competitive and requires a great deal of dedication.

Whereas there are precious few venues for nightly paid performances of classical music, paid jobs for jazz pianists in nightclubs, bars, and restaurants are more common, especially in urban areas such as Chicago, New York, and Kansas City. Helpful degrees are piano performance and jazz piano.

## Resource

*JazzTimes Education Guide*

www.jazztimes.com

- Select "Jazz Guides" from top menu
- From pull down menu, select "Jazz schools"

## Rock/Popular/Country/Christian

In these idioms the ability to compose becomes more significant. Excellence in technique may not be as essential as individual style, artistic vision, and innovation. Good business skills are necessary as is a willingness to travel. Location may be of importance, such as establishing oneself in New York, Memphis, Nashville, or Los Angeles. The relatively new field of Christian music is expanding and attracting larger audiences. Degrees are not necessarily required for these careers and perhaps not as important as getting that "big break." We all know of rock artists who seem to be more show than skill, but in reality these fields are also highly competitive. Although degrees would not be required in most situations, the more musical training one has and the higher the level of skill, the better.

## Resources

*The Christian Country Music Association*

www.ccma.cc

*Country Music Association*

www.cmaworld.com

*International Association for the Study of Popular Music*

www.iaspm.net

*Reason to Rock*

http://reasontorock.com

This is an excellent site with many helpful links.

## Studio Musician: Television/Movies/Commercials/Video Games/Recordings

Only the top musicians are hired to record music for television, movies, commercials, video games, and recordings. Therefore only the very top pianists can consider this as a career option, understanding that the market is extremely limited. There are recording studios all over the country, doing a variety of types of recording, with the most significant hiring being in New York and Los Angeles. Where a movie studio might hire an orchestra of 110 players to record a movie soundtrack, only a few of those players would be piano/keyboard players. Musicians in this field are hired for individual jobs, and do not have a set income from any one employer. For the top musicians in this field, the pay can be quite lucrative; for others, additional sources of income may be needed. The job requires the ability to work unpredictable hours in a multitude of diverse settings. A pianist in this profession must have excellent sight-playing and improvisation skills, an advanced knowledge of keyboard technology, and must be considered entirely reliable by the contractors who do the booking. Some recording studios require the ability to learn music directly from a recording rather than from a score. Degrees that are well-suited are piano performance and jazz piano.

## Resources

Forest, Greg. *The Complete Music Business Office.* Vellejo: Mix Books, 1999. Distributed by Hal Leonard Corporation.

This book is written with performing musicians, such as members of bands, in mind. It gives advice on business contracts and managing a performing career. A supplemental section in the back of the book includes spreadsheets and tax forms, Library of Congress forms, and helpful lists of trade unions, guilds, and associations; clinics, workshops, and seminars; trade periodicals; booking and talent agencies; music publishers and catalog administrators; record distributors; information for licensing on the web and recommended readings. The CD contains all of the forms, spreadsheets, contract examples, and templates discussed in the book.

**WEBSITES**

*The American Federation of Musicians*

www.afm.org

*The Recording Musicians Association*

www.rmaweb.org

## Conductor

The most plentiful opportunities for conducting exist in a junior high/middle school, high school, or university setting. Becoming the conductor of a major symphony orchestra is as difficult to achieve as becoming a world-renowned concert pianist. There are not many major symphonies, the jobs do not become available often, and musicians from all around the world apply for open positions. Although someone gets those jobs, if a student expects to be conducting the New York Philharmonic by the time they are 30, a supportive yet honest discussion is needed.

Large orchestras often employ assistant conductors; there are many smaller professional orchestras in mid-sized cities as well as a vast number of chamber orchestras, community orchestras, and community bands. On the choral side, there are a few major vocal ensembles, and a far larger number of community and church choirs. Conductors also direct the pit orchestras of opera companies, ballet companies, and musical theater productions.

Although the conductors of major ensembles are paid well, most other conducting positions require additional sources of income. For those who are interested in conducting, smaller groups or community ensembles serve as excellent stepping-stones during a conducting career. The student wishing to be a professional conductor will need to develop an excellent conducting technique, a broad understanding of musical styles and music history, a thorough understanding of music theory, and a wide knowledge of repertoire in her field. Degrees exist in choral conducting and instrumental conducting.

As discussed further in Chapter 46, those interested in conducting in the school system will need a degree in Music Education.

## Resources

Professional organizations tend to be specific to a certain type of conducting, such as band, orchestra, or choir. Some of the many professional organizations include:

*American Choral Directors Association*
www.acdaonline.org

*College Band Directors National Association*
www.cbdna.org

*College Orchestra Directors Association*
www.codaweb.org

*The Conductor's Guild*
www.conductorsguild.org

*National Band Association*
www.nationalbandassociation.org

# Chapter 45

# COMPOSING AND ARRANGING

## Composing

Very few composers make their living entirely from composition. Talented students can be encouraged in this field, understanding that it, too, is another crowded field with attractive, if limited, opportunities. A composer must have a unique vision and an innately creative mind, but must be grounded in an exceptionally strong music education. Requirements include the study of composition and extensive study in music theory, including counterpoint, form and analysis, and harmony. If the composer writes for instruments, further study in orchestration and an understanding of the fundamentals of all instruments will be required, with a similar understanding of vocal range and techniques for vocal composition.

Teachers are wise to take advantage of the many composition competitions (covered in more detail in Chapter 36) available to students of all ages, from elementary school to young adulthood. These competitions serve student composers well, offering valuable comments from judges and exposure to a broad variety of compositional requirements. It benefits students to become the best pianists they can if they are considering composition, as being a strong performer helps them to develop a keen sense of musicianship.

Just as there are a number of types of music for performers to explore (classical, chamber, rock, country, etc.), there are a number of venues for composition. Composers may choose to write "serious" or "art" music, or a limited few may write for movies, video games, commercials, country/western artists, etc. In addition, there is a fairly large market for educational music; works for elementary, middle, and high school band, orchestra, and choir are in high demand.

The current high-tech world serves aspiring composers well. The ability to self-publish and self-promote are enhanced by modern technology. Sites like YouTube and MySpace, as well as the ability to search the Internet, open a whole new world for those who wish to market their compositions.

In the United States, composers of serious art music are often employed at universities and have the duty of teaching composition classes and music theory. As with any university position, it is wise to have a secondary area of strength in order to be more marketable. Degrees might include bachelor's, master's, and doctoral degrees in composition, music theory, or performance.

## Resources

American Composers Forum
    www.composersforum.org

American Music Center
    www.amc.net

National Association of Composers
    www.music-usa.org

Society of Composers, Inc.
    www.societyofcomposers.org

## Arranging

Arranging music requires solid compositional tools and an understanding of form, instrumentation, and theory. Arrangers might compose simplified versions of famous works for elementary, junior high, or high school ensembles, an arrangement of a symphony for concert band, or a marching band version of a popular movie score. A small number of the very best arrangers work for the TV and movie industry. Arrangers need to be aware of all copyright laws that apply to arranging. A good arranger does far more than simplify or change the instrumentation of a piece. Top-notch arrangements require the same creativity and musical skill as other forms of composition. Degrees might include bachelor's, master's, and doctoral degrees in composition, music theory, or performance.

## Resource

*American Society of Music Arrangers and Composers (ASMAC)*

www.asmac.org

# Chapter 46

# EDUCATION

---

**M**any piano students are interested in teaching careers. Teaching is a gratifying profession that provides a reliable income and the opportunity for steady employment. Teachers receive valuable benefits such as health insurance, sick leave, and retirement options, which most performing musicians do not receive. Although some school districts may be poorly funded or understaffed, others have ample funding for the arts and boast exceptional choirs, bands, and orchestras that showcase the school. Top-quality music teachers are courted and valued in every setting—from independent studio to high school to university.

## Elementary/Junior High (Middle School)/High school

Teaching in public and private schools is both a demanding and a rewarding career choice. The degree required is a Bachelor's in Music Education, with many teachers obtaining advanced degrees. Education degrees can be in elementary music or secondary music. The secondary music degree (suitable for junior high/middle school and high school) can be in vocal or instrumental music. Some institutions offer a composite degree that certifies the teacher for general music classes, and vocal and instrumental ensembles from kindergarten through high school. Such a degree is actually a double degree and requires more than four years to obtain.

If a student anticipates teaching a number of different performing groups, preparation should include experiencing as many ensembles as possible during the college years: choir, band, jazz band, swing choir, pep band, orchestra, marching band, percussion ensemble, etc. The student will need to take private lessons on a primary and secondary instrument and study music theory and music history. A number of music methods classes are required, including vocal methods; methods classes in woodwinds, strings, brass, and percussion instruments; elementary teaching methods; and/or secondary teaching methods. Additional areas of study would most likely include choral and instrumental conducting, diction, scoring/orchestration and arranging, and advanced theory. For those who enjoy working with students, a career as an elementary, junior high/middle school or high school music teacher offers a steady income, good benefits, and the richly rewarding experience of having a profound impact on the lives of young learners.

## Resources

*American Choral Directors Association*
    www.acdaonline.org

*American School Band Directors Association*
    http://home.comcast.net/~asbda

*The National Association for Music Education*
    www.menc.org

## University

Many pianists have hopes of teaching piano in a university setting. This is an overcrowded field, with far more pianists than positions. Pianists can increase their marketability by obtaining a terminal degree (doctorate) and focusing on a strong secondary field, as most piano instructors also teach courses besides applied piano. Secondary areas might include accompanying, chamber music, theory, class piano, music appreciation, chamber music, music education (along with experience teaching in the public schools) music fundamentals, and vocal coaching. Some pianists may decide to change their primary area of focus in order to pursue a job in another field such as music history or music theory; such a switch necessitates a change in degree. Possible degrees for those interested in university teaching include piano performance, chamber music, accompanying, collaborative arts, music education, music theory, music history, and composition, and usually include bachelor's, master's, and doctoral degrees.

## Resource

*College Music Society*
www.music.org

## Independent

It is wise to encourage the dedicated piano student to consider a career as an independent teacher. Even if the student is an exceptional performer, she may need or wish to supplement her performing income by establishing an independent studio. A quick summary of the qualifications needed to be an independent piano teacher include the following:

- Strong musical training
- Top-notch skills as a pianist and musician
- A background in pedagogy
- An understanding of stylistic elements
- A solid training in music theory and music history
- Business, computer, and record-keeping skills
- The ability to devise attractive studio documents and set professional studio policies
- An understanding of all laws that affect small businesses, such as local zoning, tax, and business license laws
- A long-range plan for studio growth
- Continual professional development
- Membership in professional organizations
- A well-maintained professional teaching space
- A plan for accumulation of inventory

If students are given a solid musical background and develop sound pedagogical skills, they can eventually reap the rewards of establishing a first-rate studio. Students should be reminded of the role that location (population) plays in determining income from an independent studio. Degrees might be in the field of piano performance, piano pedagogy, or music education, and could include a bachelor's, master's, or doctorate.

## Resources

*Music Teachers National Association*
   www.mtna.org

*National Federation of Music Clubs*
   www.nfmc-music.org

*National Guild of Piano Teachers*
   www.pianoguild.com

## Community School of the Arts

Community schools of the arts exist in a number of cities, and offer part-time or full-time employment to instructors of applied lessons. Some of the larger community schools also offer health benefits to their full-time instructors. All of the requirements of the independent music teacher apply here, although many of the business duties become the responsibility of the school administration. Community schools offer an environment where teachers work outside of the home, network with other teachers, and benefit from the administration's efforts to maintain a budget, market the school, recruit students, and organize recitals.

## Resource

*The National Guild of Community Schools of the Arts*
   www.nationalguild.org

## Music Store

If a teacher chooses to teach in a music store rather than (or in addition to) a home studio, the degrees and requirements remain the same as for the independent teacher. In some music stores teachers set and collect their own tuition payments, and in others bookwork is handled by the store.

**PART XI**

# Chapter 47

# SERVICE

Although performing and teaching are the two areas students consider most often when planning a career in music, in reality there are a number of attractive choices. Students are well served when they have been exposed to a wide range of options from which to make an informed choice.

## Musician in Places of Worship

A rich history of religious music will be lost if more musicians do not become involved with music in their place of worship. Teachers can encourage students of all ages to perform for services, thus increasing the likelihood of professional involvement in religious music.

Different religions require different types of music, and jobs within a place of worship include positions such as the organist, choir director, cantor, or youth music director. Requirements include:

- Excellent organ skills

- Conducting skills

- A broad knowledge of sacred literature

- Excellent sight-playing skills

- The ability to harmonize, transpose, and improvise

Most musicians need to supplement income earned from working in a place of worship, although some of the larger worship settings employ full-time staff musicians who are paid well. Possible degrees include sacred music, organ performance, and conducting.

## Resources

*The American Guild of Organists*

www.agohq.org

- For certification information, select "Education and Certification" at the top of the page.
- Select "Certification Chart" from the menu on the right.

*The National Association of Church Musicians*

www.nacmhq.org

## Music Librarian

Music librarians work in settings such as a major library, music library in an institution of higher education, public library, or for some other entity such as a publisher, orchestra, music company, etc. The *Music Librarian Association* website describes the duties of a music librarian:

> The traditional responsibilities of librarians are at the heart of most music librarians' activities: organizing, cataloging, and maintaining collections; providing instruction in use of the library; answering reference inquiries; selecting music, books, journals, recordings, microforms, and sometimes manuscripts and other rare materials for acquisition. Music librarians recommend means of preservation and housing of materials in their custody and use electronic bibliographic and reference resources to their full potential.

Additional duties reflect the employer's needs, such as planning exhibits and concerts, or organizing lectures or classes.

The requirements needed to become a music librarian include a well-rounded education in music and library sciences. A bachelor's degree in music and a master's degree in library sciences often serve as a good match. The music librarian's background should include knowledge of related arts fields, humanities, languages, music literature, and music history. If the library specializes in another area such as world music, additional education in that field may be necessary.

### Resource

*Music Library Association*
    www.musiclibraryassoc.org

## Music Therapist

Although music is the primary tool used in music therapy, musical goals are not its primary objectives. Music therapy uses music to help a client in emotional, physical, spiritual, social, or physiological ways.

Often our piano students are very caring individuals and music therapy provides an excellent marriage between students' nurturing skills, their commitment to caregiving in an allied health profession, and their musical skills. Music therapists may choose specialized areas of concentration such as assisting children (e.g., at-risk youth or children with disabilities), working with the elderly (patients who have experienced a stroke, have Parkinson's Disease, or have Alzheimer's), relieving pain and stress within a medical environment (such as patients recovering from trauma, those diagnosed with depression, or women during labor and delivery), and easing the experience of dying.

**PART XI**

Music therapists are highly trained, and are required to take courses in music, music theory, music therapy, biological and behavioral sciences, and general education. In addition to the coursework, students are required to complete 1200 hours of clinical training. After individuals obtain a music therapy degree, they are eligible to pursue board certification via a national examination.

The Certification Board for Music Therapists (CBMT) issues the credential Music Therapist-Board Certified (MT-BC), which is a requirement for all those choosing to practice in the field.

The American Music Therapy website states:

> Music therapy is the clinical and evidence-based use of music interventions to accomplish individualized goals within a therapeutic relationship by a credentialed professional who has completed an approved music therapy program.

## Resources

American Music Therapy Association, Inc.

www.musictherapy.org

Hanser, Suzanne. *The New Music Therapist's Handbook.* Boston: Berklee Press, 1999. Distributed by Hal Leonard Corporation.

The book is designed for music therapists, allied health professionals, and students. Although the handbook may be used as a text, it can also serve as an introduction to the music therapy profession. Each chapter includes references, a guide to key words, and a bibliography.

## Music-Thanatology

Music-thanatology, or music for the dying, uses music to assist a patient at the end of life. As stated on the Music-Thanatology Association International website, music-thanatology practitioners:

> …provide musical comfort, using harp and voice, at the bedside of patients near the end of life. The service at the bedside is called a music vigil and is delivered by one or two highly trained music-thanatologists. Its purpose is to lovingly serve the needs of the dying and their loved ones with prescriptive music.

> Prescriptive music is live music that changes, moment by moment, in response to physiological changes in the patient. Practitioners, therefore, provide music that is tailored to each specific situation, marrying the length of a musical phrase to the cycle of respiration for example, or supporting a particular emotional process through sensitive application of harmony or rhythm, or a freedom from rhythm.

> [A music vigil helps] to ease physical symptoms such as pain, restlessness, agitation, sleeplessness and labored breathing. The vigil conveys a sense of serenity and

consolation that can be profoundly soothing to those present. Difficult emotions such as anger, fear, sadness, and grief can find unspoken comfort as listeners rest into a musical presence of beauty, intimacy, and reverence.

Since antiquity, music and medicine have a long tradition as allies in healing.

Music-thanatology and prescriptive music are contemporary deliveries continuing that same historic tradition. Music-thanatology has been developed as a palliative medical modality over the last three decades by Therese Schroeder-Sheker, the founder of Chalice of Repose Project, which is located in Mt. Angel, Oregon. The Chalice of Repose Project offers the only music-thanatology curriculum in the country, and the 50–60 students enrolled in the program each year are from North America, Europe, and Asia. Music-thanatologists work professionally in every psycho-social setting and in full- and part-time staff positions in hospitals, hospices, and long-term care facilities across the country.

# Resources

*The Chalice of Repose Project, Inc.*

www.chaliceofrepose.org

This site contains music-thanatology publications, course offerings, clinical consultations, and general music-thanatology information.

*Music-Thanatology Association International*

www.mtai.org

This site contains a partial directory of students and certified music-thanatology practitioners.

Schroeder-Sheker, Therese. *Transitus: A Blessed Death in the Modern World*, 2nd edition. Mt. Angel: St. Dunstan's Press, 2005.

Written by Schroeder-Sheker, the leading force in music-thanatology, this unique book offers insights into the ways music-thanatology contributes to a blessed death. The medieval roots of music-thanatology are presented along with the spiritual and medical benefits of music-thanatology evident today.

## Music Copyist

Music copyists provide an integral service within the music industry. Without copyists, a film with symphonic underscore could not be made. Copyists do not just "copy" a composition, note by note. The copyist's job is to notate what is intended (recognizing what notes are supposed to be on the page), much like a manuscript editor of a book. This challenge requires thorough training in all musical disciplines, including orchestration and composition. In addition, copyists must meet deadlines diligently, as a missed deadline can cost a copyist her job. As copying by hand is becoming a lost art, today's professional copyists must be proficient with a number of notation and sequencing programs, depending on the requirements of the job.

**PART XI**

Although many copyists are self-employed, some have full-time employment with symphonies, publishers, the recording industry, Broadway shows, and the film industry. A film or show copyist (or music librarian) is often required to be on site, available to make any sudden changes in the score. Like other areas of music, the copying profession is extremely competitive at the upper levels, although lower-level jobs exist in the university setting or through freelance work. Most professional copyists have a four-year music degree. Important areas of study are theory, orchestration, composition, and an understanding of chord changes/symbols in jazz and rock music.

## Piano Technician

Piano technicians tune, repair, voice, regulate, and rebuild pianos. They may work in concert halls, universities, music camps, recording studios, piano stores, independent studios, or any public or private facility where a piano is maintained. Piano technicians are usually self-employed, although some serve as full-time staff technicians, or work for other technicians or music stores. Some may have one employer, such as a large university, but most serve a number of clients. Paths into the profession are varied and include resident college programs, apprenticeships, and self-study/correspondence courses. Because entry into the profession does not require any specific degree or training, the Piano Technicians Guild has established a self-regulating system of examination. In order to become a Registered Piano Technician (RPT), an applicant must pass a series of three examinations: a written exam, a tuning exam, and a technical exam involving repairs and regulation of both vertical and grand pianos.

It is not required that a technician acquires a background as a pianist, but many do. There is always a need for high-quality piano technicians, and many technicians have more work than they can handle. Unlike other music professions such as concert pianist or conductor, which have few available jobs, there is a need for qualified technicians in every community. Similar to the independent teacher, the self-employed piano technician's clients and income reflect the quality of her work.

## Resource

*Piano Technicians Guild*

www.ptg.org

The Piano Technicians Guild has a particularly helpful website full of information for any student who may be considering this profession. It is also a helpful website for piano teachers, with information on the history of the piano, composers, piano care, and numerous helpful links.

# Chapter 48

# BUSINESS

A number of jobs exist in music business, including manager, bookkeeping agent, record distributor, record promoter, and more. This chapter discusses a few of the better-known careers in the world of music business.

## Resource

*LaCostaMusic.com*

www.lacostamusic.com

– Select "Sponsored Links" from the menu at the top of the page.

– Scroll to "Featured Sites"

## Music Retail

Many music store employees are musicians themselves. This certainly is an asset when selling instruments, books, and musical equipment, as is training in retail. Some musicians open their own stores, often with a slant toward an area of special interest to them, such as electric keyboards, guitars, or piano music. A career in music retail will be enhanced by a more advanced study of business, such as a music business degree.

### Retail Sales

Those involved in retail sales must have excellent customer service skills, a pleasing and professional phone manner, and the ability to work well when interrupted. They must be a punctual and dependable worker and reliable when dealing with cash. A thorough understanding of the store's inventory is essential and may require specialized knowledge in a given area such as vocal music, guitars, DVDs, sound equipment, piano music, or keyboards. Computer skills are often an asset.

Managers perform the day-to-day tasks of running a successful retail music business. The manager supervises and trains employees, keeps track of inventory, orders music and supplies as needed, oversees all budget and payroll issues, and supervises store marketing strategies.

Those interested in this area would do well to study both business and music, perhaps with a degree in music business.

# Resources

*Coalition of Entertainment Retail Trade Associations*

www.erlam.org

*NAMM – The International Music Products Association*

www.namm.org

*National Association of Recording Merchandisers*

www.narm.com

*National Association of School Music Dealers*

www.nasmd.com

*Retail Print Music Dealers Association*

www.printmusic.org

## Music Publishing

There are a number of companies devoted to the publishing of music-related materials such as compositions, music related texts, recordings, videos/DVDs, and music software. Publishers work to produce, finance, print, and market materials. They seek materials worth publishing, and make decisions concerning which products will be published by their company. The publisher oversees all work involving the publicity, marketing, circulation, graphic arts, distribution, and editorial needs of its products. Publishing is an attractive but highly competitive field. The various positions within the music publishing field (or within a specific music publishing company) require workers to be well rounded, understand music (possess musical skills: proficiency on an instrument, read music, understand music theory, etc.), understand copyright laws, and even possess skills in business and marketing. The publishing company as a whole must develop the ability to network within the industry, so workers in many areas must have strong communication skills. Degrees in music, journalism, public relations, business, or music business are all options.

### Editor

Editors work for a publishing company, reviewing music and often making decisions on what will or will not be published. Once a composition or book has been accepted, editing is necessary before the work is ready for publication. The editor works with the author or composer to review, rewrite, proofread, and edit material as needed. They may also oversee the production of the work as it is being published, including any art to be included, the page design, and the overall appearance of the completed product. Editors must be self-motivated and have strong writing skills, a thorough understanding of the area of music in which they work, the ability to multitask (often working on a number of projects at once), and the ability to work under a deadline. Many editors must also possess transcribing and arranging skills. There is no specific required degree, and many editors come to the profession with a variety of life experiences and educational backgrounds. Possible degrees include music, journalism, communications, English, and music business.

## Engraver

Engravers prepare music scores or text for publication. When a musical score is being prepared, the engraver uses a notation software program such as Finale® or Sibelius. The engraver is responsible for developing a pleasing, accurate, and professional looking book or score. This job has many of the same duties and requirements as a musical copyist. (See Chapter 47.) Some engravers also work with text and graphics, developing the style and layout for products such as music instructional books. Proficiency with software such as QuarkXpress® and Adobe® InDesign® is required for these additional engraving tasks.

## Business Affairs

Those employed in business affairs negotiate contracts and need legal expertise. Some positions may require a law degree, while others require a business degree. People in this area of music publishing often work with artists, authors, and even other publishers in matters of music licensing and contracts/agreements involving the payment of fees and royalties to creators of compositions, instructional or reference books, and videos/DVDs.

### LICENSING

The rights to music are bought and sold every day. Hit tunes, such as those used in radio or television advertisements, restaurants, videos, elevators, restrooms, and telephone messages, are licensed material, and as such, permission to play or print and sell them must be purchased. Copyrights protect music from any unlawful reproduction including unapproved recordings, performances, or revisions. The lyrics to songs are also protected, as is the music itself and the recordings of the music. The business affairs department reviews any requests to use licensed material, granting or denying permission, issuing contracts, and often charging fees for the permission. (For some purposes, a license may be obtained to perform music through an agency such as BMI or ASCAP.) In turn, this department may also seek out and make requests to license material from artists or other publishers.

Any print-related usage such as photocopying, arranging or adapting, and reprinting of lyrics or music requires the permission of the publisher. All published images and text from books and other media are protected by copyright laws, as are programs and other material available throughout an Internet site.

Those working in a business affairs department grant permission for the reproduction of the company's copyrighted material, often charging a fee when granting permission. On the flip side, they might also seek permission to reproduce copyrighted material from another entity and pay any fee associated with such permission.

In order to work successfully in a licensing department, a strong understanding of copyright law is required, as well as familiarity with licensing contracts and agreements, and familiarity with all legal issues concerning licensing. Degrees might include business, music, or law.

### ROYALTIES

Employees dealing with royalties ensure that song or book royalties are paid for all material in use anywhere in the world. Any song or book that is published by a company will generate royalties that need to be carefully and accurately dispersed to authors, composers, and other publishers.

## Information Technology

Those working in the information technology (IT) department of a publishing company create, maintain, and update websites; design and maintain customer databases, and troubleshoot all IT-related issues within the company.

In the area of web design, workers need to have excellent technology skills, be open to new and developing technologies, understand graphic arts, be able to problem solve, and be flexible when fulfilling the demands of the company. No specific degree is required, but those interested in web design and maintenance could have degrees in information technology, computer science, graphic arts, or information science.

Those working with database design and management must identify the database needs of the company, and be able to set up, test, manage, and modify the database. They may also be responsible for designing a system for database security. In working with a database, they must have excellent technology skills, an understanding of how to organize data, and the ability to troubleshoot. Employees in IT often have degrees in information technology, computer science, information science, management information systems, or even a master's degree in business administration.

## Transcriber

Transcribers listen to a recording of music and transcribe what they hear to the written page. Transcribers must be able to accurately create a written score of all that is heard. In many cases, the transcriber must also serve as arranger, taking a song recorded by a full band and transcribing and arranging all the parts of the band into one piano score/arrangement. Doing this requires that the person be a capable pianist, able to create a playable piano part at appropriate difficulty levels. Perfect pitch is not required, but is a strong asset. Strong aural skills and an understanding of theory are essential tools for successful transcribing. Comfort with notation software such as Finale® or Sibleius is necessary. Some computer programs assist with transcriptions by slowing down a recording of music without changing the pitch. Transcription software may also organize music into easily accessed units or loops for repeated playback of sections of material. No specific degree is required, but skills such as the ability to hear music accurately, work independently, and meet deadlines are crucial.

## Advertising and Marketing

Advertising and marketing staff members are responsible for marketing any materials the company publishes. They also are charged with identifying markets for the company's products and designing promotional materials to help sell the company's products.

# Resources

*Music Publishers' Association*

    www.mpa.org

*National Music Publishers Association*

    www.nmpa.org

## Music Technology/Sound Technician

Music technology is a growing field. University classes in this area include software applications, sequencing, and electronic composition. Courses cover creative sound production and learning to record and master professional-sounding recordings. Possible jobs in music technology are too numerous to mention, but include recording engineer, digital re-mastering editor, live sound engineer, web audio producer, studio technician, film audio engineer, record company staff, music software developer, and teacher of music technology. Sound technicians work in venues such as music studios, concert halls, university music departments, theaters, and recording studios. There are a growing number of degrees in music technology and music business.

## Resource

*Recording Industry Association of America*

www.riaa.com

## Arts Administration

A number of opportunities in arts administration exist, including serving as the director of a community school of the arts, working for local or state art's councils, orchestra management, managing an opera company, grants administration for foundations for the arts, and administrator for after-school arts programs. An arts administration position usually comes to those with a strong background in the arts and years of experience in arts-related jobs. An arts administrator must have good speaking and writing skills and the ability to work well with others. An effective administrator usually displays strong organizational skills, is able to juggle a multitude of responsibilities, has a vision for her agency, and is able to market that vision to clients, donors, and the media.

Examples of arts administration related courses include arts management, board development, program development, fundraising for the arts, and financial management. There are an increasing number of degrees offered in arts administration, especially at the master's degree level.

## Resource

*Association of Arts Administration Educators*

www.artsadministration.org

The *Association of Arts Administration Educators* (AAAE) website lists a number of universities offering undergraduate and graduate degrees in Arts Administration.

**PART XI**

# PART XII

## THE BROADER PICTURE

Outside sources of funding may be necessary in order to expand the arts opportunities within a given community. Many teachers may never have sought additional funding for a music program, feeling that this was beyond their area of expertise. This section presents ways to seek available funding for studio or community music programs.

Part XII also discusses the importance of serving our students, studios, and communities by acting as advocates for the arts. When we become dedicated arts advocates, we strengthen the musical environment of our communities while helping the arts to flourish.

Chapter 49

# ARTS FUNDING

---

The first grant application I ever wrote was for $2000 from a small organization with very specific requirements for the grant. Because the grant was available only to this organization's limited membership, I knew I had a much better chance of receiving those funds than I would have had I applied to a major foundation. The application process itself was quite simple, and when I received the funds I was ecstatic.

I have since learned that a summer camp or chamber music festival may require more funding than tuition alone can secure. Many teachers are unaware of the fact that they can apply for outside sources of funding for such programs. Just like starting composition even though we are not composers, or teaching a camp on world music when we are not musicologists, we can each learn how to apply for outside sources of funding.

Some sources are easier than others for a first attempt at outside funding. For example, if a town has a percentage of taxes that must go to the arts, there may be a very simple process of application. The potential for success is far greater if we ask our town's Visitor's Bureau for funds than if we send a request to General Motors. The larger the grant, the stiffer the competition, and usually the more meticulous and time consuming is the application process. I have written and received many small to mid-size grants, but like Babe Ruth, I have had more strikeouts than home runs.

In some cases, individuals are eligible for funding, but many times funds are available only to non-profit organizations with a 501c3 status. This does not mean that those sources of funding are not available to independent music teachers, but rather that individuals must partner with a non-profit organization when applying for such funds. There are a number of potential avenues to pursue when considering arts funding.

## Start at Home

Exploring community funding when financing a new program may uncover a number of local resources:

- City dollars designated to enhance the cultural life of the community

- Percentage of city tax money that is required to be spent on arts programs

- Service clubs such as the Elks or the Masons

- Local gaming or lottery funds

- Donations from a place of worship

- In-kind (non-cash) donations of time, money, and materials from members of the community

- Donations of food for arts-related activities (camp, open-house, reception) from supermarkets

- Local businesses

- A city Visitor's Bureau

- The city Chamber of Commerce

- City commissioners

- County resources

- A city arts group or local arts agency that allocates funding (A local arts council is an excellent group for an initial funding request.)

- A state arts council

- National music organizations (Many offer grants to individual teachers as well as to local organizations affiliated with the national. If the grant is intended for a local organization, teachers seeking funds can work together to develop the program and apply for the funds.)

- Private donors (Private donors often hear of a good idea and wish to contribute; sometimes donations come unsolicited when a new idea is well-marketed and piques the interest of someone wishing to donate to the arts.)

## Fundraising Events

Events such as a spaghetti supper, auctions, and benefit concerts are activities that can be used to raise funds for a special program or event. Usually these are developed more by groups (such as high school music boosters) than individuals. They can be labor-intensive, but when successful, they can be repeated each year.

## Direct Requests

Using a phone-a-thon or direct mailings offers another avenue for fundraising. Phone-a-thons require a great deal of time, as does developing a list of potential donors. Some arts agencies may already have such a list and be willing to partner on an arts event. Direct mailings are best done using bulk mailing or e-mail. Actively seeking private donations can be lengthy and requires patience.

## Larger Grants, Foundations, and Corporations

There is a great deal of money out there, waiting to be given away to those who are persistent. Grant writing can be time consuming, and the forms can be simple or complex, depending on the agency. Some grants are available only in specific cities or states because many corporations and foundations will give only in the area where they are centered. Living near a city with many corporate home offices (or even just one arts-minded philanthropic foundation) is advantageous for those seeking funding, whereas living in a mostly rural state offers limited opportunities for corporate or foundation funding.

Once it has been determined that a certain corporation or foundation offers funds in a given state, the next thing to verify is that the funds are available in the correct part of the state, and not just one city 400 miles away. Funds must also be available for the type of activity that is being organized.

**PART XII**

Most local libraries contain resources to help with grant research, as does the Internet. Before writing any grant, the applicant must first be sure that she, or her organization, is indeed eligible.

- What locations are eligible for this grant program?

- Does the applicant's program fit this particular type of grant? (Grants can sometimes have very specific requirements, such as arts programming only for after-school programs.)

- Does the applicant fit the criteria for this grant? (Is it necessary to be a non-profit, 501c3 organization to be eligible?)

- If non-profit status is required, what local arts agencies with non-profit status could serve as partners for this grant?

In *Great Ideas Aren't Enough: Fundraising tips*, non-profit consultant Regina Podhorin of The Leadership Group offers the following advice:

> Often in the world of nonprofit fundraising we hear the lament about the great idea that didn't get funding. Regardless of the "worthy" cause, there are often disappointments when looking for financial support. Most of these disappointments have to do with the following:
>
> - Asking the wrong group/person (mistargeting)
>
> - Asking in the wrong way (failing to follow the funder's guidelines)
>
> - Having an inadequate/incomplete description of your "product" (marketing)
>
> Whether you're looking for support for an art show, musical performance, or theater event, private and public funders will be looking for more than a good idea. They will be looking to be convinced that your good idea has social merit (what difference will it make, for whom?), that you have the skills and expertise to pull it off and that they will get a positive response (press, reputation) as a result of the work.

Podhorin, Regina. "Great Ideas Aren't Enough: Fundraising tips." *Journal of the Fellowship of Quakers in the Arts*, Issue 9 (Spring 1998).

It is imperative that applications are made only when they fit the criteria of the grant. If, for example, an application was made for funds available for an after-school music program, but the grant can be given only to organizations serving Hispanic students when the applicant's organization has none, applying for the grant would have been a waste of time.

All proposals must be sent to the correct person, at the correct address, and by the correct deadline; it is important not to overlook this basic information.

# Application Materials

When seeking funds from an outside source, some basic materials will be required:

- A completed application form and any additional written materials requested

- A résumé of the person coordinating the program or administering the funds

- Supporting materials or documentation of past efforts

- A program budget

## Application forms

Having reviewed grant applications for a state arts agency, I know that at times applicants stray from the questions that are asked, thus not providing the information necessary for approval. I have learned that in order to write a successful grant, I must answer every question as it has been asked on the application form. If the question is to define the timeline of the program, I give a detailed timeline. If I am asked to describe the goals of the program, I describe the exact goals. If a budget is requested (and it always is), I give a detailed budget. Rather than describe my program the way I feel is best, I present my program the best way I can within the framework of the questions asked. The funding agency asks their particular questions for a reason, so it is wise to offer answers within the context they seek.

## Additional written material

Every grant is different, and a variety of materials may be required, especially if the grant is sought in partnership with a non-profit organization:

- An applicant profile

- The answers to any narrative questions that are asked, such as, "Describe the impact this program will have on your community."

- A list of board members (for non-profit organizations)

- The organization's most recent financial statement

## Résumé

A résumé of the person responsible for the program and for the administration of any grant funds must, in most cases, accompany the grant application. Since a personal résumé is almost always requested, applicants should keep their résumé updated at all times.

## Supporting materials or documentation of past efforts

If the grant asks for additional supporting materials, it is wise to develop an attractive collection of past newspaper articles, studio photographs, letters from students or parents testifying to the value of the program, or any other documentation of community support for the program. Displaying these materials in an attractive binder or notebook and including a CD or DVD of performances strengthens the application by giving visual and aural documentation of the value of the program for which the funds are requested.

PART XII

365

## Budget

Most agencies have their own budget form that must be completed. The following is one example of how a completed budget form (with fictional figures) for a grant or funding proposal might look:

### PROPOSED BUDGET

| INCOME | PREVIOUS YEAR BUDGET | CURRENT YEAR BUDGET |
|---|---|---|
| Admissions | 500 | 600 |
| Corporate Support | 0 | 0 |
| Foundation Support | 0 | 0 |
| Other Private Support | 250 | 250 |
| Government Support | 0 | 0 |
| Applicant Cash-on-hand | 200 | 300 |
| Other Revenue | 0 | 0 |
| In-Kind Contributions (space) | 500 | 500 |
| Grant Amount Requested | 1000 | 1100 |
| **Total Operating Income:** | **$2450.00** | **$2750.00** |

| EXPENSES | PREVIOUS YEAR BUDGET | CURRENT YEAR BUDGET |
|---|---|---|
| Personnel | 1000 | 1200 |
| Outside Professional Services | 300 | 350 |
| Travel | 100 | 150 |
| Marketing | 100 | 100 |
| Supplies | 300 | 350 |
| Remaining Operating Expenses | 0 | 0 |
| Equipment/Capital Expenditures | 150 | 100 |
| Space Rental (in-kind) | 500 | 500 |
| **Total Operating Expenses:** | **$2450.00** | **$2750.00** |

If the program is new, the "previous year budget" column is left blank and the application must indicate that the program is in its first year. In cases where a specific form does not need to be completed, a budget still needs to be sent, possibly similar to the outline presented in Chapter 39 on music camps. When submitting a budget, it is important to remember that the income and expense totals must match. The amount submitted must be the most accurate estimate of costs and income, although the estimate may differ from the final budget once the project is concluded. Such variances are to be expected, but should not be excessive.

# Resources

Poderis, Tony. *It's a Great Day to Fund-Raise!* Cleveland: FundAmerica Press, 1996.

This book gives fundraising tips to non-profit organizations, volunteers, trustees, consultants, and anyone else working on a fundraising campaign. Poderis offers practical suggestions for success, based on over 30 years of experience as a fundraising development professional. Basic facts of fundraising, such as "Organizations are not entitled to support—they must earn it" are followed by chapters on specific types of fundraising, developing a plan, preparation for fundraising, and assessing outcomes after a fundraising campaign. Anyone interested in fundraising will benefit from Poderis's sensible approach.

**WEBSITES**

*The Foundation Center*

http://foundationcenter.org/

*Foundations.org*

www.foundations.org/

*Grant Proposal.com*

www.grantproposal.com/

*Lone Eagle Consulting – Grant Writing Tips*

www.lone-eagles.com

– Select "Grant Writing Assistance."

*Search "Nonprofit Resources Catalog" for further Internet sites*

# Chapter 50

# ARTS ADVOCACY

---

Through my experience as a music educator, I have grown to realize that my job is not only to teach those interested in music; I also feel I have an obligation to strengthen the arts in my community. This devotion to a healthy arts community reflects my belief in the important role the arts plays in all of our lives. I feel that devotion as I teach my students, when I start new programs within my community, as I work on behalf of the arts in my state, and whenever I give presentations on the national level. All of these activities are a reflection of my belief in the value of what we, as piano teachers, do for our society.

## What is Arts Advocacy?

In the strictest sense, being an advocate means "publicly supporting or defending a cause." Arts advocates educate others about the essential role the arts play in a thriving community and a healthy society. In a broader sense, being an advocate means not just speaking on behalf of the arts, but actively working to keep the arts alive in one's community. It means fostering public support for arts programs, developing new arts opportunities, and making a personal contribution to the arts environment within a community.

Without strong advocates for the arts, symphony orchestras, opera companies, and chamber groups will suffer from diminishing participation, smaller audiences, and decreased funding. Mike Greenberg's article "Enjoying this music takes time" from the *San Antonio Express-News* discusses the value of symphony orchestras and classical music. The article states that listening to classical music requires a certain amount of mental effort. It goes on to recognize the fact that since popular music is easier to listen to, many orchestras are choosing lighter programming to stay alive. In defense of the traditional classical repertoire for orchestras, Greenberg states, "A hardcore classical work lasts longer than a pop song for the same reason that a novel takes longer to read than a Post-it note."

Isn't that it in a nutshell? As promoters of classical music, we are advocating for music that is more meaningful than a Post-it® note. This does not mean that we are unreceptive to popular music, only that we see the value of music that is significant, timeless, and enduring.

What exactly can we, as activists, do to preserve the timeless and enduring qualities of the arts? We can:

- Speak within our community on the value of the arts
- Lobby legislators and school boards on behalf of the arts
- Be proactive
- Start new arts programs in our studios and within our community
- Collaborate with other arts activists
- Fundraise for existing arts programs

- Volunteer

- Vote on arts-related issues and funding

- Support other arts agencies

- Be visible and be heard

In order to be an advocate for the arts, it is helpful to think of ourselves as part of a larger, proactive group. Collaborating with others provides a stronger base of power. When we function as true advocates for the arts, we work with other community members, the school board, local politicians, and other arts activists. Although there is much to be said for "the power of one," the value of working with other music teachers to offer a collective voice cannot be overstated. Working together we have more power to enact change. The story in Chapter 15 about the Fairfax County Commissioners is a good example of that collective power.

When it comes to decisions about the arts, our individual and collective voice needs to be part of the decision-making process. For example, how many piano teachers are present when the school board makes a decision concerning music in the schools? In local politics, are music teachers aware of votes made by city commissioners that affect the arts? We need to be at those meetings. The supportmusic.com website has a quote from Dr. Dennis R. Morrow that states, "The decision belongs to those who show up." How simple, and yet how true!

LaMoine MacLaughlin, director of the Northern Lakes Center for the Arts, is the author of a pamphlet entitled *Arts Advocacy 101: A Workbook and Inventory of 101 Arts Advocacy Considerations*. MacLaughlin posses 101 questions of the arts advocate, and the following summarizes a few:

- Who in your community is publicly recognized as the strongest (vocally, financially, etc.) advocate/champion in support of the arts?

- What member of your city council is the strongest (vocally, financially, etc.) advocate/champion in support of the arts?

- Has your mayor been actively involved (as a participant, student, audience member, etc.) in the arts during this past year?

- What has been [your public school board's] overall voting record on arts/educational priority issues? How much arts funding did it approve this past year?

- What member of your public school board is the strongest (vocally, financially, etc.) advocate/champion in support of the arts?

- How well do your community civic organizations (Chamber of Commerce, Visitor's Bureau, Fraternal Organizations, etc.) understand and support... arts/educational priority issues?

- How well do your state assembly representatives understand and support arts/educational priority issues?

- How did your congressman and senators vote on arts/educational priority issues this past year?

PART XII

If we are concerned that defending the arts is not as important to our city commissioners or school boards as other issues such as juvenile crime or budget concerns, we have powerful data to help place the arts in a position of strength.

- A strong grounding in the arts is known to reduce juvenile crime.

- A strong arts community can contribute more to a city's financial health than sports events!

- The arts help make a city or town appealing to outside businesses and professionals who are looking for a high quality of life when choosing a community for relocation.

When we advocate for the arts, we advocate for far more—the health of our youth and of our community.

A recent trip to a different state opened my eyes to two vastly different approaches to the arts in neighboring communities. I gave a series of presentations to a group of music teachers from two cities that were about a 45-minute drive apart. Since one of the presentations was to be on arts advocacy, I first did some research on the arts climate in each community.

City A's website showed precious few links to any arts activities. When I called a city office to try to learn more, I was told that the school board was cutting arts classes, the new mayor was not as actively involved with the strategic plan (which included the arts) as the previous mayor, and people actually spoke of City A as a place where the arts was not a priority. In speaking with one city employee in City A, I mentioned the fact that I had learned of the local jazz festival and symphony orchestra, which should both be on an arts link on the city web page. I mentioned that this might attract professional people such as doctors to their city. The response was, "The doctors just move to City B." City A, I might add, was the state capitol.

The web page for City B immediately reflected a strong arts presence. The Office of Cultural Affairs was highlighted as a huge asset to the community, and the calendar of arts events was full of activities. Although I understand that a web page is just a form of advertisement, it does reflect the priorities within a community. City B showed pride in their arts activities, and when I spoke to members of the arts community, their conversations reflected that sense of strength and pride. Where would each of our cities fall? How would we describe the arts in our own community? If we were to go to our own city's web page, would the arts be visible? If not, we could be the intelligent and persistent voice that insists on a change.

Two particularly helpful items can be used for arts advocacy purposes. The brochure *Keep Music Education Strong* and the action kit *Support Music Community Action* come as true gifts. Someone has done a great deal of work putting the information into an accessible format and presenting it for public use. The first time I saw these materials, I was overwhelmed by what was being offered, and I highly recommend making use of these materials in any advocacy endeavor.

## Advocacy in the Studio

A strong opportunity to act as an advocate for the arts starts right in our own studios. When we help students to love Beethoven, to want to hear an opera, or to play with thoughtful musicality, we are being an advocate for the arts. When we help them to be curious learners, and open to new musical ideas, we serve as advocates for the arts. As advocates, we teach our students the beauty of music—knowledge that goes far beyond correct fingerings and carefully learned notes. We show our students that understanding music in the deeper sense requires discipline, hard work, and creativity, and that it will be well worth the journey. Perhaps the biggest contribution to the arts we make is developing lifelong lovers of music who, as adults, will attend symphony orchestra concerts, make music a part of their family, and see the arts as a critical part of their community.

Studio activities that have the potential to enhance arts awareness include:

- Employing a comprehensive approach to teaching that incorporates theory, history, improvisation, jazz, composition, etc.

- Involving students in chamber music

- Sponsoring masterclasses

- Hiring guest speakers to come to the studio

- Offering themed semesters and themed recitals

- Focusing on world music

## Developing Programs Outside the Studio

Regardless of the size or type of community in which we live, the quality of life will be improved by a healthy arts presence. Indeed, there is no such thing as a dying community where the arts are strong. The arts are just as important to smaller cities and rural areas as they are in major metropolitan areas. Someone living in a small community can be that one person who creates a fine arts program where there had previously been none, while those living in a large community can expand available artistic resources to make them more accessible or meaningful.

How could we develop a new arts program in our community? The first thing required is an idea, or more nobly stated, a vision. Any number of programs, both small and large, might be appealing:

- A new festival (such as a chamber music festival, a Bach festival, or a multi-cultural festival)

- A children's choir

- A handbell choir

- An Arts Little League

- A Renaissance Festival

- A Monster Concert

- A Play-a-Thon

PART XII

- One of the music camps mentioned in Chapter 39

- A community school of the arts (Churches or private schools sometimes have space that can be used after school, or perhaps there is a building that could be rented. Maybe there is a sponsor who would be willing to fund the start-up costs, or the school could affiliate with a local university. If we find other like-minded individuals, we can work together to create the school.)

Any new program will be an asset to our community, and we will have made a significant contribution to the arts.

## Partnerships

If we have an idea for a new program, we can work with other music teachers to develop our dream. Collaboration is often the key to success, and we can consider partnering with any number of groups within the community, from schools, to places of worship, to various businesses or organizations. For more information on partnerships, see Chapter 19 under "Networking and Partnerships."

## A Personal Story of Advocacy

My most meaningful experience as an advocate for the arts started when I first moved to North Dakota and was hired by Valley City State University (VCSU) to be a faculty member in their music department. I was asked to develop a piano preparatory department to help offset the shortage of piano teachers in the community. I started the VCSU Preparatory Department in 1994, initially with myself, one other piano instructor, and 20 students. Soon the program was expanded to include guitar lessons, an early childhood music class, and theory classes.

In the second year, enrollment was up to 40 students, but I felt somewhat constrained by the limits of my small town. Fortunately, I discovered the National Guild of Community Schools of the Arts, and decided to attend their national conference. It was indeed an inspiring and educational event. There were representatives from a variety of community schools—some large schools from major cities, and some small ones in rural communities. Some were affiliated with universities (divisional schools), and some were completely independent community schools.

I must admit, I found some of the conference to be depressing. A speaker would talk about her school's junior orchestra, senior orchestra, honors orchestra, Latino band, and African-American band. In contrast, at that particular time there were no string players at all in my small town in North Dakota; if a student wanted to study strings she had to go to Fargo, a roundtrip of 120 miles. Yet these large community schools had three student orchestras! They talked about their enrollment of 700 students, and I was proud of our 40! They discussed their latest million dollar grant or their $2.5 million a year operating budget. My budget was probably what they spent for postage, and I would never have that kind of enrollment; our town was just too small.

Seeking directors from rural community schools, I met a woman from a small community in Utah. Feeling a sense of relief, I told her how these big schools with their string programs and orchestras were depressing me. She said, "Oh, we have a string program and an orchestra." I asked her how this was so; did she have string players living in this small town who were qualified to teach? She replied "Oh no, I fly them in." "How can you afford to fly them in?" I asked. "I can't afford to fly them in; I went to the airlines and they donated the tickets. The string teachers fly in from California twice a month."

That was when my attitude changed. That was when I decided to stop feeling frustrated because I lived in a small town with limited resources. And that is also when I decided to turn our prep department into a community school of the arts. The VCSU Community School of the Arts was approved by the North Dakota State Board of Higher Education in 1996 and fully certified by the National Guild of Community Schools of the Arts in 1999. The Community School is thriving today, with a variety of arts-related programs:

- Private lessons on piano, organ, guitar, voice, woodwind, brass, string, and percussion instruments

- An annual chamber music festival

- A women's choir

- A children's choir

- A community orchestra

- Visual art classes such as painting, drawing, and ceramics

- A literary magazine showcasing the creative writings of high school students

## Rita Simo

Rita Simo's life tells an inspiring story of advocacy. In 1975, Simo decided to start a tuition-free music school in Chicago with just $625 in donations. In 1995 the school moved to an impressive $2.5 million building, funded in part by a capital grant as well as by many donations.

There are no auditions or financial reports required of parents of students wishing to enroll in The People's Music School. The school's students come from the Latino, Asian, African-American, Caucasian, and Native American neighborhoods surrounding the school. Those who are accepted sign a contract and pay a small registration fee. Each family contributes two hours of volunteer work per month such as clerical work, cleaning, or contributions to the monthly bake sale. They must also participate in one major fundraising event each semester. The students get a top-notch education as the faculty is drawn from professionals in the Chicago area, who play in orchestras and teach in nearby colleges.

That is what I consider a truly wonderful story. Although Simo retired in 2001, the school continues to be successfully run by a new director. The success of the school is due in part to Simo's foresight and her desire to go after her dream. It is also due to her ability to get people involved in her vision. The students have a certain amount of ownership in the school; donations, fundraising efforts, and contributions are made by all and are important to all. Simo is an example of one person making a difference. She has made a significant contribution to her community, to her students, and to the arts.

**PART XII**

## The Daily Activities of an Advocate

I don't believe I am being overly dramatic when I say that if we do not work as advocates, the arts as we know them will become as obsolete as the krummhorn. The music lovers and audiences of the past will be glued to their computer screens or televisions. In order to act as an advocate of the arts on a daily basis we can:

- Encourage students and their families to attend symphony orchestra concerts and go to the opera

- Take our students to museums

- Encourage students to watch public television shows on the arts

- Promote attendance at community arts events—from lectures, to masterclasses, to concerts

- Set a good example by going to these same events. If we are not visible at arts events in our community, we can be sure that others notice, and that it makes a statement about our commitment to the arts

- Give extra credit to students who attend arts events

Arranging for our students to perform in malls, museums, libraries, places of worship, senior citizen centers, or retirement communities shows them from an early age that they can contribute to the cultural life of their community. They can make a difference—what they have learned is valued.

Supporting the music programs in our school system is also of vital importance to the health of music in our community. Too many school systems are cutting funding for music, just when the proof is growing of the benefits of music study to a child's development, social skills, problem-solving skills, creative thinking, and discipline. When we work with music teachers, parents, and school boards (public and private schools), we develop a collective voice that can be heard far better than one voice alone.

The arts are a vital sign of the health and diversity within a community. They reflect our sense of that which is greater and nobler than ourselves. They reflect history, culture, and creativity. We can each ask:

- What better way to contribute to the health and energy of a community than through the arts?

- How better to stem the creeping alienation of life in front of a television or computer?

- How better to teach children about beauty, discipline, and the rewards of hard work?

- How better to provide entertainment and enrichment to a community?

- What better way is there to expose students to genius and that which is truly great?

# Resources

*Community Outreach and Education for the Arts Handbook.* Cincinnati: Music Teachers National Association, 1997.

This brief booklet offers valuable information for those wishing to be involved as arts advocates. Practical suggestions are given for being involved with arts-related votes (on local, state, and national levels), being informed on arts-related issues, serving on boards, and being involved with arts phone or letter campaigns. For those who want to do more for the arts, this book offers a solid starting point for getting involved. The booklet can be purchased by going to mtna.org/HLtext.

Cuesto, Carlos, Dana Gillespie and Padraic Lillis. *Bright Stars: Charting the Impact of the Arts in Rural Minnesota.* Minneapolis: The McKnight Foundation, 2005.

For anyone curious about the impact of the arts in a community, or the feasibility of a small group making a big difference, this short book provides gratifying stories that affirm the value of the arts. The book serves as a summary of the McKnight Foundation's study on the impact the arts had on eight Minnesota towns with populations under 13,000. As stated in the foreword, "One of the resounding themes in this report is the close connection between the arts—in a variety of forms—and community vitality. An increase in arts activity can draw new residents and businesses, boost civic participation, develop new social gathering places, and build bridges across ethnic and class divides—all of which strengthen communities. The arts can profoundly affect the ability of a town not only to survive over time but to thrive." The book, and other helpful advocacy materials, can be downloaded by going to www.mcknight.org and typing "Bright Stars" into the Search box.

Greenberg, Mike. **"Enjoying this music takes time."** *The San Antonio Express-News,* August 28, 2005.

### Keep Music Education Strong

NAMM, a not-for-profit trade association representing the international music products industry, published the *Keep America Strong* brochure, available in both English and Spanish. The sheet includes four pages of powerful quotes and statistics in support of music, such as "Students who participate in school band or orchestra have the lowest levels of current and lifelong use of alcohol, tobacco, and illicit drugs among any group in our society." The sheet can be downloaded from www.supportmusic.com/SMBrochure_eng.pdf.

MacLaughlin, LaMoine. *Arts Advocacy 101: A Workbook and Inventory of 101 Arts Advocacy Considerations,* Amery: LaMoine MacLauglin, 2001.

www.nationalguild.org

- Select "Make Your Case/Advocacy" from the top menu
- Select "Arts Advocacy 101: A Workbook and Inventory of 101 Arts Advocacy Considerations" from the menu on the right side of the page.

### SupportMusic Community Action Kit

An excellent resource published by NAMM, the kit is an excellent resource for those wishing to become more involved with advocacy. The kit includes sample correspondence, sample news releases, useful summaries of important scientific research, and public service announcements for non-broadcast use in meetings and presentations. The kit's printed manual contains tips on organizing music advocates, working with the media and lobbying local school boards, plus a wealth of support material designed for easy reproduction. A fact-filled brochure, entitled "Why Learn to Play Music?" and eye-catching printable posters feature children of all ages and abilities learning to play musical instruments.

To obtain a free copy of the *SupportMusic Community Action Kit,* download files from www.supportmusic.com.

**PART XII**

# Resources (cont.)

**WEBSITES**

*American Music Conference*
www.amc-music.com

*Americans for the Arts*
www.artsusa.org

*Artslynx*
www.artslynx.org

*ArtsMarketing*
www.artsmarketing.org

*The McKnight Foundation: Bright Stars*
www.mcknight.org
– Type "Bright Starts" into the search box

*Music Friends*
www.musicfriends.org

*National Association for Music Education (MENC)*
www.menc.org
– Select "Resources."
– Select "Advocacy and Public Policy" from left menu.

*Support Music*
www.supportmusic.com

# Appendix A: Studio Documents

## USE OF APPENDIX A

The documents in this section are offered to serve as examples of what might be included in a studio, not what should be included. It is hoped that each document will be viewed with a critical eye for what will or will not work in any given studio.

At times, I have included far more than I would use in my own studio, or perhaps worded an area more sternly than I would in my own studio. This is offered solely to show what could be presented; each teacher can then modify the verbiage to suit her own needs.

I have shown one way to compose each document when there are multiple possibilities. Please use what is offered in Appendix A as a starting point for developing your own personalized studio documents.

## THE UNIQUE PIANO STUDIO

**KAREN TURNER**
555 Central Avenue
City, ID 54321
Phone: 555-555-4321

uniquepianostudio@somewhere.net

# CONTENTS

# KAREN TURNER

555 Central Avenue • City, ID 54321 • Phone: 555-555-4321
uniquepianostudio@somewhere.net

## PROFILE

- Self-motivated, well-organized, high-energy approach to music education
- Skilled at establishing creative curriculum and innovative programs
- Well-developed awareness and understanding of individual learning styles
- Highly effective communicator
- Expert motivational skills; positive and flexible

## EDUCATION

| | |
|---|---|
| 1994 | Bachelor of Music in Piano Performance |
| | Idaho State University |
| | **Continuing Education:** |
| 1999–present | Piano study with Dr. David Anderson, Northern Center for Music |
| 2003 | Applications of Music Technology, Northern Community College |
| 2002 | TI:ME–Basic Skills in Music Technology |
| 1999 | Creative Keyboards, Northern Center for Music |

## PROFESSIONAL EXPERIENCE

1995–Present    Founder and Director of **The Unique Piano Studio**

- Design comprehensive curriculum, including music theory, music history, repertoire, sight-playing, chamber music, and composition
- Coordinate scheduling of multiple studio activities, including lessons, computer lab, performance workshops, recitals, and summer camps
- Prepare extensive calendar of events
- Host three uniquely themed recitals a year; provide students with opportunity to participate in festivals, competitions, community performances, and state theory exams
- Interview prospective students and families
- Establish effective studio policies and author professional studio documents
- Comply with state/local business and zoning regulations
- Determine and implement marketing strategies; prepare press releases for all studio activities
- Process billings, registrations, and correspondence
- Maintain financial and tax records;  manage yearly budget

1999–Present    Initiate and direct **The Unique Studio Summer Camps**
(Camps to date: Baroque Dance Music, Jazz Styles, Beethoven the Revolutionary, The Romantic Era, Rhythm Skills, Eccentric Ensembles)

## HONORS

| | |
|---|---|
| 2005 | Teacher of the Year, Idaho Music Teachers Association |
| 2004 | Contribution to the Community Award, City Chamber of Commerce |

page 1

380

# KAREN TURNER

## PROFESSIONAL ACTIVITIES

### Performances

| | |
|---|---|
| 2006 | Duo Piano Recital, City Recital Series |
| 2004 | Piano Trio Recital, Our Savior's Church |

### Presentations

City Music Teachers Association

| | |
|---|---|
| 2008 | Favorite Piano Repertoire – Panel Member |
| 2005 | Chamber Music for Elementary Students |

### Student Activities

1995–Present   Idaho Federation of Music Clubs, Junior Festival
          100% superior and excellent ratings
         Idaho Music Teachers Association, State Theory Exams
          Students score in upper 10% annually
         Idaho Composition Competitions
          3rd place winner, Elementary Division, 2006
          1st place winner, Senior Division, 2004
         National Guild of Piano Teachers, annual auditions
          100% student participation

## PROFESSIONAL AFFILIATIONS

1995–Present   Music Teachers National Association
         Idaho Music Teachers Association
         Idaho State Competitions Coordinator, 2006–2008
         City Music Teachers Association

1995–Present   National Federation of Music Clubs
         Idaho Federation of Music Clubs
         Local Festival Chair, 2004–present

1995–Present   National Guild of Piano Teachers

### Certifications

2000–Present   Nationally Certified Teacher of Music, Music Teachers National Association

## SERVICE TO COMMUNITY

| | |
|---|---|
| 2000–Present | Present annual programs to Rotary Club and Optimists Club |
| 1999–Present | Member of Handbell Choir, Our Savior's Church |

## TECHNOLOGY

Technology applications used regularly in teaching and administrative duties:
      Microsoft® Word, PowerPoint®, Excel®, Finale®, e-mail, and the Internet.
Programs used in computer lab: Music Ace, Music Ace 2, Music Lessons 1 and 2,
      Band-in-a-Box, Auralia, and Finale.

## REFERENCES

*References are available upon request.*

# THE UNIQUE PIANO STUDIO

KAREN TURNER, NCTM

555 Central Avenue
City, ID 54321
Phone: 555-555-4321
uniquepianostudio@somewhere.net

555 Central Avenue
City, ID 54321

## KAREN TURNER

Karen Turner holds a B. M. in Piano Performance from Idaho State University.

She currently studies piano with Dr. David Anderson at the Northern Center for Music.

Turner is a member of a number of professional organizations, including:

City Music Teachers Association

Idaho Music Teachers Association

Music Teachers National Association

Idaho Federation of Music Clubs

National Association of Music Clubs

Turner has served as the Idaho State Competitions Coordinator and the Local Junior Festival Chair and is an MTNA Nationally Certified Teacher of Music.

Karen Turner has been named the Idaho Music Teacher Association's Teacher of the Year and has received the Contribution to the Community Award from the City Chamber of Commerce.

Turner is respected for her creative approach to curriculum and the positive learning environment of her studio.

# I TEACH MUSIC

Not because I expect you to
be a great performer

Not because I expect you to
play or sing all your life

Not so you can relax and
take it easy

But so you will be human

So you will be sensitive

So you will be closer to God

So you will have something
to cling to

So you will have more love, com-
passion, gentleness and good…

In short, more life.

Of what value will it be to make
a prosperous living unless
you know how to live?

—Author Unknown

# THE UNIQUE
# PIANO STUDIO

INDIVIDUAL PIANO LESSONS

GROUP LESSONS

THEORY

AURAL SKILLS

SIGHT-PLAYING

COMPOSITION

COMPUTERIZED WORKSTATION

MIDI KEYBOARD

COMPOSER OF THE MONTH

MUSIC HISTORY

THEMED RECITALS

COMPETITIONS/FESTIVALS

# THE UNIQUE PIANO STUDIO

## STUDIO POLICY 20__ – 20__

### TUITION

Tuition for private music lessons covers _____ weeks of study, from _____ to _____ and is payable in _____ equal monthly payments. Tuition covers the following services:_____
_____

A late-payment fee of $_____ will be deducted from the Book and Activity Deposit for all tuition not received by the ___th of the month. Students starting mid-semester will have their tuition pro-rated. Checks may be made payable to: **The Unique Piano Studio**. Tuition will be adjusted annually.

### BOOK AND ACTIVITY DEPOSIT

A $_____ Book and Activity Deposit is due at registration. This deposit will be used for all book expenses and activity fees during the year and will eliminate the need to pay additional monthly charges. If the funds are used in full, a copy of the charges will be mailed and another deposit will be requested. Monies not utilized will be refunded when lessons are discontinued.

### CALENDAR

A calendar of studio events, holidays and non-lesson weeks will be provided in the Studio Assignment Notebook. Please refer to this calendar for important studio dates.

### MISSED LESSONS

Refunds, credits, or make-ups will not be given for lessons or classes missed or canceled by the student. When the student has a conflict, he or she may use the Studio Swap List to arrange a swapped lesson time with another student.

### STUDIO SWAP LISTS

Understanding that students sometimes have conflicts, and at the same time realizing the importance of attending lessons faithfully, a studio swap list will be published. Students who choose to be on the swap list will receive a copy listing the names, lesson times, and phone numbers of all students requesting to be on the swap list. Students can then rearrange lessons for important and unavoidable conflicts. Please notify me in advance of any swapped lesson times.

### STUDIO OPPORTUNITIES

**Performance, theory, and camp opportunities:** There will be three **Unique Piano Studio** recitals a year. Other performance opportunities may include: community performances, Junior Festival, Guild, recitals sponsored by local or state music organizations, and state and national competitions. Performance opportunities are incentives to help students set and attain worthy goals. My goal is to help students develop self-confidence, stage-presence, and discipline while expressing musical creativity. Students are also invited to participate in the state theory exams and in the various summer camps offered through the studio.

**Group lessons:** Group piano lessons are offered in two formats: weekly group piano lessons and a combination of weekly private and group lessons. Students attending group lessons have an added responsibility to their group, including faithful attendance and preparation of group materials.

**Computer lab:** Students wishing to study music theory, music history, composition, aural skills, and world music in the computer lab may sign up for weekly time in the lab. A variety of programs and levels are available so that each student can work independently and at his/her own pace. The computer lab is designed to give **The Unique Piano Studio** students exposure to areas needing more time than the weekly applied lesson allows. Use of the computer lab is covered by an additional fee of $_____ per month.

**Studio music library:** Students wishing to borrow music from **The Unique Piano Studio** Lending Library may do so by checking out materials for a maximum of two weeks. The lending library serves as an excellent tool for sight-playing materials, previewing repertoire, and listening to CDs.

## PRACTICE EXPECTATIONS

Students are responsible for practicing their full assignment and preparing the lesson that has been assigned them. Students must also remember to bring the following materials to lessons:

- The Unique Piano Studio Assignment Notebook
- Double-pocket folder for handouts
- All books currently in use (even if no piece is assigned in a book that particular week)

### Guidelines to facilitate effective practicing:

- Maintain practice time at a daily minimum arranged with me.
- Give practice time the same priority as homework.
- Schedule practice at a regular time every day.
- When desired, break practicing into smaller sessions to help maintain concentration.
- When practicing, avoid distractions such as television, pets, visitors, phones, or interruptions for chores.
- Regularly review all items listed in the Studio Assignment Notebook as it serves as a guide to weekly practice and learning.

## PROPER GROOMING, PROPER DRESS, AND PROPER STUDIO USE

- Keep fingernails short, as long nails impede good hand position.
- Keep hands clean and germ-free out of respect for the other students using the piano; washing hands before the lesson is recommended.
- Avoid wearing immodest clothing.
- Remember to remove wet boots/shoes at the door.
- Use the hallway restroom when needed; parents and younger siblings are welcome to use the studio waiting room.

## INVOLVEMENT OF PARENTS OR GUARDIANS

- The adult's most important role is to listen to the student with encouragement and enthusiasm. I recommended that parents or guardians sit down with the student at least once a week to see that all assignments are practiced and to offer support.
- Parents or guardians should provide a well-tuned piano (at least once a year), a metronome, and a quiet place to practice.
- The parent's or guardian's responsibilities include bringing the student to lessons on time, and picking them up on time.

- Cars may be parked in the studio driveway only. Zoning laws do not permit on-street parking.

- Parents are encouraged to call me if there are any concerns or questions. It is my goal to give your child a positive learning experience in a supportive and musical environment. Calls can be made 7:00–9:00 pm to 555-555-4321, or I can be reached by email: uniquepianostudio@somewhere.net

ONE COPY OF THIS FORM IS INCLUDED IN THE STUDIO ASSIGNMENT NOTEBOOK. PLEASE SIGN THIS COPY AND MAIL WITH THE REGISTRATION FORM AND PAYMENT TO:

The Unique Piano Studio
555 Central Avenue  •  City, ID 54321

I HAVE READ AND AGREE TO THE TERMS OF THE CURRENT UNIQUE PIANO STUDIO 20__-20__ STUDIO POLICY STATEMENT AND REGISTRATION FORM.

Signature _____
(Parent, Guardian, or Adult Student)

Date _____

# THE UNIQUE PIANO STUDIO

## CALENDAR OF EVENTS 20__ – 20__

| | |
|---|---|
| Thursday, September 1 | Lessons begin |
| Saturday, October 29 | Idaho Music Teachers Association Competitions<br>Individual Times TBA<br>State University |
| Wed – Fri, November 23–25 | Thanksgiving Holiday |
| Sunday, December 12 | Chamber Music Recital<br>3:00 p.m., Sterns Retirement Home |
| Monday, December 13 | Studio Recital – Chamber Music<br>6:00 p.m.–7:30 p.m., City Recital Hall |
| Monday, December 19 | Winter Holiday begins |
| Monday, January 9 | Lessons resume |
| Saturday, February 18 | Studio Recital – Music of the Masters<br>6:00 p.m.–7:30 p.m., City Recital Hall |
| Saturday, February 25 | Federation of Music Clubs – Junior Festival<br>Individual times TBA<br>State University |
| Wednesday, March 22 | Spring Holiday |
| Thursday, March 23 | Spring Holiday |
| Sat – Wed, April 1–5 | No lessons – National Conference<br>National Competitions |
| Saturday, May 20 | State Theory Examinations<br>Individual times TBA |
| Saturday, May 27 | National Guild of Piano Teachers – Auditions<br>Individual times TBA |
| Sunday, June 4 | Studio Recital – Composition Highlights<br>6:00 p.m.–7:30 p.m., Schmitt Music, City Recital Hall |
| Friday, June 9 | Last day of lessons |

# THE UNIQUE PIANO STUDIO

## REGISTRATION

Student's name _____

Date of birth (under 18 only) _____

Student's cell phone _____

Previous years of study_____

Student's email address_____

Home phone _____

Home address _____

Street _____

City _____ State _____ Zip Code _____

Billing address (if different)
Street _____

City _____ State _____ Zip Code _____

Parent or guardian name _____

    Daytime phone _____Cell phone _____

    E-mail address _____

Parent or guardian name _____

    Daytime phone _____Cell phone _____

    E-mail address _____

Are there any personal circumstances of which I should be aware (special needs, health problems, etc.)?  No _____  Yes _____ ( I am enclosing a confidential explanation.)

Are there any family religious beliefs that might impact repertoire choices or performance dates? If so, please explain: _____

_____

_____

_____

**Tuition:** Tuition for the year covers ___ weeks of music study. Lessons are offered from _____ to _____. Please check the desired length and type of lesson:

**Private**

_____ 45 minute $_____.00 a month for _____ months

_____ 60 minute $_____.00 a month for _____ months

**Group**

_____ 60 minute $_____.00 a month for _____ months

**Combination Private and Group**

_____ 45 minute private + 60 minute group

$_____.00 a month for _____ months

**Computer Lab**

_____ 60 minute $_____.00 a month for _____ months

**A $_____.00 Book and Activity Deposit is due upon registration.** Additional funds will be requested when the current funds have been used. Any unused funds from the Book and Activity Deposit will be refunded if the lessons are discontinued.

**Scheduling: Please complete and return the enclosed Lesson Request Form.**

## IMPORTANT

- Please return the first month's tuition, the Book and Activity Deposit, the Lesson Request Form, the signed Registration Form, and one signed copy of the Studio Policy, due by August ___, 20_____.

- Make checks payable to **The Unique Piano Studio**.

- Refunds, credits, or make-ups will not be given for lessons missed or canceled by the student.

- The above student may _____ may not _____ be included on a lesson swap list.

_____    _____
(Signature of Parent, Guardian, or Adult Student)    Date

I give permission for the student's picture to be used for publicity purposes.

_____    _____
(Signature of Parent, Guardian, or Adult Student)    Date

I have read and agree to the terms of the current Unique Piano Studio Registration Form and Studio Policy Statement.

_____    _____
(Signature of Parent, Guardian, or Adult Student)    Date

**THE UNIQUE PIANO STUDIO**

## PRACTICE AGREEMENT

Student's name _____

Having discusssed the importance of dedicated practice with my teacher, I agree to commit myself to _____ minutes of practicing a day for _____ days a week.

I make this commitment for the entire year and understand the benefits that consistent practicing will bring to my piano study.

_____          _____
Student Signature                          Date

# THE UNIQUE PIANO STUDIO

## SWAP LIST

**Monday**
| | | |
|---|---|---|
| 3:00 | Debbie Smith | 555-5551 |
| 4:00 | Linda Anderson | 555-5552 |
| 4:45 | Time Not Available | |
| 5:30 | Steven Jones | 555-5553 |
| 6:15 | Susan Thomson | 555-5554 |

**Tuesday**
| | | |
|---|---|---|
| 3:00 | David Samson | 555-5556 |
| 3:45 | Barbara Jones | 555-5557 |
| 4:45 | Nancy Becker | 555-5558 |
| 5:30 | Joe Hoffman | 555-5559 |
| 6:15 | Donna Perkins | 555-5560 |

**Wednesday**
| | | |
|---|---|---|
| 3:00 | Roxanne Williams | 555-5561 |
| 3:45 | Dennis Brown | 555-5562 |
| 4:30 | Valerie Harrison | 555-5563 |
| 5:00 | Susan Nelson | 555-5565 |
| 6:00 | Jody Park | 555-5566 |

**Thursday**
| | | |
|---|---|---|
| 3:00 | George O'Neil | 555-5567 |
| 4:00 | Patty Ross | 555-5568 |
| 4:45 | Sara Wagner | 555-5569 |
| 5:30 | Patty Boyle | 555-5570 |
| 6:30 | Shelley Goodman | 555-5571 |

**Friday**
| | | |
|---|---|---|
| 3:00 | Kay Stein | 555-5572 |
| 4:00 | Time Not Available | |
| 5:00 | David Foster | 555-5573 |
| 6:00 | Nathan Foster | 555-5573 |

**THE UNIQUE PIANO STUDIO**

# STUDENT INTERVIEW FORM – BEGINNING STUDENT
(Questions to be asked by the instructor of the student)

Name _____

Name you prefer to be called _____

Age _____ Date of birth _____ Grade in school _____

What after-school activities do you have? _____
_____

How is your leisure time spent? _____
_____

Why do you want to take lessons? _____
_____
_____

What are your favorite types of music? _____
_____

Have you had any previous musical training, such as on another instrument? _____

If yes, please describe. _____
_____

Instrument(s) to be used by the student at home _____
_____

Have you been playing piano on your own? _____

If yes, can you play anything for me now? _____

(If not, teach the student a simple piece by rote and record any observations.)

Observations: _____
_____
_____
_____

Can you sing a song?  Observations: _____
_____
_____

General observations about the student: _____
_____
_____

# THE UNIQUE PIANO STUDIO

## STUDENT INTERVIEW FORM – TRANSFER STUDENT
### (Questions to be asked by the instructor of the student)

Name _____

Name you prefer to be called _____

Age _____ Date of Birth _____ Grade in School _____

What after-school activities do you have? _____
_____

How is your leisure time spent? _____
_____

Why do you want to take lessons? _____
_____
_____

What are your favorite types of music? _____
_____

How many years of lessons have you had? _____

Why did you change teachers? _____
_____

How much are you accustomed to practicing per day? _____

Instrument(s) to be used by the student at home _____
_____

Have you had any previous musical training, such as on another instrument? _____

Describe: _____
_____

What would you like to play for me now? Observations: _____
_____
_____

Can you sing a song? Observations: _____
_____
_____

Observations about theory and technique: _____
_____
_____

General observations about the student: _____
_____
_____

# THE UNIQUE PIANO STUDIO

## PAYMENT RECORD

| STUDENT | SEPT | OCT | NOV | DEC | JAN | FEB |
|---|---|---|---|---|---|---|
| Linda Anderson | $ | | | | | |
| Nancy Becker | | | | | | |
| Patty Boyle | | | | | | |
| Dennis Brown | | | | | | |
| David Foster | | | | | | |
| Nathan Foster | | | | | | |
| Shelley Goodman | | | | | | |
| Valerie Harrison | | | | | | |
| Joe Hoffman | | | | | | |
| Barbara Jones | | | | | | |
| Steven Jones | | | | | | |
| Mary Lee | | | | | | |
| Susan Nelson | | | | | | |
| George O'Neil | | | | | | |
| Jody Park | | | | | | |
| Donna Perkins | | | | | | |
| Patty Ross | | | | | | |
| David Samson | | | | | | |
| Debbie Smith | | | | | | |
| Kay Stein | | | | | | |
| Kay Stein | | | | | | |
| | | | | | | |

# THE UNIQUE PIANO STUDIO

## LESSON ATTENDANCE RECORD

| Monday | Name | 9/5 | 9/12 | 9/19 | 9/26 |
|---|---|---|---|---|---|
| 3:00–4:00 | Debbie Smith | — | 9/12 | U | 9/26 |
| 4:00–4:45 | Linda Anderson | — | 10/22 | 9/19 | 9/26 |
| 4:45–5:30 | Patty Boyle | — | 9/12 | 9/19 | 9/26 |
| 5:30–6:15 | Steven Jones | — | 9/12 | 9/19 | 9/26 |
| 6:15–7:00 | Susan Thomson | — | 9/12 | 9/19 | 9/26 |
|  |  |  |  |  |  |
| **Tuesday** |  | **9/6** | **9/13** | **9/20** | **9/27** |
| 3:00–3:45 | David Samson | 9/6 |  | 9/20 | 9/27 |
| 3:45–4:45 | Barbara Jones | 9/6 |  | 9/20 | 9/27 |
| 4:45–5:30 | Nancy Becker | 9/6 | 9/13 | U | 9/27 |
| 5:30–6:15 | Joe Hoffman | 9/6 | 9/13 | 9/20 | 9/27 |
| 6:15–7:00 | Donna Perkins | 9/6 | 9/13 | 9/20 | 9/27 |
|  |  |  |  |  |  |
| **Wednesday** |  | **9/7** | **9/14** | **9/21** | **9/28** |
| etc. |  |  |  |  |  |
|  |  |  |  |  |  |
|  |  |  |  |  |  |
|  |  |  |  |  |  |
|  |  |  |  |  |  |
|  |  |  |  |  |  |
|  |  |  |  |  |  |
|  |  |  |  |  |  |

**THE UNIQUE PIANO STUDIO**

## SCHOLARSHIP APPLICATION RECORD

Student's name _____

Parent's or guardian's name _____

Phone: (wk) _____ (hm) _____ Cell phone: _____

A copy of the form verifying acceptance into Free/Assisted Lunch Program is enclosed. _____

**THE UNIQUE PIANO STUDIO**

## NOTICE OF OVERDUE FUNDS

Student's name _____

Amount overdue _____

A $_____ late fee has been deducted from the student's Book and Activity Deposit.

Please send the overdue amount in the enclosed self-addressed and stamped envelope by _____ in order to avoid additional late fees.
(date)

Checks are to be made to **The Unique Piano Studio**.

## THE UNIQUE PIANO STUDIO

# LESSON INQUIRY/PHONE INQUIRY

Student's name _____

Age _____ Year in school _____

Parent's or guardian's name _____

Relation to student _____

Phone: (wk) _____ (hm) _____ Cell phone: _____

Beginner _____ Transfer _____

Years of prior lessons _____ # of prior teachers _____

Reason for transfer _____

_____

_____

Days and times available for lessons _____

_____

_____

Main goals for piano lessons _____

_____

Date and time set for interview _____

_____

Observations/comments after phone conversation _____

_____

_____

_____

_____

# THE UNIQUE PIANO STUDIO

## WAITING LIST

Date inquiry made _____

Student's name _____

Age _____ Prior years of piano _____ Level _____

Parent's or guardian's name _____

Home phone: _____ Cell phone: _____

Preferred date/time for lessons _____

Comments: _____

_____

_____

 THE UNIQUE PIANO STUDIO

## STATE THEORY EXAMS – ACHIEVEMENT RECORD

| STUDENT | LEVEL '06 | SCORE '06 | LEVEL '07 | SCORE '07 | LEVEL '08 | SCORE '08 |
|---|---|---|---|---|---|---|
| Linda Anderson | 3 | 98 | 4 | 100 | 5 | 97 |
| Nancy Becker | 1 | 90 | 2 | 91 | 3 | 90 |
| Patty Boyle | 5 | 92 | 6 | 94 | 7 | 95 |
| Dennis Brown | 8 | 99 | 9 | 97 | 10 | 97 |
| David Foster | 1 | 92 | 2 | 90 | 3 | 96 |
| Nathan Foster | 9 | 100 | 10 | 100 | 11 | 100 |
| Shelley Goodman | 1 | 91 | 2 | 95 | 3 | 97 |
| Valerie Harrison | 2 | 97 | 3 | 100 | 4 | 99 |
| Joe Hoffman | 2 | 93 | 3 | 90 | 4 | 92 |
| Barbara Jones | 6 | 94 | 7 | 99 | 8 | 92 |
| Steven Jones | 9 | 92 | 10 | 95 | 11 | 92 |
| Mary Lee | 5 | 100 | 6 | 99 | 7 | 100 |
| Susan Nelson | 1 | 97 | 2 | 99 | 3 | 98 |
| George O'Neil | 4 | 93 | 5 | 96 | 6 | 95 |
| Jody Park | 7 | 100 | 8 | 92 | 9 | 99 |
| Donna Perkins | 2 | 90 | 3 | 93 | 4 | 92 |
| Patty Ross | 2 | 99 | 3 | 100 | 4 | 98 |
| David Samson | 9 | 95 | 10 | 98 | 11 | 100 |
| Debbie Smith | 8 | 96 | 9 | 92 | 10 | 90 |
| Kay Stein | 1 | 100 | 2 | 98 | 3 | 98 |
| Kay Stein | 5 | 91 | 6 | 94 | 7 | 92 |
| | | | | | | |

**THE UNIQUE PIANO STUDIO**

# NATIONAL FEDERATION OF MUSIC CLUBS JUNIOR FESTIVAL

| STUDENT | LEVEL '06 | SCORE '06 | LEVEL '07 | SCORE '07 | LEVEL '08 | SCORE '08 |
|---------|-----------|-----------|-----------|-----------|-----------|-----------|
| Linda Anderson | P 4 | S | E 1 | S | E 2 | S |
| Nancy Becker | P 1 | S | P 2 | S | P 3 | S |
| Patty Boyle | Med | E | MD 1 | S | MD 2 | S |
| Dennis Brown | D 1 | S | D 2 | S | VD 1 | S |
| David Foster | P 1 | E | P 2 | E | P 3 | S |
| Nathan Foster | Med | S | MD 1 | S | MD 2 | S |
| Shelley Goodman | P 1 | E | P 2 | S | P 3 | S |
| Valerie Harrison | P 1 | S | P 2 | S | P 3 | S |
| Joe Hoffman | P 3 | E | P 4 | S | E 1 | S |
| Barbara Jones | P 2 | S | P 3 | S | P 4 | E |
| Steven Jones | E 1 | E | E 2 | S | E 3 | E |
| Mary Lee | MD 1 | S | MD 2 | S | D 1 | S |
| Susan Nelson | P 1 | S | P 2 | S | P 3 | S |
| George O'Neil | E 1 | E | E 2 | S | E 3 | S |
| Jody Park | E 4 | S | Med | S | MD 1 | S |
| Donna Perkins | P 2 | S | P 3 | E | P 4 | E |
| Patty Ross | P 3 | S | P 4 | S | E 1 | S |
| David Samson | VD 1 | S | VD 2 | S | MA 1 | S |
| Debbie Smith | MD 1 | S | MD 2 | E | MD 3 | E |
| Kay Stein | P 1 | S | P 2 | S | P 3 | S |
| Kay Stein | E 2 | E | E 3 | S | E 4 | S |
|  |  |  |  |  |  |  |

# THE UNIQUE PIANO STUDIO

## STUDIO INVENTORY

| CATEGORY | | |
|---|---|---|
| Title | Publisher | Value |
| METHOD BOOKS: | | |
| | | |
| | | |
| COLLECTIONS: | | |
| | | |
| | | |
| BY COMPOSER: | | |
| Bach: | | |
| | | |
| | | |
| Beethoven: | | |
| | | |
| John Robert Poe: | | |
| | | |
| SEASONAL: | | |
| | | |
| TECHNIQUE: | | |
| | | |
| SCALES/KEYBOARD SKILLS: | | |
| | | |
| WORKBOOKS: | | |
| | | |
| | | |

# THE UNIQUE PIANO STUDIO

## LENDING LIBRARY RECORD

| Loan Date | Item Loaned | Student's signature | Date returned tcher. init. |
|---|---|---|---|
| | | | |
| | | | |
| | | | |
| | | | |
| | | | |
| | | | |
| | | | |
| | | | |
| | | | |
| | | | |
| | | | |
| | | | |
| | | | |
| | | | |
| | | | |
| | | | |
| | | | |
| | | | |
| | | | |
| | | | |
| | | | |
| | | | |
| | | | |
| | | | |

# THE UNIQUE PIANO STUDIO

# STUDENT/PARENT ASSESSMENT OF TEACHER

Student's name (optional): _____

Dates being assessed: _____

| **Teaching assessment** | Needs improvement <—> Satisfactory |
|---|---|
| The teacher shows a genuine interest in the student's progress. | 1  2  3  4  5 |
| The teacher works to develop a positive relationship with the student. | 1  2  3  4  5 |
| The teacher chooses age and developmentally appropriate material. | 1  2  3  4  5 |
| The teacher creates an environment conducive to learning. | 1  2  3  4  5 |
| The teacher explains new concepts clearly. | 1  2  3  4  5 |
| The teacher presents material with enthusiasm. | 1  2  3  4  5 |
| The teacher resolves technical challenges effectively. | 1  2  3  4  5 |
| The teacher presents a broad understanding of historical styles. | 1  2  3  4  5 |
| The teacher explains music theory effectively. | 1  2  3  4  5 |
| The teacher incorporates innovative programs into the studio. | 1  2  3  4  5 |
| The teacher gives clear instructions on effective practice habits. | 1  2  3  4  5 |
| The teacher provides positive performance opportunities. | 1  2  3  4  5 |

| **Professional assessment** | |
|---|---|
| The teacher starts and ends lessons on time. | 1  2  3  4  5 |
| Studio policies are explained clearly. | 1  2  3  4  5 |
| Studio policies are consistently enforced. | 1  2  3  4  5 |
| Invoices and written communications are presented in a timely and effective manner. | 1  2  3  4  5 |
| The teacher is open to communications about the student's needs. | 1  2  3  4  5 |

**Observations**

Rate the student's enjoyment of piano lessons.        1  2  3  4  5
Please explain:


Rate the student's progress during this period.       1  2  3  4  5
Please explain:


Do you have any concerns or suggestions for change?
Please explain:

# THE UNIQUE PIANO STUDIO

# TEACHER'S ASSESSMENT OF STUDENT'S PROGRESS

Student's name: _____

Dates being assessed: _____

**Lesson Preparation and Attitude**　　　　　　　　　Needs improvement <—> Satisfactory

| | |
|---|---|
| The student shows a genuine interest in piano. | 1　2　3　4　5 |
| The student works to develop a positive relationship with the teacher. | 1　2　3　4　5 |
| The student completes assignments on time. | 1　2　3　4　5 |
| The student takes suggestions well. | 1　2　3　4　5 |
| The student approaches new material with enthusiasm. | 1　2　3　4　5 |
| The student asks questions when needed. | 1　2　3　4　5 |
| The student comes to lessons with a positive attitude. | 1　2　3　4　5 |
| The student brings all necessary materials to each lesson. | 1　2　3　4　5 |
| The student arrives on time for lessons. | 1　2　3　4　5 |

**Practice and Memorization**

| | |
|---|---|
| The student uses an efficient system for practicing. | 1　2　3　4　5 |
| The student practices the agreed upon amount of time. | 1　2　3　4　5 |
| The student has high standards for accuracy. | 1　2　3　4　5 |
| The student memorizes pieces systematically. | 1　2　3　4　5 |
| The student has pieces memorized well in advance of performances. | 1　2　3　4　5 |
| The student takes advantage of studio performance opportunities. | 1　2　3　4　5 |

**Musical Elements**

| | |
|---|---|
| The student incorporates expressive phrasing into assigned pieces. | 1　2　3　4　5 |
| The student uses expressive dynamics in assigned pieces. | 1　2　3　4　5 |
| The student pays attention to sound concepts/tone at the piano. | 1　2　3　4　5 |
| The student incorporates stylistic accuracy into assigned pieces. | 1　2　3　4　5 |
| The student executes accurate and stylistic pedaling. | 1　2　3　4　5 |
| The student completes music theory and history assignments. | 1　2　3　4　5 |
| The student works diligently on technique. | 1　2　3　4　5 |
| The student demonstrates rhythmic accuracy. | 1　2　3　4　5 |
| The student carefully observes finger markings. | 1　2　3　4　5 |
| The student works well on improvisation and composition. | 1　2　3　4　5 |
| The student practices sight-playing on a weekly basis. | 1　2　3　4　5 |

**Observations:**

# THE UNIQUE PIANO STUDIO

555 Central Avenue • City, ID 54321
Phone: 555-555-4321
uniquepianostudio@somewhere.net

# CHAMBER MUSIC RECITAL

## THE UNIQUE PIANO STUDIO

## CERTIFICATE OF MERIT

# ROXANNE WILLIAMS

## FOR A JOB WELL DONE!

_Karen Turner_

Date _____

# THE UNIQUE PIANO STUDIO

# PRESS RELEASE

For Release:  December 5, Arts Page
Contact: Karen Turner, 555-555-4321; uniquepianostudio@somewhere.net

## Students to Present Chamber Music Recitals

Students from The Unique Piano Studio, directed by pianist Karen Turner and The Dolce String Studio, directed by violinist Beth Leinen, will present two chamber music recitals in the upcoming week.

Turner and Leinen first collaborated last year as members of a local trio ensemble with cellist David Hagen. "We enjoyed the experience so much, we decided to share the joys of chamber music with our students," said Turner. "It has been a real pleasure to see them develop a love of chamber music. We are all looking forward to the upcoming recitals." For the last three months, Turner and Leinen have been offering chamber music classes in addition to their students' regularly scheduled private lessons.

The students will be performing for residents of the Sterns Retirement Center on Sunday, December 12th at 3:00 pm. All residents of the facility as well as any visitors are welcome to attend. The Sterns Retirement Home is located at 344 North Main Street.

On Monday, December 13 the students will give a recital at 6:00 p.m. in the City Recital Hall located at 554 3rd Avenue NW. The recital is free and open to the public and will be followed by a reception.

The recitals will feature chamber works by Carse, Corelli, Tartini, Köhler, Klengel, Clementi, Haydn, Mozart, and Schubert. Students performing on the programs include pianists Linda Anderson, Dennis Brown, Valerie Harrison, and Patty Rose. Violinists include Hannah Johnson, John Chong, David Stein, Natalie Anderson, and Corey Wood. Brandon Winters, Cindy Hillier and Devon Lee will perform on viola and Stewart Green, Kim Lee, and Ricardo Ramirez will perform on cello.

For more information, please contact The Unique Piano Studio at 555-555-4321.

YOU ARE CORDIALLY INVITED TO

## THE UNIQUE PIANO STUDIO
# CHAMBER MUSIC RECITAL

# THE UNIQUE PIANO STUDIO
in partnership with
# THE DOLCE STRING STUDIO

# SUNDAY, DECEMBER 13, 20__
6:00–7:30 p.m.
City Recital Hall

*The recital is free and open to the public.*

# THE UNIQUE PIANO STUDIO

**An innovative studio dedicated
to an enjoyable and comprehensive study of piano
and the love of music-making**

## STUDIO CURRICULUM

- Individual piano lessons
- Computer lab
- Chamber music
- MIDI keyboards
- Competitions/Festivals
- Music theory

- Composition
- Music history
- Aural skills
- Themed recitals
- Sight-playing
- Technique

To arrange an audition or for more information
call 555-555-4321 or e-mail
uniquepianostudio@somewhere.net

 **THE UNIQUE PIANO STUDIO**

# ASSIGNMENT BOOK

Student _____

20___ - 20___

**Week of:** _____

**Repertoire: Specific practice goals/instructions**

**Practice Log – Minutes per day**

| Mon. | Tue. | Wed. | Thurs. | Fri. | Sat. | Sun. |
|------|------|------|--------|------|------|------|
|      |      |      |        |      |      |      |

# Technique and Scale Assignments

# COMPOSER OF THE MONTH

**Month:** _____

**Composer:**

**Birthdate and Place:**

**Significant events & information:**

| Period of Music: | Dates of Period: |
|---|---|
| | |

**Description of musical style, instruments, events, etc. during this period:**

# LISTENING ASSIGNMENTS

**Month:** _____

**Listening Assignments**

1. _____

   _____

   _____

   _____

2. _____

   _____

   _____

   _____

3. _____

   _____

   _____

   _____

4. _____

   _____

   _____

   _____

5. _____

   _____

   _____

   _____

**Listening Summaries**

# LISTENING ASSIGNMENTS

**Month:** _____

### Listening Assignments

1. _____

_____

_____

_____

2. _____

_____

_____

_____

3. _____

_____

_____

_____

4. _____

_____

_____

_____

5. _____

_____

_____

_____

### Listening Summaries

# REPERTOIRE

**Method/Technique Book Title**

**Level Completed**

# POPULAR REPERTOIRE

Title                                    Composer

Memorized

419

# BAROQUE PERIOD

DATES:

### Title

### Composer

# CLASSICAL PERIOD

**DATES:**

Title

Composer

# ROMANTIC PERIOD

## Title

**DATES:**

## Composer

# CONTEMPORARY PERIOD     DATES:

**Title**                          **Composer**

Memorized

Other options to include in the Studio Assignment Book:

- Studio Calendar
- Studio Policy Statement
- Musical terms and definitions
- Scale and arpeggio fingerings
- Circle of fifths

# Appendix B: Sample Survey

This survey is reproducible and can be modified to suit the needs of any local or state music teachers organization.

# INDEPENDENT MUSIC TEACHER
# BUSINESS PRACTICE SURVEY

By Beth Gigante Klingenstein

Although some questions deal with sensitive issues such as rates, please answer all questions. The survey is anonymous and all information is collected in order to give independent teachers useful data concerning professional policies and rates.

1) How many years of teaching experience do you have?_____

2) On average, how many students do you teach in an independent studio? _____
   On average, how many students do you teach in a school setting?_____

3) What is your highest level of education?
   Music related education:
   _____ No college music courses
   _____ Some college music /minor in music/Bachelor's degree in progress
   _____ Bachelor's degree in music
   _____ Some work on Masters degree in music/ Master's /degree in progress
   _____ Master's degree in music
   _____ Some work on DMA or PhD in music/DMA or PhD in music in progress
   _____ DMA or PhD in music

   Education in areas other than music:
   _____ Bachelor's degrees in field outside of music
   _____ Master's degrees in field outside of music
   _____ PhD or other terminal degrees in field outside of music
   _____ Other

4) What is the population of the community where you teach? [These figures should be adjusted to better reflect the demographics in the area where the survey is being administered.]
   _____ Less than 10,0000
   _____ 10,000 – 50,0000
   _____ 50,001 – 200,000
   _____ 200,000 – 1,000,000
   _____ Over 1,000,000

5) What do you charge for a 60-minute private lesson? _____
   (Even if you charge by the month and not the hour, or do not offer 60-minute lessons, please compute an hourly fee so that an average can be tabulated.)

   On average, how often do your rates increase?
   _____ Annually          _____ Every 3–4 years
   _____ Every other year   _____ Every 5 years or more

6) What length lesson do you offer? Check all that apply:

_____ 30-minute

_____ 40- or 45-minute

_____ 60-minute

_____ A combination of weekly group and weekly private (please explain)

_____ Other (please explain)

7) Do you give reduced rates for students with financial need?

Yes_____/ No_____

Do you give reduced rates for siblings? Yes _____/ No _____

8) Group lessons: (Please do not include information about performance classes or theory classes, but only about group lessons on an instrument.)

How much do you charge per student per hour of group lessons? _____

(If you offer a different length of group lessons, please compute an hourly fee per student so that an average can be tabulated.)

What is the average number of students in each group lesson?_____

How often are group lessons held? _____

What length group lessons do you offer? _____

How much do you earn per year (before expenses) from group teaching? _____

9) What services do you provide for students other than a weekly lesson?

_____ Workshops

_____ Recitals

_____ Performance classes/studio classes/master classes

_____ Competitions and festivals

_____ Guild

_____ MIDI keyboards, computer lab, or workstation

_____ Ensembles

_____ Purchase of books and supplies (to be reimbursed by student)

_____ Theory classes

_____ Summer programs/camps

_____ Field trips

_____ National Music Certificate Program Examinations

_____ ABRSM or Royal Conservatory of Music Examinations

_____ State theory or keyboard skills exams

_____ Other_____

10) On average, how many hours a week do you spend on the services listed above?_____

On average, how many hours a week do you spend for music-related bookwork?

_____

On average, how many hours a week do you spend teaching? _____

11) What is your gross annual income from teaching in an independent studio? _____
(Gross income from other areas will be listed later. Gross annual income is the total of all income made in a year before deductions are taken out for taxes and expenses.)

12) What is your net annual income from teaching in an independent studio? _____
(Net income is the total income made in a year after deductions are taken out for taxes and expenses.)

13) Do you receive income from music areas other than private teaching? If so, please mark the total gross income earned from each category in a year.

_____ Religious services          _____ Royalties
_____ Workshops/lectures          _____ Adjudicating
_____ Performing                  _____ Retail
_____ Accompanying                _____ Early childhood music
_____ Retirement pension, fund    _____ Teaching in community school,
_____ Second job unrelated to music           public school, university, etc.
_____ Other (please explain on back of this page)

14) What happens to your teaching income in the summer months?
_____ Increases
_____ Stays the same
_____ Decreases slightly
_____ Decreases significantly
_____ No summer income

15) If your income decreases in the summer, which statement is true?
_____ My summer income is lower by choice.
_____ I wish I could keep my summer income more on a par with my income during the school year.

16) How do you bill for lessons?
_____ By the week
_____ By the month, altered according to each month's activities
_____ By the month, a set tuition which is the same each month
_____ By the semester or term

17) How do you bill for books, supplies, and fees?
_____ Send home notice at the lesson
_____ Bill at the end of the month
_____ Use a book and activity deposit
_____ Require students to purchase their own music

18) What is your policy concerning make-up lessons? (Check all that apply)

_____ No make-up lessons are given

_____ For extreme weather

_____ For sickness with advance notice

_____ For school activities

_____ For family conflicts

_____ For any reason with advance notice

_____ For any reason

_____ Other (please explain)

19) Do students in your studio use a swap list to rearrange lesson times?

_____ Yes

_____ No

20) Do you interview prospective students before accepting them?

_____ Yes

_____ No

21) Do you have a formal written Studio Policy?

_____ Yes

_____ No

22) Do you have a liability/umbrella policy in addition to your homeowners or renters insurance?

_____ Yes

_____ No

23) How do you obtain health insurance?

_____ Spouse's job

_____ My second job

_____ Medicare

_____ Individual policy

_____ Do not have health insurance

24) How do you save for retirement?

_____ Spouse's benefits or income

_____ My second job

_____ My IRA

_____ I don't/can't save for retirement

_____ Other (please explain)

_____

_____

_____

25) How do you feel about your income?

_____

_____

_____

26) How do you feel about your make-up policy?

_____

_____

_____

27) What do you see as the biggest problem facing the independent music teacher?

_____

_____

_____

_____

28) If you were to set up an ideal policy and business, what would it include?

_____

_____

_____

_____

Please complete the survey by (date) _____

and return to (individual's name and address)_____

_____

_____

_____

# Appendix C: Professional Organizations

Appendix C provides contact information for some of the most significant professional organizations discussed in this book.

## Associated Board of the Royal Schools of Music (ABRSM)

24 Portland Place
London W1B 1LU
United Kingdom
Telephone: +44 20 7636 5400
Website: www.abrsm.org

## The College Music Society (CMS)

312 East Pine Street
Missoula, MT 59802
(406) 721-9616
Website: www.music.org
E-mail: cms@music.org

## Early Childhood Music & Movement Association (ECMMA)

805 Mill Avenue
Snohomish, WA 98290
(360) 568-5636
Website: www.ecmma.org
E-mail: adminoffice@ecmma.org

## Music Teachers National Association (MTNA)

441 Vine Street, Suite 505
Cincinnati, OH 45202-2811
(888) 512-5278; (513) 421-1420
Website: www.mtna.org
E-mail: mtnanet@mtna.org

## The National Association for Music Education (MENC)

1806 Robert Fulton Drive
Reston, VA 20191
(703) 860-4000
Website: www.menc.org
E-mail member services: mbrserv@menc.org

## National Music Certificate Program Examinations

P.O. Box 1984
Buffalo, NY 14240-1984
(866) 716-2223
Website: www.nationalmusiccertificate.org
E-mail: info@nationalmusiccertificate.org

## NAMM, The International Music Products Association (NAMM)
5790 Armada Drive
Carlsbad, CA 92008
(760) 438-8001
Website: www.namm.org

## National Conference on Keyboard Pedagogy (NCKP)
The Frances Clark Center for Keyboard Pedagogy
P.O. Box 651
4543 Route 27
Kingston, NJ 08528
(609) 921-0371
Website: www.francesclarkcenter.org (Select "National Conferences")
E-mail: nckpinfo@francesclarkcenter.org

## National Guild of Piano Teachers (NGPT)
P.O. Box 1807
Austin, TX 78767
(512) 478-5775
Website: http://pianoguild.com

## The National Federation of Music Clubs (NFMC)
1336 North Delaware Street
Indianapolis, Indiana 46202-2481
(317) 638-4003
Website: www.nfmc-music.org
E-mail: nfmc@nfmc-music.org

## Royal Conservatory of Music Examinations
5865 McLaughlin Road, Unit 4
Mississauga, Ontario
Canada L5R 1B8
(905) 501-9553
Website: www.rcmexaminations.org

## World Piano Pedagogy Conference, Inc. (WPPC)
333 Beethoven Circle
DeFuniak Springs, Florida 32433
(850) 951-0133
Website: www.pianovision.com (Select "WPPC")
E-mail: info@pianovision.com

# INDEX

# N

# ABOUT THE AUTHOR

**B**eth **Gigante Klingenstein** is nationally recognized for her practical, humorous, and motivational presentations on the professional issues affecting today's music teacher. Her presentations have been well-received across the country, offering helpful insights for the seasoned professional as well as the novice.

Besides appearing at a number of state conventions, Klingenstein has presented extensively at national conferences, including the National Piano Foundation, National Conference on Keyboard Pedagogy, World Piano Pedagogy Conference, Association for Technology in Music Instruction, National Symposium on Music Instruction Technology, National Conference on Ubiquitous Computing, and numerous presentations for Music Teachers National Association.

Klingenstein's first book, *A Business Guide for the Music Teacher*, was followed by numerous articles in *American Music Teacher*, as well as articles in *Keyboard Companion*, *The Piano Adventures Teacher* and music reviews in *Piano and Keyboard Magazine*.

Beth Gigante Klingenstein received a bachelor's degree in piano performance from Syracuse University and a master's degree in piano performance from the University of Michigan. Klingenstein maintained an independent music studio for 28 years, and in 1994 moved from the Washington D.C. area to North Dakota, where she currently serves on the music faculty of Valley City State University and is the Founding Director of the VCSU Community School of the Arts. In the spirit of lifelong learning, Klingenstein started work on a PhD in Educational Leadership at the University of North Dakota just before completing this book.